GOVERNMENT IN TENNESSEE

GOVERNMENT
IN
TENNESSEE
FOURTH EDITION

Lee Seifert Greene
David H. Grubbs
Victor C. Hobday

THE UNIVERSITY OF TENNESSEE PRESS

"Knowledge, learning, and virtue [are] essential to
the preservation of republican institutions"
—*Tennessee Constitution*, Article XI, Section 12 (as worded before the amendment of 1978)

Library of Congress Cataloging in Publication Data

Greene, Lee Seifert, 1905–
Government in Tennessee.

Bibliography: p.
Includes index.
1. Tennessee—Politics and government—1951–
I. Grubbs, David H., 1929–   . II. Hobday,
Victor C., 1914–   III. Title.
JK5225 1982.G7   320.4768   81–16428
ISBN 0–87049–338–8   AACR2
ISBN 0–87049–339–6 (pbk.)

For Dorothy Kuersteiner Greene, Opal Greene Lamb,
and Ruby Greene Parsons
·
For Florence B. Grubbs
·
For Elizabeth Price Hobday

Preface

Most of what we said in the preface to the third edition remains true for the fourth. This book is directed to the general public. We still hope, for the sake of both our meager royalties and a long-held conviction that government is worth studying, that students will find this edition readable and useful. We think they will; any other statement would be more modest but less honest. We are not particularly writing for our colleagues in the political science fraternity, although we hold to the opinion that this volume may be useful for them from time to time. We are deeply indebted to many of those colleagues, whose painstaking research has provided us with bits and pieces of wisdom and understanding. Throughout the volume our heavy indebtedness is thankfully acknowledged as the results of their labors are used.

For the sake of protecting the authors, if for no other reason, it is helpful to say what this book is not. It is not an attempt to present the political theory underlying the behavior of the State of Tennessee, although some of that theory, both as to the structure and as to the proper functions of the state, may appear from the description of its organs and their operations. It is not a book on the politics of Tennessee, although some chapters have been given over to this subject and we have expanded our comments on the relation of Tennessee politics to Tennessee government. It is not a history of the functions performed by the state and its agencies, nor does it include a careful critique of the successes and failures of Tennessee policy. All of these subjects are worthy of the attention of political observers; indeed, it is regrettable that so little of this type of exploration has been undertaken. But we do believe that the policies of government should be studied and we have dealt with such matters insofar as we could. We wish that a more extensive treatment of policies had been possible. We are forced to confine ourselves to what we can now reach and grasp. We stand in need of longer lives, wealthier publishers, and more patient readers.

The writer of history faces the particular difficulty of determining what happened, and the critic is entitled to think that the author often misses some of the data. The political scientist faces the same difficulty, and the more deeply he penetrates into his subject the more modest he may become about his certainties. But he faces another trouble, similar to that encountered by the physicist. His subject will not stand still. We beg our readers' indulgence if our portrait of Tennessee neglects some of the postures taken on by our model in the last of the seventies and the beginning of the eighties.

We wish particularly to express our indebtedness to Dr. Robert Avery, the coauthor of the first two editions. This edition has relied heavily on his work. A great many people have assisted us with information and critical comment. We wish especially to acknowledge the help of Dr. Sam Smith, Professor of History, Tennessee State University; Mr. Leonard Bradley, former student and since then experienced civil servant of the State of Tennessee; Dr. John Ewing, Dean, Agricultural Experiment Station, the University of Tennessee; Mr. J.J. Mynatt, former Director of the Legislative Council Committee; Mr. Ralph J. Harris, Executive Director, Tennessee County Services Association; Mr. William Koch, Director of Personnel, State of Tennessee; Mr. Herbert J. Bingham, Executive Director, Tennessee Municipal League; Mr. Robert Lovelace and Mr. Eugene Puett of the Municipal Technical Advisory Service, the University of Tennessee; Mr. Walter Lambert, Special Assistant to the Executive Vice-President, the University of Tennessee; Mr. Harlan Mathews, Treasurer of the State of Tennessee; Dr. Hyrum Plaas, Professor of Political Science, the University of Tennessee; Mr. Robert Freeman, Assistant Director, East Tennessee Development District; Mr. T. Mack Blackburn, former Executive Secretary to the Supreme Court of Tennessee; Mrs. Sammie Lynn Puett, Commissioner of Human Services; and many others.

We wish to express our special thanks to the reference librarians of the University of Tennessee, who, under the direction of Robert J. Bassett, have patiently endured our demands upon their time and their extensive knowledge.

Contents

Illustrations

Maps

Photographs

Cartoons

Chart

Tables

GOVERNMENT IN TENNESSEE

1

☆ ☆
☆

Beginnings

TENNESSEE WAS ADMITTED AS THE SIXTEENTH STATE IN THE UNION IN JUNE 1796. Before her admission into the federation of states, the area had been a part of the colony and the subsequent state of North Carolina, and her institutions recall the experience and history of that state. After a brief experience with an independent state—the State of Franklin—and the cession of the territory to the United States by North Carolina, Tennessee became, for a time, the "Territory of the United States South of the River Ohio." It was a territory that presented the increasing stream of settlers both opportunity and hardship. It was covered with forests; some of the upland land was poor, but the bottomlands were inviting. Great rivers were the principal routes for settlement, and water was to prove one of the state's great resources. There was coal, and other minerals. The climate was, on the whole, welcoming.

The State of Tennessee covers 42,244 square miles. Here lived, in 1980, 4,590,750 people, largely native white, increasingly urban, and principally employed in nonfarm occupations. A temporary fort was built in what is now Tennessee at Fort Prud'homme, north of the present city of Memphis, in 1682, but the settlement of Tennessee, begun in the succeeding century, was directed to Middle and East Tennessee, reached by pioneers who moved down the trails from Pennsylvania and the Piedmont areas of Virginia or who followed the French Broad into the Tennessee area from Asheville, North Carolina. West Tennessee was not opened to settlement until the signing of an 1818 Indian treaty.[1]

In 1980 the population of the state was rather evenly divided between the three Grand Divisions; East, 38.5 percent; Middle, 32.9 percent; and West, 28.6 percent. These figures were about what they were in 1970, and we may

[1]Stanley J. Folmsbee, Robert E. Corlew, and Enoch L. Mitchell, *Tennessee, A Short History* (Knoxville: Univ. of Tennessee Press, 1969), ch. 4.

1

consider it likely that the distribution of population among the Grand Divisions is likely to remain rather stable. The state's population expanded, from 1960 to 1970, by about 10 percent. From 1970 to 1980 the growth continued at a rate of 16.9 percent. The growth is steady, but it is not as spectacular as that of some of the states to the South and West. Tennessee shares (but not heavily) in the flight to the Sun Belt. All the same, the growth rate in Tennessee in the seventies substantially exceeded the 11.4 percent rate for the United States as a whole.

The black man is a political and economic factor in many states. And so he is in Tennessee, although fewer in number here than might be assumed. In 1980, 15.8 percent of Tennessee's people were black. This represents a slight increase over 1970. Some 726,000 Tennesseans are black (as of 1980), overwhelmingly urban. The distribution of the black population among the three Grand Divisions is uneven; West Tennessee accounted for 59.4 percent of the black population in 1980, Middle Tennessee, for 25.2 percent; and East Tennessee, for 15.4 percent. West and Middle Tennessee account for most of the nonurban black population of the state. Shelby County contains almost 45 percent of the state's blacks, but substantial black populations exist in Madison, Hamilton, and Davidson counties. Throughout the United States, the blacks have tended to concentrate—or sometimes to be stranded—in the central cities of metropolitan areas; that is the case in Tennessee as well. Blacks are therefore increasingly significant in the politics of the big urban areas, especially in Memphis. The significance is apparent in both local and Congressional elections. In some counties of the state there is almost no black population, and in many of them the number of blacks has never been high. Here racial questions have never played much of a role in politics.

In the last half-century Americans have moved in large numbers to urban or metropolitan areas. The character of that movement is changing, for much of the migration is now to the fringes of the big cities rather than to the cities themselves. But the movement is to urbanization, away from rural life and rural occupation. In 1860 almost 96 percent of the people of Tennessee lived in rural areas; since then urban growth has been steady. In 1980 2,850,000 people lived in the Tennessee portion of the six standard metropolitan statistical areas that lay wholly or partly in the state. From 1960 to 1970 the urban population of the state increased by 23.6 percent, while the rural population declined by 4.9 percent. In 1970, Tennessee was over 58 percent urban. (Figures for 1980 are not yet available).

Tennessee has had three constitutions; it lives now under the constitution of 1870, somewhat amended by the succession of constitutional conventions that have come along beginning in 1953. The first constitution, that of 1796, was modeled on the fundamental laws of North Carolina and Pennsylvania. It was typical of the state constitutions of its day in providing for three branches of government, with a preeminent legislature and a weak governor, but it foreshadowed a growing sympathy for democracy, a sympathy more fully evidenced in the second constitution, written in 1834 and adopted in 1835. An interesting but, for that day, not unusual provision of the 1796 constitution had been the requirement that land, if taxed, could be taxed only on acreage, not on value.[2] Thus, the owners of the bottomlands sought to protect themselves from the rapacity of their less fortunate neighbors, but this protection was given up in 1835. The democratizing influence of the Jacksonian era was apparent in the constitution of 1834–35, as indeed it was in other Southern states. Property qualifications were removed from all offices. County officials were to be elected by the voters in their jurisdictions, or appointed by the popularly elected county court. This constitution was slightly amended in 1853, and again in 1865.[3]

(★★★)

The principle of the sovereignty of the people governs the whole political system of the Anglo-Americans.

ALEXIS DE TOCQUEVILLE (1835)

DURING THE 1860s Tennessee was a principal theater of the struggle for the survival of the United States. A border state and the last to secede from the Union, Tennessee, because of its location and its waterways, was bound to become a major battleground of the Civil War. The east–west division of the state, even then evidenced in economic life, was reflected in the political differences on the issues of Unionism and Confederacy. East Tennessee, with its mountains and small-scale farming, was sympathetic to the cause of the Union throughout the period; West Tennessee, allied in economics and social structures with the Deep South, was overwhelmingly Confederate.[4]

In May 1861 the General Assembly, acting on the recommendation of Governor Isham G. Harris, passed an ordinance dissolving the federal relations between Tennessee and the United States. The people, voting on June 8, 1861 (the second vote on secession), adopted the declaration and annulled laws binding the state to membership in the Union. The Assembly

[2]On the constitution of 1796, see the third edition of this work, Univ. of Tennessee Press, 1975, 10–13.

[3]On the constitution of 1834–35, see third edition, 13–15.

[4]Philip M. Hamer, ed., *Tennessee: A History, 1673–1932* (New York: American Historical Society, 1933), vol. II, ch. XXXIV; see also Stanley J. Folmsbee, Robert E. Corlew, and Enoch L. Mitchell, *History of Tennessee* (New York: Lewis Publishing Co., 1960), vol. II, ch. XXVII; and Mary Emily Robertson Campbell, *The Attitude of Tennesseans toward the Union, 1847–1861* (New York: Vantage, 1961), 206–7.

had already moved to make Tennessee a part of the Confederacy, and by the end of summer the complete affiliation of the state with the other seceding states was accomplished.

About 105,000 persons voted for the separation to about 47,000 against. Seventy percent of the dissenting votes were cast in East Tennessee.[5] There was evidence that a greater number of dissents might have been registered in other areas had it not been for the intimidation of Union sympathizers by those who favored separation.[6] The people of East Tennessee did not readily acquiesce in the decision, but proposals for a separate state of East Tennessee came to nothing. The divisions of the state thus evidenced a century ago have played a role in Tennessee politics ever since.

Tennessee was the only seceding state to escape a military reconstruction. The amendment to the state constitution in the early part of 1865 abolishing slavery in the state and prohibiting the legislature from recognizing the right of property in man, together with the state's ratification of the Fourteenth Amendment in 1866, prompted Congress to restore the state to the Union. A constitutional convention, having been authorized by the people, met in Nashville in January 1870. The constitution produced by this convention, ratified by a vote of 98,128 to 33,872,[7] has been the fundamental law of the state for over a century.

The product of the convention was a document patterned on the constitution of 1834. That constitution, in turn, closely followed the general principles and outline of that of 1796. The people of Tennessee are therefore living today under a government in many ways originally designed for use in the eighteenth century. Since the original framers of the fundamental law limited themselves generally to statements of basic organization and jurisdiction, the 1870 document has continued to be highly usable, in spite of certain undesirable features. The major departures in 1870 from the 1834 document were alterations of the suffrage provisions, limitations on the length of sessions of the General Assembly, and curtailment of the governor's power in regard to the state militia—all reactions to the recent history of government in the state. The main purpose of the convention was to reunify the state; insofar as constitutional revision could achieve it, the results were satisfactory. Tennessee's constitution of 1870 remained unamended until 1953.

The constitution of 1870 is a comparatively short document as state constitutions go. It contains eleven articles including changes made in 1953 and later. There is evidence of considerable disorganization in the arrange-

---

[5]Hamer, 550, gives the vote 108,511 to 47,238; Caldwell quotes it 109,399 to 47,233; Joshua W. Caldwell, *Studies in the Constitutional History of Tennessee*, 2d ed. (Cincinnati: Robert Clarke Co., 1907), 275. Folmsbee *et al.*, *Tennessee, A Short History*, show the favorable vote to be about 105,000. All agree on the relative strength of the East Tennessee vote.

[6]Hamer, 547.

[7]*Ibid.*, p. 657; Folmsbee *et al.*, *Tennessee, A Short History*, 374–77.

ment of the constitution, a result of the patchwork of the conventions that have rewritten it. Parts of it are archaic. Dueling is, in effect, prohibited by the Tennessee constitution,[8] and ministers of the gospel who are, "by their profession, dedicated to God and the care of souls, and ought not be diverted from the great duties of their functions,"[9] are made ineligible for the General Assembly, a clause found in other eighteenth-century constitutions.[10] (This provision, borrowed from the North Carolina constitution, has been held in violation of the federal constitution by the Supreme Court of the United States). "No person who denies the being of God, or a future state of rewards and punishments, shall hold any office in the civil department of this State."[11] These provisions, reminiscent of an earlier time, are quaint but largely innocuous.

Article I of the constitution is devoted to a declaration of the rights of the individual within the state. (These rights are declared by Article XI, section 16, to be forever inviolate and excepted from the general powers of government.) Herein are the statements of principles of democratic self-government, the guarantees of religious liberty, freedom of speech, press, and assembly, security against search and seizure of private property by civil authority without proper warrant, the subordination of military to civil authority, the definition of the rights of individuals accused of crime within the state, and the prescription of procedural safeguards for all persons before the law. The boundaries of the state are outlined in section 31. The last two sections, 33 and 34, are in substance the constitutional amendments of 1865. They prohibit slavery and involuntary servitude except as punishment for crime and restrain the legislature from making a law that recognizes the right of property in man.

General qualifications for suffrage and officeholding as contained in the constitution of 1870 added some restrictions on legislative interference. Religious and political tests for officeholders, other than an oath to support the constitutions of the United States and Tennessee and the requirement of a belief in God and in the rewards and punishments of a future life, were prohibited.[12] The right of suffrage was so fixed that it could not be denied to any person who met the constitutional requirements of age, residence, and poll-tax payment "except upon a conviction by a jury of some infamous crime, previously ascertained and declared by law, and judgment thereon by court of competent jurisdiction."[13]

---

[8]*Constitution of Tennessee*, 1870, Art. IX, sec. 3. Hereafter this constitution is referred to by article and section only.

[9]Art. IX, sec. 1.

[10]See Ralph A. Wooster, *Politicians, Planters, and Plain Folk: Courthouse and Statehouse in the Upper South, 1850–1860* (Knoxville: Univ. of Tennessee Press, 1975).

[11]Art. IX, sec. 2.

[12]Art. I, sec. 4; Art. IX, sec. 2.

[13]Art. I, sec. 5.

The constitution, following a familiar American pattern, states that government "shall be divided into three distinct departments: the Legislative, Executive and Judicial."[14] In no case, except where the constitution directs it, can one of the branches exercise the powers belonging to either of the other two.

From the beginning the Tennessee governorship has been a position that permitted great flexibility and discretion in the exercise of administrative power. The governor is instructed by the constitution to execute the laws, but very little else is said about him. The major duties of the governor derive from the statutory rather than the constitutional law of the state. A number of powers assigned to him are typical of those of the American executive in all governmental units. He is commander-in-chief of the Tennessee army and navy (clearly no great navy is available to him), and he has the constitutional authority to appoint his military staff officers. He is allowed to grant reprieves or pardons to any person convicted of a crime. He can veto legislation, but his veto can be overridden by a majority of all the members elected to each house of the legislature. He makes temporary appointments to those offices that are regularly filled by the legislature in case a vacancy occurs when that body is not in session. He may call special sessions of the legislative body. Tennessee is one of the few states in the Union whose constitution does not provide for a lieutenant governor, an office that corresponds to that of the vice-presidency. In case of the inability of any governor to serve out his term, the speaker of the Senate succeeds him.[15]

The 1870 constitution placed several minor restrictions on the powers of the governor, although his authority was left, for the most part, to definition by the General Assembly, as was the case in the preceding constitution. Governor William G. Brownlow had suspended the writ of habeas corpus on occasion, so the convention stipulated that the Assembly should have the sole power of determining the emergency that would require the suspension of the writ.[16] It was provided that the militia could not be called into action except in case of invasion or rebellion, and then only when the Assembly should declare by law that the public safety required it.[17] The threats and practice of Brownlow's Radical government of declaring martial law in areas that failed to support the governor's program were fresh in the minds of the delegates.

During the Brownlow administration the Assembly had been in long, almost continuous session for the greater part of four years. In the ensuing reaction, the sessions of the Assembly were indirectly limited, a limitation

[14]Art. II, sec. 1.
[15]Art. III, sec. 12. By statute the speaker of the Senate is now designated lieutenant governor, but the designation adds little, if anything, to the speakership.
[16]Art. I, sec. 15.
[17]Art. III, sec. 5.

that would prove irksome to those who would like to have a legislature permanently in session. The constitution required that the Assembly meet biennially and that the legislators receive $4.00 per day plus traveling expenses to and from the capital. No members could be paid more than seventy-five days of a regular session, nor for more than twenty days of an extra session.[18]

A procedural restriction of legislative activity was also introduced into the new constitution. Omnibus bills—bills that carry provisions covering a multitude of subjects—were prohibited. The title of a bill could cover one subject only, and no bill could embrace more than the subject stipulated.[19]

The Tennessee legislature, the General Assembly, was divided by the constitution into two popularly chosen houses, the Senate and the House of Representatives. The maximum number of representatives was put at ninety-nine, and the Senate was limited to a membership of not more than a third of that number. An enumeration of qualified voters every ten years is directed by the constitution, the results to be used as a base for reapportionment of the members in an equitable manner by the legislature. With few exceptions the legislative body determines its own organization and prescribes its own rules of procedure. Speakers must be elected in both houses, bills must follow a designated form, and the passage of a bill through three successive readings in each house was carefully outlined. (The provision on three reading's was altered in 1978.) Members of the Assembly are protected from petty interference on civil grounds with their duties in the legislature.[20]

The scope of the legislative power of the General Assembly may be broadly defined as being all that is necessary for state government. Inasmuch as all powers not delegated to the federal government by the Constitution of the United States are reserved to the people or left to the states, the potential field of state legislation is a vast one, although progressively hemmed in by the expanding powers of the national government. Many state constitutions have hedged in the legislative power with restrictions that have long ceased to be realistic in the face of demands by the people for expanded services from the state. The Tennessee constitution, however, contains only a few restrictions on the powers of her government, and those are chiefly concerned with the field of taxation and the use of public money. The general property tax receives express constitutional sanction, and the constitution of 1870 required that all property be taxed according to value at the same rate. The constitution also allowed for the taxation of merchants and of privileges of a business nature, and until 1953 it made provisions for the levy of a poll tax, payment of which was made a requisite

[18]Art. II, sec. 23.
[19]Art. II, sec. 17.
[20]Art. II, *passim*.

for voting in the state. Farm products could not be taxed while they were in the possession of their producer or vendee.[21] Certain prohibitions on the investment of public money are laid down in the constitution, there being a restriction against investments in privately owned corporations and a limitation on the issue of bonds on the credit of the state for financial assistance of railroad companies.[22]

The constitution gives the Assembly explicit duties relating to the organization and management of local government. Instructions for the formation of new counties are included in the document, and some county boundaries were redrawn by the convention itself.[23] The constitution also made provision for the election of county sheriffs, trustees, registers, and justices of the peace and directed that certain other county officers should be appointed by the county court.[24]

It was long the practice of the Tennessee legislature to provide for the government of municipalities through the passage of special or local legislation that involved the most perfunctory attention from the Assembly as a whole, in that the body acted almost automatically on the recommendation of the delegation in the legislature from the locality involved. Tennessee is one of the few states that retains this procedure as a principal method of governing municipalities (although some changes were made in 1953). The constitution requires that corporations be formed under general laws,[25] but court interpretation of this section exempted municipal corporations from its application, and so by judicial interpretation gave constitutional sanction to the system of special legislation.

The Assembly is given certain nonlegislative powers. The House of Representatives has the power of impeachment over the governor, all judges in the state, the state attorneys, the state treasurer, the comptroller, and the secretary of state.[26] Impeachment proceedings are, briefly, formal accusations of official misconduct. They are preferred by the House, which takes the responsibility of electing three of its members to prosecute the trial. Trial on impeachment charges is held before the Senate with the chief justice of the Supreme Court presiding unless, of course, he is being tried. Conviction requires a two-thirds vote of the Senate. Impeachment has been vary sparingly employed; the last case occurred in 1958.

The secretary of state, state treasurer, and the comptroller of the treasury are elected by a joint ballot of the Assembly.[27] Inasmuch as the administrative department of the government is not outlined in the consti-

[21]Art. II, sec. 28.
[22]Art. II, secs. 31, 33.
[23]Art. X, sec. 4.
[24]Art. VII, sec. 1.
[25]Art. XI, sec. 8.
[26]Art. V, secs. 1–4.
[27]Art. III, sec. 17; Art. VII, sec. 3.

tution, legislative participation in the appointment of other administrative officials is left to legislative determination, through the passage of statutes that establish the departments and agencies of the state. The powers of the legislature over appointments may be limited by the doctrine of the separation of powers; state constitutional law on this subject is, so far, obscure.

The constituent power of the Assembly involves inaugurating the process for amending the constitution.

The judicial power of Tennessee is "vested in one Supreme Court, and such Circuit, Chancery and other inferior Courts as the Legislature shall from time to time, ordain and establish."[28] The Supreme Court is composed of five members, not more than two from any Grand Division who are elected at large by the people for eight-year terms. To be a judge of the Supreme Court, it is necessary to be thirty-five years of age and to have been a resident of the state for five years before election. The judges of this court designate one of their own number to preside as chief justice. Decisions of this body require the concurrence of three of the judges. The Supreme Court meets in Knoxville, Nashville, and Jackson, hearing cases on appeal from lower courts exclusively.

The judges of the circuit, chancery, and other lower courts are elected by the voters of the districts or circuits over which their respective courts have jurisdiction. Such judges must be thirty years of age and must have been, before election, residents of the state for five years and of the circuit or district for one year. They serve for eight-year terms.

Judges are subject to removal from office by a concurrent vote of both houses of the General Assembly, each house voting separately. This action, however, requires a two-thirds vote of the membership of each house and has rarely been used. The last attempt to remove a judge by this method occurred in 1978; it failed.

We are accustomed to describe our constitutions as the fundamental law and to make them harder to establish or to change than ordinary.
HARVEY WALKER (1960)

TENNESSEE GOVERNMENT OPERATED for about eighty years without a change in the fundamental law. The amending process, carefully outlined in the constitution, set up formidable hurdles for constitutional amendments. These proved insurmountable before the convention of 1953.

[28]Art. VI, sec. 1.

The perilous journey of a constitutional amendment in Tennessee under the original amending clause began with a proposal made in either house of the Assembly, requiring only a majority of the members elected to each house to gain first passage. The amendment, duly recorded, was then stored in mothballs until six months before the election of the next Assembly, when the constitution required that it be published. These requirements for delay and publication were probably inserted to allow both the electorate and the representatives to give each measure calm deliberation; no doubt it was thought that the support or nonsupport of the proposals should become a campaign issue at the time of the next election. The second Assembly could pass on the amendment favorably with a two-thirds majority of the members elected to each house. Finally, the proposed amendment was to be referred to the people for a vote on adoption or rejection. Before 1953 the Tennessee constitution required that the people must ratify a proposed amendment by a majority of all those voting for representatives. The effect of this provision was to count as negative all those who expressed no opinion on the amendment. (In 1953, this final vote was changed to a majority of those voting for governor in that election.)

The constitution of 1870 added a sentence to the amendment section of the 1834 document. The latter had no provision for calling a constitutional convention, and the 1870 constitution was written under the legal justification of the clause found in the first section of the Declaration of Rights allowing the people to alter, reform, or abolish their form of government. The 1870 constitution specifically empowered the General Assembly to submit to the people the question of a constitutional convention to "alter, reform, or abolish" the existing fundamental law. Under this provision a majority of all votes cast on the convention issue is sufficient to call a convention. From 1870 to 1952 twelve attempts to call conventions failed. It has been the practice of the Assembly to pass two simultaneous acts, the first submitting the issue of calling a convention to the people, and the second providing for the election of delegates thereto. Apparently the General Assembly could limit the powers of the convention by specifying in its proposal those sections of the constitution or those subjects on which the convention could propose amendments.

From 1875 to 1935, we know of twenty proposed amendments to the Tennessee constitution that failed to pass in the second legislature. In this period ten amendments passed the two legislatures but failed to receive the extraordinary majorities necessary for approval by the voters. Thereafter numerous further attempts to amend the constitution by legislative action on single issues failed either in the second legislature or in the referendum process, and it became thoroughly clear that this form of amendment could not be successfully used (although this record of failure has not kept legislators from trying it). It is surprising that legislators still try to use this procedure; repeated attempts have been made to use this clause, even after 1953. The latest such use of this procedure began in 1979, when several amendments were initiated. It is reasonable to assume they will never make it. A number of other amendments were proposed to the legislature, but were not adopted.

Tennessee's 1870 constitution has been remarkably durable. Extensive amendment has not been necessary as there was little padding of the 1870 constitution with statutory material, nor were there many major restrictions or limitations on the operation of government. The number of times a constitution has been amended is no criterion of its excellence or even of its adjustment to present demands on government. In some states frequent amendments have hacked away at the fundamental principles of a constitution until they have become obscure. The Louisiana constitution until 1975 was an outstanding example of this practice, as that of California still is. An amending procedure that allows change in the constitution with little more effort than change in the statutory law is not conducive to a stable, well-defined system of fundamental law. It was fear of the instability allowed by easy change that prompted the framers of the Tennessee constitution to make it the most difficult of all state constitutions to amend. But by making the Tennessee system as extremely difficult as it is, the framers sacrificed the possibility of ready adjustment to social change.

Eight of the proposals in the early history of attempts to amend the constitution were concerned with the popular election of certain constitutional officers: the comptroller, the treasurer, and the attorney general. The first two, under the constitution, are elected by a joint ballot of the General Assembly; the last is appointed by the Supreme Court. These attempts to place the government of the state more directly under the authority of the people (and incidentally to lengthen the ballot, a practice that has been in considerable disfavor in the past fifty years) substantially ceased with the 1911 proposals for amendment. The extension of the term of governor, however, has been a constant aim of amending attempts. A number of proposals have been made to alter the restrictions on the taxing powers of the General Assembly. Some of these attempted to secure the classification of property (finally successful in 1972), a change that would allow the imposition of differing ratios of assessment to actual value on various kinds of property in consideration of their differing income-producing characteristics. One proposed change that failed would have authorized the adoption within the state of a progressive income tax; this issue has not gone away. The earliest proposed constitutional change regarding the taxing power would have allowed the exemption of manufacturers from taxation by local governments, a proposal apparently prompted by the desire for new industry. A number of proposals were directed toward adding to the powers of local government and changing its general structure. Some amendments have been directed to the suffrage: one in 1915 was designed to permit women to vote in the state, a goal later achieved by the passage of the Nineteenth Amendment to the United States Constitution; one, in 1945, would have abolished the poll tax. Remaining proposals have been concerned with such matters as prohibition, the amending process, and the earmarking of revenue sources for highways.

Beginning in 1945, further determined attempts were made to amend the constitution. The governor was authorized at this time to appoint a Constitution Revision Commission to propose amendments. The commission expressed the view that a general revision or a new constitution was not necessary, recommending instead that the legislature propose a convention with authority to revise only certain sections of the constitution. The specific revisions suggested by the commission applied to such matters as the amendment process, the taxing powers of the legislature, apportionment of senators and representatives, the legislative quorum, compensation of legislators, the governor's term, the veto power, suffrage, municipal home rule, and city–county consolidation.[29]

The commission's report was published in 1946 and submitted to the 1947 legislature. One member of the seven-man commission, although signing the report, appended a statement to the effect that he doubted the wisdom of five of the commission's basic proposals. A further negative view was expressed in an opinion of the attorney general to the effect that the General Assembly was without power to propose a limited convention. The 1947 legislature failed to take action on the commission's report.

In the slow and imperfect process of political adjustment to social need . . . the Constitutional Convention of 1953 has made a conspicuous contribution . . . .

FRANK GOAD CLEMENT (1953)

IN 1949 THE GENERAL ASSEMBLY proposed to the voters a constitutional convention limited to the specific subjects on which the Constitution Revision Commission had recommended change. For this referendum, the General Assembly ordered a special election that year, but the proposal was defeated by a small margin—65,417 against holding a convention and 62,483 in favor of a convention. In 1951 the General Assembly again proposed the calling of a limited constitutional convention; this time it ordered that the referendum be held on the same day as the statewide direct primary in August 1952, and this referendum resulted in a majority vote for the convention, 196,376 to 106,583.

[29]*Report of the Constitution Revision Commission* (Nashville: Nov. 1946).

The ninety-nine delegates to the convention were elected by the voters in November 1952 from the same ninety-nine districts from which members of the lower house of the General Assembly were elected. The convention met in April 1953, organized, and spent approximately two months considering the subjects specified by the General Assembly. Eight amendments were submitted to the voters at a special election in November 1953; all eight received a majority of the vote and were proclaimed by the governor as part of the constitution on November 19, 1953.

Delegates to the convention included personalities not ordinarily found in the General Assembly. Party and factional lines were not as clearly drawn among the delegates as they ordinarily were among legislators; in many communities candidates came forward who were not habitually legislative candidates, and many veteran legislators were missing from the convention roster. All the same, many well-known political figures were present. The convention was thought to be an able one. Three ex-governors were delegates: Ben Hooper (one of the few Republican governors), Jim McCord (who was forced by his wife's illness to resign early in the sessions), and Prentice Cooper, who became president of the convention. Governor Cooper narrowly defeated Cecil Sims of Nashville for this post; Mr. Sims had been a member and secretary of the Constitution Revision Commission of 1945. Some able veteran legislators were on hand. Two professional political scientists (C. C. Sims and Frank W. Prescott) were delegates experienced in public affairs.

The contest over the presidency was sharp, but both major candidates were Democrats. The vice-president of the convention, elected by acclamation, was a Republican. Governor Frank G. Clement favored the candidacy of Prentice Cooper for president of the convention, but aside from this it is fairly clear that the governor did not seek influence in the deliberations.

Divergent opinions appeared most sharply in the convention on the question of lowering the voting age to eighteen years and on the issue of home rule. On the latter question, the Tennessee Municipal League represented an active interest group before the convention, but aside from this one case, interest groups were not very evident. It could not be said that the issues dealt with by the convention were noncontroversial, but they were not the kind to invite the attention of special groups in the state.

The convention was at its most conservative with respect to the amending process. The difficult path of single amendments was left substantially unchanged; in the future such single amendments must be approved, after action by the two sessions of the legislature (as previously was the case), by a majority equal to a majority of the total vote for governor, instead of the majority of the vote for representatives (as was formerly the case). The new version of the amending process made it perfectly clear that a convention could be called with jurisdiction limited to specific subjects, but conventions are limited to one every six years.

The pay of the legislature was increased to $10.00 per day, and expense allowances were likewise raised; raises or reductions by legislative action were permitted. (The grant of authority to raise legislative pay has since then been generously used.)

The convention edged toward a stronger executive by establishing a four-year term for the governor; but at the same time, it made a governor ineligible to succeed himself. In a lengthy and carefully drafted clause, the governor was empowered by item veto to reduce or disapprove a sum appropriated by a particular item or clause, a power that since then has been plentifully employed. The General Assembly may reinstate such items by a majority of all the members elected to both houses.

The chief effect of the suffrage amendment was to strike out the poll tax as a prerequisite for voting. This step was actually no more than a contribution to clarity, for the statutes had already eliminated the poll tax in Tennessee. The minimum period of residency in the county necessary for voting was reduced from six to three months.

The convention undertook its sharpest departure from past practice when it revised state–local relations. Amendment Six put a sharp restriction on special legislation by providing that no special act concerning a county or city could be passed without a provision making its validity dependent upon approval by a two-thirds vote of the local governing body or by a simple majority in a local referendum. Furthermore, the amendment stipulated that no special act may remove the incumbent from a municipal or county office, abridge his term, or alter his salary during his term.

This fairly drastic change in the constitution failed to satisfy the strong pressures for home rule for cities, backed by the Tennessee Municipal League. Eventually, therefore, the convention developed a longer clause on home rule which provides that any municipality can, by ordinance, submit the question of adoption of home rule to popular local referendum. Once home rule has been adopted, the General Assembly may act with respect to such municipality only by laws that are general in terms and effect. A home-rule municipality may amend its charter or adopt a new one providing for its organization and powers, but no charter provision so adopted may be inconsistent with the general acts of the state. Such general acts do not, however, bind the home-rule city with respect to compensation of city personnel. The taxation powers of home-rule cities may not be enlarged except by general act of the legislature. The methods of creating, enlarging, merging, consolidating, and dissolving municipalities may be provided only by general act. A procedure is set up for local home-rule charter commissions. The General Assembly was prohibited from authorizing municipalities to tax incomes, estates, or inheritances, or to impose any tax not authorized by sections 28 or 29 of Article II of the constitution. Such was Amendment Seven, perhaps, along with Amendment Six, the most significant of all the changes made by the 1953 convention.

Late in the closing days of the convention the delegates added one final amendment. Number Eight empowered the legislature to authorize the consolidation of any or all municipal functions with county functions providing that such was made dependent upon concurrent majorities inside and outside the municipality, a requirement that, in most cases, has hamstrung consolidation moves.

Incrementalism and gradualism are far more characteristic of American experience in revising . . . constitutions than drastic alterations.

ALBERT STURM (1973)

IN 1958 THE VOTERS of Tennessee, starting a trend for conventions every six years, authorized another limited constitutional convention which convened in July 1959. The convention's agenda was restricted to three subjects: (1) lowering the voting age from twenty-one to eighteen years, (2) establishing a four-year term for sheriff without limitation as to the number of terms permitted to the same individual, and (3) establishing a four-year term for the office of trustee (county treasurer). The convention rejected the proposal to extend the term of office of sheriff and to permit unrestricted terms, and it voted to retain the twenty-one-year age minimum for voting. It approved the four-year term for trustee subject to ratification by the voters in the general election of November 1960. This amendment received ratification and became effective September 1, 1962.

In the special session of 1962 called to deal with apportionment (the basic drive being to preserve rural powers) and the governor's suggestion for a constitutional convention, the legislature started the machinery for a convention to be held in 1965. A referendum on the call in the fall of 1962 having approved the proposal, the convention met in 1965. By this time it was clear that reapportionment of both houses of the General Assembly would have to be based on population in order to comply with Supreme Court decisions, so the convention turned to other matters. It proposed, among other things, four-year staggered terms for senators, the apportionment of the Assembly on the basis of population, the division of counties into districts where counties had two or more representatives or two or more senators, the calling of special sessions if requested by two-thirds of each house (as well as when requested by the governor, as previously provided), "split" sessions of the legislature, and annual salaries for legislators. These proposals were adopted in 1966.

After an appropriate call and the convening of still another convention in 1971, the constitution was again amended by an overwhelming popular vote in 1972 to order a classified property tax. The convention that adopted this proposal was severely restricted in what it could do by the enabling legislation, and the convention itself was heavily dominated by the Farm Bureau Federation, a strong proponent of sharp limitation of the property tax on farms. The Tennessee Municipal League and the Tennessee County Service Association also worked for the convention and for the amendment; their motives were not so readily apparent. The legislative call for the convention had included four other proposals involving reform of the judiciary, changes in local powers, changes in the sessions of the legislature and the succession of the governor, and the lowering of the voting age to eighteen, but all of these ideas were rejected by the voters, who refused to authorize the constitutional convention to deal with them. The 1971 convention was therefore confined to a consideration of the classified property tax. The popular vote on the other proposals offered strong indication that the voter of Tennessee was still not ready for sweeping changes in his fundamental law, and it could have indicated some weariness with the persistent procession of conventions that has taken place since 1953.[30] If so, such weariness went unheeded, for another convention met in 1977.

A lengthy, sometimes stormy, and almost continually controversial convention met in the summer and fall of that year. In the scope of the subjects covered it surpassed the first limited convention of a quarter-century earlier. It turned over to the voters for a special election on March 7, 1978, thirteen proposals, of which the electorate approved twelve.

A number of issues before the convention excited controversy, but the calling of the convention itself was triggered to a large degree by the determination of the state Supreme Court to enforce the limit on interest rates set in the constitution, a limit that threatened to close down small loan businesses and that the banking interest found irksome, at least. Bankers in Tennessee enjoy political clout when they are aroused, and they worked for the convention. Enough other items were added to the call to produce substantial changes in the fundamental law of Tennessee.

Proposal 10, which was approved by the voters, removed the 10 percent interest rate maximum in the constitution, required the legislature to set a rate, and temporarily reinstated the 1969 consumer loan law that the Supreme Court had ruled invalid. Proposal number 4 revised one of the

---

[30]Constitutional activity in the states generally has been summarized in Albert L. Sturm, *Trends in State Constitution-Making 1966–1972* (Lexington, Ky.: Council of State Governments, 1973).

revisions of 1953: it kept the governor's term at four years but allowed a governor to succeed himself. It was so written as to apply to the incumbent, Ray Blanton, whose administration had been under heavy fire. The voters approved this proposal. In the late spring of 1978, Blanton withdrew anyway, possibly (although he never said so) convinced that he could not make it.

In another respect, the 1977–78 proposals revised an earlier amendment (made in 1966); the "split" session of the legislature that provided for a period exclusively devoted to organization was abandoned. The voters approved.

In a section that attracted the nationwide attention of weary taxpayers, the convention proposed, and the people adopted, the requirement of a balanced budget; it also banned deficit spending and keyed increases in future spending into the growth in personal income. Bonds were permitted, but the first year of financing was required to be provided for with the authorization of the bonds. A ruling from the office of the attorney general had already held that the constitution prohibited deficit spending, on the basis of an old and not very clear decision.

The convention also took advantage of its opportunity to repeal a number of outmoded or invalid provisions of the 1870 document. The voters approved removing the ban on interracial marriage and the segregation and poll-tax clauses. The poll tax as a prerequisite for voting had long since disappeared, even before a national amendment had prohibited it. The racial clauses had been rendered invalid by federal action. (These matters were in proposals 1 and 6.)

Proposal 7 lowered the voting age from twenty-one to eighteen, which had already been required by federal amendment, but a provision was included that prohibited registration on the day of the election. In adopting this proposal the voters signalled that they disliked the proposals of President Carter for "quickie" registration. Considering how long it had taken Tennessee to get voter registration in the first place, it is understandable that Carter's proposals looked like a return to the corrupt election administration of earlier times.

Proposal 2 removed some venerable legislative procedures. Now that the voters have approved, legislative bills need not be signed by the speaker in open session and bills need no longer be "read" three times; "consideration" and voting are required three times. Proposal number 6 gave the governor ten days—instead of the old five—to decide whether or not to sign a bill.

Proposal 3 increased the amount of property exempt from court-ordered bankruptcy, a matter of importance only to an unfortunate few.

Proposal 11 set the stage for a far-reaching reorganization of county government, replacing the ancient nonintegrated county machinery with medium-sized county legislative bodies and a county executive. The constitutional officers were preserved, and a county executive, county clerk, and an assessor of property were added to the list (a forward step in a backward direction—like the advance of the defeated Austrian general). The sheriff was now given a four-year term and allowed to succeed himself (the sheriffs had been trying for that for over a decade). All this was approved, but legislative action was required—and this was to cause confusion and litigation.

But proposal 13—reform of the judiciary—was defeated at the polls. The proposal would have reduced terms to six years (from eight), provided nonpartisan elections for trial judges, consolidated the confusing system of trial courts, and required all judges to be lawyers. The "Missouri plan" would have been applied to all appellate judges. A prohibition against changing a judge's pay during his term would have been removed. A Court of Discipline and Removal would have allowed the court system to remove errant judges. Legislative approval of Supreme Court rules would have been required (an important element in the defeat of the amendment). The attorney general would have been chosen by the governor.

This proposal was defeated in a fairly close vote. The trial lawyers, the big-city bar, and the Supreme Court didn't like it. Blacks feared the threat of legislative reduction of pay for judges who handed down unpopular decisions. So the ancient complications of the Tennessee judiciary continue.

The voting patterns on these issues invite entertaining—but dangerous —speculations. County majorities against the judiciary proposition were widespread, but some approval was evident in East Tennessee, which has lived long under the domination of a heavily Democratic judiciary. Knox County approved, but the other big three counties rejected the proposal.

The spending limit proposal swept the state, losing only in a few central counties, largely on the Highland Rim. All the big counties went for it, somewhat surprisingly considering the concentration of the poor in those areas. But the total number voting in some places was low enough to support the notion that the disadvantaged voter did not speak up—one way or another.

The removal of the interest rate ceiling received its widest support in East and West Tennessee. Why?—no answer is apparent.

County government changes received support in all three Grand Divisions, but were rejected in some areas including Highland Rim counties and in Hamilton and Davidson. Davidson already had a reformed government, and Hamilton had gone part way along the road of county modernization.

2

☆ ☆
☆

The Unalienable and Indefeasible

THE AMERICAN STATE CONSTITUTION-MAKERS OF THE EIGHTEENTH CENTURY never failed to include in their fundamental laws numerous clauses designed to protect the private citizen from the ruler's abuse of power. Both the Constitution of the United States and that of North Carolina of 1776 contained statements of rights considered to be fundamental. As finally adopted on February 6, 1796, the Tennessee constitution included a bill of rights—thirty-two sections now incorporated in Article I. These rights were carried over in the constitution of 1834 with no more than minor changes. An addition made in 1865 prohibited slavery and forbade the legislature to pass any law "recognizing the right of property in man." A few states have added to their bills of rights matters of contemporary concern such as right-to-work clauses, freedom of association, or equal rights regardless of sex; Tennessee has not, and the political climate plus the difficulty of amendment makes such additions unlikely.

The constitutional convention of 1870 was primarily concerned with reconstruction. Although the Declaration of Rights was little changed, such changes as were made reflect the problems of that day. Political tests for officeholding, except for an oath to support the federal and state constitutions, were prohibited. The right of suffrage was strengthened. Religious and political tests for jury service were prohibited. The General Assembly was given control over the suspension of the writ of habeas corpus. Martial law, "in the sense of the unrestricted power of military officers, or others, to dispose of the persons, liberties or property of the citizen," was prohibited. Such words as "freeman" and "free white men" were changed to "men" or "citizens" or "persons." The amendments of 1865 were included.

⊛

The Fourteenth Amendment gave an express sanction, hitherto lack-
ing, to the principle of equality; on the other hand, the due-process
clause merely added the federal guaranty to a principle already famil-
iar under state constitutions.

ERNST FREUND (1917)

THE TWO CONSTITUTIONS under which the people of the United States
live—the national and the state—furnish the bases for these governments,
and both contain guarantees of private rights. The Tennessee Declaration of Rights affords no protection against the acts of the federal
government, nor do the first eight amendments of the Constitution of the
United States protect the people from the acts of state governments. Other
sections of the federal constitution, however, limit state action in the
interest of liberty. An example will illustrate the matter: a person may not
be deprived of life, liberty, or property except by due process of law. This
protection against unlawful acts of the federal government is secured by
the Fifth Amendment of the Constitution of the United States. Similarly
acts of the state government are limited not only by the constitution of
Tennessee, but also by the Fourteenth Amendment of the federal constitution. Thus certain liberties are twice guaranteed. This dual protection is not
without significance. State bills of rights are still important, but people
have become so used to looking to the federal government for civil rights
action that they forget that state constitutions contain similar guarantees.
By way of the federal constitution's Fourteenth Amendment in particular,
the federal courts exercise a control, when called upon to do so, over the
actions of state and local authorities, particularly with regard to freedom of
religion, freedom of press and speech, and the rights of persons accused of
crime.

Courts are one of the agencies that may be relied on for the enforcement
of private rights. But in the last analysis the protection of private rights
rests upon the degree of support that those rights receive from the public.
In the United States such support is somewhat uncertain and uneasy.
Support for free speech receives only a qualified acceptance from Americans, particularly from persons of lower educational levels. People of
higher educational levels are more tolerant of diversity than is the general
public, but inasmuch as educated sectors of the population are politically
more active than less fortunate groups, freedom of speech is at least
afforded a degree of support in politically active classes.

The Tennessean's bill of rights is known as the Declaration of Rights; it
consists primarily of thirty-three of the thirty-four sections of Article I of
the state constitution. These rights may be classified as (1) political, (2)

personal, and (3) property rights. These three categories overlap, but the division is useful.

Some rights are primarily procedural; they guarantee certain methods of doing business. Such are the rights of accused persons. Other rights are concerned with the substance of things, such as freedom of speech; we refer to these as substantive rights.

Liberty, as a principle, has no application to any state of things anterior to the time when mankind have become capable of being improved by free and equal discussion.

JOHN STUART MILL (1859)

THE FIRST SECTION of the Declaration of Rights sets forth the doctrine of popular sovereignty and proclaims the right of revolution. The second section vigorously denounces "the doctrine of non-resistance against arbitrary power and oppression" as being "absurd, slavish, and destructive of the good and happiness of mankind." The principles here stated are those of the American Revolution; the debt of the framers of the constitution to the ideas expressed in the Declaration of Independence is obvious. Such clauses are statements of principles; they cannot be effectively used as limitations. We operate on the assumption that the popular will is expressed in the constitution and in statutes passed by the legislature. The "unalienable and indefeasible right to alter, reform, or abolish the government in such manner as they may think proper" must be limited to constitutional methods. If, however, free government came to an end, the people might be morally justified in using other than constitutional means to restore it; indeed, an obligation to resist tyranny may be assumed. It is hardly necessary to say that in such a case a man's attempt and failure to restore free government could easily result in his execution—although he might go to his death with a clear conscience. In practice, the statement of revolutionary principles in our state constitution, although a reminder of our heritage, has no day-to-day usefulness.[1]

If the doctrine of popular sovereignty is to have meaning and if political democracy is to be preserved, it is essential that people must enjoy freedom of the press and speech, freedom of assembly, and freedom to vote and hold office. Our bill of rights does contain provisions of an enforceable sort that aid in preserving political independence. Freedom of the press and of speech is guaranteed in the Declaration of Rights, and such freedom is enforceable. At the same time it is recognized that such freedom

[1]*West* v. *Carr,* 212 Tenn. 367 (1963).

is not absolute and that citizens are "responsible for the abuse of that liberty."[2] Thus, for example, publishers of newspapers may be punished for contempt if "pending the trial of a case" they "publish matter for public circulation which is calculated to impede, embarrass, or affect the orderly trial and disposition of the case being heard."[3] Freedoms of speech and press do not grant one the privilege of committing a criminal libel; nor do they allow defamation or protect one from civil liability for libel and slander. These rights do not permit sedition.

The right of assembly is embodied in the provision that "citizens have a right, in a peaceable manner, to assemble together for their common good, to instruct their representatives, and to apply to those invested with the powers of government for redress of grievances, or other proper purposes, by address or remonstrance."[4] This right is also limited; the assembly must be "peaceable."

An example of an issue requiring an interpretation of this right is provided by a case in which the right of assembly, together with the right of petition, has been held to protect a group of citizens, who petitioned two officials to revoke a merchant's license, from the merchant's subsequent suit for damages charging the group with civil conspiracy after the illegal revocation of the license by town officials. However, the court indicated that had the citizens acted with malice the decision might have been otherwise.[5] The right of assembly is undoubtedly more far-reaching than this case indicates. It must be broad enough to cover all peaceable political meetings and all other meetings of citizens designed to promote the "common good," "to instruct their representatives," or to petition "for redress of grievances." We have seen in recent actions concerning civil rights how important the right of assembly may be.

Of all the rights or privileges fundamental to a democracy certainly none is more important than the right to vote. Whether the vote is a right or a privilege may be debatable, but our own state constitution uses the word "right." The Declaration of Rights provides: "[The] elections shall be free and equal, and the right of suffrage, as hereinafter declared, shall never be denied to any person entitled thereto, except upon a conviction by a jury of some infamous crime, previously ascertained and declared by law, and judgment thereon by court of competent jurisdiction."[6] This section does not stand alone; it must now be read with Article IV, section 1, as amended in 1953 and 1978. The right to vote is denied to those convicted of infamous crime, but this disability may be removed. The right to hold office is

[2]Art. I, sec. 19.
[3]*Tennessee Code Annotated*, hereafter referred to as *TCA*, annotation to 23–9–102. See also *Tate* v. *State*, 132 Tenn. 131, 136 (1915).
[4]Art. I, sec. 23.
[5]*McKee* v. *Hughes*, 133 Tenn. 455 (1915).
[6]Art. I, sec. 5.

protected by the provision "that no political or religious test, other than an oath to support the Constitution of the United States and of this State, shall ever be required as a qualification to any office or public trust under this state." Discrimination against particular parties and religions is thus proscribed,[7] but Article IX, section 2 requires that civil officers believe in God and a future state of rewards and punishments. A cynic could remark that some officials appear to believe in a present state of rewards.

Bills of attainder, ex post facto laws, and laws impairing the obligation of contracts, are contrary to the first principles of the social contract.

JAMES MADISON (1788)

CERTAIN RIGHTS that have been listed above as political freedoms may clearly be classified as personal. But the list of personal freedoms is even more extensive.

The third section of the Declaration of Rights provides:

> That all men have a natural and indefeasible right to worship Almighty God according to the dictates of their own conscience: that no man can of right be compelled to attend, erect, or support any place of worship, or to maintain any minister against his consent; that no human authority can, in any case whatever, control or interfere with the rights of conscience; and that no preference shall ever be given, by law to any religious establishment or mode of worship.[8]

A sensational interpretation of this section arose in the famous Scopes case, which gave certain Tennessee affairs wide and lasting news value. A statute had made it unlawful to teach in any tax-supported school any theory that denied the divine creation of man as taught in the Bible.[9] John Scopes, a theretofore obscure teacher, was convicted for violation of the statute; the Supreme Court of Tennessee reversed the judgment but upheld the statute. "The plaintiff in error was a teacher in the public schools of Rhea County . . . . He had no right or privilege to serve the State except upon such terms as the State prescribed. His liberty . . . to teach and proclaim the theory of evolution, elsewhere than in the service of the State, was in no wise touched by this law."[10]

---

[7]Art. I, sec. 4.

[8]Art. I, sec. 3.

[9]*Public Acts,* 1925, ch. 27.

[10]*Scopes* v. *State,* 154 Tenn. 105, 111 (1927). The statute was eventually repealed. A 1973 act requiring "equal time" for theories of creation other than evolution, including but not limited to the Biblical version of creation, was held to be unconstitutional as violative of the federal and state constitutions; *Steele* v. *Waters,* 527 S.W. 2d 72 (1975).

A later case is more explicit on the subject of religious freedom. A Tennessee statute provides: "It shall be unlawful for any person, or persons, to display, exhibit, handle or use any poisonous or dangerous snake or reptile in such a manner as to endanger the life or health or any person."[11] Members of the Holiness Church, who believed in snake handling as proof of faith and as a means of evangelism, were indicted and convicted of violating the act by handling rattlesnakes. The Supreme Court upheld the conviction.[12]

Conflicts between religious belief and public health measures arise from time to time, but reasonable health measures will ordinarily prevail.[13] As interpreted by the Supreme Court, the state constitution permits limited religious observance in the public schools, even over the objections of a few persons and even though the observance has something of a sectarian character.[14]

The Declaration of Rights provides:

> That the people shall be secure in their persons, houses, papers and possessions from unreasonable searches and seizures; and that general warrants, whereby an officer may be commanded to search suspected places, without evidence of the fact committed, or to seize any person or persons not named, whose offenses are not particularly described and supported by evidence, are dangerous to liberty and ought not to be granted.[15]

The statutes of Tennessee are detailed in their prescription of warrants and warrants of arrest as well as in authorizing arrests. A search warrant is issued only after a cause is shown to be probable; it must describe the place to be inspected. Evidence obtained as a result of an unlawful search cannot be used in court against a defendant.

A warrant of arrest is issued by a magistrate when he is satisfied "that the offense complained of has been committed, and there is reasonable ground to believe the defendant is guilty thereof . . . ."[16] A person who is arrested is taken before a magistrate or placed in jail pending a hearing. If arrested and confined in jail, a person is not to be treated with "unnecessary rigor."[17] If taken before a magistrate, he will be discharged if the magistrate

---

[11]*TCA*, 39–2208.

[12]*Harden et al.* v. *State*, 188 Tenn. 17, 25 (1948). Such practices have not completely died out; an instance of the sort occurred in Cocke County in 1973. Late in 1974 the Court of Appeals did hold (possibly on the principle of one fool the less, one angel more) that a man who wanted to handle snakes could do so, provided he did not test his faith by endangering someone else. See also *State ex rel. Swann* v. *Pack*, 527 S.W. 2d 99 (1975).

[13]See *Gamble* v. *State*, 206 Tenn. 376 (1960).

[14]*Carden* v. *Bland*, 199 Tenn. 665 (1956); see also Joseph W. Harrison, "The Bible, the Constitution, and Public Education," *Tennessee Law Review* 29:3 (Spring 1962), 363–418.

[15]Art. I, sec. 7.

[16]*TCA*, 40–704.

[17]Art. I, sec. 13.

finds that no offense has been committed or that no probable cause exists for charging the defendant. If the defendant is charged, he will be sent to jail unless the offense is bailable and he is able to provide sufficient bail. At this stage the defendant comes again under protection of the Declaration of Rights, which provides "That all prisoners shall be bailable by sufficient sureties, unless for capital offenses, when the proof is evident, or the presumption great."[18] Even one charged with a capital offense is bailable when proof is not evident or the presumption is not great. The right to bail is lost after conviction, but the court still has discretion to grant it. In any case, excessive bail must not be required.[19]

The purpose of either confining the accused or requiring him to furnish bail is to ensure his appearance at court. If he is to be prosecuted, additional protection is afforded by the Declaration of Rights. It is provided "That no person shall be put to answer any criminal charge but by presentment, indictment or impeachment."[20] A misdemeanor is not a criminal charge within the meaning of this section, but all misdemeanors, just as all felonies, may be prosecuted by indictment. "An indictment is an accusation in writing presented by the grand jury of the county, charging a person with an indictable offense."[21] A presentment is similar to an indictment and serves the same purpose. The requirement of an indictment or presentment protects the accused from standing trial on groundless accusations. It also serves to fulfill the constitutional right of the accused "to demand the nature and cause of the accusation against him, and to have a copy thereof."[22]

The "accused hath the right to be heard by himself and his counsel . . . ."[23] The right to be heard is a very real right—a genuine hearing is required. Not only does the accused have a right to be heard, but he must be present in any court of original criminal jurisdiction that tries him, and he may be allowed to be present in appellate courts to plead his case. A defendant may argue his own case, but he is entitled to be heard through counsel. Counsel must have time to prepare the defense. If the defendant is not able to employ his own counsel, he has a right to have the court appoint counsel. Furthermore, counsel "shall be allowed access to the defendant at all reasonable hours."[24] If the defendant requests permission to testify in his own behalf, he is a competent witness, but his failure to testify does not operate against him. If he wants to testify, he must do so before he offers

---

[18]Art. I, sec. 15.
[19]Art. I, sec. 16.
[20]Art. I, sec. 14.
[21]*TCA*, 40–1701.
[22]Art. I, sec. 9. This article does not apply in misdemeanor cases; *Jordan* v. *State*, 156 Tenn. 509 (1928).
[23]Art. I, sec. 9.
[24]*TCA*, 40–2004; compare also *Johnson* v. *State*, 213 Tenn. 55 (1963).

any other testimony. The accused also has "the right . . . to meet the witnesses face to face . . ."[25] and "to have compulsory process for obtaining witnesses in his favor."[26]

In prosecutions by indictment or presentment, the accused has a right to "a speedy public trial, by an impartial jury of the County in which the crime shall have been committed . . . ."[27] The Declaration of Rights also provides "That the right of trial by jury shall remain inviolate, and no religious or political test shall ever be required as a qualification for jurors."[28] A speedy trial "means a trial as soon after indictment as the prosecution can, with reasonable diligence, prepare for it, without needless, vexatious, or oppressive delay, having in view, however, its regulation and conduct by fixed rules of law, any delay created by the operation of which rules does not in legal contemplation work prejudice to the constitutional right of the accused."[29] The right of jury trial does not apply to certain misdemeanors unless they involve life or liberty, to certain summary proceedings, to contempt proceedings, or to suits in chancery court.

The defendant is entitled to be tried in "the County in which the crime shall have been committed . . . ."[30] The accused "shall not be compelled to give evidence against himself."[31] He does not have to testify unless he wants to do so, but if he does testify he may be treated as any other witness. A person may never be forced to testify against himself unless the state grants him immunity from prosecution arising from the testimony.

If the accused should be convicted he would find himself protected by still other provisions. No cruel and unusual punishment could be inflicted on him.[32] The court rarely, if ever, voids a punishment as "cruel and unusual" in Tennessee, but it has declared its power to do so.[33] At common law a person attainted by conviction of crime forfeited all his property to the state, and because his blood was considered corrupted he could not inherit property nor could anyone inherit property through him. Thus his dependents and heirs suffered for his crime. This ancient harsh injustice has been overcome by the constitution of Tennessee, which provides that the conviction of the accused shall not "work corruption of blood or forfeiture of estate."[34]

[25]Art. I, sec. 9. The right to meet witnesses refers to prosecuting witnesses only; *Petty* v. *State*, 72 Tenn. 326 (1880).

[26]Art. I, sec. 9.

[27]*Ibid.*

[28]Art. I, sec. 6. See also sec. 8, which guarantees every man "the judgment of his peers."

[29]*Arrowsmith* v. *State*, 131 Tenn. 480, 488 (1914).

[30]Art. I, sec. 9.

[31]*Ibid.*

[32]Art. I, sec. 16.

[33]*Brinkley* v. *State*, 125 Tenn. 371 (1911).

[34]Art. I, sec. 12. See *Fields* v. *Metropolitan Life Ins. Co.*, 147 Tenn. 464 (1922), for a discussion of this section.

The Supreme Court of the United States has moved increasingly in the direction of the view that the Fourteenth Amendment of the federal constitution guarantees in the state courts the kinds of criminal trial procedure that are required of federal courts in the Fourth, Fifth, Sixth, Seventh, and Eighth amendments. For example, the Court now holds that indigents must be furnished counsel in felony cases.[35] Coerced confessions are frowned upon,[36] and the Court has tightened requirements for legal search and seizure.[37] The Supreme Court of the United States outlawed the discretionary death penalty in 1972, and as a result Governor Winfield Dunn commuted to long imprisonment the sentences of death then pending for Tennessee prisoners. After further litigation, involving other states, in the Supreme Court of the United States, a limited death penalty act was passed in 1974; subsequently this act was also invalidated as to punishment and the pre-1973 law was reestablished. The death penalty situation remains obscure in Tennessee, as elsewhere.[38]

The Declaration of Rights does not limit its protection of personal rights to accused persons only. It provides that "the privilege of the writ of habeas corpus shall not be suspended, unless when in case of rebellion or invasion, the General Assembly shall declare the public safety requires it."[39] The purpose of the writ of habeas corpus is principally to secure the release of a person from unlawful custody or to discover the cause of his custody. It is designed to give him a hearing on the question of whether his imprisonment is lawful. The application is made by the person, or by someone acting in his behalf, in a petition to any judge of the circuit or criminal courts, and in some cases of equity jurisdiction it may be made to chancellors. If it appears from the petition that the petitioner has grounds for release, the court will issue a writ of habeas corpus, addressed to the person alleged to be holding the petitioner in unlawful imprisonment. This person is ordered to bring the prisoner and appear with him before the court at a designated time. At that time a hearing before the court will determine whether the imprisonment is lawful.

The Declaration of Rights prohibits *ex post facto* laws.[40] A classic definition of these laws was stated by Chief Justice John Marshall as follows: "An *ex post facto* law is one which renders an act punishable in a manner in which it was not punishable when it was committed."[41] Thus any

[35]*Gideon* v. *Wainwright*, 372 U.S. 335 (1963).

[36]Compare *Ashcraft* v. *Tennessee*, 322 U.S. 143 (1944); for a comprehensive study of confessions, see Otis H. Stephens, Jr., *The Supreme Court and Confessions of Guilt* (Knoxville: Univ. of Tennessee Press, 1973).

[37]See *Mapp* v. *Ohio*, 367 U.S. 643 (1961).

[38]On various federal cases, see Thomas R. Dye, Lee Seifert Greene, and George S. Parthemos, *Governing the American Democracy* (New York: St. Martin's Press, 1980), 155–56; for the invalidation of the 1974 act, see *Collins* v. *State*, 550 S.W. 2d 643 (1977).

[39]Art. I, sec. 15; *TCA*, Title 29, ch. 21, for statutes on the writ of habeas corpus.

[40]Art. I, sec. 11.

[41]*Fletcher* v. *Peck*, 6 Cranch 87, 138 (1810).

law providing punishment for an act that was innocent when committed would be an *ex post facto* law, as would be any law that increased the punishment for an act after its commission or that changed the rules of evidence or procedure so as to make conviction easier after the act was done. In short, an *ex post facto* law is a retroactive criminal law, one made applicable to acts, evidence, procedure, or punishment to the detriment of one accused of crime committed before the passage of the law.

A person cannot be twice placed in jeopardy of life or limb for the same offense.[42] The purpose of this rule is to protect an individual from being harassed by multiple prosecutions for a single offense. An accused is in jeopardy the minute the jury is sworn to try him on a valid indictment before a court of competent jurisdiction. The constitution provides that he shall never again be placed in such a position for the same offense, but there are certain well-recognized exceptions to this provision. A defendant cannot plead former jeopardy in a subsequent trial after the jury, before reaching a verdict in the preceding trial for the same offense, has been discharged with his consent, or by the court because of necessity, or because of failure to agree on a verdict.

An accused in one jurisdiction cannot plead that he has previously been in jeopardy in another jurisdiction for the same offense. A conviction by the federal government will not bar a state conviction for the same offense. In reality these are cases of two jurisdictions, although they arise out of the same act. Thus one criminal act can be in violation of the laws of two governments, and in such a case either or both may punish the criminal without violating the prohibition against double jeopardy.[43]

There can be no imprisonment for debt.[44] A debt has been defined as an obligation arising out of a debtor–creditor relationship either by express contract or by legal implication.

No man's services can be taken without compensation.[45] No citizen except one in the armed forces may "be subjected to punishment under martial or military law."[46] Citizens "have a right to keep and to bear arms for their common defense; but the Legislature shall have power, by law, to regulate the wearing of arms with a view to prevent crime."[47] Soldiers may not be quartered in any house in time of peace "without the consent of the

[42]Art. I, sec. 10.

[43]The Supreme Court of the United States has held that the same offense cannot be made the basis for one conviction under state law and another under a municipal ordinance; *Waller v. Florida*, 397 U.S. 387 (1970). Action of a criminal character in a municipal proceeding followed by state criminal action is double jeopardy; *Nashville and Davidson County v. Miles*, 524 S.W. 2d 656 (1975).

[44]Art. I, sec. 18.

[45]Art. I, sec. 21.

[46]Art. I, sec. 25.

[47]Art. I, sec. 26.

owner; nor in time of war but in a manner prescribed by law."[48] Slavery, except as punishment for crime, is prohibited.[49]

⊛

*The great and chief end . . . of men's uniting into commonwealths . . .
is the preservation of their property.*

JOHN LOCKE (1690)

PRIVATE PROPERTY has been jealously guarded from the very beginnings of government in this country, and the Declaration of Rights of Tennessee continues this policy. Some provisions relating to property stipulate that it may not be "taken, or applied to public use" without the consent of the owner or his representatives or "without just compensation being made therefor,"[50] that no man may be deprived of his property "but by the judgment of his peers or the law of the land,"[51] that for an injury a man "shall have remedy by due course of law,"[52] and that the obligation of a contract shall not be impaired.[53]

Private property rights are not absolute. The state has a right, subject to the limitation that compensation be paid, to take private property for public use. The exercise of this right of eminent domain must be authorized by the legislature. In the absence of a clear abuse of power the courts will not interfere with the legislature's determination (quite generously provided) that it is necessary to take property or with its decisions as to what shall be taken, although the legislature must provide for the award of compensation.[54]

No man may be "deprived of his life, liberty, or property, but by the judgment of his peers or the law of the land."[55] A multitude of cases involving this provision of the constitution have been heard without a clear, concise, and comprehensive definition of "law of the land" having been reached. The constitution, the common law that is in effect, and all valid statutes constitute this general body of law of the state. No person may be deprived of life, liberty, or property except on the basis of that system of law which is generally and impartially applied to all the people of

[48]Art. I, sec. 27.
[49]Art. I, secs. 33, 34.
[50]Art. I, sec. 21.
[51]Art. I, sec. 8.
[52]Art. I, sec. 17.
[53]Art. I, sec. 20.
[54]A reasonable exercise of the police power is excluded from the operation of this limitation. Police power is generally defined as the power to protect the health, safety, and morals of the people. See *Spencer-Sturla Co.* v. *Memphis*, 155 Tenn. 70 (1927).
[55]Art. I, sec. 8.

the state. Arbitrary class legislation is prohibited, but a reasonable classification is permitted. This is to say that, although in general law must apply to all persons, the state may distinguish between butchers and bakers and candlestick makers and may apply special regulation to each class. The basis for any classification, however, must be natural and must rest on some substantial difference between classes.

The "law of the land" means the same as "due process of law."[56] Because of this protection no person may be deprived of life, liberty, or property by the arbitrary action of any agency of the state or in any manner except after opportunity for a hearing and upon the judgment of a tribunal of competent jurisdiction.

The Declaration of Rights sets forth "That all courts shall be open; and every man, for an injury done him in his lands, goods, person or reputation, shall have remedy by due course of law, and right and justice administered without sale, denial, or delay. Suits may be brought against the State in such manner and in such courts as the Legislature may by law direct."[57] This provision, however, does not mean that all controversies must be heard by the judicial branch of the government. Certain contests, such as election contests, may be tried by other agencies—city councils or boards of commissioners—even though their judgments may not always be final. Circuit courts have jurisdiction in all cases not otherwise provided for, and they have appellate jurisdiction over inferior tribunals. As a general rule the courts must be available for a judicial determination of all controversies either in the first instance or on appeal. The legislature may provide, however, that the findings of fact and other actions by administrative boards and similar agencies of the state shall be final. In such cases the courts of the judicial branch of the government will not disturb the findings or acts, provided always that the administrative agency arrived at its finding or decision without exceeding its authority, without fraud, and after providing for a full and fair hearing.[58]

Except as provided for in the federal constitution, no state may be sued without its consent. The Declaration of Rights provides such consent, but only "as the Legislature may by law direct."[59] The legislature would have this power even in the absence of the constitutional provision because, unless otherwise limited, it exercises the sovereign power of the state. The legislature has established a procedure for claims against the state.

[56]*State* v. *Staten*, 46 Tenn. 231, 244 (1869).
[57]Art. I, sec. 17.
[58]See *Ford Motor Co.* v. *Pace*, 206 Tenn. 559 (1960).
[59]Art. I, sec. 17. See *TCA*, 20–13–102, for statute prohibiting suits and 9–8–101 ff. for provisions on the Board of Claims.

Finally, the constitution provides that the obligation of a contract may not be impaired and that a retrospective law may not be made.[60] When persons enter into contracts, either among themselves or with the state, they do so on the basis of laws in existence at the time, and they incur certain known obligations and obtain certain contractual rights. The state is prohibited from damaging or impairing these obligations by subsequent legislation. At the same time, this constitutional limitation does not inhibit the reasonable exercise of the police power by the state.[61] Obviously it would be intolerable for private persons to be able by their contracts to prevent the state from carrying out its essential functions for protecting public health, safety, and morals.

---

[60]Art. I, sec. 20. Cf. *Massey* v. *Sullivan County*, 225 Tenn. 132 (1971).
[61]*Shields* v. *Clifton Hill Land Co.*, 94 Tenn. 123 (1894).

3

☆ ☆
☆

Vox Populi

IN TENNESSEE THE BASE OF DEMOCRACY HAS ALWAYS BEEN BROAD. IN THE early history of our nation it was not uncommon to find many states where only those who held property of a certain value could vote; and at one time church membership, or at least the profession of a Protestant faith, was in some states made requisite for voting rights. In the State of Tennessee property qualifications were abolished by the 1834 constitution. Religious qualifications never existed, but for several years during the Reconstruction period the voter was required to show that he had never supported the Confederate cause.

⊛

The right of citizens . . . to vote shall not be denied . . . by any state on account of race, color, or previous condition of servitude . . . or sex . . . failure to pay poll . . . or other tax . . . or on account of age [if eighteen years or over].
EXCERPTS FROM AMENDMENTS 15, 19, 24, 26, CONSTITUTION OF THE UNITED STATES

THE CONSTITUTION OF THE UNITED STATES originally left the prescription of federal, as well as state, suffrage requirements to the individual states; according to its terms, all those persons eligible to vote for the most numerous house of the legislature in a state are also eligible to vote for specified federal officers.[1] The federal constitution does, however, place certain restrictions on the state. For example, by reason of the Fifteenth and Nineteenth amendments to the federal constitution, no person may be deprived of voting privileges by reason of sex, race, color, or previous condition of servitude. Federal statutes contain extensive regulations of

[1]*Constitution of the United States,* Art. I, sec. 2 and Amendment 17.

32

federal elections. Amendment Twenty-four outlaws the poll tax as a prerequisite for voting for federal officeholders, and Amendment Twenty-six lowers the voting age to eighteen for all elections. Contrary provisions in the Tennessee constitution, invalidated by federal law, were removed in 1978. Tennessee secured a certain notoriety by being the thirty-sixth state to ratify the Nineteenth Amendment (on woman suffrage).

Control over elections and voting requirements, once clearly left to the states, and more and more passed to federal authority by amendments, has been still further shifted to national decisionmaking by federal court decisions and federal statutes. The sudden proposal and ratification of the Twenty-sixth Amendment, at a time when doubts were rising about the wisdom of entrusting the franchise to the eighteen-year-olds, followed a downright fantastic decision of the Supreme Court of the United States that pulled a "right" to the eighteen-year-old vote out of the vague theories of natural law—surely one of the strangest decisions ever to come out of an activist Court.[2]

Who should vote? To make this inquiry is to go to the heart of the problem of government.

JASPER SHANNON (1949)

IN THE NATION TODAY certain voting qualifications are common to the various states. United States citizenship is now a uniform prerequisite for the suffrage, although at one period during the heavy influx of foreign immigrants this was not true. For a period after the Civil War, loyal aliens were allowed to vote in Tennessee.[3] In addition to citizenship, voters must have reached the age of eighteen.[4]

Each state demands that citizens shall have established residence within its boundaries before they exercise their voting privilege. In Tennessee the constitution as amended in 1978 gives the General Assembly the right to set a period of residence as a prerequisite for voting.[5] Requirements for residence have varied among the states from six months to two years, but the reasoning behind all the requirements is identical. Strangers in a community cannot be aware of all the issues nor sufficiently familiar with

---

[2]*Oregon* v. *Mitchell,* 400 U. S. 112 (1970).

[3]Caldwell, 287, citing *Public Acts of Tennessee,* 1866–67, ch. 37. Hereafter the *Public Acts of Tennessee* are referred to as *Public Acts.*

[4]For a more complete account of voting requirements, see Dye, Greene, and Parthemos, 205–08. The change to eighteen from twenty-one is recognized by *TCA,* 1–3–113, reproducing ch. 162, sec. 3 of *Public Acts,* 1971, and *TCA,* 2–2–102, reproducing *Public Acts,* 1972, ch. 740, sec. 1, and 1973, ch. 327, sec. 2.

[5]Art. IV, sec. 1 as amended.

the candidates to share in the elections of that community immediately upon their arrival there. Transients are not desirable participants in local elections. In the Voting Rights Act Amendments of 1970, Congress provided that citizens could not be deprived of the right to vote for presidential electors because of durational residence requirements; this statute, subsequently upheld,[6] did permit thirty days between registration and voting. (This same statute outlawed literacy tests for all elections, but that change did not affect Tennessee, which had no literacy tests anyway.) Tennessee's durational residence requirements for voting for state and local officers were held unconstitutional in 1972.[7] Using a standard of "compelling interest," the Supreme Court of the United States held that Tennessee did not need to impose residency requirements of one year in the state and three months in the county, as it had done, and that such requirements violate the equal protection clause by inhibiting travel and subjecting newcomers to the state to improper requirements. The Court thought a thirty-day residence requirement was enough to provide proper election administration. Since this case, the Court, with a change in its personnel, has become less rigid in its limit on durational residential requirements, permitting, in some cases, fifty or sixty days. Still, it is clear that the states are no longer completely free to set their own standards on residence.[8]

Large numbers of persons within the state fail to meet the requirements of citizenship or age, and should not, therefore, be allowed to vote. In order that persons who do not meet these requirements may effectively be prohibited from exercising the privileges of the ballot, to prevent the living from voting under the names of the dead, to prevent individuals from voting more than once, and otherwise to secure honest election administration, a system of registration for voters has been developed. By act of the 1951 General Assembly, as subsequently amended, registration is now required of all voters in Tennessee. Such registration is continuous and permanent; that is, when a voter is once registered he does not need to reregister unless he changes his residence, changes his name, or fails to vote in a statewide election during a period of four successive calendar years. Registration takes place at designated polling places during certain periods, and at other times persons may register at the offices of the county election commission. It is a criminal offense for a voter to register if he is not entitled to be registered or to attempt to vote on the registration of some other person, to change or forge the registration records, or to commit other similar offenses against the principle of an honest ballot. The enforcement of the registration act is in the hands of the county election commis-

---

[6]*Oregon* v. *Mitchell.*

[7]*Dunn* v. *Blumstein,* 405 U. S. 330 (1972).

[8]See *Modernizing Election Systems* (Lexington, Ky.: Council of State Governments, 1973), 1–5.

sioners.[9] Early in his administration, President Carter proposed easing registration requirements, even to the point of permitting registration on election day. It was a gesture to the poor, the uneducated, and the careless. In the vernacular of Tennessee, this was a "dog that wouldn't hunt," and in 1978 the Tennessee constitution was amended to prevent such "quickie" registration, but if Congress ever follows the Carter lead (which seems unlikely), undoubtedly the Tennessee provision will be overruled. A valid federal statute is superior to a state constitution.

For many years the Tennessee voter was required to meet one further qualification before he could cast his ballot: he had to offer evidence that he had paid his poll tax for the preceding year. After a series of limiting statutes, the poll tax as a voting prerequisite was finally deleted from the state's fundamental law in 1953. The federal amendment on this subject was passed after Tennessee had disposed of the question.

$$\bigodot$$

The function of supplying personnel is accomplished through intricate and decentralized organization . . . a hierarchy of . . . party committees . . . [and a] series of conventions.

BONE AND RANNEY (1963)

ELECTION LAW HAS BEEN a matter of abiding interest, an interest excited both by the public desire to assure honest procedures and by party desire to secure advantage. Of all the concerns of the legislature, election administration is one of the few that arouses party-line response.[10] The election laws of Tennessee were codified for the first time in the Code of 1858. In the reconstruction following the Civil War, Governor Brownlow, in order to suppress opposition, managed with the aid of the legislature to limit the franchise and control the election machinery, but this phase passed rapidly. In 1890, following the spirit of the time, a major addition was made to the election laws by the Dortch Ballot Law, which incorporated the main features of the secret (or so-called Australian) ballot. By some the Dortch Ballot Law has been seen as an element in the discouragement of black voting. This statute, much amended, remains the basis of Tennessee election law. The Tennessee ballot is often quite long, particularly in the primaries. The form of the ballot, whether on paper or on the now widely used voting machine, is set by the county election commission, under some general restrictions (it appears that some counties disregard the general law at times). The form of the ballot can be an office block system or the party

[9]*TCA*, 2–2–108 ff.
[10]See Harry F. Kelley, Jr., *Dimensions of Voting in the Tennessee House of Representatives in 1967* (Knoxville: Bureau of Public Administration, Univ. of Tennessee, 1970).

column system, but, in any case, it makes party distinctions easy enough for the voter to detect and use them. Voting by computer punch cards is being used in some counties.

In 1907 an administrative apparatus was provided by the creation of a State Board of Elections with power to appoint the county commissioners of elections who had formerly been appointed by the governor. Campaign expenditures were first regulated in 1927. In 1937, the county primary election commissions were created. In 1959 a Coordinator of Elections was established in the office of the secretary of state.[11] Finally in 1972 the election law was very generally rewritten.

Before that revision one of the most distinguishing features of Tennessee elections was the separation of the administration of the primary from that of the general election. The primary was a party affair. Each party had its own primary, with its own elaborate machinery. The candidates paid county primary election expenses. The election machinery, both general and primary, was the subject of party combat in the legislature, and changes of detail were frequent. We do not intend to furnish here a blow-by-blow account of this internecine warfare but will confine ourselves to a statement of the election machinery as it was set up in 1972, although the past history of changes in this machinery does not augur too well for its future stability. Apparently the parties have felt in the past that tinkering with election administration will somehow give them an advantage over their opponents, although it is difficult to agree with this belief without suspecting improper manipulation of election results.

Public officials may be chosen by majority vote within a given jurisdiction or by a plurality. The latter, in a many-cornered race, can be less than a majority, and in Tennessee many electoral decisions are in fact made in this way. The effect of plurality elections is especially striking in the election of a governor. In 1958, Buford Ellington was nominated by only an eight-thousand-vote margin over his two major opponents, Andrew "Tip" Taylor and Edmund Orgill. Four years later, Frank Clement won by a plurality over William Farris and "Rudy" Olgiati. In 1974, Ray Blanton eked out a narrow plurality in a Democratic free-for-all with over a dozen contestants. In 1978, with three prominent candidates, Bob Clement, Jake Butcher, and Richard Fulton, Clement and Butcher came to the wire together, with Butcher a narrow winner. In times past, the Democratic nominee was assured election in November; and so, Tennessee has had a long record of governors chosen by a minority. But whether the final (or general) election is by majority or plurality, some way must be found to cut to some reasonable figure the scope of choice. The selection of candidates is a proper function of a political party, and political parties do play a

[11]Legislative Council Committee, *Study on the Election Laws* (Nashville: The Council, 1966), 4–5, 7.

prominent role, but not an exclusive one. In Tennessee, as in many other states, the selection of candidates is a fairly open process.

Political parties, aware of the dangers to party unity involved in allowing several members of the same party to run simultaneously for the same office, sought in the early history of this country to select candidates by means of the party caucus, in which party leaders in a joint, and often enough a secret, meeting formulate slates of candidates. Procedure of this sort locks out the party rank and file, and in a short time the caucus disappeared from use as a means of nomination. The political convention, a method of nomination still employed by the national parties in picking presidential and vice-presidential candidates, was then tried, although even this system has been subjected to increasing criticism. The convention system requires the selection of delegates to a general meeting at which candidates are nominated; usually when this system is used in a state, the statewide convention is based upon conventions at the lower levels of government, which, in addition to selecting delegates for the state convention, also nominate party candidates for local office.

One of the governmental reforms instituted by the "Progressive" movement of the first two decades of this century (a movement that supported the income tax, the regulation of railroads, the short ballot, and the like) was the direct primary. First tried in Tennessee by the Democrats in 1908, the direct primary was made compulsory in 1909.[12] In the primary races various candidates who are members of the same political party announce themselves for office, and primary elections are held to determine which of them is most acceptable to supporters of the party. Party primaries are thus party affairs, but the membership of American parties is so uncertain that it is difficult to confine the voting strictly to party members.

In Tennessee the candidates of statewide political parties for the offices of governor, United States senators and representatives, public service commissioners, and state senators and representatives must be chosen by the direct primary. A statewide political party is a party that had one candidate for a statewide office in the past four years who polled 5 percent or more of the total votes cast in the most recent gubernatorial election, or a party that has a membership equal to at least 2.5 percent of the total vote cast for governor, as shown by petitions.[13] Over its history Tennessee has been divided usually between two parties, but third parties are by no means unknown, and independent candidacies are common, although not usually successful.

[12]Folmsbee et al., Tennessee, A Short History, 438; Legislative Council Committee, Study on Election Laws, 5.
[13]TCA, 2–1–104(27).

On the Run-Off Election Proposals. Artist: Sandy Campbell in the *Tennessean*.

The above formula puts the figure low enough to cover significant organizations.

Parties are not required to conduct primaries for offices other than those mentioned above, although they may do so,[14] and some counties have compulsory local primary laws. Party primaries for local offices are omitted for the weaker party in some Tennessee counties. Democrats in West and Middle Tennessee customarily use the primary for local offices. It is also used to some extent in East Tennessee Republican counties, although the convention method is sometimes used there. In two-party counties both Republicans and Democrats are likely to use the direct primary. Private acts allow for variations in primaries. Even for statewide offices, it appears that primaries are not always held in every county. For example, in the August elections of 1972, no Republican primary for United States senator was held in Clay or Hardeman counties, and no Republican primary for public service commissioner was held in Clay, Hardeman, or Van Buren counties.[15] In 1978, however, Republican primaries for these posts were held in all ninety-five counties. In 1980 Republican primaries were held generally throughout the state, although there were no candidates in some Assembly districts.

Forty-two states use some kind of "closed" primary, one in which only party members may vote. Actually it is hard to keep "closed" primaries closed. In Tennessee the law requires that a person be a bona-fide member of the political party in whose primary he votes or that he states his allegiance to and his intention to affiliate with that party. In practice this requirement is as elastic as a rubber band, for the voter has only to request the ballot for either party's primary in order to vote in that primary. Seldom indeed is a voter challenged to show that he belongs to the party in which he seeks to vote. In effect, therefore, Tennessee has an open primary, and there seems little disposition to change to a closed one.[16] The national Democratic party in 1972 adopted rules that would penalize a state without a closed primary; in 1976, the party rules specified that all feasible steps must be taken to restrict participation in the selection of delegates to Democrats, but there is no indication that such steps mean anything in Tennessee.

In this "open" situation raids by one party on another are quite common, although hard to document. It is pretty clear that Republicans went into the Democratic primary in 1966 to help in nominating Frank Clement over Ross Bass for the U.S. senate,[17] and Jake Butcher encouraged such

[14]*Ibid.*, 2–13–203.

[15]Election report of the coordinator of elections.

[16]An act of 1972 requiring a voter to state the basis on which he is voting when he applies for a ballot was repealed in 1974. In practice a voter must state his choice of a party in order to get the right ballot or to use the voting machine.

[17]Lee Seifert Greene, *Lead Me On: Frank Goad Clement and Tennessee Politics* (Knoxville: Univ. of Tennessee Press, 1982).

crossovers in 1978 in the close contest for the nomination for the governorship. It is virtually certain that not all of the voters who helped to make George Wallace the Democratic choice in Tennessee for candidate for president in 1972 were Democrats. In every primary election voters shop around a good deal, and election officials, without inquiring as to earlier votes, readily issue whichever party ballot the voter asks for.

In spite of widespread doubts about the wisdom of holding presidential primaries, the legislature came to feel that Tennessee ought to have one, and a 1971 statute provided for it. An attempted repeal of this statute was vetoed by Governor Dunn in 1974. As amended, the law now requires that a presidential preference primary be held for each statewide political party in May before the November presidential election; the primary precedes by a short period the usual dates of the nominating conventions. The candidates whose names appear on the presidential primary ballot are those certified by the secretary of state, acting in his sole discretion, as those generally recognized as candidates, or those persons for whom nominating papers have been signed by at least 2,500 persons. A person certified as a candidate may withdraw his name by affidavit to the state election commission. The primary is binding on delegates to the convention for the first two ballots, for statewide delegates on the basis of statewide results, and for congressional district delegates on the basis of district results, with some obligation for two further ballots on the basis of the candidate's strength or wishes. But this provision may be unenforceable, as the 1972 Democratic convention indicated, when in spite of an overwhelming popular vote in Tennessee for Wallace as the Democratic candidate, a few of the more dedicated McGovern delegates refused to obey the primary vote, perhaps partly on the basis that a good many Republican voters went into the Democratic primary to vote for Wallace.[18] Participation in the presidential primary is often low, and proposals to abolish that primary surfaced in the legislature in 1981.

(★★★)

Free and honest elections are the very foundation of our republican form of government.

Mr. Justice Douglas
U. S. v. Classic, 313 U. S. 299, 329 (1941)

As a result of the 1972 legislation, election administration is now entirely in the hands of the state and county election commissions. The composi-

---

[18]Wallace sentiment in Tennessee is described in Lee S. Greene and Jack E. Holmes, "Tennessee: A Politics of Peaceful Change," in William C. Harvard, ed., *The Changing Politics of the South* (Baton Rouge: Louisiana State Univ. Press, 1972).

tion of the election commissions has long been a subject of contention and change, and there is little guarantee that the present arrangements will endure.

With the exception of the presidential primary, primary elections in this state for candidates for federal, statewide, and legislative offices are held on the first Thursday in August in the even-numbered years. Before the election, prospective candidates for statewide offices file nominating petitions bearing the signatures of at least twenty-five voters with the state election commission and with the chairman of the party's state executive committee. Independent candidates (by no means unknown to Tennessee elections) file with the state election commission. Candidates for primaries in elections other than statewide file with the county election commissions. The state election commission certifies the names of candidates for statewide positions to the county election commissions, who place names on the ballots.

The general election for county officials and for judges is held in August on the same day as the primary for statewide offices. If county primaries are held for county offices, they take place in late spring.

At the apex of the election machinery is the state election commission. The commission's composition has undergone frequent changes over the years, but as provided by the statute effective in 1979 the commission consists of five members, chosen by the General Assembly for terms of four years. Three members are selected from the majority party, and two

Chart: Election Administration System in Tennessee

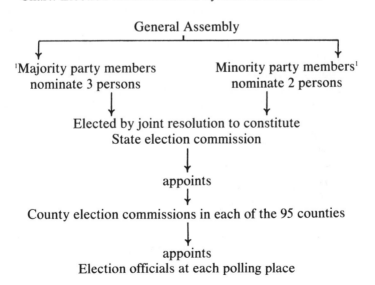

General Assembly

¹Majority party members nominate 3 persons

Minority party members¹ nominate 2 persons

Elected by joint resolution to constitute State election commission

appoints

County election commissions in each of the 95 counties

appoints
Election officials at each polling place

from the minority. The majority party is that party that holds the most seats in the General Assembly; the party holding the second highest number of seats is the minority party. No more than two members shall be from the same Grand Division of the state. The persons elected to the state commission are first nominated by a joint House-Senate caucus of the parties to be represented on the commission.

For each county in the state, the state election commission chooses five election commissioners, not more than three of whom may be from the same political party. Majority members of the county commissions are chosen by the majority members of the state commission, and minority county members by the state minority members. Members of the legislature from each county are to be consulted before the selections are made. Appointments are for two years. Since the Democrats are usually the state's majority party and therefore control the state election commissions, this same party has held the majority in the county commissions; this has been true even in counties whose politics are dominated by the Republican party. A sharp change in the practice occurred in 1965, when the Republicans as a reward for their support of Governor Clement's choice for the speakership of the Senate, Jared Maddux, were, by statute, given two of the three commissioners (at that time the number on the county commission) in all counties carried by Barry Goldwater in 1964.[19] The change was stated in general terms so as to call for further adjustments after later presidential elections. A 1972 law provided that three of the five commissioners shall be members of the political party that polled the most votes in that county, and the other two, members of the party polling the second highest vote in the most recent election for governor. In 1977, under the Blanton administration, the law was again changed to require that the majority party be in the majority in all counties.

The detailed administration of elections and voter registration devolves upon the county election commissions. They select the persons who man the polls. Some central coordination of election administration is provided by the coordinator of elections in the office of the secretary of state, but his powers are small, and holders of this post give few signs of active interference in local affairs.

In the United States one of the weakest features of the electoral process is evident in administration of the elections. This is true of Tennessee as well as of other states. Weakness of administration may be the result of general slipshoddiness or of conscious corruption. Tennessee's election laws, although they overemphasize local administration, are not entirely inadequate in themselves, but the statutes provide no very reliable guarantee that local management will be either competent or honest.

[19]Greene, *Lead Me On.*

The 1972 statute provides a lengthy list of punishable offenses designed to guarantee honest elections. These include breaking up political meetings, bribing voters, taking part in political activity that interferes with state business, and even betting on elections. Penalties are substantial, but cases are seldom brought. This may mean, of course, that offenses do not occur often, but vote-buying has been common enough in the past. The littering of public property with campaign "literature" is especially common. In 1947 the legislature created an election commission to study the election laws and administration of the state; this commission reported "it is common knowledge that the administration of elections in Tennessee has been accused by allegations of many irregularities, sharp practices and frauds."[20] The old system of party-run primaries added to the confusion and possibility of corruption. Lack of central authority meant that local practices varied from place to place with no possibility of uniform interpretation of the law and no pressure for honest and competent local administration. Some of these weaknesses have been corrected. The election law has been rewritten and rearranged. A coordinator of state elections has been created, although his powers over local officials are still very limited. Voting machines and electronic registration equipment have been authorized, and over half the counties use voting machines. All elections, including the primaries, are now run by the county election commissions. Still, the quality of administration at the county level varies, and the training and competence of local officials remain problems. In 1978, a number of indictments for vote fraud were returned in troubled and troublesome Polk County, and all members of the county election commission resigned.

⊛

The will of the people . . . practically means the will of the most numerous or the most active part of the people.

JOHN STUART MILL (1859)

LOW VOTER PARTICIPATION has been characteristic of the South; it is at its lowest in the Deep South. Tennessee as an Upper South state shows a history of low participation, but its voters are more active than their neighbors further toward the Gulf of Mexico. The low voter participation has been explained in terms of the degree of party competition, the suppression or discouragement of the blacks, the comparatively low socioeconomic condition of the South, and sometimes, such explanations as these failing, low turnout has simply been attributed to political cul-

---

[20]*Study on Election Laws,* 5, 6.

ture—supposedly a term denoting habits.[21] For a short time after the Civil War, the bitter policies of Brownlow operated to disfranchise his opponents, but thereafter for some two decades participation in presidential elections ranged around 70 to 80 percent. Around 1890, changes in the ballot laws requiring the use of the printed ballot and the imposition of the poll tax were accompanied by a drastic drop in voter participation, particularly in Middle and West Tennessee. What effect the poll tax had is very unclear.[22] Some figures on Tennessee participation in presidential elections are shown in the following tabulation:[23]

Year	Percentage of Adult Population (Male Only before 1920) Voting in Tennessee
1892	58
1900	54
1904	46
1920	31
1924	20
1936	28
1940	30

But whatever the reasons for low participation in voting in the past, the record in recent elections is better. In the 1968, 1972, 1976, and 1980 presidential elections the participation record of Tennessee voters was 53.7, 43.6, 49.6 and 50.1 percent of the civilian population of voting age, as compared to the figures for the United States as a whole of 60.9, 55.5, 54.3 and 51.8 percent.[24] In the general election of November 1976, in Tennessee as elsewhere in the United States, fewer voters cast ballots for elections of members of the national House of Representatives. In 1976, for example, when the presidential election attracted about 50 percent of the Tennessee voting population, the U. S. representatives drew the interest of only 42 percent. The contests for representatives get even less attention in the years when no presidential candidates are running. In 1978, 34.3 percent voted for Tennessee representatives.[25] Of course, it must be remembered that some of the Congressional districts of Tennessee present no contests.

[21]For an extended discussion of voter turnout, on which the literature is quite extensive, see Lester W. Milbrath, "Individuals and Government," in Herbert Jacob and Kenneth N. Vines, eds., *Politics in the American States: A Comparative Analysis*, 2d ed. (Boston: Little, 1971), 32–44.

[22]Greene and Holmes, 171–73.

[23]Jasper Berry Shannon, *Toward a New Politics in the South* (Knoxville: Univ. of Tennessee Press, 1949), 31, quoting *Hearings before a Subcommittee of the Committee on the Judiciary*, U. S. Senate, 77 Cong., 2 sess., on S. 1280 (Washington: Government Printing Office, 1942), 55–60.

[24]*Statistical Abstract of the United States, 1980*, 517.

[25]*Ibid.*

There has been little point in coming out to vote for John Duncan in the second district or Joe Evins in the fourth, for generally no one of any political stature ran against these candidates, who represented respectively Republican and Democratic strongholds with a long history of party loyalty.

In the conservative reaction to the excesses of Reconstruction, various measures were taken to discourage Negro voting; in the process, poor whites were also inhibited, and some scholars consider that the measures were directed as much toward poor whites as toward blacks. But black voting did continue, especially in the large cities. Negro blocs were formed, under control of both black and white leaders. Beginning with the Roosevelt period, blacks everywhere turned to the Democratic party. With the civil rights push of the Lyndon Johnson administration, Tennessee blacks began to register and vote, and blacks gained public office, locally and nationally.

In 1978, Shelby County blacks, led by the machine developed by the Ford brothers, gave lopsided votes to Jake Butcher, and there is evidence of heavy black support for him in other counties. It seems likely that this heavily publicized support produced some white backlash, particularly in West Tennessee.[26]

In a state or section where party contests are weak, it might be expected that the primary would attract more interest than the general election. That is not true in Tennessee. Primaries often draw as few voterss as do general elections and sometimes even fewer. A very sizable portion of as do general elections and sometimes even fewer. A very sizable portion of the adult population of Tennessee is simply not interested in voting.

[26]See reports of the coordinator of elections.

4

☆ ☆
☆

Behind the Ballot

Political recruitment is a prime function of political parties.

BONE AND RANNEY (1963)

POLITICAL PARTIES ARE UNKNOWN TO THE CONSTITUTION OF TENNESSEE, but they are a necessary part of the political process here as well as in all the other states. Their organization is to a large degree dictated by custom, but inasmuch as they are an integral part of the nomination and election machinery, they have been increasingly regulated by statutes.[1] The latest statutory regulation of parties in Tennessee was enacted by the General Assembly in 1972 effective in 1973, but because this is a sensitive partisan area we may expect that the increasing disposition of the legislature to tinker with party machinery will bring about further changes from time to time. The 1972 act defined the offices for which party primaries must be held as those of the governor, public service commissioner, members of the General Assembly, and members of Congress. No person may appear on the ballot as a candidate of a party for these offices or other offices for which voters vote in more than one county unless the party concerned is a statewide party and unless he is nominated in substantial compliance with the primary laws. Provision is made for local party nominations.

The 1972 statute provides that voters in the party's primary in each state senatorial district elect one man and one woman as members of the party state executive committee for terms of four years beginning September 15. This means a state executive committee of sixty-six members, a body too

[1]Cf. William Goodman, *Inherited Domain: Political Parties in Tennessee* (Knoxville: Bureau of Public Administration, Univ. of Tennessee, 1954).

large to serve as an "executive." The statute implies more open and public competition than is actually present in many areas.

The first executive committee of a new political party is to be elected at a statewide convention of the party after it becomes a statewide political party. That committee holds office until the next election at which members of the executive committees of all parties are to be chosen.

The statute gives only a sketchy outline of the duties of the state executive committee, indicating that the committee shall act as the state primary board and that it shall appoint the county primary boards, but because elections, including primary elections, are now run by the county election commissioners, the state and county primary boards, which originally administered the party primaries, seem to have been robbed of their former significance, although they still exist.

The statutes are silent on the structure of the parties below the state level; organization is left to custom and to party rules. The basis of the party structure is the voting precinct, an area in which all voters go to the same polling place. These are subdivisions of the county district, which, in turn, are subdivisions of the counties created by the county courts.[2] In cities, the ward is used in place of the district. The lowest party organization is the county executive committee, which is also a larger organization than the name "executive committee" would imply; it is based in the large counties on precinct party meetings open to all party members and often very poorly attended and loosely run. Precinct meetings generally constitute precinct (or ward) committees made up of persons present. Except when spasmodic efforts at reform are in the air, the precinct meetings will be managed by and for party regulars, for the general public neither knows nor cares how these precinct meetings are conducted. Party membership is a vague concept and the meetings are fairly open to anyone who wishes to come. During the McGovern upheaval in the Democratic party, the precinct meetings were often taken over by nonregulars; for the Democrats in the ensuing elections the result was not a happy one. The city wards and county districts in the large counties are allowed a number of votes on the county executive committee in relation to votes cast for the Democratic candidate for governor in the last election. At times the number of persons attending the precinct meetings will be less than the number of votes allowed the precinct on the executive committee. In the small counties a mass convention is called and those attending will elect themselves to the county committee. Republican procedure is similar; in the large counties

[2]The county districts are the successors to the old civil districts that were formerly the units for election of JPs to the county courts. The reapportionment of the county courts made necessary by judicial decisions resulted in the requirement by the legislature that the county courts create new county districts. The old civil districts were left as they were for record-

county convention delegates are elected in subcounty conventions; in small counties, the county convention and the county executive committee are identical.

Both parties employ state and Congressional district conventions. Aside from the choice of delegates made by the convention, the meetings are not ordinarily very significant, for the parties offer no programs, and candidates for important offices are chosen in the primaries. In 1972, however, the state convention of the Democratic party was a stormy affair, the scene of an attempt to impose a quota system on the organization.

A major function of the Democratic state convention was formerly the selection of delegates to the national convention. The delegates so selected were certain to be the active party leaders of the state, and the delegation was likely to be under the chairmanship and usually the effective control of the governor. In the preparations for the unruly Democratic National Convention of 1972 this scheme was changed. Eighty percent of the delegates to this national convention were selected by Congressional district conventions, which in themselves were made up of the delegates to the county conventions, and the state convention selected the remaining 20 percent of the national convention delegates.[3] The county conventions were made up of delegates from the precinct conventions, and the precinct meetings were open to anyone claiming to be a Democrat. In 1972 control of the whole selection process passed out of the hands of the professionals as the structure was invaded at the grass roots by young people, blacks, women, and others largely independent of and unsympathetic to control by old-line professionals. Many of the leading old-time Democrats were thoroughly snubbed, not to say "stomped"! Given this free-for-all and the "quota" scheme for representing blacks, young people, and women, the Democratic delegation in 1972 was quite a different collection from those of the past. The resounding defeat of George McGovern and the well-known lack of persistence of reforms led to some reaction. Professional politicians are back in the party machinery, and the revolt of 1972 has dwindled. Still, women are active,[4] as they were even before 1972, and black politicians are more evident than they were. Indeed the most powerful machine in Memphis is now the Ford machine, dominant among the black voters. It is the amateur and the nonpolitical young who lack staying power. (This is not to imply that the Tennessee politician is middle-aged or old; quite the contrary, there are plenty of young contenders for office.) The presidential

---

keeping purposes. County election commissions may change precinct boundaries. *TCA*, 5–1–110, 5–1–112, 2–3–102.

[3]See Kenneth Fulton, ed., *Democrats in Convention 1972: Official Program for the Thirty-Sixth Quadrennial National Nominating Convention of the Democratic Party*, 233. See also Charles A. Zuzak, *Presidential Nominating Procedures* (New York: National Municipal League, 1974), sect. on Tennessee.

[4]Half the delegates to the Democratic national convention of 1980 were women.

primary law now requires the election of delegates to the party national convention according to the votes secured by the candidates in that primary, but the Supreme Court of the United States has now made it clear that national parties are not bound by state laws.

American parties are exceedingly loose aggregations where individual energy and initiative can produce victories.[5] This is certainly true of Tennessee politics. For substantial periods of Tennessee history, individual enterprise in the Republican party had little chance of paying off except in East Tennessee, but the Democratic party offered scope to the ambitious. Typically, each candidate built his own personal organization, sometimes on what remained of the machine of a defeated, dead, or exhausted political figure. Frank Clement and his first campaign manager, Buford Ellington, built Clement's political organization on the machine that had supported Jim McCord.[6] Personal machines exist inside a party. When, in 1972, John J. Hooker, Jr., made one of his unsuccessful tries for the governorship and Albert Gore lost his seat in the Senate, the two men, although both Democrats, showed little or no desire to cooperate. Personal machines may split up on the death or retirement of a leader. When Estes Kefauver's heart artery broke, some of his forces gravitated to Ross Bass, while Frank Clement and M. M. Bullard claimed others.[7] Shifts in the old Clement–Ellington organization were apparent in 1978, when, in the gubernatorial primary campaign, some former allies of Frank Clement deserted his son, Bob, to cleave to Jake Butcher. And it seems clear that in the 1978 general election some Clement Democrats helped to make Lamar Alexander governor. The pattern of shifting factions in the Democratic ranks is duplicated among Republicans.

The tourist, warmly welcomed by an area avid for his expenditures, was advised by billboard upon his entry that he was now in the "three states" of Tennessee.

GREENE AND HOLMES (1972)

WHEN BUFORD ELLINGTON WAS governor of Tennessee, the tourist crossing Tennessee's borders was met by a large sign welcoming him to the "three states" of Tennessee. No doubt he was puzzled, unless he happened to know that Tennessee history and politics repeatedly recognized, officially and unofficially, the presence of East, Middle, and West Tennessee. Every

[5]See Dye, Greene, and Parthemos, ch. 8.
[6]Greene, *Lead Me On.*
[7]*Ibid.*

incoming governor has felt it essential to change the welcoming signs, and Governor Dunn struck out the "three states," stating that Tennessee needed to emphasize unity (a loss for an interesting diversity). Eliminating the signs did not do away with the diversity, but it is easy to overemphasize the differences, both culturally and politically. Still some differentiation is there, and the effects are still to be reckoned with in political planning. East Tennessee was never particularly hospitable to blacks; slaves were held there, but not in numbers comparable to Middle and West Tennessee. East Tennessee has been poor, whether from the lack of physical resources or from deficiencies of the population, a matter that has exercised the historian. Of course, diversities obtain inside the Grand Divisions. In West Tennessee, the sandy forested land of Benton County produced an economy unlike the old cottonlands in the Mississippi borderlands of West Tennessee. And along the infertile sandy ridges of Henderson County, as one ironic and knowledgeable local figure put it, "Only the best people are Democrats."

The differences between the regions were sharply focused by the conflicts of Civil War and Reconstruction, and the patterns of politics set then continued to be reflected in the allotment of voters between the Republican and Democratic parties until the 1970s. East Tennessee became and remained Republican. Middle and West Tennessee, once hosts to substantial numbers of Whigs, became and remained Democratic (because the Republicans were associated with a bitter reconstruction period), although the Democratic pattern can be broken, as the Populist vote of 1892, the Wallace vote of 1968, and the elections of Dunn and Alexander demonstrated. In 1892 and 1962, seven decades apart, the populist strength was evident in Middle and West Tennessee, over broad areas.[8]

But these regional patterns, once such a stable feature of the political landscape, have lost some of their former shape. Since the Civil War an island of Republicanism has persisted in a few counties along the western portion of the Tennessee River, but this island has now been extended to cover substantial sections in West Tennessee, including portions of that ancient stronghold of the Democrats, Shelby County. Indeed, all the great urban areas have now become disputed territory, where Republicans contend with Democrats in a type of contest quite familiar to other sections of the country—the conflict between the central city and the suburbs, and the conflict, more or less submerged, between blacks and whites. Middle and West Tennessee Democrats seem to be getting used to voting Republican—so far, only the political sky has fallen. And as the regional pattern has altered, the relations between the governmental institutions in Nashville have suffered a change quite probably long-range in effect. Recent

[8]See Greene and Holmes, 165–200.

elections indicate that the suburbs of Nashville and Memphis add strength to the Republican party.

Lamar Alexander's victory in 1978 raised Republican hopes to a high pitch. The young Republican not only carried most of the traditional Republican counties, but he also made notable dents in Middle and West Tennessee and carried all four big metropolitan areas. His victory can be attributed to several factors: the aura of scandal in the Blanton years, the possible shift of Clement votes to the Republicans, suburban Republicanism, the backlash to Butcher's ties to the blacks in Memphis, and, just possibly, a growing tide of Republicanism in the nation. But through all this the Democrats retained firm control of the state legislature.

Protest or independent candidates have appeared on Tennessee's presidential ballots in nineteen of the last twenty elections.
GREENE AND HOLMES (1972)

SPASMODIC DESERTIONS from Republican and Democratic orthodoxies are far from unknown in Tennessee. Desertions of this type have unquestionably originated in racist politics (although usually not in other forms of ethnic animosity), but race is not the only issue, for economic views, principally of the Populist variety, have moved the voters to unusual positions. The revolts against two-party orthodoxy have usually been temporary and brief, but they have been frequent enough to indicate a political substratum of some permanent significance.

Independents often appear on Tennessee ballots; when such candidacies are for local offices (or even when independents run in Congressional districts, as they sometimes do) not too much significance need be attached to their presence. But when such independents surface on presidential ballots, more notice is justified. In twenty of the last twenty-one presidential elections, independent or third-party candidates have appeared. Most of these have drawn very few votes, but five of them drew over 3 percent of the total vote in Tennessee:

1892	Populist (Weaver)	10.8 percent of total vote
1912	Progressive (Theodore Roosevelt)	23.2
1924	Progressive (La Follette)	3.5
1948	Dixiecrat (Thurmond)	13.4
1968	American (George Wallace)	34.0

In the campaign leading to the election of President Truman in 1948, certain dissident elements in the South, aroused by the President's civil rights program, decided to forsake their traditional allegiance to the Democratic party. These elements were placed in a most uncomfortable position.

They could not very well join the Republican party, and in leaving the Democrats they were compelled to establish a third party. As they had little chance of winning a popular majority in the country as a whole, their only hope was to throw the election of the President into the House of Representatives and thus secure some consideration of their point of view without actually joining the ranks of the Republican party. The effort failed completely, for Truman was elected and the Dixiecrats, as the dissidents were known, merely read themselves out of their own party with no place else to go.

It is significant that Tennessee Democrats by and large avoided this move. With one or two exceptions, the principal figures among the Tennessee Democrats (although some of them publicly deplored the President's civil rights program) stood by him as the official candidate of the party for the office of President. Not only does this indicate that the Tennessee Democrat is less of a "Southern" Democrat than has often been supposed, but it may indicate also that he is more astute. The Dixiecrat rebellion produced no more than a ripple in Tennessee; one presidential elector voted for the party's candidates in 1948. Tennessee Democrats are still members of the national party in good standing and in good repute; their influence in national politics was not diminished by the revolt and may even have been enhanced by the loyalty to the national party standard that Tennessee exhibited during a period of internal party strife. In the 1952 Democratic National Convention the Democratic delegation took positions generally unfriendly to the remnants of the Dixiecrat movement.

George Wallace, former governor of Alabama, was in and out of the Democratic party, depending upon the state of his satisfaction with the party and his estimate of his own fortunes. Wallace's intrusion into Tennessee started in 1964. In that year, he announced his intention to campaign for the presidency in every state, but eventually he withdrew. But in 1968 Wallace did run for the presidency, the nominee of the American party, an organization officially formed in Tennessee during a convention held in Knoxville in late August 1968. Tennessee had no presidential primary at this time. When Wallace appeared as a presidential candidate in November, he was the American party's only candidate in Tennessee, but he was a strong one. Tennessee law required over 57,000 signatures to put Wallace on the ballot; more than 90,000 were secured. Volunteer campaigners for Wallace were active in every county in the state.

Wallace's appeal to the voter was a continuation of the populist appeal —an anti-intellectual approach, geared to the common, the "little" man, unfriendly to racial mixing of all kinds, resentful of central government, favoring "law and order." Nationally, Wallace polled 13 percent of the popular vote, but in Tennessee, Wallace captured 34 percent of the popular vote, considerably more than had been shown by any other third-party candidate since the Civil War. Wallace came in second to Richard Nixon in Tennessee; the Democratic candidate, Hubert Humphrey, came in third. Wallace's strength in Tennessee, on a county basis, lay in the sections of the state that have been considered one-party Democratic in the South. Middle and West Tennessee were Wallace country in 1968; the Republican counties of the state remained true to their historic allegiance. A substantial number of the Middle and West Tennessee counties that could be considered one-party Democratic were carried by Wallace, and he captured a number of counties, mostly in West Tennessee, that have in recent years shown signs of being competitive two-party areas. The geographical pattern of the Wallace vote was similar to the pattern of Populist party strength in 1892. The presence of the Wallace vote in those sections of the state that historically have had a considerable number of blacks is evident, but it must be remembered that the blacks have been leaving these counties (outside the urban areas); therefore the Wallace vote, if racial in character, is based upon racial compositions of the past rather than of the foreseeable future.[9]

Wallace returned to the Democratic party for the presidential campaign in 1972; he emerged the overwhelming choice of those Tennesseans who voted in the state's first presidential primary in the spring of that year. In this primary a substantial number of normally Republican voters undoubtedly crossed over to vote in the Democrat's preferential jamboree. The results were spectacular. Wallace carried every county in the state—rural, small town, and big urban. His votes ranged from percentages in the upper 40s to 90 percent in one small county. The highest majorities were in Middle and West Tennessee (with the one exception of Sevier County in the East), exactly what one would expect from the geography of Wallace country. Later in the year, Tennessee went overwhelmingly for Richard Nixon; McGovern carried only five counties—four on the Rim and the Tennessee River west of Nashville and one on the Highland Rim to the east of Nashville.

The American party has virtually disappeared in Tennessee. In the western portion of the state the party has been able to offer candidates for local offices, for the General Assembly, and for the national House of Representatives, but there is little evidence to indicate a breakup of the traditional contest between the two major parties.[10]

---

[9]We are much indebted for the material on Wallace and the American party in Tennessee to Paul H. Holmes, "The American Party in Tennessee—1968–1971: A History of Its Development and a Portrait of Its Leadership," master's thesis, Univ. of Tennessee, 1973; see also Greene and Holmes.

[10]Paul Holmes, *passim.*

Of the candidate's resources the most essential is the intangible personal appeal.

WILLIAM BUCHANAN AND AGNES BIRD

ISSUES MAY BE IMPORTANT in politics, but personalities and political families (the Taylors, the Gores, the Clements, and their relatives with other names) are more interesting. The people—their quirks, their foibles, their loves and hates—submerge the issues, both in campaign and in the historical accounts. At the state and local levels personalities overshadow issues partly because, while the issues may be there, they are more humdrum than national controversies, even though they may be quite vital for day-to-day existence. In many races the search for controversies sometimes takes on an almost pathetically desperate tone, as candidates suggest foolish or impossible solutions to insignificant or nonexistent problems. Nevertheless, issues do exist and some of them have torn the state and its society apart. These soul-scarring conflicts are generally national in scope, their expression in Tennessee no more than a part of national controversy and indecision.

In its early history Tennessee was affected by the widespread movements of the time—the expanding democracy, tariffs and banking controversies, internal improvements. Of course, the most pervasive and devastating issue of all was slavery, its preservation or abandonment, its limitation or expansion, and the effects of these matters on the nature and even continuance of the federal system. The Tennessee struggle over secession was crucial for the pattern of state politics, and the alignments established at that time persist into the present.

A similar conflict, deeply and bitterly felt, raged around the control and prohibition of the liquor traffic. In the early years of the present century this issue split the Democratic party and opened the way to a temporary assumption of power by the Republicans. It explains the direction taken by Tennessee in certain national elections. And the final solution—to leave decisions in this area to local option—merely transfers to local politics what once moved the state.

If other controversies are lacking, a fight can always be stirred up on taxes. For years Tennesseans have been confronted by the question of the personal income tax; the dispute over its possible adoption is by no means dead, and possibly the insatiable demand for governmental expenditure may bring the tax into being. By all signs it is highly unwelcome at the present. In the Democratic primary of 1978, every candidate for the governorship came out flatly against the income tax.

But issues in Tennessee have relatively little to do with day-to-day party alignments, and in most areas the voters and their representatives do not divide on issues in accordance with party lines. At the same time, voters appear to identify candidates as "conservative" or "liberal" and at least part of the time to vote for such general orientations rather than for personalities.[11]

The hatreds of political struggles are persistent in Tennessee. Beginning with the rivalries between William Blount and John Sevier, when Tennessee statehood was in its inception, it is possible to trace a series of political conflicts over lifetimes. The Sevier faction in what was originally known as the Republican party (predecessor to today's Democrats) transferred its enmity from Blount to Jackson. Polk succeeded to Jackson's friends—and his enemies. After the Civil War, the Democrats suffered a prolonged division between a conservative industrialist faction, the older "machine" crowd, and a third group of populist outlook. In the present century the Democrats have been divided into two groups that in recent years could be roughly identified as the conservative Clement–Ellington force and the somewhat more liberal wing exemplified by Ross Bass and John J. Hooker, Jr., heirs and associates of Estes Kefauver and Albert Gore.[12] But this dichotomy seemed to break up in 1974. The Democrats fielded over a dozen candidates in the primary of that year, and one would be hard put to locate any definite ideological separations. On the score of issues, there was little to choose between Clement, Butcher, and Fulton, the three leading Democratic contenders for the governorship in 1978. Aspirants for the top rung of the ladder in Tennessee always make deep obeisance to the need for better roads and schools, and all pledge to attract new industry and to operate efficiently. It is a wearisome litany that carries little excitement or conviction. Television has tended to degrade issues still further, for the advertising firms that the candidates employ come up with slogans that mean no more than any other sale of soft soap. Issues were more clearly articulated in the days of the stump speech in the courthouse square—days now gone.

In Tennessee, campaign tactics have relied heavily on personal attacks. There is no reason to suppose that Tennessee politicians are more vituperative than their fellows in other states, but certainly they need not fear having to give place to anyone in their use of invective, charges and countercharges, and general vilification of the enemy. Crump and Browning were talented masters in this medium. Given this type of incessant harping on the evil deeds of the opposition, it is not surprising that the public mingles with its enjoyment of the fracas a general disbelief in the

[11]See William Buchanan and Agnes Bird, *Money as a Campaign Resource: Tennessee Democratic Senatorial Primaries, 1948–1964* (Princeton: Citizens' Research Foundation, n. d.), 40 ff.

[12]Compare Buchanan and Bird, 75–77.

charges and in the one who makes them. Because of this skepticism, the politician, in spite of his obvious services to society, suffers from a certain amount of disrespect. No doubt, like his government, he is traditionally viewed as a necessary evil.

Campaign styles differ from one candidate to another. Before the advent of television with its meaningless spot announcements and tasteless jingles the candidate had to rely on stump-speaking—the "hustings"—on hand-shaking, on food—"clambaking"—on entertainment (not surprisingly, country music is an old standby), and on advertising by every means available, but certainly by billboard. These means are time-honored. Debates have been commonplace (and still persist), and, curiously enough, opponents sometimes traveled together. Such a team was formed by the Taylor brothers, Alf and Bob, who moved around the state together for their debates for the governorship.[13] Some candidates are dead serious; some are storytellers. Bob Taylor acquired a wide reputation as a racon-teur; indeed, one of Taylor's political opponents, Governor Ben Hooper, allowed that Taylor's principal qualification was his ability to tell stories.[14] Dignity is not a quality much sought, appreciated, or evidenced, but some candidates have had this trait; Austin Peay is said to have been both dignified and candid.[15] The aura of the governorship, whether possessed or sought, has not prevented some candidates from slipping into the role of entertainer. Bob Taylor played a country fiddle; so did Albert Gore, Sr., at times. Governor Gordon Browning was glad to sing "The Tennessee Waltz," not only because he liked to sing, but also because the perfor-mance could garner votes. Browning's appearances fastened the Tennes-see Waltz in the imagination of people outside the state, and Frank Clement had to endure being greeted by the musical signature of his principal opponent in some of his speaking appearances outside the state.[16]

Oratory has been a handle to greatness and preferment. The outstanding example of the orator in recent times was Governor Clement. His some-what old-fashioned eloquence was the result of deliberate training, plan-ning, and execution, practiced from boyhood on. His mastery of the technique not only brought him the governorship three times (with some luck, plus a sharp intelligence and very hard effort), but also made him the keynote speaker of the Democratic National Convention in 1956, there exacting even from the skeptics a grudging acknowledgment of his mastery of the medium.[17] But Clement was by no means alone. Browning was an

[13]Daniel Merritt Robison, *Bob Taylor and the Agrarian Revolt in Tennessee* (Chapel Hill: Univ. of North Carolia Press, 1935), 61–62.

[14]Ben W. Hooper, *The Unwanted Boy: The Autobiography of Governor Ben W. Hooper*, ed. Everett Robert Boyce (Knoxville: Univ. of Tennessee Press, 1963), 69–70.

[15]Observations made to the senior author by the late James P. Hess of the Univ. of Tennessee.

[16]Greene, *Lead Me On.*

[17]See William L. Davis, "Corruption vs. Morality: A Rhetorical Analysis of the Campaign

able speaker, and an exceedingly rough campaigner, particularly in the 1954 primary. McCord had a good voice and beautiful diction. Ellington, by study and practice, became a good speaker.[18] Kefauver, by contrast, was a dull, plodding performer, who succeeded by other techniques. Unquestionably, television has altered campaign techniques, but the local surfacing of would-be orators from time to time indicates a continued faith in the speech from the stump. At the same time, as the career of Frank Clement is examined, it is difficult to avoid a feeling that Clement was born out of his time and that the abilities so much admired from the days of Webster to Bryan were beginning to lose their effect on the national scene, even though these abilities continued to be useful in Tennessee through the 1960s.

The Tennessee politician cannot be stereotyped. Frank Clement outgrew his boyhood shyness to become the extrovert par excellence. Buford Ellington, an equally able politician, was reserved and remote, although he could throw off this attitude in a campaign. Prentice Cooper seemed shy and dignified, but he was far from shy when it came to asking for political support. Estes Kefauver, no spellbinder, was a great handshaker. McKellar, in his old age, was crabbed and agressive. Crump could be bitter and vengeful, but he could show a geniality that was far from feigned. Ross Bass and Ray Blanton, short-tempered both, inflicted self-wounds at times. Bob Clement, in 1978, suffered from a youthful appearance that made him, then thirty-four, seem twenty-five. All of these men have made contributions to a history of campaigning filled with interest and marked by unrelieved turmoil.

The most obvious conclusion to be drawn from . . . campaign histories is the comparative impotence of money, in and of itself, as a campaign resource.

BUCHANAN AND BIRD

THE TENNESSEE STATUTORY LIMITS on campaign expenditures that once existed (they have now been repealed) bore little resemblance to actual practice; allowable expenditures were far below what could be considered reasonable, and candidates appeared to pay little attention to the requirements. It has been difficult to tell how much is spent on campaigns. One study of campaign expenditures in U. S. senatorial campaigns from 1948 to

---

of Frank Goad Clement for Governor of Tennessee, 1952,'' master's thesis, Wake Forest Univ., 1972; and Stephen Dean Boyd, ''The Campaign Speaking of Frank Clement in the 1954 Democratic Primary: Field Study and Rhetorical Analysis,'' diss., Univ. of Illinois , 1972.

[18]Interview, Lee S. Greene with Charles Lockett, Knoxville, June 25, 1980.

1964 estimated that an average cost of a primary campaign per candidate was $210,000, or about seventy-five cents per vote. But costs of a campaign can go very much higher than this figure, and in some cases can be very low. Perhaps the lowest of recent years was the 1964 reelection campaign of Senator Albert Gore, who spent an estimated $20,000. We have had very little material on gubernatorial campaign costs, but they have probably been of the same order as the costs of a senatorial race. In the 1974 gubernatorial primary, expenditures of significant candidates ranged from $200,000 to over $1 million and there is little reason to expect an early decline in these costs.

Financial disclosure acts were passed in 1975 and 1976; these have been superseded by the Campaign Disclosure Act of 1980. The legislation requires candidates to file with the state librarian lists of contributors and the amounts they contributed, with some exceptions for small contributions. Such lists are open to public inspection, but totals are not provided and overall reports are not made, so the information is not kept in readily usable form.

The sources of campaign funds are varied. Some money accompanies the support that candidates receive from organized pressure groups of various kinds. Organized labor in Tennessee cannot exert unified pressure, and, like labor elsewhere, the labor organization cannot deliver the labor vote. But financial support from labor can be substantial. At various times in Tennessee organized labor has supported Kefauver, Gore, Browning, and Clement. It was reported to have contributed $25,000 to the campaign for governor conducted by Mayor P. R. Olgiati of Chattanooga. Ross Bass had labor support and money in his campaign for the Senate in 1964 when, it is thought, Bass received over $50,000 from labor. The lists published since 1975 show large numbers of small contributors. A Negro bloc supported Bass in 1964 and even raised money for him, a departure in Tennessee affairs, where blacks had been more likely to receive than to give.

Businessmen and organizations have contributed to many different kinds of candidates, not all of them conservatives. In the 1964 senatorial campaign Governor Clement, in a bid for the Senate seat left vacant by Kefauver's death, raised funds from the sources usually available to gubernatorial candidates. Such candidates draw on contributions from state employees, more or less compulsory, and on contributions from firms that do business with the state. The state purchasing laws are not tight enough to prevent some picking and choosing among firms competing for state business, and both locally and on a statewide basis contributions are made in the "lively expectation of favors to come." In the Clement campaign of 1964, the candidate's contributors included attorneys, automobile and auto parts dealers, oil distributors, tractor and implement dealers, insurance men, and bankers. This kind of contribution, always somewhat suspect, earned a good deal of public distaste during the disclosures that followed the 1972 campaign of President Nixon; it is, however, a common source of money for campaigns in Tennessee as well as in the entire country. In campaigns involving regulatory agencies, where not much general public interest is involved, probably the main source of money is the business firms that are subject to regulation. This is said to be the case with campaigns for membership on the Public Service Commission of Tennessee.

Most Tennessee campaigns for important statewide offices call forth indignant charges of solicitation of public employees for campaign war chests. The whole pattern brings the merit system into question. Yet it is certain that pressure is brought to bear to get employees to contribute; it is not so certain that reprisals are taken against those who do not give. Five percent of one month's pay has more than once been suggested as an appropriate contribution from a state employee.

Local campaign contributions can sometimes be built up on the basis of the favors the local community has received, or hopes to receive, from the officeholder, and it is often charged that a reluctant community can expect little from a successful candidate. Such statements were made concerning the Clement administration, but if they were true, they describe practices probably used by others as well.

Campaign funds are spent for newspaper advertisements, radio and television, billboards, and for overhead campaign expenses, including travel. Amounts spent on these various items vary from candidate to candidate, depending in part on the campaign style. Expenditures on television are substantial, and billboards are costly. Expenditure is only loosely coordinated; local campaign agencies act much on their own initiative. Since money is spent without too much regard to need, a good deal of it is thrown away in areas already friendly to the candidate. There has been some outright vote-buying in Tennessee, but this practice appears to be on the decline.

It is quite evident that money cannot win an election. Money is necessary to put the candidate in the minds of the voters, but the candidate cannot be put across with money alone. He must have a high degree of personal appeal, as Governor Clement had for much of his career and as Senator Estes Kefauver generally enjoyed, or he must be on the right side of the controversial issues, as Senator Bass was, for a short time. Money is useful and to a degree essential, but in Tennessee, as elsewhere, it is not the critical element in the election.[19]

[19]We are heavily indebted for these comments on campaign funds to Buchanan and Bird, *Money as A Campaign Resource*. These comments are substantiated by the Democratic and Republican primaries of 1974.

⊙

Americans of all ages . . . constantly form associations.

ALEXIS DE TOCQUEVILLE (1835)

THE PARTY STRUCTURE can be called the half-visible government; the voter knows the party exists, but he is quite unfamiliar with the details of its functioning. The operations of pressure groups and special interests within the politics of the state are even less well understood by the average voter. Yet these groups are fully as important as the political party organization is in determining what rules go on our statute books and how they are enforced. In most states, and Tennessee is no exception, an act is passed by the General Assembly, not because its passage has been promised by one or the other of the parties (in the government of the state the party platform as such either does not exist or counts for practically nothing), but because some particular group in the state wants the act passed and can persuade the legislature to move.

A full list of the groups in the state able and willing to bring pressure to bear upon political officials would give a fairly complete picture of the social and economic character of the population. A few are mentioned here. To begin with, something of a conflict of interests revolves around the governmental agencies themselves. Perhaps as significant as any is the potential rivalry between rural and urban interests. This rivalry has not reached the pitch in Tennessee attained in certain other states, but it exists and seems to persist in spite of the increasingly urban character of the state. All levels of government need funds; generally speaking, the cities of the state appear to need new sources of revenue more than the counties do. It is to be expected therefore that city officials and their friends will seek to convince the legislature that sources of revenue should be set aside for municipal use. In the past the cities of the state have been underrepresented in the apportionment of seats in the state legislature. Reapportionments since the U. S. Supreme Court held in *Baker* v. *Carr* that apportionment is subject to judicial review have corrected this imbalance, but the results of that change are not entirely clear. Experienced observers in this and other states have noted that urban interests often fared better with rural legislators than with those representing suburban concerns. The chief opposition to annexation to central cities, for example, has come from the suburban areas in Knoxville, Chattanooga, and the "Tri-cities" region.

The potential conflict of interest between cities and the rural sections is expressed in part by the formation of groups of officials or governmental units organized to carry through legislative programs. Thus, organizations of county judges and other county officials exist, some fairly strong, and others loose and informal; one of the principal functions of these groups to date appears to be to watch the legislative program as it affects counties. These county organizations seem to be growing and strengthening. In

Tennessee the county interest is represented by the Tennessee County Services Association, which has become increasingly active and aggressive, although, for the most part, it acts in cooperation with the Tennessee Municipal League. The League has grown politically powerful during the past quarter-century. It has an active legislative program involving, among other matters, an allocation of sources of revenue to municipalities sufficient to enable them to meet the ever mounting demands upon their services. In addition, it carries on some research and has entered into arrangements with the University of Tennessee to provide technical advice and assistance to municipal officials. Other groups of city officials have formed organizations; so far they have few legislative programs, but if such develop they will probably be carried on through the Tennessee Municipal League. Nevertheless Tennessee officialdom is less well organized in this way than are the officials of many other states.

Cities do not present a united political front. On the contrary, it is by no means unusual in American states for very large cities to be allied against smaller cities in various aspects of legislative lobbying; the same situation exists to some degree at the federal level. In Tennessee a latent conflict of this sort exists, but the Tennessee Municipal League has been instrumental in keeping a large degree of harmony between the divergent interests. It is apparently true that Memphis has pursued its own way somewhat independently of other cities, but even here the conflict between large and small cities has not reached the intensity that has developed in certain other sections of the country where a single big city will often be lined up on one side with the rest of the state on the other. The nature of our population distribution in Tennessee means, however, that certain types of governmental questions, especially those involving organized labor, may receive more sympathetic attention from the large cities, where the more powerful forces of labor are located.

Perhaps one of the most interesting types of organizations that were active in behalf of legislation in past years is exemplified by the associations of policemen and firemen in the large cities of the state. In the past the legislature, by special acts, was able to alter municipal charters in great detail. The legislature by this means often set the minimum salaries of municipal employees. Hence, policemen and firemen, if organized in such a way as to be influential with the legislature, were able to get that body to set salary scales that they could not obtain from city councils. Organizations of policemen and firemen used to campaign actively for their own interests at sessions of the General Assembly. Amendment Six to the constitution, made in 1953, by decreasing the amount of special legislation, substantially altered the influence of such city employee organizations. In the 1970s, governmental employee organizations are supplementing whatever lobbying they do with more direct action. Memphis, for example, experienced a disastrous strike of firemen in 1978, and threats of such direct action have occurred in other big cities.

Teachers are considered by some observers to constitute one of the most powerful of the interest groups in the state, although they do not always get all they want. This has become true of other states as well. In Tennessee the interests of the teachers of the state as a whole are represented by the Tennessee Education Association, thought of, by some observers, as tough and ruthless. In addition, the teachers of each Grand Division have influential organizations of their own. Not only do the teachers themselves, with their friends and relatives, make up a large bloc of voters, but they have also commanded a large measure of public support and sympathy, for they have always been seriously underpaid and they perform a service in which the public has always been deeply interested. Hence, their combined political power has come to be very considerable, but their incessant demands encounter some resentment and resistance. Pressures from University and college teachers are added to those from elementary and secondary school teachers; but, left to themselves, university faculties exercise little political strength.

Beginning in the 1950s, the black voters of Tennessee began to register and go to the polls in increasing numbers. A principal spokesman for the black interests was the Tennessee Voters Council, in which Avon Williams, Russell Sugermon, Ben Hooks, and A. W. Willis were prominent members. The council arranged meetings at which candidates could appear to seek endorsement. Governor Clement and soon-to-be Senator Howard Baker were among those who sought black approval. The council did not escape internal disagreement or rivalry from other black organizations, and it could not guarantee to deliver the black vote intact, but it was significant enough that candidates courted its favor. In the 1970s, the political machine of the four Ford brothers in Memphis became highly significant. It was an important factor in giving Jake Butcher the nomination for governor in 1978 over Bob Clement, but the support thus given Butcher undoubtedly cost him heavily among white voters in the ensuing general election in which he was defeated by Lamar Alexander, the Republican candidate. The experience helped to accustom West Tennessee counties to voting Republican.

One of the changes in Tennessee political life from the late 1960s on is the increase in the numbers of black elected officials. In 1979 there were slightly over one hundred black officeholders, including one U. S. representative, several legislators, members of county, city, and school governing bodies, and a few judges. Most of these are found in the metropolitan counties, but a few are found in smaller communities. Their constituencies are likely to be principally black.

The private organizations that from time to time have legislative or other programs of concern to public agencies must be almost innumerable. Some of these organizations are extremely active; one might say that they are in continuous session. For example, the Tennessee Farm Bureau Federation, representing the most powerful of the farm groups in the state, exercises a profound influence on the course of state politics, in spite of the decline in farm population, as was shown clearly in the constitutional convention of 1971; there is good reason to assume that the Federation, dominated by large farmers, has close ties to banking, credit, and insurance interests. Various industrial groups are actively represented in Nashville, especially during the sessions of the General Assembly. The railroad interests, represented by the Tennessee Railroad Association, are careful to see that their concerns are brought to the attention of the legislature by paid counsel; in former days the railroads had local lawyers throughout the state on their payrolls. The truckers have had a strong influence in state politics. Frank Clement's first contest against Gordon Browning was a straight-out fight between the truckers supporting Clement and the railroad-backed Browning. The Tennessee Manufacturers' Association maintains a Nashville office and presents its views on matters before the legislature. The Tennessee Taxpayers Association forms a permanent organization to study governmental administration from the point of view of securing the most for the expenditure of the government dollar. Business groups include the Tennessee Motor Transport Association, the Tennessee Malt Beverage Association, the Wine and Spirits Wholesalers of Tennessee, the Tennessee Retail Merchants Association, and many others. One of the chief clerks of the legislature for many years was the acknowledged representative of beer interests. Labor unions have organized committees that take positions on legislative matters of concern to their membership. Labor's general spokesman is the Tennessee State Labor Council. The Tennessee Valley Public Power Association is a spokesman for publicly owned utilities. When they wish, bankers exercise pressure, as they did in the calling of the 1977 convention. The League of Women Voters makes its views known to members of the General Assembly. The Assembly is the focus for the pressures of the community organized into a variety of associations reflecting a complete cross section of the life of the state.

By and large the organization of our society is such that the most powerful and cohesive organizations are those that have particular objectives related quite closely to occupational groupings in society. For the most part the groups that lobby in the General Assembly do not attempt to represent the interests of society as a whole. In other words, most of them have axes to grind. How do matters of general concern, or matters that do not serve particular selfish interests, get consideration? Some such matters probably do not get attention. Some considerations of general public good are kept before the eyes of the legislature by the administrative agencies of the state. Thus, the hospital needs of the state will be supported by the Department of Public Health, and recreation interests will be supported by the Department of Conservation. Then, too, some of the interest groups who seek benefits for themselves are able at the same time to bring their interests into line with the desires of the general public. Teachers, for example, when they campaign for living wages for themselves, are able with some truth to say that a better paid teaching profession might mean a better education for the children of the state, although proof of this statement is not available. Public employees who advocate sound retirement pensions undoubtedly serve sound public personnel administration at the same time. Then, too, there is no reason to suppose that the members of the legislature are mere automatons subject to any particular pressure that may be put upon them. They will come to the sessions of the General Assembly with some views on public welfare.

Organizations exist that represent the public interest somewhat more altruistically than do many of the organizations we have just mentioned. The League of Women Voters, although not large numerically, is able to exercise some influence in public affairs; it supports no clear economic interests, unless it be those of the upper-middle-class consumer. The Council of Social Agencies has worked actively to improve the adoption laws of the state, without having had any interest in the matter except the improvement of the conditions under which children may live in our state. Nevertheless, in spite of these examples, it is true that the organization of our society fosters pressure and lobbying groups that work behind the facades of our political parties. It would be difficult to alter this arrangement. For example, labor unions could secure an improved position for themselves by seeking lower prices as well as by seeking higher wages. In the nature of things, however, it is easier for labor unions to secure an increase in their own wages than to bring about decreased prices for consumers as a whole. Consequently, who would not expect labor unions to press for immediate wage increases? The truth is, our society is organized from the point of view of the producer, not from the point of view of the consumer.[20]

---

[20]An analysis of interest group activity is provided by John C. Wahlke, Heinz Eulau, William Buchanan, and LeRoy C. Ferguson, *The Legislative System: Explorations in Legislative Behavior* (New York: Wiley, 1962).

5

Tribunes of the People

A QUARTER OF A CENTURY AGO AN EDITORIAL IN ONE OF THE KNOXVILLE newspapers reflected forcibly its opinion of the legislature. "For our part," said the statement, "and we think many citizens will share our view, the sooner the Legislature closes the safer the state's population will feel. While every legislative body does some good and necessary things, the public welfare usually takes a good many beatings before any session is concluded."[1] Such an attitude toward the people's representatives is nothing new. In 1888 the governor of Mississippi contemplated a call for a special session of the legislature to raise some additional funds. His adviser warned: "Don't, please don't call the legislature back. I will pay my pro rata share rather than have them here again. Yes, I'll subscribe $10 to make up the deficit if that body never meets again. Besides if the governor were to call them back, the people would arise and hang him, and it would be a case of justifiable homicide."[2] There is little reason to think these opinions are any less widely held now than they were then. If these sentiments are a correct gauge of popular attitudes toward the legislature, the proposals being heard these days for a professional full-time, year-round legislature are not likely to be welcome. When the legislature is in session an aura of uncertainty and instability spreads over society; when the legislature goes home, at least the rules of the game are clearer, even if not always well regarded.

[1]*Knoxville Journal*, Feb. 24, 1949.
[2]Quoted in Thomas D. Clark, *The Southern Country Editor* (Indianapolis: Bobbs-Merrill, 1948), 295.

*State legislatures today have emerged from obscurity into the spot-
light of professional and public attention.*

MALCOLM JEWELL (1968)

THE GENERAL ASSEMBLY of Tennessee is a bicameral legislature; it is
composed of the Senate and the House of Representatives. In this respect
Tennessee is like most of the other states of the Union; all states, with the
exception of Nebraska, now have two-house legislative bodies.

Legislative bodies of more than one house, even of more than two, grew up
in the early history of representative government as a means of providing
recognition of different classes, or interest groups, within the community.
The framers of the federal constitution adopted the device of two houses as a
compromise between the principle of equality of states and that of representation according to population. Hence, where diverse interests are thus
balanced against each other, a solid argument can be put forward for a two-
house legislature. It is argued, too, by the friends of bicameralism, that the
two houses furnish a check on each other, and therefore the passage of harm-
ful and poorly drafted bills may be retarded. The most important force making for the retention of the dual plan in Tennessee is simply that we have had it
since 1796, and the people are not disposed to make any drastic changes in
the structure of the legislative body. The unicameral legislature now excites
little interest in the United States.

The House of Representatives is composed of ninety-nine members, the
exact number set by 1966 amendment. The number of senators may not
exceed one-third the number of representatives and is at present thirty-
three. The number in the Tennessee General Assembly is not too far from
the average among state legislatures and seems to be adequate.

The constitution specifies certain qualifications for a member of the
General Assembly. He is required to be a citizen of the United States, to
have been a citizen of Tennessee[3] for three years, and to have been a
resident of the county or district "he represents [for] one year immediately
preceding the election." A representative must be at least twenty-one
years of age and a senator at least thirty.[4] In addition to those positive
requirements, the constitution disqualifies certain persons from serving in
the legislature. No collector or holder of public funds may serve until he
"shall have accounted for and paid into the Treasury all sums for which he
may be accountable or liable."[5] "No judge of any Court of law or equity,

[3]Citizens of the United States acquire citizenship in a state by residence therein. Residence
means living in a state with the intention of remaining.

[4]Art. II, secs. 9, 10. There is a slight difference in the residency requirements for the two
houses in that representatives are required to be residents of the county, and senators of the
county or district represented, but sections 5a and 6a require that members be qualified voters
in their districts.

[5]Art. II, sec. 25.

Secretary of State, Attorney General, Register, Clerk of any court of Record, or person holding any office under the authority of the United States, shall have a seat in the General Assembly . . ."[6] Other provisions disqualify ministers and priests (this provision has been ruled to violate the federal constitution), atheists, and duelists, including those who send or accept a challenge to fight a duel or aid and abet in fighting a duel.[7] Thus is the purity of the General Assembly preserved.[8] Whether the qualifications are actually possessed is a matter to be decided by each house; each house is the judge of the qualifications of its own members, and the legislature has not been too cranky about some of the out-of-date restrictions. The state courts will not review a house's determination of the qualifications of its members, but the federal courts have done so.[9]

Some very practical qualifications are in force, qualifications unexpressed in the constitution. The would-be legislator must be either otherwise unemployed or engaged in some business that he can leave for several weeks each year, although the increased pay of legislators has enabled a few persons to act as full-time members of the Assembly. And he must have whatever it takes to get elected.

The members of the House of Representatives of Tennessee "hold their offices for two years from the day of the general election"; as a result of the 1966 amendment, members of the Senate are elected for four-year staggered terms.[10] Some critics favor a longer term for both houses partly on the ground that an election contest every two years places an undue burden on the officeholder. He should, they feel, have a longer period in which to adjust himself and build the record he must stand on.

The once unbelievably low pay of Tennessee legislators was a source of criticism for many years. One of the amendments adopted in 1953 raised legislators' compensation to $10.00 per day and $5.00 per day for expenses —a total of $15.00 per day. As a result of later amendments plus statutes the pay of the legislator is now slightly over $8300 annually, and his expense money is substantial. Speakers of the two houses receive additional compensation. Legislative pay for a time was tied to a kind of cost-of-living measurement.

Legislators are entitled to participate in the state retirement system, although they are not required to become members. Those who join the current system receive coverage under social security.

---

[6]Art. II, sec. 26.

[7]Art. IX.

[8]No member of the legislature may, during his term, accept any office or place of trust, except that "of trustee of a literary institution," filled by appointment by the executive or General Assembly. Art. II, sec. 10. No person may hold more than one "lucrative office" at a time, but offices in the militia and of justice of the peace are not considered "lucrative." Art. II, sec. 26.

[9]Art. II, sec. 11; *State ex rel. v. Shumate*, 172 Tenn. 451 (1938). See *McDaniel* v. *Paty* 435 U. S. 618 (1978), reversing Supreme Court of Tennessee.

[10]Art. II, sec. 3.

Legislators in Tennessee are usually male, and ordinarily Protestant. They are not therefore a proportionate image of Tennessee's census characteristics. Exceptions to the rule have been very few. The Senate of the 91st General Assembly (1977–79) included one woman and three Negroes, Edward Davis of Memphis, John N. Ford, also from Memphis, and Avon Williams of Nashville, one of the most colorful and controversial members of the Assembly and a strong and relentless spokesman for the increasingly self-conscious blacks. All of these returned to the 92nd Assembly. The woman was Anna Belle Clement O'Brien, of Crossville, sister of the former governor, Frank Clement. She also returned to the 92nd, after facing a tough campaign. The 91st House included three women, one of whom was black, and eight black men, all returned to the 92nd. In the 1979–81 House, two women were Democrats; one Republican; and the blacks were Democratic (one did not identify his party). The black House members all came from Hamilton, Shelby, and Davidson counties. The women represented districts in Shelby and Knox counties. The number of blacks and women now appears fairly stable in both houses.

The legislature is middle-aged. Almost half the Senate in the 91st General Assembly was between 41 and 50. Among House members of the 91st, the vast majority ranged from 31 to 60, (31–40: 27; 41–50: 32; 51–60: 21). The very young and the very old are not numerous.

Religion plays no role in Tennessee legislative politics. Protestant sects claim the majority of the legislators as members; this is roughly reflective of the religious climate of the state, but has no further significance, for sectarian differences appear not to agitate the General Assembly. But if sectarianism is not present, religious background probably does account for some legislative attitudes.

Tennessee legislators are engaged in occupations essentially of a middle-class nature. In the 90th Assembly less than half of the members of each house were lawyers; practically all the rest were widely scattered over various middle-class occupations, contractors, insurance agents, accountants, engineers, teachers, physicians, funeral directors, and bankers. Farmers and skilled workers were rare. There were a few students. A few individuals considered themselves full-time legislators. The point has been made that, in the country generally, legislators come from second-run elites, not from old established wealth and position.[11] That appears to be the case in Tennessee as well, although a few members come from families with a tradition of participation in politics.

As a usual thing, Tennessee legislators were born in Tennessee, and those who were not were born in neighboring states; there are exceptions,

---

[11]See Table 6 in Thomas R. Dye, "State Legislative Politics," in Jacob and Vines, 178, quoting Wahlke et al., *The Legislative System.*

however, and there is little evidence that birthplaces some distance away get any attention in political campaigns.

Turnover in the General Assembly, according to a study prepared in 1967 for the American Assembly,

> is high enough to give some worry from the point of view of securing and keeping experienced people. Of the 33 senators elected in the autumn of 1966, 13 had served in the preceding Senate; 8 had served in the House in the preceding Assembly, and 5 others had served in some preceding Assembly (House or Senate), a total of 26 experienced persons. Seven senators will come into the Senate as freshmen legislators. The experienced senators in the 85th include a former speaker of the Senate and a former prominent candidate for speaker. Consequently the picture one secures of the Senate is that of experience, rather than turnover. The situation in the House differs rather sharply from that in the Senate. In the 85th, of the 99 elected representatives, 43 served in the preceding House, and one served in the House at some previous time. Consequently, a majority of the House will consist of freshmen members.[12]

In the years 1962 to 1971, the average percentage of new members in the Senate was 43.8; in the House, 51.2. This was a high turnover rate compared to other states. Turnover in this period was related to the frequency of elections, to low compensation, and to the frequency of reapportionment. But turnover now seems less of a problem. In 1977, 77 percent of the House members and 94 percent of the senators could show prior legislative experience.[13] The situation in 1979 was similar. The Senate of the Ninety-second Assembly (1981–83) contains only one freshman member. In the House only eleven of the ninety-nine members are new, a remarkably low turnover and a high degree of continuity.

Frequent turnover has also been characteristic of the speakerships of the two houses over the long pull of Tennessee history, but some signs of change are evident here also. Speaker John Wilder of the Senate has been in office since 1971, and House Speaker Ned McWherter, since 1973.

It would be easy to exaggerate the effects of turnover. The Assembly has for years contained members of long experience, some of widely recognized capacity. Many of these members—James Cummings, Walter Haynes, McAllen Foutch, Hobart Atkins, James Bomar, Jared Maddux, John Bragg, Ernest Crouch, Tom Garland, to mention a few—served long periods and shared power with the speakers and the governors. At the same time the legislature of the past lost able people, such as Eugene Collins, James Bomar, and Tom Johnson, because they needed to build

[12]Malcolm E. Jewell and Lee S. Greene, *The Kentucky and Tennessee Legislatures* (Lexington: Dept. of Political Science, Univ. of Kentucky, 1967), 31–33. The conclusions reached in 1967 still have some significance although conditions have improved. The relatively high turnover in the Tennessee legislature is confirmed by Alan Rosenthal, "And so They Leave: Legislative Turnover in the States," *State Government* (Summer 1974), 149.

[13]For the 1977 figures we are indebted to a paper given at Gatlinburg in 1979 by Paul Hain, supplied to us by Thomas VanDerwort.

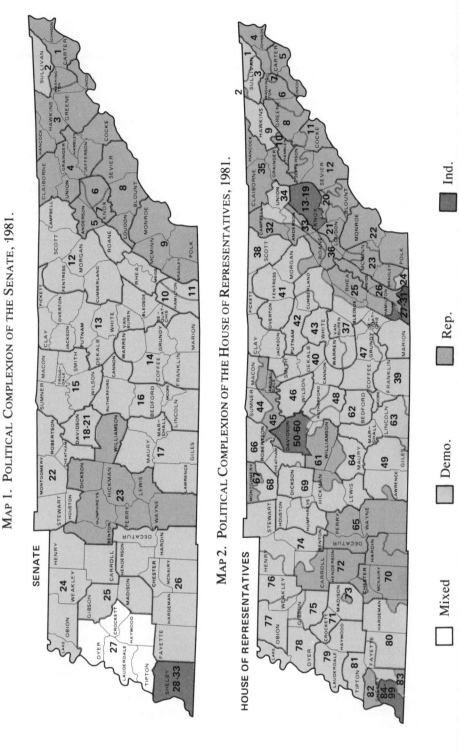

MAP 1. POLITICAL COMPLEXION OF THE SENATE, 1981.

SENATE

MAP 2. POLITICAL COMPLEXION OF THE HOUSE OF REPRESENTATIVES, 1981.

HOUSE OF REPRESENTATIVES

Mixed   Demo.   Rep.   Ind.

careers elsewhere (Johnson moved to the Legislative Council Committee, where his experience was still available to the Assembly). Reapportionment resulted in the loss of some of the members of the Assembly, notably the able former floor leader and speaker of the House, W. L. Barry.

Democratic domination of the legislature is of long standing, although reapportionment and the growth in the number of voters who are acquiring the habit of voting Republican has lessened the gap between the number of Democrats and that of Republicans. The elections to the Senate of the ninety-second Assembly, produced 20 Democratic members, 12 Republicans, and 1 Independent. In the House these figures were 58 Democrats, 39 Republicans, and 2 Independents. This gives the Democrats a comfortable, although not an overwhelming, majority, but the significance of this arrangement must not be exaggerated, because legislative decisions are not ordinarily made on straight party lines.

Primary elections for the General Assembly are held in August; party candidates picked then compete in November. Competition for seats in the General Assembly is often limited—a reflection, possibly, of disinterest or distaste for politics. In some instances veteran legislators acquire reputations large enough to discourage competition. In the 1978 elections, the speakers of the two houses had no competition, either in the primary or in the general election, and that would be true of some other veteran legislators. The lack of competition appears in two ways: in some districts, one of the two parties puts up no candidates; in some districts, only one candidate runs in the primary. For example, in the primary election of 1980, the Democrats fielded no candidates at all in two Senatorial districts (vacancies occurred in sixteen seats). The Republicans had no candidate in seven Senatorial districts in 1978, but they missed only one district in 1980. This situation is a reflection in part of the traditional territorial division of the parties in the state—a division that is still significant in spite of some erosion. It would surprise no one that Democrats sometimes pass up the opportunity to run for districts one and three, which are in Upper East Tennessee. It is a bit more surprising that there was no Democratic candidate in 1978 in the thirty-first Senatorial district in Shelby County, but one must reflect that the Shelby suburban voters are getting used to voting Republican. The districts where no Republicans felt impelled to run in the primary of 1978 were in Hamilton County, on the eastern Highland Rim, certain districts in Nashville and south of Nashville, and districts in West Tennessee and Shelby County. It is not always certain that a lack of a Republican candidate is because no Republican has a chance at any time, but it is clear enough that in some of these districts, Republican chances are mighty slim. All the same, it is well to remember that party allegiances are shifting in Tennessee, and what looked like a Republican desert in 1978 showed tender blossoms in 1980 (a banner year for the GOP).

For the House of Representatives, the figures are still more striking. In 1980 the Democrats put up no candidates in seventeen districts, and the Republicans passed up twenty-six, this in a year when the Republicans made a deliberate play for greater strength in the Assembly. The geographic imperatives were at work for the House as well as for the Senate.

So much for the lack of candidates. But in a large number of districts the party candidate faces no primary contest. In 1980 for the Senate primary, ten Democrats ran without any contest within their own party; fifty-eight Democrats ran for the House without contest. In that year, in the Republican primary, twelve persons ran unchallenged by rivals for the Senate; for the House, fifty-five Republicans were unchallenged. All of this spells something less than a relentless popular urge to get into the legislature.

Where there is no candidate in the primary, there is no contest in the general election. In the 1978 general election, when 17 Senate vacancies existed, there were no contests in eight cases (in two other cases, an independent contested for a seat). About half the Senate seats went to winners without contests. Except for three independent candidacies, forty-seven House seats were uncontested. In almost half the districts, House seats are allotted without challenge. In some of these cases, there would have been no challenger either in the primary or the general election. Clearly membership in the legislature is not universally sought. But challenges in 1980 reduced the number of uncontested seats, as the party ballot grew sharper. In many cases the uncontested seats are in districts within the metropolitan areas where there is some good evidence of division of seats on a party and racial basis among the districts in the areas.

(⋆⋆⋆)

Logically, in a society grounded on representative government, it would seem reasonable that a majority of the people of a State could elect a majority of the State's legislators.

Reynolds v. Sims, 377 U. S. 533, 565 (1964)

THE RELATION OF a legislature to its people is intimately connected with the schemes of apportionment. The determination of how many people each legislator shall represent might be a simple mathematical process of dividing the number of legislators into the population, determining the number of people to be represented by a legislator, then drawing district lines. Unfortunately matters are not so easily ordered.

Several devices of representation may be utilized in a democratic community to reflect its varied interests. Representation on a geographical basis has been used throughout the United States for both national and state bodies. One form of geographical representation is used in the United

States Senate, where each state, without regard to its size or population, is allowed two representatives in the legislative body. This basis of representation was, and is, a compromise between the interests of the large and small states. Geographical representation allows for the presentation of minority points of view attributable to the differences in sections within the political community.

Not all political opinions are attributable to the general environment in which individuals live. Social position, occupation, and economic considerations influence individual opinion profoundly. During early British history, Parliament was roughly representative of a few broad classes. The modern counterpart of special interest representation in American government has taken on an extralegal character. Pressure groups take an active part in specialized legislation by sending representatives of their particular interest to present their positions before the lawmakers. Some modern governments have recognized the variety of interests determined by affiliation in economic or social groups and have made formal provisions for representation on that basis in the form of boards, tripartite commissions, and the like.[14]

American government practice in the past has been shaped to allow for some apportionment of representation on the basis of population. Thus, in the composition of Congress, the House of Representatives is apportioned according to population. As a result of decisions of the United States Supreme Court, it is now clear that only population may be used as a basis for representation in the state legislatures, and this principle has been extended, with some restrictions, to political subdivisions.

The framers of Tennessee's 1870 constitution provided that the General Assembly should be reapportioned every ten years, beginning in 1871.[15] As now amended, the constitution sets a figure of ninety-nine for the House and provides that the Senate shall not exceed one-third of that figure. The Senate currently numbers thirty-three. The constitution provides for combining counties where necessary to form districts of the proper size, but it prohibits the division of counties in the apportioning of Senate or House seats made up of more than one county. A constitutional amendment of 1966 provided for districts within counties that have two or more representatives or senators.[16] The provision preventing the splitting of counties for seats has been superseded by federal court orders.[17] Under the 1870 constitution the basis for apportionment was the number of qualified voters, but the present basis for apportionment, following the decisions of

---

[14]On the legal aspects of tripartite commissions, see Kenneth Culp Davis, *Administrative Law and Government* (Minneapolis: West, 1960).

[15]Art. II, sec. 4, as it stood before amendment.

[16]Art. II, secs. 5, 6.

[17]*Kopald* v. *Carr*, 343 F. Supp. 51 (1972).

the United States Supreme Court, is now population, for both houses.[18] The state constitution, as a result of amendment, preserves the right of the General Assembly to apportion one house on some basis other than population,[19] but this provision is a dead letter.

No means of enforcement of the apportionment provisions was expressly provided for, and the General Assembly was responsible for its own reapportionment. These instructions to the legislature seem relatively simple, but from the point of view of human nature they require the accomplishment of an almost impossible task. As adjustment to account for population shifts requires that certain districts shall have less of a voice than they have previously enjoyed, some legislators are voted out of jobs. To ask that a man voluntarily deprive himself of power is to ask a considerable self-sacrifice. Thus the constitutional intentions regarding reapportionment were not carried out, until the judiciary finally insisted on reform.

Apportionment developed into a running battle between the courts and the legislature. For years, the last general reapportionment had been that of 1901 on the basis of the 1900 census.[20] After 1900 two major population trends within the state produced the rapid expansion of the four large metropolitan areas and many medium-sized cities, and the continued expansion of East Tennessee. East Tennessee was seriously underrepresented in the House of Representatives. Middle Tennessee was overrepresented significantly, as was West Tennessee, with the exception of Shelby County.[21]

For a long time no method of relief for malapportionment was available other than through the General Assembly. The Assembly was dominated by rural elements, symbolized by the power exercised for many years of I. D. Beasley, James Cummings, and Walter Haynes, all small town Democrats. The governor had no way to control this matter except through his influence, and the subject was too ticklish for him to touch it, even if he wanted to. It can be taken for granted that governors like Prentice Cooper, Gordon Browning, Jim McCord, and Buford Ellington had no uncontrollable itch to reapportion and Frank Clement probably felt the same way. The courts rather steadfastly refused to act, and indeed court action in the matter presented unusual difficulties. The state Supreme Court resolutely

[18]Art. II, secs. 4, 5, 6.

[19]Art. II, sec. 4.

[20]*Public Acts,* 1901, ch. 122, and even this apportionment was badly done.

[21]Evan A. Iverson and Lee S. Greene, "The Apportionment of Legislative Seats," *Papers on Constitutional Revision,* Vol. II, University of Tennessee *Record, Extension Series 23:3* (Knoxville: Bureau of Public Administration, 1947). Henry N. Williams, "Legislative Apportionment in Tennessee," *Tennessee Law Review* 20 (April 1948), 235–45, shows that there were inequities under the 1901 law. Sixteen counties entitled to a single representative were placed in joint districts.

refused to dictate or direct action.[22] Faced with this impasse, a group of Tennesseans commenced action in the federal courts, and after a good bit of legal maneuvering, in a precedent-breaking decision the United States Supreme Court held in 1962 that the federal courts could take jurisdiction in the matter of Tennessee legislative apportionment.[23] The decision had country-wide repercussions. In Tennessee, following the Supreme Court ruling, a special session was convened in late May 1962 to reapportion the legislature. Reapportionment acts were passed that partially, but only partially, relieved existing inequities. A three-judge federal court, on June 22, 1962, accepted the reapportionment for the 1963 legislature, but ordered that legislature to reapportion once more, criticizing the 1962 act as "a crazy quilt, . . . inexplicable either in terms of geography or demography."[24]

In 1963, dominated still by rural politicians, the legislature tried again but was challenged in court on the grounds that both houses should have been apportioned on the standard of population. The district court indicated that approval of a reapportionment could be forthcoming if at least one house were set up on a fairly strict basis of population, but even this feature was lacking in the 1963 act. Subsequently the court adopted a plan submitted by the plaintiffs against the legislature's 1963 statute. Then in 1964, in a case involving Alabama, the U. S. Supreme Court indicated that both houses of the legislature must be apportioned on a population basis.[25] The regular session of the legislature in 1965 failed to deal further with reapportionment, and Governor Clement called a special session to deal with the issue. (He had always resisted the idea of special reapportionment sessions in the past because he felt the Assembly would meet and do nothing important—a reasonable position considering the domination of rural forces). The reapportionment achieved by the special session was approved by the federal district court, but was challenged successfully in the state Supreme Court because of its violation of the Tennessee constitution's prohibition against dividing counties into senatorial districts[26] (a provision since invalidated by federal court decisions).

After the results of the 1970 census were available, the apportionment job had to be done over again. Democrats controlled the General Assembly, and in the drawing of Assembly district lines they did what they could to favor Democrats. The federal district court, asked by the Republicans to overturn the Democratic apportionment law, made a few corrections, accepted the plan for the 1972 elections, but warned the General Assembly

[22]*Kidd* v. *McCanless*, 200 Tenn. 273 (1956); cert. denied by U. S. Supreme Court, 352 U. S. 920 (1956).
[23]*Baker* v. *Carr*, 369 U. S. 186 (1962).
[24]*Knoxville News-Sentinel*, June 23, 1962.
[25]*Reynolds* v. *Sims*. 377 U. S. 533 (1964).
[26]The state case is *Williams* v. *Carr*, 218 Tenn. 564 (1966).

to come up with an approved plan for later use; such a plan was adopted in 1973.[27] Some further adjustments were made in 1974.[28] In the 1972 apportionment county lines were crossed in setting up districts, disregarding the prohibition in the Tennessee constitution. Under the 1972 act the average population of a Senate district was 118,914 (with a 3.68 percent variation from the largest to the smallest); for the House the comparable figures were 39,638 average size and 4.26 percent maximum variation.[29] During the 1970s, the Assembly continued to tinker with district boundaries, making minor adjustments here and there, sometimes with trivial or, on occasion, racial objectives. Some of these realignments were overruled by federal courts, which continue to ride herd on the legislature.

The districts as set by the General Assembly are contiguous—they are not split up in an attempt to disadvantage the minority party—but they are not always compact. That is to say, some of the districts take odd shapes that indicate the manipulation of boundaries for political or other reasons. Actually, such odd shapes do not necessarily indicate that political chicanery has been practiced. Natural contours, such as rivers —the Cumberland in Nashville, the Tennessee in Knoxville and Chattanooga —could account for some of the odd shapes, and the necessity of equalizing population among the districts may call for some of the unusual configurations. But political unlikes are sometimes put together. Thus one of the districts in Knoxville puts the students at the University of Tennessee in the same district with Sequoyah Hills, one of the areas of old wealth (mitigated, it is true, by the presence of numbers of university faculty, whose views tend away from the extreme right). The fact that separation of races by residence is still the rule in Tennessee cities means that normally whites and blacks are not mixed together in the same district. There is no busing of voters.

The 1980 census called for further rearrangements. The Tennessee population center moved eastward as Middle and East Tennessee became more significant than formerly. A rapid population growth occurred in the counties adjacent to the central metropolitan counties—areas likely to vote Republican—and consequently readjustments for the 1980s became necessary. The General Assembly's first painful attempt to reapportion resulted in an act that Governor Alexander vetoed because of a number of errors it contained, such as overlapping of districts and unrepresented areas. The Assembly then met again and passed a new act, apparently free of such errors, and this act, acceptable to the governor, will stand unless challenged in court.

[27]*Public Acts,* 1973, chs. 161, 403.
[28]*Public Acts,* 1974, chs. 600, 649.
[29]Figures prepared by Legislative Council Committee.

Reapportionment has been accompanied by political change in the State of Tennessee; it is not clear that this change has been caused by reapportionment, but surely the reapportionment has facilitated the change. The urban population has now received its share of the legislative seats; at the same time the creation of single-member constituencies has split urban areas into districts, and the suburbs have been separated from the central cities. Reapportionment has been accompanied by a resurgence of the Republican party, and probably the party was helped by the changes in the legislative structure. As a result the Republicans have representatives from areas once solidly-Democratic, most notably the suburban sections of Shelby County. At the same time the Republican area outside Shelby County in the lower half of West Tennessee has been widened. With the growth of the Republican party, the party battle in the legislature has become more evident, and when in 1970 a Republican governor was chosen, the legislature, which remained in the hands of a Democratic majority, asserted the independence normal to two-party situations. (Actually that independence commenced to develop as early as 1965 and began to reach full bloom during the first years of Governor Ellington's last term.)

But how much difference these changes made in the actions of the legislature is not so clear. It was never completely clear that the disenfranchised sections of the state or segments of the population suffered materially in policy matters before the case of *Baker* v. *Carr*. For example, cities worked happily enough with the malapportioned legislature, and the Tennessee Municipal League was never a strong proponent of reapportionment. The league, representative of the incorporated towns and cities, has good reason to fear the unfriendliness of the unincorporated suburbs. Still, on policy questions in the future, one can expect a shift in the climate in a legislature now truly based on population rather than on traditional sectionalism.[30]

(★★★)

I love Speaker Rayburn, his heart is so warm,
And if I love him he'll do me no harm.
So I shan't sass the Speaker one least little bitty,
And then I'll wind up on a major committee.

ANONYMOUS (1958)

LEGISLATURES, AS IN THE CASE of all deliberative bodies, can arrive at

---

[30]Compare Greene and Holmes, 192–99, and Jewell and Greene, 34–37. The literature on reapportionment is now enormous. Especially important for Tennessee is Richard C. Cortner, *The Apportionment Cases* (Knoxville: Univ. of Tennessee Press, 1970); this work deals in detail with the development of the Tennessee issue that triggered the whole course of reapportionment nationally. A particularly extensive work is Robert G. Dixon, *Democratic Representation: Reapportionment in Law and Politics* (New York: Oxford Univ. Press, 1968). See also Richard Claude, *The Supreme Court and the Electoral Process* (Baltimore:

decisions only through the use of an operating mechanism. Provision must be made for the selection of officers to guide and direct the proceedings, and all business must be transacted under established rules of procedure. If the most effective work is to be done, staff must be provided to perform the many duties incident to carrying on work, and there must be an established pattern of sessions for the transaction of legislative business.

The organization of the two houses of the Tennessee General Assembly is the same. On the opening day of each new session each house is called to order by the clerk of the previous session. After new members are sworn in, the houses proceed on constitutional authority to elect their speakers.[31] This election is usually routine. No real contest is involved, for the speakers have already been designated by the majority caucus, but when, as has happened in recent years in Tennessee, the parties are evenly divided in a house or a party split occurs, a few party desertions can shift the election of the speaker from one party or faction to another. Other officers of the legislature such as the clerks are also predetermined by the caucus.

The most important official in each house is the speaker. For something like a generation the speaker in each house (the chief official of the Senate is also called "speaker" in Tennessee) was a person acceptable to the governor and may even have been designated by him. But restiveness under gubernatorial control developed, reaching serious proportions in 1965; the governor no longer controls the choice of speakers. The speaker presides over the house, preserves order, recognizes members, puts questions to the house, and refers bills to committees.[32] The speaker's power over committees is very significant. Unless otherwise directed he appoints all committees and designates the chairman of each. He is an ex officio member of each committee. In addition to its officers, each house is provided with the services of approximately twenty employees who serve in the various capacities of chief clerk, engrossing clerk, bill clerk, or public relations personnel. The speakers have become powerful, particularly Speaker McWherter of the House. McWherter has been a determined partisan, and his power has rivaled the governor's.

Each house is guided by rules that are adopted for each session. These rules specify such details as the duties of the speaker, the order of business,

---

Johns Hopkins Univ. Press, 1970). See Timothy G. O'Rourke, *The Impact of Reapportionment* (New Brunswick, N. J.: Transaction Books, 1980); see also James C. Coomer, "The Impact of Reapportionment on the Tennessee Legislative Process: An Analysis of the Tennessee General Assembly, 84th and 85th Sessions," diss., Univ. of Tennessee, 1975.

[31]Art. II, sec. 11.

[32]These powers are provided for in the Rules of Order of the two houses. Tennessee is the only state in which the presiding officer of the Senate is called the speaker. In most states the term "president" is used to designate the incumbent of this office.

the conduct required of members, rules of debate, motions that may be made, treatment of bills, and committees used. The nature of the parliamentary practice is indicated by a rule in each house providing that, in the absence of other rules, *Robert's Rules of Order* will apply. The rules may be rescinded or amended by a two-thirds vote of the members present, but only on one day's notice. They may be suspended at any time by a two-thirds vote of members present.

The General Assembly once met in session beginning on the first Monday in January after the election.[33] In 1968, annual sessions started; the length of the session is not specifically set by the constitution, but a practical limitation is imposed by the constitutional provision limiting the expense and travel pay of members to 90 days for a regular session (interpreted to cover the two-year period), excluding the organizational session, and to 30 days for any special session (these limits were formerly 75 and 20). In practice the legislature uses about half its paid time each year.

The regular session of the General Assembly may be supplemented on extraordinary occasions by special sessions called by the governor, or by the speakers on request of two-thirds of the members. The call must state the purpose of the session, and the legislature, when called by the governor, is limited to the purpose he states.[34] Any number of special sessions may be called, but the members receive pay for only thirty days of each. Special sessions have always occurred with relative infrequency, and the annual session may eliminate any need for them.

The heart of any legislative body will be found in its system of committees. Bills that receive approval of these committees are likely to be passed; bills that committees disapprove of are almost always killed simply by the committee's failure or refusal to report them to the house. Unwanted bills are killed by inaction—"pigeonholed" or "bottled up."

Before 1955 the committee structure had grown to the point where it was badly in need of overhaul. At one time the House of Representatives had 46 standing committees, and the Senate 35, unequal in both size and importance. For example, in the session of 1947 the House of Representatives Committee on Corporations had seven members, while the Committee on Agriculture had thirty-eight. In the session of 1949 three Senate committees had seventeen members, a majority of the Senate membership, while several committees had eight members.

A progressive reform took place in 1955 when the number of standing committees of the General Assembly was reduced to seventeen in each house. Beginning in the 1969 Assembly the number of committees was reduced to seven in the House and six in the Senate, plus committees on

[33]Art. II, sec. 8, before amendment.
[34]Art. III, sec. 9; Art. II, sec. 8.

calendars and rules in each house; the numbers were later increased. The House committees (in addition to the Committee on Calendar and Rules) are (as of 1979–80) those on agriculture; commerce; conservation and environment; education; finance; ways and means; general welfare; government operations; judiciary; labor and consumer affairs; state and local government; and transportation. In the Senate, as of 1979–80, the standing committees are commerce and labor; education; energy and environment; finance, ways and means; general welfare and human resources; government operations; highway planning, development, and safety; judiciary; and state and local government. The committees vary in both size and importance, but in keeping with the size of the Senate, they are all small. All bills that clear Senate committees are eventually brought to the floor.

Committee loads differ markedly. The committees on transportation and agriculture are not active, and probably there is not too much reason for having them. Committees on finance, ways, and means, on education, on the judiciary, and on state and local government are more significant. The Committee on Finance, Ways, and Means is especially important, as it is likely to be in any legislative body. In Congress the use of seniority for committee assignment (a seniority acquired through long tenures of some members of Congress) results in the development of expertise in substantive fields among committee leaders. Some of this expertise is evident among Tennessee legislators, although the high turnover and the relative unimportance of seniority in committee assignments limit the degree to which expert knowledge can be acquired.

A key committee in the House of Representatives is the large Committee on Calendar and Rules that controls the flow of legislation through the House. This very large committee consists of the chairmen, vice-chairmen, and secretaries of the standing committees, plus a chairman, vice-chairman, and secretary of the committee itself, who do not have to be officers of any of the standing committees.

In the House each member serves on two standing committees, but the committee size varies somewhat. The larger committees include finance, ways, and means; state and local government; and education.

In the past, committee chairmanships were shared to a degree between the parties, but in the 88th General Assembly and subsequent Assemblies the speaker of the House has appointed Democrats to the chairmanships of all House committees, a logical enough extension of the principle of party politics that nevertheless was greeted by howls of dismay from the Republican side. All vice-chairmen and secretaries of the committees have also been Democrats, with the result that Republicans were squeezed off the calendar committee. As the result of pressure from fellow Democrats, plus the fact that an ambitious Republican party attempted to deprive him of his seat in 1980, Speaker of the Senate John Wilder in 1981 decided to play rough and adopted the practice of naming only Democrats to the chairmanships in the Senate. Furthermore, he ousted from the committee leadership in 1981 those Democrats who had opposed him for speaker.

The Assembly offers little chance for a further and wider career in politics. Most legislators cannot expect a chance at the governorship, or even a cabinet position. Ambition does not find a necessary outlet from the Assembly to the United States Congress. Of course, exceptions exist. Some legislators become candidates for governor, but the careers of Clement and Dunn indicate clearly enough that the governorship may be reached by other routes. Indeed, avoidance of the legislature may spare a candidate for governor the burden of past enmities. (Early on, Clement was advised to forgo a legislative career for precisely this reason.)

The legislature of the 1970s recovered its independence from the governor, and the trend promises to continue in the 1980s. Although Democrats can no longer count on controlling all branches of the state government, the General Assembly is still usually Democratic. But, whatever the governor's party ties, the Assembly no longer bows to his wishes. It picks its own officers, selects its own committees, determines its own policies, keeps nonmembers off the floor, and even exercises some oversight of administration. The two speakers wield power. Party identification is stronger. Committees are active and influential. As in the past, some members retain their seats over long periods and by reason of long tenure coupled with ability become significant political figures. Among such figures the two speakers must be counted, as well as experienced and sometime controversial figures such as John Bragg, Anna Belle Clement O'Brien, Tom Garland, Jim White, and Victor Ashe.

6

☆ ☆
☆

Mandates and Methods

THE GENERAL ASSEMBLY IS THE STATE'S PRINCIPAL LEGISLATIVE BODY. IT legislates; but what is legislation? It is not easy to distinguish legislative from other functions. One author adopts the view that the legislative process is "the phase of government which initiates proposals affecting public policy, deliberates upon questions of general public concern, decides what shall or shall not be done, and enunciates law. This concept may not be wholly satisfactory, but it will do as well as any . . . ."[1] Not only does the legislator decide "what shall or shall not be done," but he also decides who shall do it, how it is to be done, and when. This is not to say that all these decisions should always be made by legislative bodies. As a general rule many of them should be delegated to the discretion of the administration. Legislative bodies are able to determine general policy, but they are not well constituted to go successfully beyond that point.

⊛

The power of the legislature is limited only by the Constitution . . . .
Quinn v. *Hester,* 135 Tenn. 373, 380 (1916)

AS IS TRUE OF ALL OTHER states of the United States, in Tennessee the constitution separates the powers of government and distributes them among the legislative, executive, and judicial branches;[2] the legislative authority is vested in the General Assembly. The Supreme Court of Tennessee has clearly indicated the great extent of this authority: "It is fundamental and axiomatic that a State legislature is the reservoir of all the

[1]Chester C. Maxey, *The American Problem of Government* (New York: Crofts, 1934), 213–14.
[2]Art. II, sec. 1.

82

reserved power of the people, except as it may be limited and circumscribed by the State and federal constitutions. The reverse is true of the federal congress, which can only exercise such power as is expressly or impliedly conferred by the constitution of the United States."[3] The authority of the General Assembly does not rest upon the limits of the federal and state constitutions. In other words, the powers of the legislature are inherent. A glance through the index of the code of Tennessee indicates the vast scope of this authority and the multitude of subjects on which it is exercised.

Even though, generally speaking, the constitution does not bestow legislative powers upon the General Assembly, sometimes the document can be quite specific. For example, Article XI, section 13 specifically states that the General Assembly shall have power to enact statutes for the protection and preservation of game and fish. Article II, section 28 authorizes the legislature to levy and collect certain specific kinds of taxes. But it is true, nontheless, that most of the power of the legislature will not be found spelled out in the fundamental law.

The constitution does contain specific restrictions upon the legislative power. The entire Declaration of Rights is a restriction upon the legislature as well as upon the other branches of government. The constitution also contains numerous specific restrictions on the legislature's power over local government, particularly with respect to county government. The constitution sets up certain restrictions on taxation such as the statement in Article II, section 30 that "no article manufactured of the produce of this State, shall be taxed otherwise than to pay inspection fees." The legislature is forbidden by section 8 of Article XI to suspend general laws for the benefit of particular individuals. No laws may be passed for the benefit of particular individuals that are inconsistent with the general laws of the state. The legislature has no power to create a corporation or to diminish or increase the powers of such corporation by special laws. These are some of the more important examples of restrictions on legislative power scattered throughout the state constitutional document.

How may we distinguish an act of administration from an act of legislation? Legislation is the process of establishing a general rule governing the future conduct of a particular group of people. It has the characteristic of generality, both as to people and as to time. It is intended to endure. Administration, on the other hand, is a process that involves taking specific actions in particular situations, such as the appointment of persons, the provision of funds, the arrest of delinquent persons, the signing of a payroll, and so on. Considerable confusion has arisen in the minds of the

[3]*Ledgerwood* v. *Pitts,* 122 Tenn. 570, 588 (1909).

public regarding the proper role of governmental officials through a failure to consider the differences between these categories of action, as well as a failure to remember that legislative agencies do more than legislate.

The powers of the Tennessee legislature include some powers that could be considered administrative. Thus, the Assembly is authorized by the constitution to elect the state treasurer, the secretary of state, and the state comptroller of the treasury. Appointment activity of this sort is purely administrative in content.

Two much more important powers of the legislature that may be considered administrative in character are those authorizing the expenditure of funds and appropriating the money to carry through the projects authorized. The latter, particularly, should be classified as an administrative power; yet it is, at the same time, one of the fundamental bases on which the ultimate authority of the legislature rests.[4]

The legislature may also authorize the establishment of new administrative agencies, prescribe their internal structure in more or less detail, provide for methods of appointment of various officials, and otherwise fill out the details of the governmental structure of the state where the constitution is silent. The Tennessee constitution sets no limitation as to how far the General Assembly may go in regulating details of this sort. One might also note that, within the limitations prescribed by the constitution, the legislature may organize and establish counties, rearrange county boundary lines, provide for municipal government in great detail, and generally regulate the entire pattern and procedure of the subdivisions of the state. Here again comparatively few limitations on the Assembly's authority are to be found in the constitution.

As a final element in the administrative authority of the legislature, we should note that the Assembly may, if it wishes, exercise varying degrees of supervision over the agencies that it has established by calling for reports from them, by subjecting them to periodic or occasional investigations, or by prescribing in more or less detail what the funds appropriated to them may be spent for.

Until recent years the General Assembly of Tennessee has made rather sparing use of its administrative powers. It has left most appointments to the governor, without even the familiar safeguard of Senate confirmation. It has rarely conducted investigations into state agencies, having been much less active in this respect than Congress, although activity of this kind is beginning to occur. But if political conflict between the legislature and the governor develops, the legislature has a considerable reserve of power at its disposal.

[4]Dr. Grubbs and Dr. Hobday consider this power to be legislative in character.

Through local legislation, that is, legislation that deals with the structure and operation of local government, the Assembly once actively interfered in local matters; since the adoption of constitutional amendments in 1953, the Assembly is somewhat less active in such affairs.

Impeachment and trial is a little-used process, borrowed from English practice and embedded in the American constitutional system, for removing officials from office for crimes and misdemeanors. Impeachment is the action of bringing charges, and trial is the process of passing on the impeached person's guilt or innocence. Impeachment and trial are not devices for punishment, but rather a means for getting rid of an official by removing him from office and, in some cases, debarring him from office-holding in the future.

The House of Representatives has the power of impeachment. The governor, judges of the courts, chancellors, attorneys for the state, the treasurer, the comptroller, and the secretary of state are liable to this action. They may be impeached if they, "in the opinion of the House of Representatives, commit any crime in their official capacity which may require disqualification . . . ." The Senate has the power to try all impeachments. The chief justice of the Supreme Court presides unless he is being tried, in which case the senior associate judge presides. A two-thirds vote of the senators sworn to try the case is required to convict. Conviction can result in only two penalties—removal from office and disqualification to hold any other state office. Conviction, however, is no bar to further prosecution under the criminal laws of the state. The legislature has the power to relieve the penalties imposed on any person disqualified from holding office by a conviction on impeachment.[5]

Tennessee politicians have not been greatly addicted to the use of impeachment and trial. The last case—the impeachment, trial, and conviction of Judge Raulston Schoolfield of Hamilton County in 1958—would probably not have occurred had it not been for the sensational revelations and charges of the McClellan Committee of the United States Senate. In the course of its explorations of the misdeeds of certain elements among organized labor in the United States, the committee took evidence and made reports concerning practices in Judge Schoolfield's criminal court in Chattanooga, noting particularly the testimony of certain labor officials regarding alleged bribery. Governor Clement was impelled by the committee's activities (its counsel was the young Robert Kennedy, and one of its members was the counsel's brother, John F. Kennedy) to authorize an investigation of Judge Schoolfield by prominent Nashville lawyer Jack Norman, who had been a longtime backer of Clement's political opponent, Gordon Browning. Norman's assistant was John Jay Hooker, Jr., who in

[5]Art. V., secs. 1–5.

later years was to run twice for the governorship and once for the United States Senate. Norman's report was a devastating attack on Judge School-field. In a special session called by Governor Clement, Judge Schoolfield was impeached on twenty-four counts, involving charges of accepting bribes, mixing in county politics, altering sentences, disregarding the verdicts of juries, and behaving inappropriately for a judge both on and off the bench. The Senate, after trial, convicted the judge by the necessary two-thirds vote on three counts, counts that involved the acceptance of a gift of a car, political activities of the judge, and a general charge of misconduct on and off the bench. On six other charges ordinary majorities for conviction were entered, but the two-thirds majorities necessary for action were not obtained. Judge Schoolfield was removed from office, but he was not prohibited from filling office in the future. He had, however, been disbarred, and his status as a lawyer has not been restored.[6]

The entire sweep of democratic experience is represented in legisla-tion. Virtually no activity today can avoid a brush with law . . . .

WILLIAM J. KEEFE (1966)

CONSIDERING THE BREVITY of the legislative session, it is hard not to be impressed by the number of matters that come to the attention of the General Assembly and are acted upon in the seemingly short span of its sessions. How burdensome is the legislative workload? From what sources does the legislative program emanate? What are the pressures brought to bear upon our lawmakers in terms of the general interest and the interests of private groups?

Table 6–1 shows the number of private and public bills enacted by sample sessions of the General Assembly from 1937 through 1979.

The volume of public bills enacted over the past two decades has increased; annual sessions have been accompanied by an increase in activity. In comparison, the number of private acts decreased sharply in the 1955 session and thereafter stayed at a comparatively low figure in spite of a tendency of some members of the Assembly to overlook or disregard the amendments of 1953. Constitutional Amendment Six of 1953 restricts special legislation by making the validity of such legislation that affects a county or municipality dependent upon a two-thirds vote of the local governing body or upon popular local referendum in the local unit of government affected by the legislation. It also prohibits such acts that remove a county or municipal officer, abridge his term, or alter his salary

---

[6]This case has been described in detail in Greene, *Lead Me On.* The account there is based on official records housed in the State Library and Archives.

before the end of the term. Amendment Seven established home rule for cities. This shift in legislative interest away from matters of local concern

TABLE 6-1
NUMBER OF PUBLIC
AND PRIVATE BILLS ENACTED IN CERTAIN SESSIONS,
TENNESSEE, 1937-1979*

Bills Enacted

Session	Public	Private	Total	Private Acts Disapproved Locally
1937	309**	905	1,214	
1947	238	878	1,116	
1953	269	592	861	
(Amendment restricting local or private legislation adopted Nov. 3, 1953)				
1955	347	420	767	77
1959	332	373	705	84
1963	390	293	683	59
1965	367	294	661	49
1967	402	303	705	37
1968	234	195	429	24
1969	340	193	533	21
1970	265	151	416	40
1971	440	203	643	13
1972	428	220	648	26
1973	409	161	570	10
1974	401	225	626	33
1975	381	196	577	29
1976	468	101	569	16
1977	495	161	656	11
1978	451	161	612	6
1979	443	173	616	12

*Includes regular session only.
**Many bills enacted in the regular session of 1937 were erroneously listed and numbered as public bills when in fact they were private bills. Since they are also listed as private, the total given is an overstatement.

may have had a strengthening influence upon state lawmakers by directing their attention to more general considerations.

The number of laws enacted during a session does not, by itself, provide a clear indication of the workload of the legislature, for many bills are introduced that never become law. Such bills may be killed on third consideration; some are withdrawn; a few are vetoed by the governor. In one session of the Ninety-first General Assembly (1979) close to 3,000 bills were introduced in the two houses, but only 443 public acts and 173 private acts were passed. The attrition rate was substantial. The range of subject matter covered by bills is staggering. Heavy activity is recorded on elections, counties, public planning, criminal procedure, education, health and safety, and insurance, among other things. Matters spread over the sublime and the ridiculous, from naming a state rock, dealing with bear hunting in Cocke County, regulating blind bidding on movies, to weightier but usually highly detailed issues of high moment.

Why this flood of legislation? The answer must be partly guess-work. The Assembly does more than set up general guide-lines of policy. It is constantly setting up detailed instructions for administrators, tinkering with the code of laws, altering a few words here and there, issuing new regulations for human behavior in a complex and shifting society. And, it must be added, ambitious legislators feel they must make some mark; this is done by passing something. Repeal has small appeal. Furthermore, a single subject may produce a briefcase full of bills, even though only one may pass. Finally, the legislature responds to the small army of lobbyists that seek special benefits in Nashville. The result is the annual thick volumes of public and private acts.

The Tennessee General Assembly for a number of years met in a split session. The first session (limited to fifteen days by constitutional provision) was an organizational session that took place every two years for the purpose of electing speakers and other officers. After a recess following the organizational session, the legislature came back together in Nashville and the business of legislating began. When the legislature met again the following year, legislative business continued. What was pending at the end of the first annual session was carried over into the next. The sessions were limited because expenses could not be paid beyond ninety legislative days of a regular session. (Although "session" is used often to mean the annual meeting, here it is interpreted to mean ninety days over the two-year period; it does not include the thirty legislative days allowed for a special session.) The organizational session was continued by the constitutional amendment of 1978, but the "split" feature was abolished.

Where do bills come from? The legislator may prepare his own, with or without the assistance available to him from the attorney general's office or the staff of the legislature and its committees, or he may sponsor legislation recommended by the executive branch or some interest group. Local bills may be prepared by persons or groups back home. During the prolonged period when the General Assembly was dominated by the governor, the most important bills were prepared by or with the assistance of persons in the administration, and that practice can be expected to continue to a marked degree, even though executive domination is much less evident now than it once was. Local bills are likely to pass unless opposed by groups at home; they are not valid now unless the consent of the local governing body or the local electorate is secured.

Proposals for bills may come from interest groups—the "lobbies"—which constitute a familiar feature of all legislative bodies. A weak beginning in the control of lobbying organizations was made in an act of 1965.[7] The act calls merely for registration of lobbyists and the disclosure of their employers. The filing of accounts and the prohibition of contingency fees are not provided for by the statute, although such controls have been established in a number of states.

Genuine deliberation is possible among a few people; a mass meeting can only listen to harangues.

JOHN WAHLKE (1966)

THE PROCEDURE OF the houses of the General Assembly is generally similar to that in legislative bodies throughout the world. For that matter it is about the same as in any well-conducted meeting of any body that proposes, deliberates on, and passes measures. Certain procedural requirements are laid down by the constitution of Tennessee. Beyond these, each house is authorized to determine its own rules.

The constitution states that each house may determine its own time of meetings and adjournments provided neither house may, without the consent of the other, adjourn "for more than three days, nor to any other place than that in which the two Houses shall be sitting." Two-thirds of the membership constitutes a quorum in each house, "but a smaller number may adjourn from day to day, and may be authorized, by law, to compel the attendance of absent members." Each house may punish its own members "for disorderly behavior, and with the concurrence of two-thirds, expel a member," but not twice for the same offense. Either house "may punish, by imprisonment, during its session, any person not a member, who shall be guilty of disrespect to the House, by any disorderly or any contemptuous behavior in its presence."

[7]*Public Acts,* 1965, ch. 187; *TCA*, Title 3, ch. 6.

A bill may originate in either house, but before it becomes law it must be passed on three different days in both houses. Prior to 1978 a requirement of three readings on different days was designed to give the members adequate notice of proposed legislation and to prevent surprise. By a 1978 amendment, the "reading" is now changed to "consideration". No bill may become law until it receives on final passage a majority vote in each house of the membership to which the house is entitled, is signed by both speakers, and receives the governor's approval. If a bill is rejected, "no bill containing the same substance shall be passed into a law during the same session." This familiar rule of parliamentary law allows for final disposition of matters after consideration. A bill is limited to one subject, and that subject must be expressed in the title. This requirement makes it easy for the legislator to determine the subject of a bill, prevents the passage of bills on hidden subjects, and simplifies the reference of bills to committees. "Each House shall keep a journal of its proceedings, and publish it, except such parts as the welfare of the State may require to be kept secret; the ayes and noes shall be taken in each House upon the final passage of every bill of a general character, and bills making appropriations of public money; and the ayes and noes of the members on any question, shall, at the request of any five of them, be entered on the journal." All meetings are open to the public unless the business "be such as ought to be kept secret."

Both houses of the legislature use essentially the same procedure for the enactment of statutes. The process starts with the introduction of a legislative proposal—a bill—in either of the two houses. A bill may involve new law on a new subject, or amend or repeal existing law. The bill may be general, covering a group, a class, or all persons under the jurisdiction of the state, or it may be private, special, or local (these three terms are used interchangeably), covering a single place, or occasionally, in past usage, a few designated persons. At the appropriate point in the order of business any member may introduce a bill. The bill is "read" (since 1978, "considered") by title, number, and names of sponsors. In the past, administration bills could be identified by the sponsors, who were generally the administration floor leaders. This constitutes the first of three considerations. After a second consideration, again by title and number, the speaker will refer the bill to the appropriate committee, if it is a general bill. The speaker is authorized by the rules to refer local bills if he thinks they require it, but almost none ever goes to a committee.

Unless a committee has the consent of a majority of the House, it may not meet while the House is in session. Meetings of committees are announced by the clerk or posted on bulletin boards. After consideration the committee may report the bill, recommending passage, rejection, or amendments, or it may simply report the bill without any recommendation. A recommendation carries great weight and almost invariably determines the fate of the bill. If a committee neglects to report a bill after seven days, the bill may be recalled by a majority vote of the members to which the house is entitled. In such a case the bill is treated as having no recommendation by the committee. After a bill has been reported by the committee, it is considered a third time. When the legislature was dominated by the governor, legislative committees wielded little power and usually did not meet regularly. Now that the legislature has declared its independence of the governor, the committees have become important, and some of them have become powerful. Hearings are now a much-used feature of committee procedure.

At the appropriate time in the order of business, the bill, having been reported by the committee and given a time by the Calendar Committee (or in the case of local bills, on any day after the second reading), may be called up for third consideration, when the bill may be debated or have various motions applied to it. The bill may be committed to a Committee of the Whole, and, if so, the rules provide that "the bill shall be read throughout by the Clerk, if demanded by any member, and then again read and debated by clauses, leaving the preamble to be last considered . . . After report, the bill shall again be debated and amended by clauses before its final passage." The constitution, as we have seen, requires that final passage be by a majority of the entire membership to which the houses are entitled, and in the case of general and appropriation bills the ayes and noes must be taken. At the request of any five members the ayes and noes on any question are to be entered in the journal.

After passage on third consideration in the House of Representatives, (or vice versa), the bill is sent to the Senate. If the Senate passes the bill on third consideration it will be returned to the House and thence sent to the governor. If the governor signs it the bill becomes law. If he holds it for ten days (Sundays excepted), it becomes law unless the General Assembly adjourns within the ten-day period. If the legislature adjourns before the ten-day period is over, the governor may sign or veto the bill, but if he does not exercise the veto within the said ten days, the bill will become law without his signature. If the governor refuses to sign the bill, he must return it to the house of origin together with his objections in writing. If the governor vetoes the bill, it may still become law if repassed by a majority of all the members elected to each house. The governor may veto or reduce items of appropriations bills.

Getting the bill to the governor was, of course, conditioned on Senate passage of the bill. The Senate could have refused passage, or it might have passed the bill with amendments, or substituted another bill. If so, the bill would have been returned to the House of Representatives for vote on the amendments or substituted bill. If the two houses failed to agree, the bill would be sent to a conference committee appointed by the two speakers.

One of the most important agencies for enhancing the importance of state legislatures has been the legislative council, based on ideas generated in the early 1920s. Tennessee's General Assembly established a Legislative Council Committee in 1953. The council was composed of the speakers of the two houses, plus eight senators appointed by the speaker of the Senate and fourteen representatives appointed by the speaker of the House. Functions of the council included provision of legislative reference, library, and bill-drafting services; the preparation of studies and recommendations on legislative procedures and facilities; research related to important problems for the consideration of the General Assembly; and related services. The Legislative Council Committee did not escape criticism. Newspapers attacked it for subservience to the governor. Its studies were sometimes thought to be inadequate, and some highly controversial issues were ignored. In fact, however, the council served a useful purpose, and its studies have generally been worth respect; many resulted in useful legislation. But eventually the council came under the attack of legislators who wanted a more partisan approach to policy questions, and the council abolished itself in 1977. Its functions were split up, and operations are now more politically motivated. The Nintieth General Assembly created a Legislative Services Committee composed of ten members, the speakers serving as cochairmen, with two members each from the majority and minority parties in each house chosen by the speakers to serve as the remaining members.

The most progressive state legislatures have long since established bill-drafting bureaus. In Tennessee, the attorney general and his staff have in the past aided in drafting bills for members of the General Assembly requesting such assistance. But this program of assistance did not operate as an organized bill-drafting service as such; rather it represented a form of technical aid that must be fitted into the workload of the attorney general's office as time permited. At present, the legislature's Office of Legal Services drafts most legislation.

We have been able to discern the beginnings of the development by legislatures of review and evaluation mechanisms and processes.

ALAN ROSENTHAL (1974)

IN THE NATURE OF THINGS one of the most significant points of conflict between the legislative branch and the executive in any state that uses the theory of separation of powers is the budget and the subsequent appropriations. One of the arrangements for determining how the state will spend money involves the presentation of proposals for expenditure—the budget—by the executive to the legislative branch, the passage of appropriations by the legislative branch authorizing expenditures, the spending of funds by the executive departments, and the auditing of those expenditures after they are made, to see that the law has been obeyed, by an official responsible to the legislature. Our constitutional provisions recognize this pattern of relationships in part. In particular, our constitution provides for a comptroller of the treasury, jointly elected by the two houses of the General Assembly for a two-year term; this official may logically be expected to be the auditor responsible to the legislature.[8] The constitution also provides that appropriations are to be made by the legislature,[9] but it makes no specific mention of the possibility that those appropriations might be based on a budget presented by the governor. These deficiencies have been remedied by statute, however, so one could say that the formal arrangements in Tennessee coincide with the main currents of administrative theory and practice in the United States. The formal arrangements did not always correctly reflect the actual practice; in truth, for many years the governor dominated both budget preparation and the action of appropriations, and in addition the General Assembly normally elected to the position of comptroller a person named by the governor. Under the regimes of Clement and Ellington, the comptroller was William R. Snodgrass, who in many respects became the spearhead of the technical know-how that distinguished those administrations, and who continued in office after their administrations. Comptroller Snodgrass, under the actual arrangements of the time, was as much the servant of the governor as he was of the legislature; in a period when the Assembly followed the governor's wishes, it was essential that the comptroller be a staff man of the governor, even though constitutional arrangements implied a degree of independence that could not actually be exercised.

When the legislature began to assert its independence, as it did in the sixties, one of the signs of change, potentially the most important, was the creation of the Fiscal Review Committee in 1967. The committee consists of the two speakers, the two chairmen of the Senate and House committees on finance, ways, and means, and four senators and seven representatives elected by the houses separately, so as to reflect the ratios in the houses between the two parties. The committee elects its own chairman and vice-chairman. The comptroller of the treasury is designated as the secretariat or staff of the committee, but it is allowed to select added staff—it has in fact an executive director and personnel of its own.

[8]See Lee S. Greene, "Tennessee's Second State Reorganization," *National Municipal Review* 26:7 (July 1937), 1–4.
[9]Art. II, sec. 24.

The committee is empowered to call for financial information from the administrative and executive offices during the process of budgetary preparation, as well as to give help to the legislature during the appropriation process. To some extent, therefore, the committee is inserted into the process of budgetary preparation before the appropriation stage. It may study work programs, allotments, reserves, impoundment, and other aspects of the whole process of fiscal policy and administration.[10]

During the past decade legislatures and their memberships have been subject to harsh criticism, much of which has been deserved.

ALAN ROSENTHAL (1974)

THE DISCUSSION UP TO this point might indicate that legislative procedure is largely a rather impersonal, somewhat mechanical matter of constitutional provisions, statutes, and rules. Such an impression would be decidedly misleading. Long experience shows that the constitution may be followed to the letter but avoided in spirit. Rules may be suspended. The uninitiated may be impressed by the casualness with which most sessions are conducted, and they may often wonder where most of the members are. Indeed, the entries in the journal give a picture of the legislature that is in striking contrast to what the visitor observes. For example, the constitution long provided that a bill shall be read on three different days, and the journal showed that any given law was read three times, but the visitor who wanted to hear a bill read would have listened in vain. Other instances of differences between formal requirements and actual procedure abound. For example, most bills are emergency bills; obviously this does not make sense.

Improvement in legislative procedure has been effected in recent years, and a few changes were made by the 1978 amendments. The provision that a bill must be limited to one subject and that the subject must be recited in the title was inserted in the constitution as a means of preventing legislators from slipping items not fully known or understood by other legislators or the public into bills whose passage is assured. In spite of this laudable objective, the provision causes some trouble, for the questions of what is a single subject and whether it is described in the title are difficult to answer. That means litigation; the courts must then determine whether the constitutional provisions have been observed, and many an act otherwise sound

---

[10]For an early view of the committee's role, see Fiscal Review Committee, *The Legislator's Role in Budgeting* (Nov. 29, 1968). Hyrum Plaas and Charles A. Zuzak, *The Budgetary System in Tennessee,* 2d ed. (Knoxville: Bureau of Public Administration, Univ. of Tennessee, 1977).

may be contested, perhaps successfully, on the ground of its caption. A way out of this particular situation is by no means easy to find.

Perhaps the most serious criticism that could have been offered on legislative procedure in the past, at least from the point of view of the way in which the legislature was originally intended to work, was that the legislature has relied too much on the governor for leadership. The legislature met only once in regular session during its two-year term. Each regular term brought a new legislature. Before the legislature met it had no organization, no officers, and no leadership. As a result, the General Assembly generally looked to the governor to tell it what to do. It was once even common practice for the legislature to name men chosen informally by the governor to fill the few appointments that the legislature had the power to make itself. In 1965 the Senate revolted against the governor; the governor's candidate for speaker, Jared Maddux, was finally selected, but the governor never gained full control of the legislature during that session, and some signs of restiveness were apparent in the special session of 1966. Republican strength mounted in the legislature chosen in the fall of 1966, and in the 1968 election the Republicans managed to elect as many members to the House as did the Democrats (one independent held the balance of power). A Republican was elected speaker of the House. And in 1970, although the Democrats managed to retain supremacy in the legislature, Republican Winfield Dunn was elected governor; the subservience of the legislature to the governor was thoroughly eliminated by these events. The legislature remained independent, even after Democrat Ray Blanton succeeded Dunn in 1975, and it seems likely to stay so. A Republican, Lamar Alexander, began a four-year term as governor in 1979; the legislature continued to be dominated by Democrats, who have made it quite clear that they will not be "bossed" by Alexander or any other governor. As the 1980s began, signs of partisan squabbling between the governor and the Assembly abounded.

In the past, legislators have been very badly housed and were given no staff assistance. This situation has been entirely altered. Private offices are now provided in Nashville, and some delegations maintain headquarters at their home stations.

A nonprofit organization, the Citizens Conference on State Legislatures, has made a fairly elaborate comparative analysis of the procedures of state legislatures and has published the results. In the process the conference ranked the state legislatures on several matters. These rankings need not be taken as absolutely valid, but they furnish us with some basis for evaluating Tennessee rules and practice. Overall the Tennessee General Assembly ranks twenty-sixth among the states. Ranks were also assigned to five major characteristics. Of these, Tennessee ranked thiritieth in the category titled Functional Legislature, consisting of matters such as staffing, the amount of time available to the legislature, structure, facilities, procedures, decorum, and the like. The conference ranked Tennessee forty-fourth on accountability, eleventh on being informed, ninth on independence, and twenty-sixth on effective representation. The ranking on independence is surprising given Tennessee's history, but the ranking is made on the basis of legal powers and capabilities, not on the basis of actual behavior. Because the entire survey necessarily was unable to penetrate deeply into legislative behavior, all rankings must be taken with caution. [11]

The conference report made specific suggestions for improvement in each state; those suggestions were directed toward the creation of a highly paid, competent, and highly independent legislature, and the suggestions must be considered in that light. Some of the suggestions made for Tennessee are now in operation; others are not, and some of them would probably not be acceptable to Tennessee voters. For example, the report was critical of Tennessee legislative salaries; it suggested that no state should pay less than $10,000 per year to a legislator. A salary of that size would not be very welcome in the present climate of Tennessee. The report also recommended that an ordinary majority or the presiding officers of the legislature be empowered to call special sessions. In view of the fact that the General Assembly now meets every year, the need for special sessions is hardly overwhelming. The suggestion that each legislature establish a Washington office is also not likely to be tremendously popular in Tennessee. (A Washington office was set up by Blanton—it was not very busy or significant and Governor Alexander closed it down.) The expansion of staff assistance for the Assembly should receive support. Some of the conference's suggestions might make for greater party cohesion in the legislature, but party control in Tennessee is traditionally not especially strong, and suggestions pointed in that direction may run against the grain. Generally, the feeling is justified that Tennessee did not come off too badly in the conference study. [12]

In the seventies the legislature struggled with the problem of ethics. The conflict-of-interest laws are weak, but it is difficult to devise a system that will not injure the chances of getting able legislators. In 1978, a stronger ethics bill by Senator Ashe failed to secure a constitutional majority in the Senate. Senator William Baird said it would make the legislature an expensive professional body, since it prevented members from doing business with the state, and Senator Baird had a point. Nonetheless, the uncertainty of the Assembly in the face of questions regarding ethics and conflicts of interest contributes to its low prestige with the voters. So far the legislature has not been able to resolve this difficult dilemma. In recent

[11]Citizens Conference on State Legislatures, *State Legislatures: An Evaluation of Their Effectiveness* (New York: Praeger, 1971), 40, 317.
[12]The specific suggestions for Tennessee are contained in pp. 317–23.

years, behavior that has ended in judicial action has forced the Assembly into disciplinary activity. Representative Robert J. Fisher was expelled from the House of Representatives after conviction for extortion. Senator Edgar H. Gillock has been tried twice—as yet inconclusively—for extortion, but so far has not been removed. Representative Emmitt Ford was convicted of mail fraud and sentenced to 20 months in prison in 1981 and resigned under pressure, with a threat of possible expulsion in the background. He talked of appealing his conviction and of running again.

The organization of the General Assembly is based upon the existence of the two-party system in Tennessee, but party affairs and interests do not dominate the policy making of the legislature. Except for rare events, the Republicans are the minority party in the legislature, and, on those occasions when party considerations determine policy, Republicans are at a disadvantage. But divisions in the legislature frequently disregard party lines. Reapportionment, which might be expected to be a party issue, is also an issue between rural areas and the great cities, and on this issue the Republicans and Democrats of Shelby and Davidson are at one with the Republicans and Democrats of Knox. Annexation law will produce conflict between the central cities and suburbia. And it must not be forgotten that a good deal of the legislative work concerns matters on which party divisions make no sense, and on which the parties take no stand. Tennessee parties do not produce platforms; they merely provide a mechanism for the political ambitions of individuals. Members of the legislature consult their consciences, their constituents, and the ever active pressure groups.

Perhaps it is the pressure group with its influence that raises the greatest doubt about legislative behavior. The public and the idealist do not give up hope of locating a "general interest" however difficult it may be to define. But the legislature seems either bound to the "special interest" or to parochialism. The suburban legislator is more concerned to protect his few thousand constituents from municipal taxation than to foster the proper development of the great cities where an increasing number of Tennesseans live. The black politician judges affairs from a racist view, having learned his lesson from the whites. The late "Mr. Jim" Cummings once gave as the secret of his political success the fact that he did what was best for Cannon County. But he, like others, often found in his program room for wider considerations, and so—painfully—tenable, but often niggling, compromises have been reached.

7

☆ ☆
☆

The Power, The Honor, and the Trouble

OF THE THREE BRANCHES OF GOVERNMENT, THE LEGISLATIVE, JUDICIAL, AND executive, the latter is undoubtedly the most conspicuous and best known to Tennesseans. Yet—and this is also true of many other states—the Tennessee governor, regarded in terms of the written constitution, is surely no more significant than the legislature and possibly much less so. The first state constitutions were designed to downgrade the executive power. The authors of these early documents had suffered some bad experiences with powerful colonial governors, and they deliberately shifted power to the legislature. Even now, close to two centuries later, Tennessee's constitutional arrangements show forth the lively suspicion of a strong executive.

The constitution of Tennessee, like other state charters, reflects the idea of the separation of powers, and our courts strive to preserve this doctrine. Nevertheless, partly because of our equal reverence for the idea of checks and balances and partly because of the absolute necessity of getting on with the business of government, our legislative, executive, and judicial branches cannot be clearly distinguished or their powers neatly separated. The legislature is not exclusively concerned with legislation; executives do more than carry out the laws.

It is the responsibility of the legislature to determine the general policy of government, to decide the course of government actions, to prescribe what is to be done or prohibited. It is the responsibility of the executive to see that the will of the legislature is accomplished. For example, the legislature provides for the control of banking institutions and of firms dealing with investments. But the statutes are not self-enforcing. If nothing more is done, the statutes will go unheeded, except insofar as private persons may sue individual firms. It is an executive function to see that something more is done—to see that the machinery of government is set in motion to the end that the public is protected. This description reduces the executive function to its simplest terms—terms that do not always appear to correspond to reality. Thus we might expect the executive function to be the exclusive province of the ''chief executive'' and his subordinates, but in practice we find that it may be performed by boards, commissions, independent officers, the legislature, or even by the courts, often on the initiative of local officials. Further, although we might expect the ''chief executive'' to be exclusively concerned with the enforcement of the legislative policy, we find the governor participating in the formation of policy with the use of his budgetmaking power, his formal veto, and his informal political power, and we find him exercising authority, such as his power to pardon, free of legislative control.

The governor has no inherent power to appoint officers, and he has no power of appointment except that vested in him by the constitution or by statute.

HEADNOTE, *TCA*, VOL. 1, P. 597.

FOR MOST CITIZENS, the governor is the focus of state political attention. He is expected to provide leadership to the entire state and to represent the state at high levels with other governors and with federal officials. His ceremonial and symbolic status is superior to that of all other state officials. As the one individual who stands at the apex of the executive branch, he speaks with authority and usually without fear of contradiction by any subordinates. This preeminence rests partly on the constitution, heavily on the statutes; it is strengthened by the conditions and activities of political parties.

One must read the daily correspondence of the governor to realize how strongly he is felt to be the leader of the state in a personal as well as a political sense. Hundreds of letters a day reach the desk of a governor. In these letters may be read the woes and tribulations, hopes and defeats of the people of the state, and their reaching out for the regard and aid of the one individual in the state who seems to them to have the power to respond to their needs. All kinds and classes turn to the chief executive, from the ambitious attorney who hopes for judicial advancement and the banker who seeks his share of the state's funds for his institution, to the near-destitute who need jobs, money, and medical aid. One group of schoolchildren demanded, by postcard, that Governor Clement exert himself to increase their recess time. In a large number of instances, possibly most of them, the governor is unable to respond favorably; he does not have the vast powers attributed to him in the writers' minds. But most governors insist that all, literally all, the letters be answered; an enormous number of the replies are signed by the governor personally. This volume of correspondence attests powerfully to the preeminence of the governor's position in the minds of the people of his state; the governor is the only official who can fulfill the public's emotional need for a final benevolent and potent authority.

The Tennessee constitution devotes relatively little attention to the executive branch; the space accorded the governor is modest indeed. Some nine distinct powers are granted the governor, two of which are very broad. Article III, section 1 vests the "Supreme Executive power of this state" in the governor, and section 10 of Article III states that "He shall take care that the laws be faithfully executed." These statements of authority are capable of very considerable expansion by interpretation, providing the interpreter takes a broad view of executive power. In fact such a broad view has been rooted in the statutes, and little occasion has arisen for judicial definition of "the supreme executive power." A potential conflict arose in 1981 when some members of the legislature advocated taking from the governor and lodging in the Assembly the power to make interim appointments to the judiciary. It is conceivable that such a proposal would violate the separation principle.

Both the broad grants of authority and some specific ones are similar to those found in most other states. The more specific grants include the governor's power as "Commander-in-Chief of the Army and Navy of this state and of the Militia"; his power to grant reprieves and pardons, except in impeachment cases; to require written information from officers in the executive branch; to convene the legislature in special sessions and control the agenda of such sessions; to give information to the legislature and recommend measures for its consideration; to fill vacancies in the offices of treasurer, comptroller, and secretary of state on an interim basis; and to veto legislation.

The Tennessee governorship was a weak office in our early history. Some puzzlement was expressed that Andrew Johnson should have wanted the job.[1] The strengthening of gubernatorial powers in Tennessee, as in all states, is a product of the twentieth century and, to a significant extent, came about as a result of administrative reform. Before 1923, the administrative structure of state government was a hodgepodge of some sixty bureaus. Under the leadership of Governor Austin Peay and with the advisory assistance of a prominent consultant in public administration, the legislature established an administrative scheme that significantly strengthened the governor as a chief administrator. The trend toward strong administrative leadership continued—except for a brief interlude of reaction during the terms of Governor Hill McAlister (1933–37)—until

[1]Hugh Blair Bentley, "Andrew Johnson, Governor of Tennessee, 1853–57," diss., Univ. of Tennessee, 1972, 24 ff.

about 1965. Governor McAlister, in a throwback to an earlier day, campaigned on a platform condemning the concept of a powerful executive and, true to his promises, succeeded in getting the legislature to restrict the executive power. For example, one measure required Senate approval of the appointment of heads of administrative departments. Another removed the important executive functions of budgeting and accounting from the supervision of the governor, placing them under the comptroller of the treasury, a post responsible not to the governor but to the General Assembly. Not only did this serve to weaken the governor's administrative powers, but it also put the comptroller in the incompatible position of auditing his own accounts. This digression from the concept of strong executive leadership was short-lived. In 1937, Governor Gordon Browning succeeded in obtaining legislative approval of an administrative reorganization plan along the lines of the 1923 act. Further changes have occurred since then that affect executive authority and responsibility. The reorganization of 1959 was one of the more extensive ones.

Gone are the days, if indeed they ever existed, when the office of governor could be well managed by the ordinary person. Rapidly increasing activities of the state, coupled with the enormous growth of administrative functions, make successful government dependent upon the competence of the chief executive. Constitutional qualifications are held by many, but only a few people can measure up to the actual requirements of the office. The constitution provides that the governor must be at least thirty years old and a citizen of the State of Tennessee for "seven years next before his election." In addition, the governor must believe in the existence of God and in "a future state of rewards and punishments" in order to hold the office. No duelist or anyone who has in any way participated in a duel is ever eligible for the office; nor can any member of the Congress or holder of any state or federal office serve as governor at the same time.[2]

Candidates for governor of the State of Tennessee are chosen by primary elections held in August. A plurality is enough to nominate; the effects of these arrangements were particularly striking in 1974 when twelve candidates competed in the Democratic primary. Proposals for runoff elections have come up in the legislature from time to time but have never attracted much support; would-be candidates appear to like the system as it is.

The state, although unpredictable in national politics, has been most likely to go Democratic in gubernatorial elections; only five Republicans have managed to become governors in the present century. However, two of the three elected between 1970 and 1978 have been Republican.

[2]Arts. III, IX. The clauses on religious beliefs reflect the Calvinism of the frontier; see Thomas Perkins Abernethy, *From Frontier to Plantation in Tennessee: A Study in Frontier Democracy* (Chapel Hill: Univ. of North Carolina Press, 1932), 136–37.

Starting in the middle 1960s, a process began that led to the strengthening of the legislature. Since there is a sort of seesaw power struggle between the legislature and the governor, it was nearly inevitable that the governor's power would be diminished relative to that of the legislature. A constitutional amendment in 1978, on the other hand, added luster to the governor's office by permitting successive terms. From 1953 until 1978, the governor was not allowed to succeed himself. He could run for the office again, but only after having sat out for four years. Now the governor can succeed himself once, but then must stand aside for four years to be eligible for a third term.

Anyone who holds the office of governor must meet the constitutional requirements for that office. It is quite impossible to define other qualifications with any degree of certainty. One could, of course, arrive at a "typical" governor by examining the various characteristics of all governors, but, aside from the statistical exercise, the results would be fruitless. There is no assurance that the "average" would have any better chance at election than any other. The kind of man wanted in any given year by the voters of the state is quite beyond statistical tabulation.

To have a reasonable chance of election, a candidate must be affiliated with, and usually an active participant in, either the Democratic or the Republican party. A candidate must demonstrate the prowess necessary to marshal his personal and party forces in the primary elections; thereafter he must meet an equally competent opponent of another party. Very considerable financial resources must be available to a candidate, either from his own purse or from those of his supporters. Until 1969 the statutes prescribed a campaign expenditure limit of $25,000, a figure so ridiculously low and openly and routinely violated that it was removed by the General Assembly in that year (no substitute figure has been provided). It was estimated that a gubernatorial primary campaign in 1974 would cost the backers of each candidate somewhere between $300,000 and $350,000, but in fact much heavier expenses were incurred. If the candidate were required to obtain a clear majority of the vote in the primary (as could be the case if the critics of the current system succeed in getting a runoff after an inconclusive primary), the successful contender would be even more powerful, but he and his friends would be poorer, since a runoff campaign would call for another tug on political pockets.

A governor is inaugurated in January following the November election, the same month the legislature convenes. From November to January the incoming governor goes through a more or less hectic period depending on how cooperative the incumbent chooses to be. Governor Ellington, who had been a rival of the unsuccessful Democratic candidate, John Jay Hooker, aided with a smooth transfer to the Dunn administration, something of a surprise because it was the first transfer of office from one party to the other in half a century.[3] The increasing complexity of government makes it essential that the transition be as smooth as possible.

⊛

The governor's ascendancy is attributable at least as much, and probably far more, to his role as state political leader as it is to legal constitutional arrangements.

WILLIAM J. KEEFE (1966)

TENNESSEE POLITICAL LIFE is intensely factional and personal. Party organization is loose, intermittent, and weak. But when an individual has succeeded in seizing the nomination for the governorship and when he has followed this victory by winning the general election, he will be considered leader of the party by title certainly, and almost always in reality. As leader of the party a governor can exercise powers beyond his weak constitutional status. Many of those powers are set forth in statutes, but their presence in the statutes, although partly the result of administrative logic, can also be explained on the basis of party leadership.

Parties are strengthened by unity and cohesion, weakened by bickering and civil war. If the governor entertains any hope of seeing his legislative program adopted (and the voters will hold him responsible for that adoption), he must be able to keep his party members faithfully behind him. When the governor leads a party that controls the legislature, he may rest somewhat easier than otherwise, but nothing can be taken for granted. When the opposing party holds a majority in even one house of the General Assembly, the governor's power is bound to be diminished, but his party leadership may be enhanced because of the outside threat—a familiar feature of group struggle everywhere.

A governor may dispense numerous rewards and punishments to assist in keeping his forces together. These same methods can also be used to tempt opposition members to support the governor's program. Appointment of people sponsored by his party colleagues, support of pet bills of party members, and the judicious choice of locations for state buildings, parks, highways, and the like are the prime means for inducing a cooperative spirit among the stiff-necked and the stubborn-hearted.

The political party machinery is likely to be heavily influenced by the governor through key appointments or suggestions for important party offices. In Tennessee the electoral machinery has been dominated by the

[3]See Leonard K. Bradley, "Gubernatorial Transition in Tennessee: The 1970–71 Experience," master's thesis, Univ. of Tennessee, 1973; see also *Gubernatorial Transition in the States* (Lexington, Ky.: Council of State Governments, 1972).

parties, although recent statutes may alter this condition. The party has been generally in the hands of a few activists, and it appears that the mass-oriented reforms of the McGovern era of the Democratic party were little more than a temporary aberration.

The personality of the governor may be significant in holding the party together, although it is foolhardy to generalize about the entertaining and diverse characteristics of Tennessee politicians. Governor Prentice Cooper gave the impression of being a shy, introverted man, hard to know, although interesting when his intitial reserve was penetrated. Governor Browning was a vigorous and colorful man, rough and tough, but sensitive to wounds. Governor Clement possessed the "shining knight" image in his youth, a handsome man whose powerful voice and intense oratory were major factors in his sudden rise to power. Governor Ellington was quiet (although, when he wished, he could "press the flesh" in handshaking tours), dignified, and inclined to inaccessibility during the late years of his life and his governorship. Some observers have thought that the Democratic party suffered during Ellington's final term, when, troubled by ill health, he appeared to lose interest in the party organization. Clement was inclined to be conciliatory toward his enemies; Ellington was made of tougher stuff.

Governor Dunn was perceived as a friendly, outgoing, articulate person who enjoyed the position. Governor Blanton's personality seemed to cause him no end of difficulties. His constant conflicts with the media undoubtedly flawed his administration. He had the misfortune of being perceived as exceedingly arrogant and stubborn. His handling of the matter of a pardon for a family friend became the symbol of his approach to his office. The general irritation his actions caused among the public finally led to his unceremonious disappearance from office and the swearing in of Lamar Alexander a few days ahead of schedule. Governor Blanton was convicted on various charges after he left office. Governor Alexander's personality was a plus for him. He appeared to enjoy the limelight and the gentle jab and thrust of political dueling with the Democratic leadership of the legislature, but, as his administration went on, he made some mistakes in his handling of instances of misbehavior by his subordinates.

As party leader, the governor is a force to be reckoned with in national politics. With vast amounts of federal funds potentially available for expenditure within the state, an alert governor can obtain the state's "fair share" of such resources. This may be especially true when his party controls the national government, although the evidence of such a "Washington connection" is far from overwhelming.

An important aspect of the governor's political base and power is the extraparty organization that each governor must develop at the county level. During the campaign for office each major candidate will ordinarily select one person in each county to be responsible for the campaign in that county. This will usually evolve into a small campaign committee. The winning candidate would be an ingrate indeed if he chose to dismiss such loyal, energetic workers with a mere "thank you." The regular political parties take somewhat of a backseat and the candidate's own organization is the dominant force. Ordinarily, in the general election, there will be an overlap between party regulars and the campaign committee.

When the new governor is sworn in, the county political committees become a screening and recommending mechanism for applicants for state jobs. Since the word "patronage" has unsavory connotations, these committees are generally given some more acceptable title, if, indeed, their existence is acknowledged at all. Governor Blanton probably made as overt and extensive a use of such committees as any governor in recent memory, but every governor follows essentially the same practice. Blanton's committees were apparently involved in some of the more controversial actions of his administration in high-level personnel firings. The fact that Roger Humphreys' father was chairman of a patronage committee lent a good deal of credence to the view that political connections had much to do with Governor Blanton's commutation of Humphreys' sentence for first-degree murder.

Governor Alexander's county-level committees have had a very low profile early in his administration, undoubtedly a result of his campaign attacks on the patronage committee system as well as of the public reaction to that system, but no governor can really escape the pressures of his local supporters. They are not in politics for love alone.

A new trend . . . in the twentieth century . . . a hunt for ways of overcoming . . . fragmentation . . . settled on the governors as a solution.

HERBERT KAUFMAN (1963)

THE POLITICAL AND administrative authority of the governor rests heavily on his sweeping powers of appointment. The most important appointments within the governor's authority are those of the commissioners of the departments. He also has the power to make interim appointments to judicial posts, and this authority has been highly significant. (In 1981 attempts were made in the Assembly to deprive the governor of this authority.)

In addition, his patronage includes posts on various boards and commissions. In 1979 some 170 such bodies were in operation in Tennessee, with hundreds of memberships available for the exercise of the governor's appointing power. Roughly half these boards are of little significance, but some, such as the university governing boards or the Alcoholic Beverages Commission, are extremely important.

The gubernatorial appointing power rests not on the constitution, for little specific power is given the governor there, but on the statutes. Until the middle of Governor Dunn's administration (1972), the Tennessee governor had a virtually unlimited power of appointment. Beginning then and extending through the Blanton administration into that of Governor Alexander, the reinvigorated legislature put more and more limitations on the governor's power of appointment, or, more to the point, asserted its prerogative to participate directly in the appointment process. The most dramatic examples of this were in connection with the establishment of the Tennessee Energy Authority and in the controversy surrounding the restructuring of the Pardons and Paroles Board in 1979. An example of how tightly the legislature can control appointments by the governor when it chooses to do so is the 1978 act relating to the appointment of Wildlife Resources Commission members. Each appointee must be confirmed by the House Conservation and Environment Committee and the Senate Energy and Natural Resources Committee. They then must be approved by a joint resolution of the General Assembly. Further, if the governor should make an interim appointment to fill a vacancy resulting from an expired term, the member whose term has expired will continue to serve until the new appointee has been properly confirmed by the legislature. Even so, the governor's power of making appointments to the numerous boards and commissions is basically undiminished.

A major change has occurred during the last two decades in the governor's role in the election of legislative and constitutional officers by the General Assembly. Under Clement and Ellington, it was clearly understood and for the most part accepted that the governor would informally name the comptroller, the treasurer, and the secretary of state as well as the speaker of each house.

The first serious challenge to that practice came when Senator Frank Gorrell stood for the position of speaker of the Senate (and lieutenant governor). Governor Clement had endorsed Senator Jared Maddux. Gorrell lost the ensuing battle, but a trend began that led gradually to the legislature resuming fully its constitutional authority. Governor Dunn involved himself in the race for comptroller when TV personality Floyd Kephart nearly succeeded in defeating William Snodgrass, a longtime incumbent in that office. Neither Blanton nor Alexander played any role in the selection of officers by the legislature.

The attorney general is selected by the Supreme Court—a unique arrangement among the fifty states. The governor is in a very weak position in dealing with this high-level official. Some critics find this method of selection inadequate, but defenders of this arrangement point out that there has never been a scandal in the office of the attorney general. The governor has no control over the Public Service Commission members, who are elected by the people—the only state executive officials, other than the governor, elected on a statewide basis.

The governor's appointive power is strong in the judicial as well as in the executive area. Even though the general practice and tradition in Tennessee is to elect judges, many vacancies occur during terms because of death, resignation, or retirement. Such vacancies are filled by gubernatorial appointment. It has been alleged that some judges who do not wish additional terms resign before the end of their present ones so as to enable the governor to make appointments. In 1971, the General Assembly adopted the Missouri Plan of judicial selection for the appellate courts. Subsequently, the Supreme Court was excluded from coverage under that plan. For interim appointments, an Appellate Court Nominating Commission now provides the governor with three names from which he chooses one to fill the vacancy. Except for appellate courts (the Court of Appeals and the Court of Criminal Appeals), the governor has broad powers of interim appointment throughout the judiciary. Once appointed, a judge in the appellate courts has rarely been unseated in subsequent elections. The governor's power over judicial interim appointments has been exercised in the past under pressure from lawyers and with due regard to sectional and even subsectional interests; the correspondence with governors preserved in the archives of the state indicates clearly the desire of various sections for representation on the appellate courts.[4] The adoption of the Missouri Plan at the appellate court level has had the effect of limiting the governor's freewheeling discretion, but it has not eliminated that discretion, either in Tennessee or in Missouri.

The Tennessee governor, like all governors except the governor of North Carolina, has a general veto power. No bill can become law without being "presented to the governor for his signature." If he signs the bill, it becomes law. If he does not approve of the bill, he returns it with his objections to the house of origin where it may be reconsidered. If it passes both houses by a majority of the members elected to each house, the bill becomes law without the governor's signature. The governor is given ten days in which to veto a bill. If he does not return a bill "within ten calendar days (Sundays excepted) after it shall have been presented to him," it becomes law without his signature. A bill passed during the last ten days of a session shall become law unless disapproved by the governor within ten days following adjournment.[5] These same provisions apply to joint resolu-

[4]Governor Dunn followed the practice of clearing all local judicial appointments with local bar associations, a practice often used by governors.
[5]Art. III, sec. 18.

tions and orders except those pertaining to adjournment or to proposals of specific amendments to the federal constitution.

The item veto, which was added to the governor's power in 1953, is designed to allow the governor to eliminate or reduce items in appropriation bills without having to veto entire bills. The governor of Tennessee may reduce or disapprove any item or part of an item in any bill appropriating money, but the General Assembly has the opportunity to override the item veto as it can override general vetoes. The time limits on the item veto are the same as those on the general vetoes. Fiscal riders may be attached to nonfiscal bills, but they likewise are subject to the gubernatorial snickersnee.[6]

When the governor's item veto power is combined with his broad constitutional powers of providing information to the legislature and the power, given him by the legislature, to submit a budget, the result is a very substantial package of fiscal control. His authority is backed up by powers to impound and to transfer certain funds. During the Dunn administration the General Assembly put some constraints on executive control over transfer of funds from one section (or code) of the appropriations to another, requiring the consent of any two of the comptroller of the treasury and the two speakers.

The veto power of the governor appears weak because it can be overridden by the same majority required to pass the bill in the first place. In fact, it is substantial. The very act of disapproval by the governor may change some minds. The publicity that the veto gains may cause others to alter votes originally given hesitantly or with reluctance. In 1973 a liquor-trade bill rattled through both houses virtually without debate or opposition, deprived of illuminating publicity. The veto killed the bill; its sponsors apparently did not relish the prospect of unfavorable public notice that would be called up by an attempt to override. Inasmuch as Governor Dunn was a Republican executive faced with a Democratic General Assembly, it might be supposed that his vetoes would not stick easily; actually his record on this score was quite good. None of his vetoes on bills passed in 1971 was overridden. Two vetoes on the legislative apportionment bills passed in 1972 were overridden, but of course apportionment presents some highly partisan issues, and overrides could be considered normal in the political situation of that moment. Four of the vetoes of bills passed in 1973 were overridden, including the governor's rejection of the repeal of the Missouri Plan for the Supreme Court—again a highly partisan matter, where the Democrats were attempting to retain control of the state's highest court (they succeeded). Nine acts passed in 1974 were enacted over the veto, and the governor also suffered defeat on some of his item vetoes.

---

[6]Cf. Frank W. Prescott, "The Executive Veto in Southern States," *The Journal of Politics* 10:4 (Nov. 1948), 667.

One of the most significant of these vetoed and repassed acts was that relating to the establishment of a new medical school at Johnson City, an issue involving deep sectional rivalries.

Governor Blanton's record on regular (nonitem) vetoes was, for 1975, fifteen vetoes with three overrides; 1976, twenty vetoes with no overrides; 1977, eight vetoes with one override; and 1978, fourteen vetoes with five overrides.

Governor Alexander's experience with vetoes during his first year in office may be a little surprising in view of the fact that he faced a legislature dominated by the Democrats. In 1979 Governor Alexander vetoed only three bills; none was overridden. Eight bills became law without his signature.

Governor Alexander's veto messages sometimes slapped the legislative cheeks with vigorous satire and sound sense. In May 1979, he wrote on one veto message: "I hereby veto . . . the so-called 'Walgreen's Bill.' This bill is designed to keep Walgreen's . . . from applying for a license to operate a liquor store . . . . Walgreen's sin is that it is an 'out-of-state' corporation. . . . What if other states' laws made it illegal for New Yorkers to sleep in Holiday Inns, for Kansans to use ALCOA aluminum, or Ohioans to visit the Grand Ole Opry . . . [horrid thought] . . . It is not as if Walgreen's arrived from outer space yesterday. The company has done business in Tennessee for 52 years at locations everywhere." And on another veto, "I can find no public purpose served by raising from twenty-five dollars to fifty dollars the amount of money a lobbyist can spend on a legislator or other state official without reporting it." The third veto was provided at the request of the author of the act to permit a desirable revision.

⊛

No one could state where legislative power as such left off and executive power began.

LEONARD D. WHITE (1948)

THE DOCTRINE OF separation of powers implies that the legislature shall determine what public policy is to be; the governor is to see that this policy is implemented. But however insignificant the governor may have been in our early history, he has long since been thought of as the leader of the state and is expected by the voters to be, as he actually is, the principal initiator of policy both in and out of the legislature. The governor's power as policy leader rests upon his constitutional power to send messages to the General Assembly and to call it into special session, the latter a power never too much used and now of less significance since the legislature began meeting annually in 1968. His constitutional power is supplemented by significant statutory authority with respect to the annual budget.

In the first two-thirds of the twentieth century the governor was the leader of the majority party in the legislature. A growing independence in the legislature, noted in the late 1960s under both Clement and Ellington, was spurred on when Winfield Dunn, the first Republican governor in many years, faced a legislature still basically under the control of the Democrats. But even with this altered situation, both members of the legislature and the general public continue to expect the governor to provide leadership to the executive branch and policy direction to the state. The governor's role in policy initiation has been institutionalized; it is not completely dependent on the character of the incumbent.

Still the governor is no dictator. Even in the heyday of gubernatorial power, in the flush years of control by the Clement–Ellington combination, the governor had to have support in the General Assembly. In that body, the leadership, in partnership with the governor, was rather tightly held by a few veterans of the legislative battles. The partnership of those days may have appeared to be one-sided. Increasingly the legislature has asserted its power and broadened its interest in what happens in the state when the members pack up and leave the rumors, the entertainment, and the excitement of Nashville to return to their constituents. The work of the Fiscal Review Committee and the two Finance, Ways, and Means Committees meeting separately and jointly evidences the concern of the Assembly that their version of "the faithful execution of the laws" be heeded.

$$\textcircled{\tiny ★★★}$$

[Washington] understood good administration to be characterized by integrity, system, energy, reliance on facts, relative freedom from detail, and due responsibility to [the legislature].

LEONARD D. WHITE (1948)

THE GOVERNOR'S ROLE in the policymaking process is somewhat seasonal — most evident when the legislature is in session. His job as chief administrator is a year-round affair. State services—such as law enforcement, hospital care, and the custody of those in correctional institutions—must be provided on a daily, even on an around-the-clock basis. For these services the governor is ultimately accountable. To assist him in his complex and burdensome task, the governor has a staff, a number of commissioners who are heads of the various departments, and ultimately the entire bureaucracy.

The chief administrator of any large and complex organization needs aides. Tennessee governors have long utilized a staff for this purpose, though each incumbent has reshaped the staff to some extent to fit his own interests and style. Certain specialists such as the governor's legal counsel, information director, administrative assistant, and personal secretary are found in the most recent administrations. These individuals, usually referred to as the governor's staff, can make important contributions to his effectiveness.

The legal counsel is needed since the attorney general is not an appointee of the governor and is not likely to be a close confidant, even when he is of the same party. The counsel is especially busy during the legislative session when the implications of legislative measures must be carefully examined and the governor kept well posted.

A governor must have public relations advice if he is to be viewed favorably by his constituents. Rarely does the governor write all of his own speeches; someone must help with that task. The governor's staff must include persons with political savvy. Governor Clement was served in this way by members of his family, particularly his father, Robert Clement, and his sister, Anna Belle; the latter was a member of his official staff.

The office of the governor has been enlarged by the creation of a number of staff divisions. An important addition was the Office of Urban and Federal Affairs, developed by Governor Ellington as a mechanism for dealing with federal aid programs and, as something of an afterthought, providing some mechanism for coping with urban programs. (The office was eliminated by Governor Alexander.)

Governor Dunn added a policy planning unit to his office. Under Governor Blanton, the Policy Planning Staff continued and grew in importance. This unit aids the governor in developing, expressing, and securing approval for his policies. It helps to determine legislative priorities, guiding the working of legislative proposals for the administration and securing legislative approval. Once the desired legislation is enacted—and the administration is still a principal source of legislative activity—the unit works with affected departments to secure enforcement of the policy thus expressed in legislation. This unit advises the governor regarding vetoes and often drafts the veto message. It works very closely with the State Planning Office, and this arrangement has continued with the Alexander administration. The State Planning Office is also directly under the governor. The creation of staff divisions in the principal executive office is the natural outcome of the governor's need for assistance, but their proliferation can present the governor with the new task of coordinating the coordinators.

Even though the organizational chart for the governor's office might look substantially the same from governor to governor, that does not mean that each governor uses his staff in the same way. Governor Dunn worked closely with the staff, most of whom he knew personally. He knew which projects the Policy Planning Staff aides were working on and would not hesitate to contact them directly when he needed information. He depended on his staff to brief him thoroughly so that he could make his decisions on sound information.

Governor Blanton showed little interest in the details of policies and programs. He depended on his staff to take responsibility for developing a policy proposal, getting it through the legislature, and seeing to its implementation. He had no substantial list of programs that he wanted to achieve. Rather, his top staff made suggestions and Governor Blanton approved or disapproved each proposal. He depended heavily on a small handful of staff people to see to the running of the machinery of government. His policy planning director, Jack Strickland, became the "man to see" in policy and major administration matters, whereas others of his staff became the key figures in appointments, political problems, and the like.

Governor Alexander had served as a top staff aide to Senator Howard Baker and is probably the only Tennessee governor in recent times to have had such experience. His view of staff is much like Governor Dunn's, and he works with them closely in developing his policy positions. His staff contains a strong representation of people with work experience in the mass media. Alexander himself had journalistic experience, and it appeared that his predecessor's running battle with the press was something to be avoided if at all possible.

But mercy . . . is enthroned in the hearts of kings

The Merchant of Venice

THE ONLY POWER exercised by the governor that exhibits a judicial characteristic is the pardoning power. The constitution provides that the governor "shall have the power to grant reprieves and pardons, after conviction, except in cases of impeachment."[7] With this one exception the pardoning power of the governor is absolute. It belongs exclusively to him and cannot be abridged. The governor can of course have assistance from his staff in making decisions in this area. The power includes conditional pardons. The Supreme Court has held:

> The power to grant an absolute pardon includes the power to grant a pardon on condition, especially since it is the right of the convicted person, to whom the

[7]Art. III, sec. 6.

pardon is offered as an act of grace, to refuse to accept it if unwilling to comply with the conditions imposed.[8]

A pardon cannot be effective until after conviction—that is to say, after a verdict of guilty. While the governor's power over pardons is complete, he is advised by the Board of Pardons and Paroles. This board, reorganized by a statute of 1979, consists of fulltime paid professional state employees who are expert in criminal rehabilitation. Governor Dunn followed the policy of acting only after receiving the advice of the board. Governor Blanton wrote an entirely new chapter on the subject of the pardoning power. The Tennessee Constitution refers to pardons and reprieves but does not mention commutations, which are reductions in the sentences imposed on convicted persons. The mounting controversy surrounding Governor Blanton's promise to pardon Roger Humphreys caused the governor to retract that promise just prior to the 1978 gubernatorial election. Not many weeks after the election, it became known that he was likely to commute Humphrey's sentence to time served.

After his term had ended (somewhat precipitously in a move by legislative leaders to prevent further last-minute pardons) Blanton was indicted and later convicted for illegal actions relating to the sale of liquor licenses, and persons connected to him confessed or were convicted of trafficking in clemency.

Was a commutation separate from the pardoning power or merely one form of that power? The answer was thought to be important because the Pardons and Paroles Board made recommendations to the governor regarding such matters and some thought the board's action was binding on the governor. The law clearly stated that that was not the case. The prevailing view was and is that the power to pardon, which all agree is absolute in the case of the Tennessee governor except for impeachment cases, includes the power to reduce sentences through commutation. Governor Blanton used this form of the pardoning in the Humphreys case.

As a result of newly inaugurated Governor Alexander's effort to block Governor Blanton's "midnight commutations" a number of court cases ensued. Prisoners who had received commutations and were to be released were still in prison. Their suits for release went to the Tennessee Supreme Court, which upheld the validity of the Blanton commutations. The broad pardoning power of the governor remains absolute and intact.

Capital punishment has been a thorny political issue in Tennessee as in other states. Even though a number of people have been given the death sentence in recent years, executions have not been carried out. Governors Clement, Ellington, and Blanton used their authority to block executions, and the legal situation nationally had made the death penalty inoperable

---

[8]*State ex rel. Bedford* v. *McCorkel,* 163 Tenn. 101, 105 (1931).

during Governor Dunn's administration. Governor Clement had deep feelings against capital punishment and made repeated attempts to have it abolished. In 1965 he took matters into his own hands by commuting to ninety-nine years the death penalty laid on five prisoners. Governor Blanton apparently intended to commute the death penalties of ten prisoners on death row but was prevented from doing so by the early swearing in of Governor Alexander. Governor Dunn advocated the reinstitution of the death penalty after it had been found unconstitutional by the United States Supreme Court, and the 1973 General Assembly enacted a statute designed to reestablish the punishment; the act, however, was declared unconstitutional by the state Supreme Court early in 1974. Still another, sharply limited act was passed in 1974. The difficulties of developing a capital punishment law whose provisions assure fair and nondiscriminatory implementation, uninfluenced by race or income, raise questions whether the penalty can ever be equitable. Governors in the past have found themselves in an extremely difficult position when faced with an imminent execution; some have felt the role of surrogate executioner an insupportable burden. So long as the death penalty is operable, the governor cannot escape the life-or-death power implicit in the authority to pardon or commute.

A number of administrative offices, usually the old and more important ones, are . . . provided for in [state] constitutions.

WILLIAM McCLURE (1916)

IN THE GOVERNMENTAL system of the United States the president is the only chief executive. In many states, though, while the governor is the chief executive officer, other executive or administrative officers chosen by popular vote are potential or actual rivals. The choice by voters of such officers as lieutenant governor, secretary of state, auditor, superintendent of banking, or commissioner of education is quite usual. In Tennessee the situation is different; other than the governor the only popularly elected executive or administrative officers are the three members of the Public Service Commission.

The constitution, however, does provide for three officials, two of whom could be considered to belong to the executive branch of the government even though they are elected by the legislature. These three officials—the secretary of state, the treasurer, and the comptroller of the treasury—are responsible to the legislature, an arrangement that is necessary and proper for the comptroller, but of doubtful validity in the case of the others. A fourth official, the attorney general, normally included in the executive branch, is elected, in Tennessee's case, by the Supreme Court.

The secretary of state, elected by a joint vote of the General Assembly for a four-year term, is the chief record keeper for the state. It is his duty to keep "a fair register of all official acts and proceedings of the government."[9] This assignment includes such matters as maintaining official copies of all bills and resolutions of the legislature and keeping the enrolled draft of the Tennessee Code, executive orders of the governor, and administrative regulations of the various departments. The secretary is responsible for having legislation printed and bound. His department records deeds to state property, grants, and corporation charters; preserves records of county civil district boundaries; and affixes the state seal to various official documents upon approval by the governor. The secretary of state, through his appointee the coordinator of elections, is responsible for administering the electoral process and certifying and keeping election returns.

The treasurer's function has gradually shifted emphasis. In the days of unsound banks, the treasurer concerned himself with placing the state's funds in banks not likely to collapse in a panic, no doubt with due attention to rewarding banks that aided party efforts. The power to deposit state funds, often at no interest in a bank of the treasurer's choosing (and to withdraw them) was a powerful political weapon. In modern times, the treasurer's job is to earn maximum revenue from interest paid on state deposits; the security of the banks or the use of deposits as rewards and punishments is less important, although it is likely that neither of these concerns will disappear completely. The law requires the treasurer to keep accurate accounts of the funds he receives and dispenses, and provides penalties for misappropriation of funds, but otherwise gives little guidance in how he shall conduct the affairs of his office.

The comptroller of the treasury, like the treasurer, is elected by a joint vote of the General Assembly for two years. It is his job to audit all financial transactions of the state administrative agencies to see that they conform to the authorizations made by the legislature. Aside from his fiscal role, the comptroller exercises significant influence in state affairs. Much of the reason for this stems from the long service, at the highest level of Tennessee government, of William Snodgrass, who came into state service in 1953 as director of the budget in Governor Clement's first administration. He was first elected to the office of comptroller in 1955 and continued in that office through many Democratic administrations and two Republican ones. During the Clement and Ellington administrations, he was one of the closest advisers to the governor on a wide range of issues, and for this and other reasons the office is given extensive responsibilities in acts passed during the fifties and sixties. With the growth in the independent spirit in

[9]*TCA,* 8–3–104.

the legislature, the constitutional officers look to that body with due deference and loyalty.

The speaker of the Senate is designated by the constitution in Article III, section 12 as the successor to the governor should there be a vacancy in that office. In 1951, the legislature by law created the office of lieutenant governor as a separate office from that of the speaker but said that at all times the speaker shall be the lieutenant governor. No duties or powers have been assigned to the lieutenant governor, and he can be considered only a potential executive officer; he is by law a legislative officer until he becomes governor. No strong interest can be observed in providing for a lieutenant governor by constitutional amendment. There is no need for one. On the subject of Tennessee governors, Jefferson's quip on government servants may be parroted: few die and none resign. The order of succession to the office of governor is the lieutenant governor, the secretary of state, and the comptroller.

8

☆ ☆
☆

The Administrative Machine

ADMINISTRATION IS THE DAY-TO-DAY BUSINESS OF GOVERNMENT THAT TAKES the handiwork of the legislature and brings it to realization in concrete situations. It is the operation of institutions, the building and maintenance of highways, the collection of statistics and data—the myriad activities of a governmental unit. It involves the management of people and materials to accomplish the purposes of the law. In many ways the problems of public administration are similar to those of private business,· and the same techniques of management and organization are often employed in both. Still, there are differences. Whereas in business the standard of success must be principally the condition of the profit column in the firm's books, in the administration of public programs other things count: service, the relative efficiency of the performing agency, and the responsiveness of the governmental agency to public demands.

In the criticism of government that is so general a feature of American life, the bureaucrat comes in for his fair share. Yet we must recognize that he is in existence because the legislator has created him. The legislature, in turn, being responsible to the people, has built the bureaucracy on a foundation of law. Public administration is based on law. Through the law the policies of government are set up, the objectives outlined, and the organization of the agency that is to administer the policy established. It is from the law, in other words, that the administrator receives his authority. The translation of the law's general principles into specific applications in concrete situations requires action from the administrator. This action, in our system, must be in accord with the law.

Public policies are carried out through rules and regulations issued by administrative agencies. Before 1974 it was difficult to know what the rules were because each rulemaking agency was the keeper of its own books. But in that year the General Assembly enacted a far-reaching law that for the first time required these many rules and regulations to be pulled together and continuously updated. Called the Uniform Administrative Procedures Act, it set up detailed provisions to guide state agencies in promulgating rules and enforcing them. It created virtually overnight a large, new body of law governing the actions and procedures of state agencies. The act was amended in 1978 to require the approval of the attorney general before a rule goes into effect. Perhaps as a token of its lack of confidence in administrative units, and probably with a desire to keep its own control over affairs, the legislature, in that same amendment, required a forty-five-day waiting period before a rule could go into effect and then only if a legislative committee had not initiated proceedings to review it.[1]

The private citizen who considers himself aggrieved by an administrator may have his "day in court." He may ask the court to consider whether the administrator has gone beyond his powers, whether he has performed his duties, whether he has been unfair. The court, by examining the law and the action of the administrator, determines whether the authority placed in the administrator by the law has been misinterpreted or exceeded.

The responsibility of the administrator enforced through the courts is reinforced by the constant surveillance of the legislature. Changes in policy, alterations in the structure of the administrative agencies, expansion or contraction of authority are all brought about by legislative action. The legislative body, which represents the people in the first instance by writing its version of the public will into statutes, retains a potentially decisive voice in the law's administration. In addition to its power of veto over rules and regulations, the authority of the legislative body over the administrative aspects of government is constantly exercised through financial control; the funds spent by administrators must be appropriated by the legislative body. The request for funds by an administrative agency is examined by the legislature, the work of the agency in the preceding year is subject to legislative criticism, and the future of the agency is determined by the appropriation of funds.

As a general rule, legislative control over administrative expenditures is implemented to some degree by an audit sponsored by and reported back to the legislative body. The degree of legislative participation in the administration of the law may be a matter of the legislature's own determination. Administrative agencies may be made directly responsible to the legislature, though the duties of a representative body, coupled with the short time ordinarily taken to perform its function, make such an arrangement generally unsatisfactory, and it is one not often employed except at the local level. Legislative participation in the appointment of officials is sometimes written into the law; legislators may also set standards for other

[1] *TCA*, 4–5–104.

personnel actions. The General Assembly in recent years has taken more interest in matters of appointment and has modified what had been an almost unlimited power of gubernatorial appointment.

The administrative organization of the state government reflects the philosophy of students of public administration in the early decades of the present century. Their schemes for structuring the public agencies were built upon military experience and thinking; they were designed to produce machinery under the direction of a commander whose orders would be based upon the advice of counsellors who had time to think and plan. It was not difficult constitutionally to place this scheme in operation in Tennessee, for, although the governor was constitutionally weak in the state, at least he had no rivals in the administrative branch. Under Austin Peay, an able and ambitious governor, the state's administrative pattern was set in 1923. That pattern, in the view of some scholars, was designed to enhance the political authority of the governor, as well as his administrative power, and doubtless it did so.[2] The state adheres basically to that administrative structure in the 1980s.

That structure is based on the existence, under the governor's authority, of a number of departments—ordinarily known as line departments—that administer, under a scheme of specialization, the major programs of the state: highways, policing, the promotion of public health, the enforcement of insurance and banking law, and so on. The heads of these departments are appointed by the governor and are responsible to him; their own subordinates in turn answer to the heads, in a system of command from the top downward and of responsibility from below upward.

Certain specialized activities—personnel, the keeping of accounts, the purchasing of supplies—are also organized into units that control the line departments but also aid them in various ways. These agencies have been called housekeeping agencies, auxiliary departments, and staff departments. In military practice the word "staff" was once reserved for thinking and planning agencies, but Tennessee state government has few agencies that are confined strictly to planning. Probably most people who study or speak of Tennessee administration think of these agencies as "staff."

The line departments are Agriculture, Conservation, Education, Employment Security, Transportation, Correction, Insurance, Banking, Labor, Mental Health and Mental Retardation, Public Health, Safety, Military, Economic and Community Development, Human Services, Tourist Development, and Veterans' Affairs. These names disclose the principal objects of state administration. Allocation of programs to these various departments is not always a simple matter, for some programs could fit into various slots. Labor and Employment Security could be put

[2]David D. Lee, *Tennessee in Turmoil: Politics in the Volunteer State, 1920–1932* (Memphis: Memphis State Univ. Press, 1979).

together, for example, and school health might fit into either Education or Public Health. Choices must be made, and those choices are often of serious concern to the people most affected and to the lobbyists who represent them.

The auxiliary, or staff, departments include General Services, Personnel, and Finance and Administration. Finance and Administration has long been regarded by many as the premier department of the state because of its responsibility for preparing budgets and monitoring expenditures. Its commissioner is one of the first named by an incoming governor because of the need for preparing a new governor's budget very early in his first administration. By reason of its work, its employees know more about what is happening throughout the bureaucracy than do other state servants. It accounts for revenues and expenditures, operates a central data processing system, plans and reviews the construction of state buildings, and serves as the primary records management unit of state government.

The Department of Revenue does not fit neatly into our definition of line and auxiliary (staff) departments. It collects funds and therefore makes direct contact with the public, but a little twisting of logic is required to think of this as "service" or even "regulation"; at the same time it does not provide aid and regulation to the other departments, as do agencies such as Personnel or General Services.

The heads of the departments, both line and auxiliary, are called commissioners. They form the cabinet. They are regarded as the governor's own team, and each new governor selects his own team. If a governor is to have any impact on the massive bureaucracy—about 50,000 employees including educational personnel—he must select people in whom he has confidence. He also has job demands from his political backers to satisfy. He needs people in whom he can repose confidence, for he will be held to account politically for the performance of his appointees. He may use his appointments of cabinet members to try to bring peace to the warring factions within his party, as Governor Blanton quite evidently did when he entered office. He must consider the claims of various regions of the state, for, whatever the signboards say (Governor Dunn changed the earlier signs that advertised the "Three States of Tennessee" to the "Great State of Tennessee"), Tennessee is still divided into three big regions that are still conscious of their separate identities. And he must consider qualifications if he is to avoid serious trouble. He also has problems of availability, for the jobs do not pay enough to attract some people. Nowadays, the demands of blacks and women must be given some thought. Governor Blanton and Governor Alexander used screening committees to help find commissioners, but, in the final say-so, it is the governor who determines the choice. The governor also has a legally free hand in the dismissal of commissioners, but dismissals are rare, and politically disturbing.

Each commissioner is assisted by deputy and assistant commissioners, their number and title varying with departments. These officials are usually politically vulnerable in a change of administration, especially if party shifts are involved. But some such officials succeed in being recognized as professionals, and survive changes of administration, or even changes of party. Such a condition is observable in the Department of Finance and Administration. Indeed, appointments of subcabinet level executives in other areas show an increasing consideration of technical competence rather than political loyalties. The political and the technical are increasingly blurred.

Some of the commissioners themselves develop staying power, particularly in offices that require professional expertise. A tradition of this sort has developed in the Department of Public Health. Governor Alexander altered past practice when he succeeded in appointing a professional administrator as commissioner of correction, a department that had long been a happy hunting ground for the professional politician.

It is to be expected that the commissioners of the health agencies will be professionals. In addition certain other departments are likely to be headed by practitioners—Agriculture by a farmer, Insurance by an insurance man, Banking by a banker. Unfortunately some of these appointments invite a troublesome conflict of interest, a subject on which newspapers and at least some of the voters are less patient than they used to be.

The commissioners form the governor's cabinet, but that may mean much or little. Governors have used their cabinets as advisers and sounding boards, or have asked their aid in pushing administrative proposals in the legislature, but they are not required to proceed in this way. Whether or not there is a "cabinet" in a collegial sense is entirely up to the governor, who may go it alone if he wants. Individually, the commissioners have the governor's confidence. Some, however, will be more important than others, partly because of personal attributes and partly because of the offices they hold, but exactly who is important will vary from time to time. The commissioners who have heavy program expenditures, such as the commissioner of transportation, are likely to be important figures. Beyond that, much rests on the personalities involved. Some commissioners are more technicians than politicians and are able to act without close supervision. Even the political commissioner is sometimes able to "buck" too much direction from his nominal boss.

The four constitutional officials, other than the governor, whose work is administrative in character—the secretary of state, the state treasurer, the state comptroller of the treasury, and the attorney general—do not much threaten the central executive power. The secretary of state and the treasurer exercise little discretion. The attorney general's functions involve a much higher degree of discretion, professional training, and experience, and his independence is offensive to some critics. The comptroller should be considered the functionary of the legislature. In any case, the constitutional officers do not impair the governor's administrative power in the degree characteristic of many state schemes, although an aggressive and independent comptroller could and probably will come into conflict with the governor, a conflict inherent in the scheme of separated powers.

The theorists of administrative organization whose ideas were followed in the organization of 1923 were generally unfriendly to boards, commissions, and independent or semi-independent authorities or agencies. They were inclined to favor a system of pyramids that would end in the authority of a single individual who could be held responsible for results. Nonetheless, such boards and independent agencies have a way of persisting like weeds in a formal garden, and this for some cogent reasons. While boards, it can be argued, are clumsy instruments for carrying on day-to-day decisionmaking, they may serve to involve numbers of people in policymaking. They also enable a top administrator to involve numbers of citizens in a program, and many administrators find this both politically and administratively useful. Boards seem justifiable and proper in the regulation of certain professions where one-person power could be dangerous.

Autonomy is more than welcome to interest groups who have something to gain from public administration. A notable example would be groups interested in schools and colleges. Independence from the normal structure of administration is often seen as a means of keeping educational institutions "out of politics." A drive for administrative autonomy may be coupled with a scheme or organization involving the use of boards or commissions.

Finally, the institution of a board may simply be a way of temporarily shelving a political "hot potato." When in doubt, create a board.

The numerous, and often obscure, boards in the Tennessee administrative system fall into three main categories: advisory boards, committees, or councils; licensing and/or regulatory boards; and policymaking councils or boards.

Advisory boards form a large group of units that technically have no policymaking power but nevertheless play an important role in the policymaking process of many departments. Over sixty such bodies with over eight hundred members function in this capacity. Examples include the Local Government Advisory Commission, the Advisory Committee for Crippled Children's Services, and the Advisory Hospital Committee. Advisory committees, set up by state law, are sometimes to be appointed by the commissioner of the department to which the committee is attached and sometimes by the governor.

Examining and licensing boards are clustered mainly in two departments. Fourteen are in the Department of Insurance where they were placed in the reorganization of 1959. Two examples are the boards of Accounting and

Examiners for Land Surveyors. Some nineteen licensing boards are found in the Department of Public Health. These health-related boards deal with the medical profession, nursing, dentistry, and other such professions.

These boards are of crucial importance to those wishing to be admitted to practice. The public policy goal is to protect the public safety by admitting only properly trained and qualified people. Examinations to test knowledge and proficiency are generally a key element in the process of being licensed. It is alleged from time to time that a secondary motive of the boards is to keep the number of practitioners reasonably small so as to prevent competition from getting out of hand and driving down prices. The fact that the professions have virtually total control of these bodies through the nomination of people for board positions lends credence to the idea. At the same time it is difficult to argue with the view that it takes professionals to police the profession. Licensing boards are at least not a direct drain on the taxpayer's pocketbook. They are self-supporting through the collection of fees paid by those seeking licenses.

The best example of a policymaking council is the Public Health Council in the Department of Public Health. The law provides that it "shall formulate the rules, regulations and policies of the department of public health."[3] This council is appointed by the governor and consists of practitioners from the major health-related professions.

The Personnel Department commissioner submits proposed rules to the Civil Service Commission for its approval or modification. The Commission is therefore in a policymaking rather than just an advisory position relative to the department. The State Board of Agriculture is given a somewhat ambivalent assignment in the law in that in some provisions it seems to have an advisory role and in others it seems to have a policymaking authority as well. For example, ". . . the state board of agriculture may prepare a statement of policy for the state department of agriculture and may present that statement . . . to the commissioner . . . and to the governor. . . ."[4] Other departments have similar units to help them formulate and adopt policies. Though they differ somewhat in duties and composition since they were established at different times by different legislatures, they follow a basic pattern; long terms are established, Grand Divisions are recognized, pertinent occupational or interest groups are represented, compensation, if any, is limited, and meetings are few.

If a more detailed organizational chart of the departments and agencies were examined, one would find a fairly typical subdivision of activity units such as exists in any large bureaucracy. Departments are made up of divisions and divisions are in turn made up of sections. Certain principles of administration are sought in developing and maintaining an effective

[3]*TCA*, 53–115
[4]*TCA*, 43–2–106.

organization. Duties ought to be clear; there should be a rational division of labor; each person and unit ought to know who its superior is; and, where possible, units dealing in the same subject area ought to be associated in one department. In many cases, these and other such principles are honored more in the breach than in the practice.

Generally speaking, the administrative structure of the state would meet with the approval of students of public administration. The structure is integrated; the responsibility for the administration rests clearly upon the governor. If anything goes wrong, he must take the blame since he has the power to correct and improve performance. And the governor's political power is enhanced, even though he must always keep a balance between the competing political factions and interest groups in the state.

Nevertheless some flaws in the administrative structure develop from time to time. Quite probably there are still too many boards even though they are much less significant than the departments. Each time a new function develops, the urge to create a board seems to get the upper hand. The reorganization of 1923 wiped out a great many of these, but if they are allowed to grow up again the 1923 job will have to be done all over again. Do the advisory boards attached to the departments serve very effectively? These committees, boards, or commissions, as they are variously termed, may be potential devices for well-tempered policy formation, inasmuch as their decisions reflect the considered opinions of several interested individuals. They may also provide an excellent device for correlation of functions within and between departments and private interests. Such correlation is achieved, of course, by including in the membership of one board interested officials or citizens from other agencies. There is, however, a definite danger of overworking the principle of commission-type policy formation and of multiplying the number of policy-determining boards to the point where they interfere with the authority and responsibility of the commissioner. The present exact scope of the powers of these boards is by no means clear, which in itself is a flaw in the organization structure.

A closer examination of the administrative organization of the state would also show that agencies are not always placed in the proper setting. On the whole, however, these maladjustments are not very numerous; the placement of functions is generally a good one.

Recent developments have tended to overload the governor's office and the Department of Finance and Administration. On the other hand, the Department of Finance and Administration has sought, with some success, to add administrative staff to the cabinet departments, so that a higher degree of decentralization could be achieved.

Administrative organizations do not stay put. Conditions and times change, and some adjustment of machinery is necessary. Consequently most of Tennessee's chief executives since 1937 have made changes in the administrative structure. Whether these changes have been necessary or whether they reflect an understandable urge to tinker with the machinery is very hard to say, but two statements may be hazarded. One, the changes have not been extensive and have not basically altered the overall design established in 1923. Two, the changes have generally taken the form of creating new departments. This latter process gives rise to some anxiety, for one of the great troubles before 1923 was the excessive number of agencies reporting to the governor. The slow but persistent creation of new departments might put us eventually back to the antiquated Model-T of 1922 in place of the streamlined job that started down the road in 1923.

The pattern of administrative organization is set by the General Assembly, and pressure-group politics are evident at times. There appears to be little need for a state organization dealing with veterans' affairs, but we have one. The creation of an urban affairs unit in the governor's office was not especially welcomed by the executive leadership of the Tennessee Municipal League, but Governor Ellington created one, nevertheless, without much advance notice that he intended to do so. (It was later abolished by Governor Alexander.) It would make some sense to transfer a relatively weak personnel department into the strong Department of Finance and Administration, but this has not seemed politically wise. A reorganization bill of 1978 was killed by the House Calendar Committee, after having passed the Senate. But in spite of political pressures the administrative structure of the state remains basically sound and controversies have been contained.

Legislators and the public generally have become alarmed by the growth of bureaucracy and so-called "sunset" laws have become popular. The General Assembly passed one for Tennessee in 1977, known as the Tennessee Governmental Entity Review Law, setting up a system of legislative review of administrative agencies every six years to determine whether the agency should be continued. It is too early to say whether much will result. The Assembly has taken some action, such as the termination of the Commission on the Status of Women and the Board of Electrolysis Examiners, but it is pretty safe to assume that most of the agencies will survive review without too much difficulty.

9

☆ ☆
☆

The Strings of the Purse

ONE ASPECT OF PUBLIC ADMINISTRATION THAT gets its full quota of attention is financial, or fiscal, administration. Citizens are deeply interested in where their tax money goes, and how, and for what. The term "fiscal administration," as we use it here, covers budgeting, accounting, purchasing, and auditing.

The budget is the life-blood of the government, the financial reflection of what the government does or intends to do.

AARON WILDAVSKY (1961)

THE TERM "BUDGET" is a familiar one to most people because they have applied it (or know that they should) to their own domestic finances. To most people the word "budget," as applied to their everyday life, means simply a record of family income and expenditures. Some go a little further by trying to cut operating expenditures whenever possible; they introduce the element of control. In government, budgeting is a major element in policymaking, a principal technique of management, and, at the national level, a factor in the general economic condition of the country. The budget is, in effect, a forecast, usually on an annual basis, of anticipated revenues and a plan for spending them. Its purpose is to provide public officials with a coherent statement of the administration's proposals for sources of revenue, and the dollar amount of support to be provided to various programs.

Constitutional provisions relating to the fiscal process include establishment of the offices of treasurer and comptroller of the treasury (each elected by a joint vote of both houses of the General Assembly for two-year terms). Statutes impose on the treasurer responsibilities for custody of state funds and maintenance of receipts and disbursements accounts, to be reconciled with "the general ledger maintained by the commissioner of finance and administration."[1] The comprehensive post-audit function of the comptroller, delegated also by statute, includes examinations to determine compliance with budgetary requirements in the expenditure of all state funds. Another constitutional provision is the prohibition against the state lending or giving its credit to, or assuming a proprietary interest in, any private or municipal enterprises.[2]

The most important constitutional provision is an amendment completely revising section 24 of article II, approved by the voters on March 7, 1978:

> Section 24. Appropriation of public moneys. —No public money shall be expended except pursuant to appropriations made by law. Expenditures for any fiscal year shall not exceed the state's revenues and reserves, including the proceeds of any debt obligation, for that year. No debt obligation, except as shall be repaid within the fiscal year of issuance, shall be authorized for the current operation of any state service or program, nor shall the proceeds of any debt obligation be expended for a purpose other than that for which it was authorized.
>
> In no year shall the rate of growth of appropriations from state tax revenues exceed the estimated rate of growth of the state's economy as determined by law. No appropriation in excess of this limitation shall be made unless the General Assembly shall, by law containing no other subject matter, set forth the dollar amount and the rate by which the limit will be exceeded.
>
> Any law requiring the expenditure of state funds shall be null and void unless, during the session in which the act receives final passage, an appropriation is made for the estimated first year's funding.
>
> No law of general application shall impose increased expenditure requirements on cities or counties unless the General Assembly shall provide that the state share in the cost.
>
> An accurate financial statement of the state's fiscal condition shall be published annually.

This amendment reflected growing public sentiment against increasing taxes, and Tennessee was one of the first states to impose constitutional restraints. The issue was strongly debated in the constitutional convention and vigorously opposed by municipal interests that saw such restrictions as potential limitations on the flow of state aid. Others argued that arbitrary limitations could severely hamper the state's capacity to deal with emerging and unforeseen problems, and held that the accountability of popularly elected representatives in the General Assembly to their constituents should be sufficient protection. The result was a compromise—instead of an automatic formula limitation, which the proponents wanted, the qualifying language in the second paragraph was added.

[1] *TCA*, 8–5–107.
[2] Art. II, sec. 31.

Five days before the vote was taken the General Assembly approved an act,[3] to be effective if the amendment were approved, prescribing as the index to measure the growth of appropriations for the 1978–79 fiscal year "the percentage change in Tennessee total personal income as determined from projections, in current dollars, made by the Tennessee Econometric Model report of the Center for Business and Economic Research [an agency of the University of Tennessee] dated December 1, 1977." One might speculate as to whether this action, taken on the eve of the referendum, was designed to influence the voters to favor the amendment. A 1979 act implements the constitutional restriction by requiring certain data in the budget document relating to budget increases, personal income, and economic growth.[4] The complexity of this act precludes summarization; the 1980–81 budget includes four tables of data to conform with its provisions.

Since the amendment grants some discretionary power to the General Assembly to vary from the rate of economic growth, its impact is presently indeterminable. It would seem to fortify conservative elements who want to reduce governmental expenditures, but the way is open for a determined legislature to appropriate funds above the formula amounts, all of which means that in this important area of governmental action representative government still prevails. The judgment of the elected representatives will determine the content and amounts of appropriation acts, but they may feel stronger pressures to justify any excesses above the formula.

Tennessee's first budget legislation, enacted in 1917 in line with a procedure inaugurated by California and Wisconsin in 1911,[5] established as an ex officio body a state budget commission made up of the governor (chairman), the comptroller, the treasurer, the state auditor, and the secretary of state. In 1923 budgeting was delegated to a division of accounts and budgets in the Department of Finance and Taxation and in 1937 to a division of budget in the Department of Administration. In 1939 the division was made a separate department. In 1959 the Department of Budgeting was abolished and its powers were transferred to a division of finance and administration; a 1961 act upgraded this division to a department under the commissioner of finance and administration and made this official also director of the budget. He is assisted in his budget responsibilities by a budget division.[6]

Until 1969 budgets were prepared on a two-year basis since the legislature met only every other year. This had the advantage of requiring only half as much budget preparation work as an annual budget system, but estimating for two years was difficult and there was too much for the legislature to

[3]*Public Acts,* 1978, ch. 614.
[4]*Public Acts,* 1979, ch. 408; *TCA,* 9–6–201 to 9–6–204.
[5]W. Brooke Graves, *American State Government,* 4th ed. (Boston: Heath, 1953), 493.
[6]The term "division" is uniformly used by administrative personnel, but the law (*TCA,* 4–3–1003) was not amended and still (1981) carries the designation "budget section."

review effectively. A statute passed in 1969 (at a time when the legislature was increasingly asserting its independence from the governor) required annual budgets.

The legal requirements regarding budget content are concise and explicit:

> The budget of the state government shall present a complete financial plan for the ensuing fiscal year, which plan shall set forth all proposed expenditures for the administration, operation and maintenance of the several departments, institutions, offices and agencies of the state government; the interest and debt redemption charges during the fiscal year. The budget shall also present proposals for capital projects to be undertaken or completed during the ensuing year, and the means of financing such projects. In addition thereto, the budget shall set forth the anticipated revenues of the state government and any other means of financing the expenditures proposed for the ensuing year.[7]

Since the governor is required by law to prepare the budget, it is called an executive budget. This function, more than any other activity of the governor, provides him with the means by which he can influence state policy, move to carry out campaign commitments, and assure a high degree of compliance by the bureaucracy with his program.

The overall guidelines for preparation of any particular budget are set by the governor. These guidelines may relate to a campaign promise not to raise taxes or they may reflect specific priorities he has in mind, such as prison reform, mental health improvements, an expanded state park system, or other special concerns. These guidelines set the tone of the administration and are utilized by the governor's top staff, both political and fiscal, in developing the budget. Through cabinet meetings and communication between the budget staff and various department budget and fiscal officers, the governor's wishes and priorities are made known.

The actual process of arriving at budget decisions in Tennessee has not been studied in detail. It is clear that the governor (and later the legislature) is under pressure from groups that want either expanded services or better salaries; teachers and local officials are among the extremely vocal groups. But it is likewise clear that new governors, eager to show some record of achievement, either welcome such pressure or think up new programs of their own. Governor Clement will be remembered for improving mental health programs (indubitably needed), and Governor Dunn promoted public kindergarten. Such positive steps are more appealing to the executive, anxious for a niche in the museum of memories, than the negative posture of sitting on the lid.

The budget staff consists of a small number of budget analysts, each of whom is assigned one or more departments or agencies to work with on a more-or-less continuing basis. The budget analyst serves as the link

[7]*TCA*, 9–6–101.

between the central fiscal office and the operating units, not only for budget preparation but also for budget execution, that is, the carrying out of the budget once it has been approved by the legislature. Each analyst becomes familiar with his assigned agencies and can provide them technical assistance as well as policy guidance. The analyst may also serve as the advocate for his agencies when fund allocation decisions must be made in the course of the budget process.

The budget timetable is set by the requirement that the governor present the budget to the legislature prior to February 1 unless it is his first year in office, in which case it must be submitted prior to March 1; the legislature can extend the deadline by a joint resolution. The law further provides that before December 1 of each year each operating agency and department must prepare estimates of its expenditure requirements along with its expenditures for the previous fiscal year and estimated expenditures for the current year.[8] Well before this time the departments begin their work on the estimates that finally reach the governor.

It is impossible to know far in advance just what the economy is going to be like during the succeeding year. Also, every fourth year, a new governor comes on the scene in the middle of the budget process (unless the governor has been re-elected for a second term, now permitted under one of the 1978 constitutional amendments). Since the election occurs after the agencies have necessarily completed most of their work, their requests may not reflect a new governor's philosophy or priorities. For these and other reasons, each department is normally asked to prepare a continuation program request and an improvement program request. A continuation program request asks that an existing program be funded at the same level as before except for normal pay and cost-of-living increases. An improvement program request calls for an expansion of existing programs and/or the addition of new programs; justification of such requests by the agency is necessary.[9] New programs are likely to be funded only if the governor is in an expansive mood or if the revenue picture appears to be especially bright. A 1977 act also requires a statement of the effect of budget requests at a level of funding at 90 per cent of the current year's appropriation[10] —a requirement likely to be significant only in periods of fiscal stringency. This is a partial approach to "zero base" budgeting.

Starting in the summer of 1972, a new approach to budgeting began whereby agencies were furnished a separate set of forms in addition to the regular ones and asked to develop a set of agency objectives to serve as

[8]*TCA*, 9–6–103. In recent years administrative instructions have set September 30 as the deadline for submitting requests to the budget division.

[9]Governor Blanton issued instructions that new programs must have the approval of his Policy Planning Staff before being included in a formal budget request.

[10]*Public Acts*, 1977, ch. 457.

guidelines for their future efforts. This approach, given the name "allocation by activity," represented a combination of concepts that had been developed over the years by budgeting specialists (sometimes referred to as "program budgeting"). The mixture of setting goals, ranking agency priorities, and evaluating program effectiveness led to some confusion and problems of compliance but nevertheless represented a determined attempt to move beyond the incremental approach to budgeting in which the basic technique is simply to use last year's expenditures as a base and add sufficient funds to take care of such things as cost-of-living increases. This approach seems to have had little impact on the budget process—the sheer magnitude of the state budget and a limited time frame make the incremental approach the only feasible one to take. Tennessee is not alone in this respect —many commentators have noted the impracticality of realizing the high aims of program budgeting.

After the departments have submitted firm requests, hearings are held with the commissioner of finance and administration and his budget staff. In line with the concept of executive budgeting these hearings were formerly held in internal private sessions. In recent years legislators have sat in on these sessions. The Fiscal Review Committee and the Senate and House Finance, Ways, and Means Committees provide each legislator with a summary of these proceedings, comparing agency requests with the previous year's estimated expenses. The governor's final budget may reflect his personal decisions on major problems and undertakings, but in large part its content is determined by the budget staff (especially by the commissioner of finance and administration) and then ratified by the governor (his many other responsibilities preclude examination of all details in a complex, voluminous budget).

The duty which is considered as belonging more peculiarly than any other to an assembly representative of the people, is that of voting the taxes.

JOHN STUART MILL (1861)

ONCE THE REQUESTS have been thoroughly reviewed and refined in the executive branch, they are printed in the budget document, which is made available to legislators and the public on the day the governor delivers his budget message. In addition to the agency requests, many other elements are included in the document, such as plans for paying interest and retiring bonded debt, estimates of revenues, and proposals for funds to pay for the expenditures.

By the time the budget is presented to the General Assembly, a number of committees and legislators are somewhat familiar with it. Even so, it goes through the legislative process like other resolutions and bills. The legislature uses the assistance provided by the Fiscal Review Committee, with its permanent professional staff, and the House and Senate Finance, Ways, and Means Committees, with their staffs. Professional staffs are especially valuable during public budget hearings where they can help balance the scales between an executive budget staff thoroughly briefed on the minutiae of the document and the legislators who, for the most part, are fiscal laymen. Though developments in recent years have seemed to some to be moving toward a full-scale legislative budget staff, it is doubtful that the legislature wants to depart from the executive budget practice, at least not in the near future. It does seem clear that present-day legislators want a great deal more information than used to be furnished before they are willing to vote on the appropriations bill.

In much of the recent past of Tennessee, when the governor was a Democrat and the legislative majority was of the same party if not always of the same faction, the governor maintained rigid control of the General Assembly and of the appropriations. Governor Clement's first administrations furnish an excellent example. No doubt the governor had to consider what the legislators might want, particularly for their own areas, but he controlled the whole process; what he finally determined upon as the expenditure plan was accepted, perhaps with some sub rosa grumbling, by the Assembly. If a member failed to go along, he was subject to reprisals, in the distribution of local favors, where it hurt. This system began to crumble in the later years of Governor Clement and again in the last administration of Governor Ellington; it was substantially altered in the administration of Governor Dunn, a Republican faced with a Democratic legislature.[11]

Many of the revisions to Governor Dunn's budgets were pet projects added by legislators with regional interests that would have caused the budgets to exceed available revenues. The governor's response was the use of his item veto power vigorously to bring the budgets into balance. In contrast Governor Blanton used the item very sparingly. The relative harmony under Governor Blanton can be attributed not only to the elimination of partisan differences between the governor and the legislature but also to improved consultation between staff personnel of the executive branch and legislative leaders of the various committees involved (who also managed to suppress amendments from the floor in both houses). The final results were appropriation acts that differed from the governor's budgets, but not nearly as much so as formerly.

[11]See Antoinette Thompson, "Legislative Review of the Budget in the Tennessee General Assembly, 1965–1973," master's thesis, Univ. of Tennessee, 1974. See also Plaas and Zuzak, *The Budgetary System in Tennessee, op., cit.*

Governor Alexander in his first year vetoed no items in the appropriations bill for 1979–80. Under severe fiscal pressures in 1980, in the bill for 1980–81 he reduced the 1980–81 appropriations rather modestly. Federal reductions in appropriations and shortage of state revenues led the governor to use the item veto extensively in 1981.

Under the aggressive and responsible leadership of key legislators, the legislature in recent years has seemed to be the dominant partner in the budget and appropriation process. However, the practice of enacting the appropriation act late in the session makes it possible for the governor to have the last word (at least negatively) through use of the item veto after the session has ended. During Governor Dunn's term there was some discussion among legislators of a recess to permit action to override such vetoes, but the idea was never pursued.

The result of the appropriation process is a bill that reflects primarily the governor's budget, with some revisions and additions resulting from the work of legislative leaders and committees. The first portion is a listing of the various state departments, institutions, and agencies and the amounts of their respective appropriations. This is followed by pages and pages of a wide assortment of provisions—from directions to compensate named individuals for various reasons (e.g., widows of CAP pilots who lost their lives while conducting a search in the Great Smoky Mountains) to a prohibition in the 1978–79 act against use of any state funds for abortions (except under very limited circumstances).

Other major policy decisions have been incorporated in appropriation acts. Examples include the decision in the 1977–78 act to award a contract for the state employees' group insurance plan on a basis of competitive bids (resulting in a shift from Provident Life and Accident Insurance Company to Blue Cross and Blue Shield of Tennessee); minimum and maximum amounts of pay increases for all state employees (including employees of all agencies and institutions receiving appropriated funds); a prohibition in the 1978–79 act against using any state funds for an airport in the Hardin Valley area of Knox County; and instructions in the 1976–77 act that engineering estimates of construction projects and funds allocated to such projects be confidential, to prevent such information from reaching bidding contractors. Some such provisions would seem to be contrary to the admonition in *TCA*, 9–6–108 that "the appropriation bill shall not contain any provisions of general legislation."

Various other actions have also been mandated by appropriation acts, such as a directive that rules and regulations governing contracting for personal, professional, and consulting services shall be promulgated by the commissioner of finance and administration, in consultation with the commissioner of personnel and the commissioner of general services and with the approval of the attorney general and the comptroller. Detailed provisions of this kind indicate a strong disposition on the part of legislators to oversee administrative matters and the use of state funds.

It would seem to be difficult to make a specific estimate of funds appropriated by the legislature, because of a large number of open-ended appropriations (for a "sum sufficient" to accomplish a designated purpose); some of these, such as for the judicial system and to pay costs of criminal prosecutions, are unqualified, but most are made subject to approval by administrative officials—usually the governor and commissioner of finance and administration; many appropriations for specific amounts are likewise made subject to approval by such officials. Other provisions authorize them to allocate from surplus funds sums sufficient to undertake new or expanded programs not funded in the appropriation act but directed by other acts of legislature, subject to the further approval by any two of three officials: the speakers of the two houses and the comptroller.

Shifting of funds between units within a department or other agency may be authorized by the governor and the commissioner of finance and administration; another provision "notwithstanding any other provision of this act" also requires approval of such a shift by any two of three officials: the speakers of the two houses and the comptroller. Transfers between departments and agencies are also authorized when approved by any two of these three officials.

Appropriations must be based upon estimates of revenue to be received in the future, and sometimes disagreements have developed between legislators and administrative officials as to the accuracy of such estimates (usually the former assert that the latter underestimate as a means of assuring adequate funds to underwrite all appropriations). Appropriations usually exceed the estimated revenues because of the certainty that vacant positions will result in actual expenditures for personnel services below the budget estimates, which are calculated on a basis of all positions being filled for twelve months.

The element of uncertainty as to whether estimates will be reached always exists, and for many years the safeguard against such an occurrence was an authorization to impound a portion of the appropriations for all agencies (usually 10 percent), which would be released a few months short of the end of the fiscal year if revenues seemed to be meeting the estimates. A new approach to meet such an eventuality was initiated in the 1976–77 appropriation act, when a $15 million reserve for revenue fluctuations was established. This has been continued in subsequent acts, with the amount increased to $32 million. This reserve is carried forward and reported from year to year as a part of the general fund year-end balance and is to be drawn on only if a shortfall in estimated revenues develops.

A general provision appropriates to each department, institution, office, or agency all "departmental revenues" collected in the course of its operations. These are defined to include all charges, earnings, contributions, and the like, as distinguished from "state revenues," which are proceeds of taxes, licenses, fees, fines, forfeitures, and other imposts laid specifically by law. Federal aid funds are likewise appropriated.

The third phase of the budgetary process is the execution stage; it relates to the implementation of the appropriation and revenue acts. If the legislature approves the budget without making any changes, some adjustments in spending patterns may still be necessary because of changes in federal policy, shifts in the economy, or other reasons. When the legislature makes significant changes in program requirements, it is even more essential to develop detailed work plans for each department indicating what is to be done and how much will be spent.

Work programs are prepared by the budget division. Budget analysts revise the original budget to reflect changes made by the appropriation act and break the annual amounts into four quarterly allotments (four equal amounts unless there is some reason to vary from this basis). Two computer printouts are furnished to the departments and other agencies, one showing the revised amounts by objects of expenditure and sources of funding, and the other showing the quarterly allotments by (1) personal services and benefits and (2) other operational expenses. A procedure is provided to permit the agencies to request changes in such work programs by obtaining approval of the commissioner of finance and administration. Unspent funds appropriated for personal services and benefits are impounded at the end of each quarter and cannot be used for other expenditures during the year.

In establishing the amounts of quarterly allotments, estimated federal aid and departmental revenues are also taken into account. The appropriation act provides that allotments must be reduced to the extent that funds from these sources fall below the estimates, but the converse does not occur if the estimates are exceeded—the amounts of the allotments are not increased. Legislative authority to fix maximum levels of expenditures is thus preserved.

Since introduction of the reserve for revenue fluctuations, the former procedure of impounding funds as a cushion against sagging revenues was abandoned for a time, to be revived in the 1981 fiscal year. Other measures to avoid a deficit situation include reducing or freezing travel funds, leaving vacant positions unfilled, and delaying purchases.

One constant control over expenditures is found in the accounting and pre-audit system. When agencies wish to appoint someone or order equipment, requests go to the personnel and budget offices, which check to see whether sufficient funds are available in the proper account and whether the expenditure is properly authorized. These controls provide a comprehensive restraint over the entire bureaucracy. The personnel department also reviews promotions, requests for positions, and so on, but these reviews relate only indirectly to money.

$$\bigodot$$

Through the accounting system current control over expenditures is exercised.

PRESIDENT'S COMMITTEE ON ADMINISTRATIVE MANAGEMENT (1937)

ACCOUNTING IS THE PROCESS of keeping track of expenditures and revenues. In broader terms, the functions of an accounting system are: to make a financial record, to protect those handling funds, to reveal the financial conditions of the organization in all its branches or purposes at any time, to facilitate necessary adjustments in rate of expenditure, to give information to those in responsible positions concerning the basis on which plans for future financial and operating programs can rest, and to aid in the making of an audit. Accounting, in addition to providing a method for preventing illegal use of funds, provides a useful tool in the planning and adaptation of work programs and is, therefore, useful as a management tool and control device.

Central accounting as the function of a single agency began in Tennessee with the administrative reorganization of 1937 when a division of accounts was created in the Department of Administration. In 1939 the division of accounts became a separate Department of Accounts. In 1959 the department was abolished and its functions transferred to an accounts section in the division (redesignated "department" in 1961) of finance and administration.

The Department of Finance and Administration performs the following principal accounting functions: (1) prescribes and maintains a general system of accounts for all state financial transactions; (2) performs a pre-audit of all expenditures to determine that they are in accordance with budget allotments, requisitions, internal agency accounts, and legal authorization; (3) issues warrants for payment of claims against the state; (4) maintains a continuous internal check of accounting operations; and (5) provides financial data for state administrators.

The treasurer receives taxes and other public monies through deposits made to his credit by state agencies. He makes reports annually to the governor in the form of financial statements, verified by the comptroller, which include a complete summary of monies received and expended for the previous fiscal year together with the year-end treasury balance. He also serves as custodian of all collateral, securities, bonds, and other valuable papers deposited with the state. A very important additional function of the treasurer's office is administration of the Tennessee Consolidated Retirement System, including management of the benefits aspects and investment of funds deposited in the system.

The process of purchasing and accounting in Tennessee runs somewhat as follows. An operating agency prepares a requisition for a needed item and sends it to the Department of General Services, which refers the requisition to the division[12] of accounts for pre-audit to determine legality and availability of unencumbered funds. Thereafter the Department of General Services takes bids. When the successful bidder has been determined, this department prepares a purchase order and sends it to the division of accounts, where the amount is recorded and a new unencumbered available balance is automatically calculated and recorded; after this is done the purchase order is returned to the Department of General Services for transmittal to the vendor. After delivery of the item the operating agency certifies this fact to the Department of Finance and Administration, which issues a warrant, similar to a check, by computer. The warrant is sent to the agency for transmittal to the person who is to receive payment; the payee then cashes the warrant at any bank in the same manner as a check would be cashed. Later, the bank is repaid by a check drawn by the state treasurer. A special bank account is maintained to cover payroll expenditures, and paychecks are issued against this account, so the intermediary warrant is not used in the payroll procedure.

The accounts division maintains a very complete accounting system utilizing computers. Monthly reports are prepared that show obligations, expenditures, revenue, and the status of budgetary accounts. These reports are distributed to the comptroller, the Fiscal Review Committee, the Department of Finance and Administration, and the agency concerned. The agency is expected to balance these reports against whatever records may be maintained within the agency. The accounts division also provides to the agencies daily reports of transactions that include essentially the same information, which must be of great assistance in the day-to-day management of agency activities.

Many modern governmental techniques—accounting and auditing requirements, procedures for letting . . . restrict the opportunities for . . . graft.

FRED I. GREENSTEIN (1964)

THE ADVANTAGES OF a central purchasing system for governmental units at

[12]Comment in footnote 6 applies here also.

all levels has been generally recognized for some time. Such a system makes possible the application of uniform purchasing standards and specifications, lower prices resulting from mass purchases, better budget and accounting control, and a check on possible fraud or favoritism in awarding purchasing contracts. Responsibility, rather than being diffused among numerous organizations, is centered in a single agency with defined standards and procedures of operation and control.

Central purchasing was initiated in Tennessee in 1923 when a division of purchases was created in the Department of Finance and Taxation. This division was transferred to the Department of Administration in the 1937 reorganization of the state government and was made a separate Department of Purchasing in 1939. In 1953 the General Assembly changed its name to the Department of Standards and Purchases.

Another change occurred in 1972 when the General Assembly abolished that department and established the Department of General Services. In addition to administering the state's purchasing system the functions of this department include management of its movable properties, food services, printing and motor vehicle facilities, federal and state surplus property programs, general public works services, central postal services, central storehouses, materials-testing facilities, and other support services not assigned by law to specific departments.

The department's purchasing division operates under rules and regulations promulgated by a board of standards (the commissioner of general services, the commissioner of finance and administration, and the comptroller). It must execute all purchases and contracts unless otherwise provided by law (e.g., construction contracts are executed by the Department of Transportation and the state building commission, and personal services contracts are executed by the Department of Finance and Administration). Awards are to be made to the "responsible and responsive bidder submitting the best bid." Factors to be considered in determining the best bid include "price, quality, purpose or use, discount, freight, and delivery date."

A procedure is established for vendors to be placed on a qualified bidders' list and for notifying such bidders when bids are to be received. Authority is delegated to agencies to make purchases under $100 for items not available under term contracts or from other state agencies, and for other specified small purchases of products and services (e.g., telephone service, freight and postage charges, and airline and gasoline credit card charges). The purchasing division is directed to obtain informal written or telephone quotations on purchases between $100 and $500 "when possible" and to take sealed competitive bids on amounts over $500 "when possible." Contracts are of two types: a one-time open-market purchase, and a term contract. The latter may be for a particular agency, a combination of agencies, or for all state agencies and local governments. An agency may issue departmental purchase orders to make purchases under term contracts established for its use.

Because sales to the state could have an important bearing on contributions to state political campaigns, state contracts and purchases are as sensitive as personnel administration, and the state has not always escaped charges of maladministration in this area. The last Browning administration (1949–53) was castigated by a legislative investigation for lax purchasing procedures, and improvements in purchasing procedure were undertaken. Yet, years later, the Blanton administration became involved in a "bid-rigging" of road contracts that reached the court and helped to discredit those disastrous four years.

An audit is an examination and verification of the accounts after transactions are completed in order to discover and report to the legislative body. . . .

PRESIDENT'S COMMITTEE ON ADMINISTRATIVE MANAGEMENT (1937)

THE FINAL STAGE in the budget cycle is the post-audit. The legislature wants to know that the funds it has asked the taxpayers to supply have actually been spent honestly and for the purposes intended by the legislature. Therefore, the books must be audited, and in Tennessee that task is assigned to the comptroller of the treasury. Responsibility for the exercise of this function is fixed by a broad grant of power:

> The comptroller of the treasury is hereby authorized to audit any books and records of any governmental entity created under and by virtue of the statutes of the state of Tennessee which handles public funds when such audit is deemed necessary or appropriate by the comptroller; and the comptroller shall have the full cooperation of officials of the governmental entity in the performance of such audit or audits.[13]

Teams of auditors work throughout the state conducting regular and spot checks of books and financial transactions. The comptroller is also empowered to make audits of any political subdivisions and their various agencies that are charged with the care and control of public funds if he deems it necessary to do so; generally, however, such audits are made at the order of local governing bodies by certified public accountants and public accountants. Such audits must be made annually in accordance with minimum standards prescribed by the comptroller, and a copy of each must be furnished to his office.

Since the comptroller's office traditionally concentrated on checking

[13]*TCA*, 8–4–109.

fiscal accountability but not the wisdom of expenditures, a gap of sorts existed, which was filled in 1967 by the creation of the Fiscal Review Committee. This committee has attempted to bring about savings through more efficient methods in governmental operations. Its responsibility is to keep the members of the legislature informed as fully as possible on all matters relating to finances. It has a small permanent staff; the comptroller serves as secretary to the committee. Accompanying this development has been increased emphasis on management audits by the comptroller's office.

The House and Senate Finance, Ways, and Means Committees hold regular hearings and carry out their own studies with the assistance of staff from the comptroller's office. The division of responsibility between the Fiscal Review Committee and the Finance, Ways, and Means Committees has not been clearly delineated. It is clear, however, that there is less concern in these committees for fiscal auditing and greater interest in what is being called program auditing; funds may be honestly and efficiently spent on a program that may have little real value. The committees have been increasingly interested in such matters in recent years—a trend that is likely to continue.

10

☆ ☆
☆

A Government of Men

MONEY AND JOBS—THESE ARE THE STUFF OF DAY-TO-DAY POLITICS, whether that be state politics, local, or private. Hiring and paying government personnel constitute an ever present concern of any organization. The term "civil service," when correctly used, refers to the employees of a government who occupy civilian, or nonmilitary, posts. In popular parlance the words are used to apply only to those employees who are under what is properly called the "merit system," whereby employees are hired, advanced, paid, and discharged on the basis of their fitness for the jobs, rather than on the basis of their politics, sex, religion, personal acceptability, or family connections.

Both the merit system and that portion of the civil service outside the merit system must take account of the hiring process, the relation of pay to the job, training for the job, the adjustment of grievances, methods of promotion, retirement, and methods of dismissal. A carefully designed merit system tries to approach these matters rationally and fairly. While it is possible to have an informal merit system, and indeed this exists in much of Tennessee government, such informality is unstable. If a merit system is worth having, it is worth formalizing.

⊛

It is very certain that, of all people in the world, the most difficult to restrain and to manage are a people of office-holders.
ALEXIS DE TOCQUEVILLE (1835)

DURING MOST OF THE HISTORY of Tennessee, the state has operated without a formal merit system, and with considerable emphasis on the spoils system. That eminent Tennessean Andrew Jackson is generally credited with having fastened the spoils system on federal employment, but, in fact, the credit does not belong exclusively to him. Every president (and every governor) has used the spoils system to some degree.

The merit system runs counter in many ways to the interests and habits of politicians and political parties. Parties exist only to a limited degree because of issues. Indeed at the local and state levels the party program—even if there is one—means very little. This is especially true in Tennessee. No instance comes to mind in recent years when the two principal parties in Tennessee have been clearly divided on any state issue that meant anything to the voter. What holds parties together, aside from habitual alliances, must be the hope of jobs, contracts, influence, and favors. The selection of state and local employees purely on merit, divorced from party connections and personal likes and dislikes, is contrary to the forces that mold the parties and party factions into a unit. No matter how much a governor may believe in the merit system, he will have difficult sledding when he attempts to put the system into operation or to enforce it rigidly. Patronage is particularly significant in large departments; departments involving natural resources, transportation, agriculture, employment security, and welfare are especially vulnerable.

In certain areas of state and local service the merit system is inappropriate as the sole basis of employment. This system cannot be expected to operate in the filling of the very top posts in a government. These posts are concerned with policy formation, and the party that controls the appointing office is entitled to select persons who will follow the lead of the party or the top appointing official, particularly if that official is the governor. It also is not easy to apply a merit system to many menial or unskilled jobs where no means for comparing qualifications are available. But in a considerable area between these two the merit system can be applied.

Before 1923, appointments to state posts were made frankly under the spoils system; the incoming political faction disposed of the jobs as it saw fit. The 1923 reorganization act led some to hope that a formal merit system would be inaugurated; the act contained provisions that made such a system possible, but nothing significant was done, and the old system continued in operation until 1937.

Complaints that the national government has usurped the functions of the states are common, and true. One of the reasons for this development is to be found in the refusal of the states to clean house. Hence, it is significant that, when the federal government, in the early days of the New Deal, entered into a program of social security after the spectacular failure of the states to cope with the Great Depression, it began to interest itself in the qualifications of the employees who would administer that part of the social security program entrusted to the states. When the Social Security Act was passed in 1935, it required that state public welfare programs receiving aid under the act be approved by the social security board, but personnel matters were excluded from this requirement. In 1939, a change was made: the Social Security Act was amended to give the board authority to approve merit system plans of the states as a condition of securing federal aid. This was to be significant for Tennessee, as well as for other states.

Gordon Browning, candidate for governor in 1936, campaigned in favor of a merit system law, and in 1937 the legislature at his request passed such legislation. Although the details of the statute were adequate in most respects, the act was not closely observed in practice, and the personnel division was not given sufficient money or time to deal adequately with patronage hunters. Nevertheless, a small beginning was made toward the creation of a merit system in some departments.

The control exercised by the national government has not been tight enough to eliminate patronage considerations entirely. A certain degree of technical competence must be possessed by employees in such departments as Human Services and Employment Security, but patronage plays a role. How much has never been made clear.

⊛

Statutes enacted by the legislative department are not self-executory. To become effective they must feel the touch of human energy, which administration alone can supply.
Bank of Commerce and Trust Co. v. Senter, 149 TENN. 569, 593 (1923)

THE 1937 ACT FAILED to satisfy some of the requirements of the federal Social Security Act as amended in 1939. At about the same time that Congress enacted the 1939 amendments, the Tennessee General Assembly passed a new civil service law, which still remains the basis for the formal merit system in Tennessee, although some amendments have been added. Tennessee law now provides for a Civil Service Commission of five members appointed by the governor for six-year staggered terms. The commission has the function of representing the public interest, approving rules and regulations, advising the governor and the commissioner of personnel, and hearing appeals from employees in such matters as dismissals, demotions, suspensions, and similar actions. The Civil Service Commission is not an administering agency and its powers are rather limited. The chief administrative officer of the system is the commissioner of personnel, a cabinet-level official appointed by the governor to hold office at his pleasure. The commissioners of personnel (both men and women have occupied this post) have generally been politically active before their appointment. The structure of the department and its relationship to the chief executive are in general accord with current thinking on the proper organization of the personnel function, which holds that the chief personnel officer should be primarily an adviser to and a functionary of the chief executive rather than a check on his authority.

The persons selected as commissioners of personnel disclose something of the governors' attitudes toward the department. Generally speaking recent governors have picked experienced fiscal persons as their commissioners of finance and administration. However, all too often the personnel commissioners have been noted chiefly for their partisan political background. Keith Hampton, a well-known political figure, and J. N. Doane, political leader of Jefferson County, were two such examples.

The organization of the Department of Personnel reflects the traditional concerns of formal personnel management; in 1981 the department was divided into divisions of examination, classification and pay, training, and intergovernmental and employee relations. In addition, there was a research division, an affirmative action office, a local classification-compensation services division, and an administrative division. These arrangements represent some minor changes from the period of the Dunn administration, but no basic differences in programs. The developments of the 1970s indicate an enhanced interest in employee training and employee relations. The local services unit indicates the increased interest of the state in aiding local personnel management, and the affirmative action division represents the interests felt in women and minority groups, a reflection of trends from the late 1960s on.

By and large, since the inauguration of the formal merit system, the coverage of employees under the act has advanced at a most deliberate pace. To begin with, the 1937 act covered the state service generally, with comparatively few exceptions, but the 1939 act gave the governor power to exempt positions during the first nine months following passage of the statute, although he also had power to extend coverage. The formal merit system at first applied only to certain divisions of the Departments of Public Health and Public Welfare, and to the unemployment compensation division and employment service division of the Department of Labor. These were agencies that received federal funds. In 1941 the Department of Safety (which includes the highway patrol) was brought under the system, and in 1945 the division of motor vehicle title and registration and the divison of criminal identification, newly created in the Department of Safety, were added. In 1947 the Department of Personnel was brought under the system. As of May 1973 the agencies under the formal merit system were the Departments of Public Health, Employment Security, Public Welfare, Safety, and Personnel, together with the divisions of juvenile probation (Department of Correction), state parks (Department of Conservation), surplus property (Department of General Services), occupational safety (Department of Labor), manpower (Department of Economic and Community Development), the Office of Civil Defense, three units (fiscal, development disabilities, and alcoholic and drug services) of the Department of Mental Health, and the research and statistics section of the Department of Labor. In October, 1976, Governor Blanton issued Executive Order 39 which essentially completed the process of including executive branch agencies under a merit system. Excluded from coverage were "deputy and assistant commissioners; administrators and directors reporting to an assistant commissioner or higher authority; other managerial staff reporting directly to an assistant commissioner or higher authority; and one confidential secretary to each appointing authority . . ." An Attorney General's opinion of January 31, 1978 stated that Executive Order 39 could be rescinded by the governor but a second, and supposedly final, opinion was issued on March 10, 1978. It reversed the earlier opinion because it concluded that the original legislation gave the governor authority to extend but not to reduce the coverage of the merit system. It must be pointed out, in any case, that many of the accepted practices of modern personnel administration were applied in Tennessee throughout the executive branch even before the Blanton administration. The extension of the formal system may reduce patronage somewhat, although ways can be found to adjust formal requirements to personal or party goals.

The business of finding the fittest persons to fill public employments . . . is very laborious, and requires a delicate as well as highly conscientious discernment.

JOHN STUART MILL (1861)

THE LOGICAL BASIS for a well-organized merit system is job classification. A system of job classification provides for a description of the jobs to be filled and a grouping of jobs by their comparative difficulty so that recruitment, examination, training, pay, and promotion, indeed most of the aspects of personnel management, can be conducted in accordance with the tasks to be performed by the employee. Tennessee has a job classification system covering generally the employees of the executive branch. It was studied and revised in 1974 and again in the early 1980s.

Equal pay for equal work is the watchword that relates a compensation plan to the job classification scheme. Tennessee executive departments operate on this system; a new and comprehensive pay plan was under preparation in 1981. The compensation of state employees is under the close supervision of the budgetary and appropriation procedure of the state, with ultimate control in the General Assembly through line-item appropriations.

The recruitment and placement division of the Department of Personnel once had the responsibility for the acquisition and placement of qualified personnel throughout the various agencies of the executive branch. The division no longer exists; its functions have been decentralized. Ideally, perhaps, job-seekers should file their applications initially with the Department of Personnel for jobs throughout the system, and the Tennessee department, like other central personnel offices, makes an attempt to fulfill this function. In practice, recruitment frequently does not work in this way, particularly in any large system, nor does it work entirely in this way in Tennessee. Various executive agencies search for personnel on their own initiative, often by use of informal and personal contacts, with the Department of Personnel used for formal approval and some advisory help. Informal recruitment of this type suffers from the disadvantages of uncoordinated effort, open to more personal and political influence and acquaintanceship than may be desirable, but it is at the same time often more effective than a more formalized approach. Such informality may sometimes counter the rigidities of a formal system, such as veterans' preference or state residence requirements.

Examinations normally include ratings of education and experience, written tests, performance tests, and interviews. The Department of Personnel uses all these methods. Examinations for most posts are administered upon request on a daily basis in selected central locations in the state, but large-scale assembled examinations are still used for positions involving large numbers of vacancies.

The American system of personnel management has always placed a high emphasis on examinations that test for the position to be filled, although testing for potential development is not completely excluded. It is not easy to devise examinations that clearly predict behavior on the job, and hence a major task of examination units is the validation of their examinations by testing the tests against the successful applicant's later performance. The Department of Personnel has an active program of this kind, conducted by industrial psychologists. Tests, including those given both by private and public agencies, have in recent years come under judicial attack in the United States, particularly from minority groups who maintain that customary testing favors persons with cultural and educational backgrounds that minority groups frequently lack. The Department of Personnel has an active and successful program of validating tests, and it is actively engaged in attempting to recruit among minority groups.

From the results of examinations, lists of persons eligible for employment are prepared. These are referred to as eligible lists or registers of eligibles. Such lists may be for original appointment, for promotion, or for reappointment. When a position is filled, the process ordinarily involves a request from the agency needing a person (the appointing agency) to the

Department of Personnel for a list of names. These names, taken from the eligible list, are presented to the appointing agency, which then selects and appoints a person from the list. The presentation of the names to the appointing agency is the process of certification.

The whole process of certification is one of the weak links in the chain of most merit systems, and it is also a point around which much argument revolves among experts in public personnel administration. It used to be customary, and still is in many jurisdictions, to require the certification of the three highest names on the list in terms of their grades. Many students of personnel management believe that the appointing agency should have a much wider choice; a few go so far as to advocate submission of all eligibles who have passed the examination. This view, of course, leaves more discretion to the appointing agency. In some jurisdictions, even though the rules may require certification of the top-ranking names, they may be disregarded in practice. If the personnel agency is not strict, it is difficult for anyone else to enforce rules of this sort. The merit system may also be circumvented by temporary appointments, provisional appointments, or by plain disregard of the existence of lists available in the hands of the personnel agency.

The Tennessee Department of Personnel supplies registers of eligibles for the whole of the executive department. For those positions under the formal merit system (officially referred to as the "classified service") lists of eligibles must be certified, although emergency appointments may be made without the use of this machinery, a practice in general use throughout the United States which recognizes a need but which is also subject to abuse. Emergency employees in Tennessee cannot remain in that status over 120 days. The department is required by law to submit five names for an open position. Emergency employees must undergo later tests. The departments not under the classified service may ask for the certification of particular persons, and lists of eligibles may be refused if sufficient reasons are given for such refusal.

Vacancies in Tennessee, except at top levels and in areas where patronage is important, are filled, when possible, by the promotions of present employees. Applicants for promotion are rated and tested, but promotions may also occur through piecemeal actions outside the formal examination procedure. This kind of promotion is a familiar procedure in personnel management throughout the country; it is flexible and workable.

The personnel system of Tennessee is not a "closed" system; that is, new employees are not compelled to enter the system at the bottom ranks and to work up through a system that excludes outsiders from all except the lower ranks. Closed systems are by no means unusual in the United States, especially in urban governments; closed systems have some desirable features, from the point of view of promoting careers, maintaining sound retirement systems, and the like, but they are unduly restrictive and it is to the interest of the state that an open system be maintained.

Discipline can be enforced over state employees by various means including demotion, suspension, and discharge. Such actions, as well as other causes, may give rise to grievances. The state has an established grievance procedure, provided for by statute. Merit system employees (those in the classified service) who are dismissed, demoted, suspended, transferred as to location or laid off, and who claim that such action is taken for political or religious reasons, or because of race, sex, national origin, or other factors unrelated to merit, may appeal to the Civil Service Commission. It is always difficult to assess the effectiveness of a grievance system. The Civil Service Commission has been rather active in hearing appeals, and employees win at least enough of their cases so that the usefulness of the appeals procedure is believable. A peak year for appeals occurred in 1980 when forty-eight appeals were filed. Seventeen were heard, of which three were won by the grievants.

Employees of the state do not enjoy a formal right to unionization and collective bargaining, although a few cases of limited bargaining have occurred. The proposed legislation that has surfaced in the General Assembly is, so far, confined to local units. Unionization and collective bargaining are inimical to certain features of the merit system. Generally speaking, the thrust of unionization is directed to limiting management discretion, including the discretion to differentiate among employees on the basis of merit. Unions are likely to seek closed personnel systems, to equalize pay wherever possible, to limit classification to a relatively small number of classes, and to emphasize seniority as the basis for personnel actions. Of course, unions will seek to establish grievance procedures and to provide ways of controlling the abuse of discretion by supervisors. Unions accept arbitration as means of settling disputes, but attempts to intrude on the impartiality of arbitrators are by no means unknown. A major purpose of unions is to raise wages and limit hours and, after this is done, to secure added fringe benefits. These union goals bring them into conflict with the elected representatives who hold the power of appropriation.

The service rating is a formal assessment of the performance of an individual employee by his supervisors. The service rating, although probably a necessary element of an adequate merit system, presents unusual difficulties. Such ratings must be based on the judgments of supervisors— some are careful, and some are not; some are harsh, and some are easy-going. Supposedly, improvement may come from the criticisms made on service ratings, but hurt feelings and bad morale may be the chief results. In any case, it would be difficult to think of any field of personnel management that has brought more discussion and less certain illumination. The service rating has been used on a rather spotty basis in Tennessee, and was discontinued in 1978. A new procedure has been devised and was ready for adoption in 1981.

A sign of the increasing interest in good personnel administration in Tennessee is the growth of attention to training. It is typical of the development of personnel management that training is recognized in personnel departmental organization after classification, recruitment, examination, and pay are acknowledged as interests of the central personnel office. Individual departments can arrange, at least to some degree, their own training programs; central agencies get around to the promotion of training only after other aspects of management have been dealt with. This has been true of personnel management in the state offices, but training is now an established division within the Department of Personnel. In 1967 a Center for Training and Development (now the Center for Government Training) was created in the University of Tennessee, directed to providing training for both state and local employees. The Center does not have, nor does it seek, a monopoly on training; state and local agencies can conduct their own programs. The state apparently makes only limited use of the Center. For many situations, training on the job is preferable to any other learning experience. In addition to the training division and the center, a special administrative organization for training has been developed in the Tennessee Law Enforcement Training Academy near Nashville. Master's degrees in public administration are offered at several state institutions.

It is always difficult to say how effective a training program is. In spite of the clear interest in training and the evident enthusiasm for further education on the part of state employees, we have a few ways of estimating whether training is effective or not. Like education in general, in-service training has to be accepted to a considerable degree on faith, adapted to needs difficult to define by means hard to validate.

The training organization of the state has its complicating features. Degree-granting programs, such as the Master of Public Administration, can be partially related to work activities, but not completely so. (At one period in the development of the joint master-of-public-administration program in Nashville by the University of Tennessee and Middle Tennessee State University, persons inside the state Department of Personnel were actively inimical to the program, although this opposition eventually disappeared.) The non-degree activities are the responsibility of the state agencies and the Center for Government Training and these are administered independently. In some ways, it might have made more sense if the center had been attached to the Department of Personnel because training of the type offered by the center is properly a part of management's responsibilities. The scheme of organization would not have been acceptable to some local government leaders, for it might have developed a move toward state supervision of localities, a move that in Tennessee has always encountered strong opposition.

The several retirement systems once operated by the state have now been combined into two main schemes, the Consolidated Retirement System and a separate system for some employees of the University of Tennessee. Various state officials and employees are included in these systems including judges, county officials, attorneys general, and others. In addition the state participates in the old age and survivors insurance system. The details of a retirement scheme are too complex to be discussed here. The schemes have been contributory (that is to say, employees make some contributions) and compulsory; proposals made by Governor Alexander to have the state pick up the tab for university and college employees were adopted in 1981. The systems generally allow for retirement at age 60, an age that, in the light of present social conditions, is probably too low. But mandatory retirement has now been dropped, except for certain classes including university teachers. Whether these exceptions are legally valid may be open to challenge. Benefits are measured by some average of highest salaries received and by years of service. The old age and survivors insurance payments are, in effect, a part of the retirement scheme because benefits paid by the state are lowered according to a formula that takes account of the OASI payments. Disability retirement is possible, and provisions are made for various types of survivors' payments.

The Consolidated Retirement System, which covers the kind of employees who have been discussed in this chapter, is administered by a board of trustees that includes the state treasurer.

The retirement funds are developed with the help of actuarial surveys, but it is not absolutely clear that the conditions of the funds are above doubt. Ideally a retirement system should involve saving enough on the part of all contributors so that retirements may be paid through the investment of those savings. But retirement schemes are authorized by legislators whose knowledge of finance is often shaky and who are tempted to confer benefits without knowing—or even guessing—what the future is likely to be. A particular trouble that governmental retirement schemes face in the last quarter of the present century is the aging of the population, the steady extension of the human life span, and the consequent increase in the number of retired persons. That the federal social security system faces this trouble is common knowledge. Tennessee's retirement systems were, like others, initiated without adequate actuarial study, but vigorous steps have been taken to correct this situation.

⊛

With regard to . . . those . . . who form the . . . professional public
servants, entering their profession . . . while young, in the hope of
rising progressively . . . as they advance in life, it is . . . inadmissible
that these should be liable to be turned out.

JOHN STUART MILL (1861)

THE CAREER SERVICE of Tennessee has shown little movement from one
division to another, a rather high turnover, and a tendency for the state to
lose its experienced administrators as they seek greener pastures in their
later years. Men predominate, although women in Tennessee are more
highly represented in the bureaucracy than are their counterparts in some
states. (At least one woman will usually be found in the governor's
cabinet.) The religion of the Tennessee bureaucrat is more likely to be
Methodist or Baptist than any other denomination. Few Catholics and few
Jews are found in the upper levels of the bureaucracy, although there is no
indication of their systematic or deliberate exclusion. Administrators are
primarily middle-class; their fathers come principally from the professions
and business; farmer and labor representatives are relatively scarce,
although the bulk of the group comes from rural areas. Most of them are
natives of Tennessee and most of them were educated there. Their educational qualifications are high.[1] Some blacks are now found in the bureaucracy.

A well-established and well-developed merit system will offer able
employees a chance of personal development and advancement during
their lifetime in public employment. Such a career service calls for conditions that guarantee that personnel actions will be taken on the basis of
merit, but it also guarantees that as an employee advances in age and
accomplishment he can secure greater responsibilities and higher compensation. Such guarantees cannot be provided if the system is too small;
council-manager government could not offer an expanding career for
managers were it not for the fact that managers move readily from one city
to another. The entire country is the career field for an ambitious professional city manager.

Careers of this type are probably not expected by the great mass of state
employees; most of them must be content with jobs that remain much the
same over the years. For them satisfaction must be sought in jobs well
done, with steady but modest increases in pay, some promotions, and

[1]This material is taken from Harry F. Kelley, Jr. and Charles E. Patterson, Jr., *The*
Tennessee Bureaucrat: A Survey of State Administrators (Knoxville: Bureau of Public
Administration, Univ. of Tennessee, 1970).

security in old age. For those who seek posts at the administrative level, something more is needed; the road must be open to jobs that offer interest; pay and security may be less important.

Improved personnel administration, improved pay, and greater emphasis on technical capacity—all evident in the state and its subdivisions——are encouraging to believers in a career system. At least since the earlier years of Governor Clement's administration, young, technically qualified people have been welcomed into the Tennessee state service. The number of such young and ambitious persons has probably increased steadily through the administrations from Clement through Alexander. Some of them have become cabinet officers and high officials in the state's educational institutions. In many ways a career open to talent is available for them in Tennessee state government. While they are not completely secure in their positions when administrations change, many of them have survived not only the change from one Democratic governor to another, but even changes from one party to the other. Party affiliation has not apparently been an overwhelming consideration in their appointment and retention.What is troublesome for careers in a state like Tennessee is that young people may reach the top too soon. If a man or woman becomes a commissioner or assistant commissioner in his thirties, where is he to go in his forties? Opportunity for federal employment is somewhat limited, since the federal career system has in actual practice some of the features of a "closed" system. There is little recruitment from one state to another, so that few young people can begin careers in a medium-sized state like Tennessee and hope for advancement to a large one such as New York or California. In this respect, at least, the "career system" possibilities of Tennessee service, although certainly superior to what they once were, still suffer from some limitations.

At the national level, the bureaucracy has become a force amounting, in the opinion of many observers, to a "fourth branch," which neither Congress nor the president can fully control. Studies of the power and independence of the Tennessee counterpart of this huge machine have yet to be made, but some influence is inherent in the bureaucratic structure. Still, it seems unlikely that the national phenomenon is exactly duplicated in the state, although it appears to be about as hard to get rid of an agency in Tennessee as in the national government.

11

☆ ☆
☆

Let Right Be Done

THE JUDICIARY IS ONE OF THE THREE LEGS ON WHICH THE THREE-LEGGED
stool of American government is balanced. The organization, powers, and
method of choice of the judiciary vary greatly in detail from state to state,
but the general pattern is the same. The basic structure of a judicial system
consists of a trial court plus an appeals tribunal. These two elements are
essential—the trial court for the routine basic decisions on controversies
and the appeals court for the thoughtful correction of the errors that
necessarily occur in the rapid working of the trial court. Additional considerations lead to features that complicate this basic structure—courts for
minor matters or preliminary actions, specialized courts for small matters
such as traffic violations or small debts, or for weighty considerations such
as criminal trials or appeals, taxation, labor issues, and the like, or the
creation of several levels of appeals. Specialized courts dealing with family
problems or the rights of children are common in American states.[1]

*The result of the geographical, historical and various other influences
on a developing court structure is a modified four-tier judicial system.*
INSTITUTION OF JUDICIAL ADMINISTRATION (1971)

THE JUDICIAL STRUCTURE of Tennessee is unusually and unnecessarily
complicated, a condition that has drawn criticism and reform efforts. A
basically complicated structure has been made more confusing by extensive use of private acts that produce numerous local variations in court
structure.

[1]Birt Waite, "The Origin and Development of the Juvenile Court," diss., Univ. of Tennessee, 1974.

The base of the judicial pyramid in Tennessee has been the justice of the peace. These courts we borrowed from the British, where they were created as long ago as the fourteenth century. In Tennessee the state constitution provided (until amended in 1978) for the election by popular vote of two justices from each of the civil districts in the county, except that three were chosen from the civil districts that included the county towns.

The justices of the peace in Tennessee served in a dual capacity; on the one hand they were the members of the county court of quarterly sessions, the basic county governing body in Tennessee (having both legislative and administrative powers), and, on the other hand (until the creation of the general sessions courts), the individual justice functioned as a judge in minor cases. Justices were not required to hold court and not all of them did. In their judicial capacity, the justices of the peace in Tennessee suffered under the same inadequacies that have characterized the JP system in the rest of the United States. They were untrained in the law; they were part-time; they served on a fee basis; they kept no complete records; and the physical surroundings of their hearings were poor and undignified. The JP system as a means of administering justice is being reformed in the United States;[2] in Tennessee the system has been replaced by the general sessions courts. In Tennessee counties, the JPs still served as members of the county court, which in most counties remained the principal governing body, until the constitutional amendment of 1978.

The legislature responded to criticism of the JP courts by creating the general sessions courts. Such courts have steadily spread over the entire state. By 1957 thirty-nine courts of general sessions had been established in Tennessee, and beginning in 1960 these courts were instituted for the whole state, excepting only six counties. As of 1980, only one county lacked general sessions judges (or an equivalent with a different name), and that one county must conform to the general pattern in 1982. General sessions courts consist of one or more salaried judges, depending on the county's size, elected by popular vote. The courts meet at stated places and times, and the fees they collect are turned in to the county treasuries. General sessions courts deal with small claims and misdemeanors, and they give preliminary hearings on felonies, determining whether there is probable cause for further prosecution. Small claims include money claims up to $3,000. In some instances the decisions of the general sessions courts may be reheard in the ordinary trial courts. The second hearings are *de novo;*

[2]See Task Force on the Administration of Justice, The President's Commission on Law Enforcement and Administration of Justice, *Task Force Report; The Courts* (Washington: Government Printing Office, 1967), 34–36. The reference to the origins of the JP is from the same commission, Task Force on the Police, *Task Force Report; the Police* (ibid.), 4; cf. also Wooster.

that is, complete new trials take place, not merely examinations of the records of the general sessions courts.

The judges of the general sessions courts are not always lawyers, but at least in the metropolitan counties the judges are legally trained and are full-time.[3]

Urban communities organized into municipal corporations generally have some sort of court of limited jurisdiction. The presiding officer of such a court may be titled a municipal judge, but in smaller cities the functions are performed in some cases by the mayor and, in others, by the recorder.

The confusions of terminology that characterize Tennessee local government are nowhere more evident than in the term "county court." There have been two county courts: the county court of quarterly sessions, which was the county legislative and administrative organ, and the county court of monthly sessions, a judicial agency. This ancient system was changed by constitutional amendment in 1978.

The monthly county court was presided over either by a county judge, elected by popular vote usually for an eight-year term, or by a county chairman, sometimes chosen by popular vote and sometimes by the justices of the peace. The county chairmen's terms varied. About three-fourths of the counties of Tennessee had county judges until the office was abolished by constitutional amendment in 1978.

The county judges of monthly sessions exercised probate jurisdiction affecting wills, executorships, and the settlement of estates. Matters affecting certain persons, such as the appointment and removal of guardians, the legitimation and adoption of children, and the affairs of apprentices, also came under the jurisdiction of this court. In certain cases the monthly county court had concurrent jurisdiction with the circuit and chancery courts. For example, such jurisdiction extended to the sale, distribution, and partition of the real estate of deceased persons, to the sale of property, and to the adoption of children. In these cases, litigation could begin in any of the courts that had concurrent jurisdiction.

Late in the last century the belief grew that special treatment should be accorded to juvenile delinquents. To use the regular courts for such persons, it was thought, was to train the young offender for a permanent career in crime. The first juvenile court was established in 1899 in Cook County, Illinois.[4] As early as 1890 the Tennessee Democratic platform advocated the separation of minors and hardened criminals in the penal

---

[3]Cf. a report of the Institute of Judicial Administration entitled *Preliminary Report of the Judicial System of Tennessee*, pt. I, *Structure and Operations* (New York, 1971). For comments on the procedure in these courts, see Hyrum Plaas, Otis H. Stephens, Jr., and James J. Glass, *The Functions of the Judge in the General Sessions Court of Knox County Tennessee* (Knoxville: Bureau of Public Administration, Univ. of Tennessee, 1973).

[4]Virginia Ashcraft, *Public Care: A History of Public Welfare Legislation in Tennessee*, University of Tennessee *Record* 50:8 (Knoxville: Bureau of Public Administration, 1947), 33.

system, but not until 1911 was a comprehensive juvenile court system authorized. As early as 1905, it is true, the state's first juvenile court act was passed, but it applied only to Shelby, Davidson, and Knox counties.

Under the general law of the state in effect until 1978, county judges or chairmen acted as juvenile judges, and in some counties, trial judges or general sessions judges acted in this capacity, but special acts have provided in a number of cases for separate juvenile courts. Oftentimes these special courts also handled divorce cases and are known as juvenile and domestic relations courts.[5]

The . . . general trial court tier is a highly variegated structural arrangement.

INSTITUTE OF JUDICIAL ADMINISTRATION (1971)

IN TENNESSEE THE PRINCIPAL trial courts of general jurisdiction (as contrasted with the minor courts and specialized courts such as the juvenile courts) are the circuit courts, the chancery courts, and the criminal courts.

Tennessee is divided into thirty-one circuits in which circuit courts sit. In the big counties of the state the circuit covers one county. The remaining circuits are multicounty. Thirteen of the circuits operate in divisions, each presided over by a single judge. Judges of these courts are elected by the voters of the circuits, which they serve for terms of eight years. The circuit courts are courts of general original jurisdiction in both civil and criminal cases. Some areas of the state, however, are provided with criminal courts that have general original jurisdiction in criminal cases.

A few instances of the jurisdiction of the circuit courts will serve to illustrate the kind of work that these courts perform. To begin with, the circuit court is a court of general jurisdiction in all those cases in which jurisdiction has not been conferred upon some other court. Thus it has exclusive original jurisdiction over felonies and misdemeanors, either according to the common law or according to statute, unless such jurisdiction has been granted elsewhere. In some instances this jurisdiction has been transferred to special criminal courts. The circuit court is also given exclusive jurisdiction to determine issues contesting the validity of wills, but only upon a certificate by the county stating that the validity of the will is contested. It has jurisdiction over demands on contracts over $50.00.

---

[5]See Institute of Judicial Administration, *Preliminary Report,* pt. I, *Structure and Operations,* "Limited and Special Jurisdiction Courts," 9c; see also *The Final Report of the Legislative Council Committee of the 80th General Assembly,* 73–74; with regard to divorce and annulment matters, the council expressed the view that jurisdiction over such cases properly belonged in the chancery and circuit courts.

The circuit court may change the names of persons; it may legitimate children and authorize their adoption; it may grant divorces; it may enter judgment on awards of arbitrators.

The circuit court has general appellate and supervisory jurisdiction over inferior tribunals. Accordingly this court may review the actions of inferior bodies, including courts, councils, and boards that have been clothed with judicial functions. Therefore a juvenile adjudged delinquent by a juvenile court may obtain a review of his case in the circuit court.

The circuit court likewise has the power of a court of chancery in equity cases unless objection is raised by the judge or one of the parties, and it has authority to abate nuisances.

In certain areas of the state deemed to have sufficient criminal court business, the legislature has established special criminal courts. At present, thirteen circuits in the state have criminal courts, and in four of these there is more than one such court. In most of these circuits the arrangement of the court is such that the circuit court judges have been largely relieved of criminal work and retain only civil cases.

Tennessee is one of the few states in the United States that still use separate courts for chancery jurisdiction. The chancery court is a vestigial remain of English judicial structure. As a separate court it has been abandoned in England and largely throughout the United States.[6]

The legislature of Tennessee has created seventeen chancery divisions. In some counties certain circuit judges act as the judges of the chancery court. In a few counties, law and equity judges are elected. Judges of the chancery court, like those of the circuit and criminal courts, are elected by popular vote for eight-year terms.

Chancery courts have exclusive jurisdiction in some matters, concurrent jurisdiction in other cases, and in some cases personal and local jurisdiction. They are primarily what we call courts of equity, and they therefore have exclusive jurisdiction in the area involving powers and privileges that rightfully belong to such courts. We have inherited equity from the English experience. Briefly put, equity was a system of justice that grew up under the administration of the English king to remedy the defects and rigidities of the common law. Equity was not limited to the remedies and rules of common-law courts but was developed in order to provide justice tempered with ethical principles. In the field of their exclusive jurisdiction, the chancery courts have an inherent common law jurisdiction over certain types of cases exemplified by cases involving the administration of estates. In addition they may administer cases involving receiverships of corporations as well as controversies between the state and corporations. Chan-

---

[6]What constitutes a separate equity court is a sufficiently complicated question so that authorities do not always agree whether separation exists; see the Council of State Governments, *State Court Systems* (Lexington, Ky.: The Council, 1970), 2–9.

cery courts have original jurisdiction with regard to boundary disputes over contiguous tracts of land where the dispute is the only issue involved. These courts also have jurisdiction over the removal of the disability of a minor. In some areas the legislature has given the chancery courts concurrent jurisdiction with circuit and county courts.

Chancery courts have personal jurisdiction in that suits may be instituted in them wherever the defendant may be found, unless some other process is prescribed by law. The local jurisdiction of courts of chancery might be generally explained by saying that the suit may be commenced in the county in which the defendant may reside or in the county where the property involved is found, but actually, because of detailed and local (special) legislation, the local jurisdiction is much more complicated than can be explained here.

It must be entirely clear at this point, that the system of courts in Tennessee at the level of the circuit, chancery, and criminal courts is extremely confused. The state affords no uniform pattern covering its entire area; in effect, various portions of the state have been given special treatment. Second, a great deal of overlapping jurisdiction has arisen between the chancery and circuit courts, as well as between the circuit and criminal courts. Although we have not given very much detail regarding the jurisdiction of these courts, enough has been said to indicate that it requires a trained lawyer to determine the exact jurisdiction of these various courts and to understand in his own particular locality which court he should select for the institution of a suit. Judicial structure at this level is unnecessarily confused, and the purposes served could be taken care of by a less complicated and more nearly uniform system.

At the top is a . . . Supreme Court . . . Immediately beneath . . . and constituting the second tier are two distinct courts of appeal.

INSTITUTE OF JUDICIAL ADMINISTRATION (1971)

AT THE LEVEL ABOVE the circuit, criminal, and chancery courts in the judicial hierarchy, the state legislature has provided two appellate courts. The Court of Appeals was originally set up in order to relieve the crowded docket of the Supreme Court. Its jurisdiction is an appellate jurisdiction only. That is to say, it hears no cases for the first time but sits only for the purpose of hearing appeals from lower courts. It has jurisdiction covering all civil cases except those that involve such matters listed in the statute as constitutional questions, the right to hold office, workmen's compensation, state revenue, ouster cases, habeas corpus, and certain mandamus cases.

The Court of Appeals is composed of twelve judges, elected by the people of the entire state for a term of eight years, according to a Missouri plan formula. Not over three of the judges may reside in any one Grand Division of the state. The court may sit *en banc,* that is, as a whole, or in divisions. When the court acts in divisions, four judges sit at Knoxville, another four at Nashville, and a third group of four at Jackson. When a matter comes before one of these divisions of the court, it can be settled just as though the decision had been reached by the entire court. This division of the court into three working units enables it to keep up on its work and thus to aim toward the purpose for which it was originally established.

Before 1967, appeals of criminal cases came directly to the Supreme Court, but in that year the legislature established the Court of Criminal Appeals, to consist of three judges; in 1969 the court was enlarged to two judges from each of the Grand Divisions, plus one judge at large. The Court now consists of nine judges. This court meets in Knoxville, Nashville, and Jackson. Its judges are elected by popular vote, according to the Missouri plan, for eight-year terms. As its name implies, this court hears appeals from the trial courts in criminal matters, but further appeals to the Supreme Court are permitted.

The constitution of the state provides that the judicial power shall be vested in one Supreme Court, and in such other circuit, chancery, and other inferior courts as the legislature shall ordain and establish. It further states that the Supreme Court shall consist of five judges, of whom not more than two shall reside in any one of the Grand Divisions of the state. The judges elect one of their number as chief justice. The court is to meet at Knoxville, Nashville, and Jackson.

The constitution also provides that the jurisdiction of this court shall be appellate only, under regulations prescribed by law, but the court may also have such additional jurisdiction as was conferred by law on it at the time of the adoption of the constitution. Like that of other judges in the state, the prescribed term is eight years, and election is by popular vote. Each judge of the Supreme Court must be at least thirty-five years of age, and he must have been, before his election, a resident of the state for five years.

As the constitution is construed by the Supreme Court, the court has only appellate jurisdiction. It is without original jurisdiction; that is, no cases may originate there, and the legislature is without power to confer original jurisdiction upon it. Cases reach the Supreme Court principally by four methods: appeal, appeal in the nature of a writ of error, writ of error, and certiorari. Under statutes dating from the early nineteenth century, an appeal may be taken from a lower court to an appellate court, and the appellate court may not refuse the appeal simply for failure to assign reasons for the appeal. An appeal in the nature of a writ of error, which dates from the year 1811, may be taken from a lower to a higher court. This appeal is simply an alternative to a writ of error as a means of securing a review by a higher court. In all cases where this type of appeal may be used, an ordinary writ of error is also available. Finally, the writ of certiorari may be used. This writ may be granted whenever authorized by law and in all cases where some inferior board, tribunal, or even a single officer exercising judicial functions, is claimed to have exceeded the jurisdiction conferred upon the agency or is acting illegally, and when, in the judgment of the reviewing court, there is no other plain, speedy, or adequate remedy. The writ of certiorari brings up the record of the case from the lower court, or agency; from this record the reviewing court determines whether the lower agency has acted within its powers or whether it has acted in accordance with the requirements of the law. The writ is used to review questions of law; it is not available for a review of questions of fact *de novo*.

You can't be thirty-two years on the bench without making some enemies.

STUDENT REMARK

THE CHOICE OF WAYS of securing judges gives trouble. An independent judiciary is desired; independence demands a certain degree of freedom from party politics. At the same time some control over judicial policymaking seems good, and judicial posts are important enough to be tempting to political parties that must exist on the availability of public jobs. When the American states pulled loose from Great Britain the new states gave the legislatures a prominent position. The colonies had suffered from powerful executives and courts, and they sought correctives; consequently the new state constitutions usually provided for the selection of the judges by legislatures, although exceptions existed.[7] The first constitution of Tennessee provided that judges were to be elected by joint ballot of the General Assembly, to serve during good behavior.

The spread of Jacksonian democracy brought about a system of popular election of judges, adopted in Tennessee by a constitutional amendment of 1853. Gubernatorial appointment continued in some states, and election by the legislature remained the pattern in a few places. As of 1970 five different patterns for the selection of judges could be distinguished in the several states: partisan election, election by the legislature, appointment, nonpartisan election, and some variation of what is known as the Missouri plan.[8] By some authorities the selection schemes considered to be most

[7]See William S. Carpenter, *Judicial Tenure in the United States with Especial Reference to the Tenure of Federal Judges* (New Haven: Yale Univ. Press, 1918), 5.

[8]Cf. Richard A. Watson and Rondal G. Downing, *The Politics of the Bench and the Bar: Judicial Selection under the Missouri Nonpartisan Court Plan* (New York: Wiley, 1969).

calculated to bring party influence to bear are those of partisan election and election by the legislature, and those that emphasize the influence of the bar and deemphasize party influence are the nonpartisan election and the Missouri plan.[9] This judgment as to the relative influence of party and of bar is probably sound in a general way; certainly the intent of the Missouri plan and of nonpartisan elections is the limitation of purely political considerations in judicial selection.

The Missouri plan has secured acceptance in a number of states since its adoption in Missouri in 1940, and a version of the plan is now used for two of the appellate courts in Tennessee. In Missouri the plan is used for the appellate courts and for certain courts in the two large metropolitan areas of St. Louis and Kansas City. Essentially the plan involves appointment of the judges by the governor from a list presented to him by commissions containing lawyers, judges, and laymen. The partial adoption of the plan in Tennessee raised constitutional issues eventually resolved by a decision of the Tennessee Supreme Court.[10]

The constitution of Tennessee provides that the judges of the Supreme Court shall be elected by the qualified voters of the state. Judges of the circuit and chancery courts and of other inferior courts (together with certain lower court clerks) shall be elected by the qualified voters of the district or circuit involved. The constitution makes no mention of the two intermediate appellate courts that Tennessee now has—the Court of Appeals and, since 1967, the Court of Criminal Appeals. The constitution gives the legislature authority to create inferior courts other than the chancery and circuit courts, and this must be assumed to cover the two inferior appellate courts. Presumably the method of selecting judges for these courts should follow the methods set up for other courts, but the constitution is not specific on this point.

The selection of the inferior court judges in Tennessee is by a ballot that shows party alignment, but whether the partisan process is highly significant as compared to lawyer influence we do not know; research in this area is still to be done in Tennessee. Selection of the judges of the Court of Appeals and the Court of Criminal Appeals is now by a form of the Missouri plan.

Before the adoption of the Missouri plan for the higher courts of Tennessee, the judges of those courts were really appointed by the governor. The situation was clearly described by Dean William H. Wicker of the University of Tennessee Law College as early as 1947:

> The explanation [of good selection] seems to be that, generally speaking, Tennessee judges are not actually selected by the electorate at large. They are appointed, and the appointing agency has considerable information as to their

[9]See Kenneth N. Vines and Herbert Jacob, "State Courts," in Jacob and Vines, 281.

[10]For a more extensive critique of the Missouri plan in the past see *Government in Tennessee* (Knoxville: Univ. of Tennessee Press, 1966).

fitness for judicial office . . . nearly 60 per cent of the regular judges who have served on our Supreme Court during the last one hundred years have been appointed by the Governor in the first instance . . . approximately one-half of the regular circuit judges and chancellors who have served during the last one hundred years were likewise appointed by the Governor in the first instance. The Governor is, generally speaking, a lawyer, and even when he is not, he almost invariably seeks the advice of judges and lawyers before making judicial appointments. Judges appointed to serve out unexpired terms are generally re-elected. Even when a judge first reaches the bench through the election route, he is not as a rule selected by the electorate. He is selected by the party leaders, and the party leaders are generally lawyers who have considerable information as to their selectee's qualifications for judicial office. The election by the people is only a formal approval of such selection by the party leaders and that approval is generally obtained in Tennessee in an election in which there is no opposition.[11]

What was true in 1947 remained true thereafter. It is clear from this description that popular vote in the ordinary sense had little influence at the appellate court level, but it is also clear that party leaders were involved in the selection process;[12] it seems probable that this involvement became heavier as one went down the scale of the judicial hierarchy. The history of the Missouri plan in Missouri indicates quite clearly that any role of the governor in the appointing process is bound to include partisan considerations.

The Tennessee version of the Missouri plan was adopted in 1971. Its provisions applied to the Supreme Court, the Court of Appeals, and the Court of Criminal Appeals. This act had the stated purpose of assisting the governor in finding qualified persons, assisting the electorate in electing qualified persons, insulating the judges from political influence and pressure, and enhancing the prestige of the appellate courts. As amended, it provides for an appellate court nominating commission, consisting of eleven members, distributed, as is usual in Tennessee, among the three Grand Divisions, four members to be appointed by the governor, three members elected by the licensed practicing attorneys in the Grand Divisions concerned, and four members appointed, two each, by the two speakers of the General Assembly. Some of the members are attorneys; some, laymen. Terms are six years and staggered. As of July 1, 1971, when the statute took effect, whenever a vacancy occurs in the three appellate courts (the Supreme Court was later excepted) the nominating commission, after holding public hearings (plus private ones, if the commission

---

[11]"Constitutional Revision and the Courts,"*Proceedings of the Sixth Annual Southern Institute of Local Government* (Knoxville: Bureau of Public Administration, Univ. of Tennessee, Jan. 1947), 14.

[12]The deep involvement of the governor in judicial appointments, even in the trial courts, is amply demonstrated by the correspondence on file in the governors' papers in the State Library and Archives, as, for example, in the papers of Frank Goad Clement. See also Greene, *Lead Me On,* ch. 4.

wishes), is to nominate three persons, from which the governor shall appoint one to fill the vacancy. The governor may require further nominations until he secures a group of three that includes one acceptable to him. Judges chosen under this plan are subject to voter approval in a subsequent uncontested election.

The adoption of a form of the Missouri plan in Tennessee appears to have been supported by important opinion from the bench. But that adoption coincided roughly with the presence of a Republican governor in the capitol building, and when that governor had an opportunity to place an appointee of his final choosing (from among recommendations made by the commission) on a Supreme Court that had consisted, 100 percent, of Democrats, a stage for controversy was set, and the presence of partisan politics in the selection of Supreme Court judges came sharply to public attention. In June 1972, Judge Creson of the Supreme Court died, and after a period of confusion, William H. D. Fones of Memphis, known as a Democrat, but listed as an independent, was appointed to the Court. In 1974, Judge Fones was elected by popular vote to succeed himself; the Court remained 100 percent Democratic, but political party controversy had been clearly introduced into Supreme Court elections.

In 1973 the Assembly, dominated by the Democrats and evidently afraid Republicans would be placed on the Supreme Court, repealed the Missouri plan as related to the Supreme Court. Governor Dunn's veto of this repeal was overridden in the legislature, and the election to the Supreme Court in 1974 developed into a genuine party contest for the first time in many years.

What happened in 1973–74 was reinforced by the events of 1980. In the summer of that year, Joe Henry, a member of the Supreme Court and a colorful veteran of the Clement–Ellington campaigns, died suddenly, and Governor Lamar Alexander, reaching for black support for the Republican party, appointed a black lawyer, George Brown from Memphis, to the court. Henry had been a resident of Middle Tennessee and some persons considered that the governor should have replaced him with a Middle Tennessean, but Alexander's appointment was ruled legal.

Brown, the first black on the Court, served only a short time. Before the August primary, the Democratic nominating committee, ignoring the appeals of Memphis black Democratic leaders to back Brown, selected a respected appellate court judge, Frank Drowota of Nashville, as the nominee of the Democrats. In the election of August 1980, Drowota defeated Brown handily, in an election that had clear racial overtones. Brown carried generally the Republican areas of the first and second Congressional districts, where evidently Republicans placed the party above racial prejudice, and his own Congressional district, the eighth, in Shelby County, where black votes, normally Democratic, went for a black who was a Republican. But Brown lost all the other Congressional districts, and there was some evidence of white backlash. Some of Brown's defeat was also attributed to a low turnout of black voters and a split in the Republican vote by reason of the independent candidacy of Larry Parrish. In any case, the Supreme Court remained 100 percent Democratic, white, and male. Governor Alexander and the national Republican chairman, William Brock, were criticized by Democrats for their active support of Brown.

As long as the state is prominently Democratic the relationship between politics and the judiciary will be somewhat obscured. When most of the top judges are Democrats and contests do not arise, the political complexion of the courts will not be evident. In 1980 the three appellate courts had twenty-six judges; twenty-three of them were Democrats. In the lower courts the political divisions roughly reflect the traditional divisions in the state.[13] The Missouri plan has as one objective the lessening of partisan politics in judicial selection. Neither the Missouri experience nor the as yet more limited Tennessee practice gives any prospect of eliminating partisan politics completely.

The Missouri plan had the aim of enhancing the role of the professionals—both on the bench and in the bar—in the selection of judges. It represents an elitist, anti-Jacksonian philosophy. In this view selection of judges by the professional will give the public a better quality of law enforcement and justice. Removing the judges from partisan political influence is assumed to have similar effects. Is this in fact the case? To this question a definite answer is probably impossible. In the first place it is not clear whether partisan selection of judges has an effect on the judges' behavior. Some studies have indicated effects of this sort, although data are lacking for Tennessee.[14] In a state such as Tennessee where the judges are overwhelmingly Democrats, it may be very difficult to show significant differences between judges based on party membership, class, or culture, and even though it is certain that predilections exist, the judges of general jurisdiction courts are bound to be governed in many instances by the past decisions of the appellate judges. Whether better judges are secured by the Missouri plan is extremely doubtful; so far Tennessee's experience with the Missouri plan has been too brief for us to draw conclusions, but some evidence exists to indicate that Tennessee judges selected before the adoption of the Missouri plan were quite as good as those selected in Missouri where that plan was used.[15]

[13]We are indebted to Chief Justice Ray Brock for information on the political affiliation of judges.

[14]See, for example, Stuart Nagel, "Political Party Affiliation and Judges' Decisions," *American Political Science Review* 55:4 (Dec. 1961), 843–50.

[15]Charles William Watters, "Judicial Selection in Tennessee and Missouri: A Comparative Analysis of the Quality and Performance of Judges," master's thesis, Univ. of Tennessee, 1961.

Few people raise questions regarding the sex or race of judges in Tennessee. By far the vast majority of judges are white men. Occasionally a Negro judge is appointed or elected; Governor Clement named Ben Hooks to the criminal court in Shelby County in 1965. It was a significant appointment, for Hooks later became the national head of the NAACP. In 1979, there were four blacks on courts of general jurisdiction—three in Shelby County and one in Davidson. Women sometimes appear as candidates, successful or not, but women judges are, so to speak, rare birds. In 1980 judges in the appellate and general jurisdiction trial courts were overwhelmingly men. Judge Martha Craig Daughtrey, a member of the Court of Criminal Appeals, was the only exception.

Judges may be removed by the legislature, by either one of two different methods, but neither method has been much used.

Our law has . . . placed this . . . two-fold barrier, of a presentment and trial by jury, between the liberties of people and the prerogatives of the crown.

BLACKSTONE, *Commentaries*

ONE OF THE OLDEST FEATURES of the Anglo-American system of jurisprudence is the jury system. Juries are of two kinds; the small, or petit, jury is an agency for determining the guilt or innocence of accused parties; the large, or grand, jury is an agency for bringing an accusation against suspected persons. Both of these agencies are referred to in the state constitution. That document provides that the right of trial by jury shall remain inviolate; it also provides that the accused person is entitled to a speedy public trial by an impartial jury of the county in which the crime was committed. The constitution contains a statement that "no person shall be put to answer any criminal charge but by presentment, indictment or impeachment"; this statement was intended to preserve the method of accusation and prosecution in use under the common law. Although the grand jury is not specifically mentioned in this passage, that means of prosecution was undoubtedly in the minds of the authors of the constitution and is still used.

We may perhaps understand the functions of these two types of juries most effectively by following a case through the courts. Let us assume that a particular person is arrested inside the limits of a city for a violation of the law. If the arrest has been made for violation of a city ordinance, he will be taken before the municipal court for trial. If the arrest was for violation of a state law, he will be given a hearing before the general sessions court. If the offense is such a minor one that the fine will be not more than $50.00, he will be fined or, if he cannot pay the fine, sent to the workhouse.[16] However, assume that the offense is a serious one, punishable by something more drastic than the $50.00 fine. In this instance he will be bound over to the grand jury. "Binding over" means that his case will next be heard by the accusing agency to which he is bound.

The grand jury consists of thirteen persons. The attorney general of the county or the district (a combination of several counties) will present to this jury the evidence that the person bound over has committed the offense with which he is charged. If the grand jury is of the contrary mind, a "not true bill" will be voted. The attorney general may take the case before the grand jury without going through the preliminary procedure in the general sessions courts.

The unfortunate individual whose case we have considered in the last two paragraphs is either free now because a not true bill has been voted, or he must stand trial because a true bill has been voted. If he is to be tried, the trial will take place in a criminal court. Here the small jury functions. This jury, consisting of twelve persons, hears the evidence presented to the court and decides whether the accused person is guilty or innocent of the offense charged. If the verdict is one of innocence, the individual is free, and he may not be tried again by the State of Tennessee for that offense. If he is held guilty by the jury, his sentence is pronounced by the judge, but he may appeal to the Court of Criminal Appeals. This court may reverse the decision of the lower court, may approve it, or may send the case back to the lower court for retrial. Appeals may then be taken to the Supreme Court of the state, whose decision will be final, unless the accused person claims that the rights guaranteed him by the federal constitution have been violated or that some other question respecting the federal constitution or laws is involved, in which event an appeal may be taken to the United States Supreme Court, providing that court agrees to hear the case.

Juries are used in civil, as well as criminal, cases. The process of selecting jurymen in the State of Tennessee is little understood by the public, and it has been made even more obscure by the practice indulged in by the General Assembly of passing special acts setting up particular procedures for particular counties, different from the procedures authorized by general law. Fortunately, in 1959, the General Assembly acted to remedy this situation by enacting the uniform jury law[17] applicable to all counties of the state except the four largest—Davidson, Knox, Hamilton, and Shelby, which continue to operate under special acts designed to meet their particular needs. Under the new law, jury lists are prepared by a board of jury commissioners in each county, and uniform procedures are

---

[16]Recent U.S. Supreme Court decisions invalidate this kind of workhouse sentence; see *Williams* v. *Illinois*, 399 U.S. 235 (1970), and *Tate* v. *Short*, 401 U.S. 395 (1971).
[17]*Public Acts*, 1959, ch. 8; *TCA*, Title 22.

established for the selection and summoning of jurors and related matters.

The jury system is an old one; we cannot say that it is respected. Its continued survival in the face of the criticism heaped upon it presents us with a puzzle not easily solved. Probably, bad as the system is in many respects, alternative methods of solving guilt or innocence have dangers that do not appeal to us.

One of the most serious indictments of the jury system as operated may be said to be the failure to secure a high grade of competence among the jurors. This is a general criticism, often made, but probably hard to substantiate. An attempt to form an adequate judgment of the competence of a single person is difficult enough; when a judgment includes a large body of persons over the country and covers a long period of time, we may properly suspect the validity of that judgment. Nevertheless some fairly clear points may be made. One of these is that the law provides for the exemption from jury service of certain groups in the community whose minds have received careful training, at least in certain special fields. Such groups include employees of the federal and state governments, teachers, physicians, and clergymen. It is thought, too, that many well-qualified persons in the community evade jury service, and it is probable that most persons who wish to avoid serving can find excuses satisfactory enough to secure the consent of the judge. We have seen, too, that the selection process for jurors is rather heavily bound up with courthouse politics; there is a danger, therefore, that jury service may become a way of making a little extra cash available to "down-and-outers" who hang around the courthouse with nothing much else to occupy their time. A final criticism of the jury system is more deeply rooted in the nature of the institution: the notion that juries heed their emotions rather than their intelligence is so well established in our folklore that it is the butt of innumerable jokes. We all grow up thinking that the successful trial lawyer is a man who can sway juries.

The court has nothing to do with the policy of legislation. The legislature intended to tax . . . and we are not at liberty to give to the act a construction that would defeat such intention.

State v. Grosvenor, 149 TENN. 158, 167 (1923)

OUR JUDICIAL SYSTEM provides for the review by the court of the decisions made by lower courts. Lawyers call this "judicial review." It is generally recognized that review of this sort is essential. Another kind of review implied by the words "judicial review" has occasioned more comment. This is the review by the courts of the validity of the acts of the legislature and the actions of administrative agents as measured against the constitution. This type of review means that a court, called upon to enforce the decision of an administrative officer or the decision of a lower court taken on the basis of that officer's or that court's interpretation of the constitution or a statute, will decide whether or not the constitution permits that enforcement.

$$\bigodot$$

There are serious weaknesses in Tennessee court structure as well as strengths.

INSTITUTE OF JUDICIAL ADMINISTRATION (1971)

THE MOST THOROUGHLY unsatisfactory feature of the Tennessee judicial system is the presence of confused, overlapping, and conflicting jurisdiction. For the most part Tennessee lawyers do not seem to be greatly disturbed by this situation; they have grown up in the environment of the courts as they stand, and they do not seem eager for change. Legal scholars, on the other hand, are clearly dissatisfied. To the general public the existing situation is confused and obscure. We have, to begin with, a set of unnecessary courts in the chancery courts. The jurisdiction of these courts overlaps that of the circuit courts. In some places we have special criminal courts, but not in all.

The courts of Tennessee, as compared with some other states, seem to give reasonably prompt service, but because the load imposed on the judges varies rather markedly from one court to another, some are overworked. The slowest courts appear to be those with an unusually high percentage of indictments for misdemeanors, partly because Tennessee prosecutors and defense counsel do not use plea bargaining as much as is done in other states. Another cause of delay exists in the fact that *de novo* trials can be had in the trial courts on appeal from the minor courts.

Drastic changes have been proposed for the Tennessee judiciary with fair regularity and perhaps with mounting insistence since the late 1940s, but change will be difficult because of the necessity of amending the constitution and the essentially technical and undramatic character of the reform proposals. Some provisions regarding the courts are found in statute law; here change is quite possible if the proposed changes have the general support of the lawyers of the state, for they are powerful enough politically to secure changes if they want them. It must be remembered, however, that the lawyers of the state have, for the most part, been trained under the judicial system as it now stands and, quite aside from the fact that legal training may seem to go along with conservative dispositions, it is not to be expected that lawyers would be eager to secure reforms that would involve changes in the procedures with which they have already become familiar.

The Institute of Judicial Administration, acting on an official assignment to study the Tennessee judiciary, recommended in October 1971 that the confusing multiplicity of state courts, exaggerated as it is by the tinkering of special acts, be replaced by a greatly simplified structure, consisting of a single supreme court, one intermediate appeals court (instead of the two we now have), one court of general jurisdiction (divided into circuits), and one court of limited jurisdiction (also divided into circuits). The report also recommended simplification of procedural forms.

Finally it may be noted that many states have provided for judicial councils, committees of the judiciary organized for the purpose of studying judicial administration and making suggestions for improvements. Tennessee established such a council in 1943.

In 1963 the office of executive secretary to the Supreme Court was established. This office is the administrative facility for all state courts and handles the fiscal affairs of the judiciary as well as other functions designated by statute and by direction of the chief justice of the Supreme Court. The executive secretary is appointed by the Supreme Court and serves at its pleasure. The creation of this office and its subsequent assumption of both fiscal and administrative responsibility for the judiciary placed Tennessee as a frontrunner in the nation among efforts to provide and maintain a judicial system free and independent from the executive and legislative branches of government.

The same powerful motives which command the observance of . . . primary moralities enjoin the punishment of those who violate them.
JOHN STUART MILL (1863)

GOVERNMENTAL AGENTS are necessary to enforce the law. Judges interpret the law and give orders for its enforcement. They do not, however, start actions themselves; they act only when issues are brought before them. The individual citizen can, of course, bring actions before the courts, seeking to enforce the law. Actually a good share of law enforcement is carried on by such individuals. But, since this is not enough, special governmental agents must be provided who are empowered to take the initiative to see that the law is carried out.

Governmental agencies must likewise have special officers whose function is to exert physical force, if that is necessary, to prevent violation of the law. These officers constitute the police. The county ordinarily has no police force under that name, but the sheriff and his deputies perform that

On Sentencing Procedure. Sandy Campbell in the *Tennessean*.

function. Generally speaking, the sheriff and the deputies are not particularly efficient as police. The sheriff is elected by popular vote for a four-year term, and his deputies are his appointees; political party allegiance, rather than ability determined by a formal merit system, is likely to be the principal consideration in employment. Furthermore the system leads to fairly rapid turnover of personnel. Under these circumstances not too much efficiency can be expected.

The smaller municipalities have one or two law enforcement officers. The larger cities of the state have police forces, where at least a certain degree of professionalization is possible.

Tennessee maintains a state police system, now under the formal merit plan of the state. This is the Tennessee Highway Patrol, created in 1929. Some states have state police forces whose enforcement power is as complete within the state as that of a municipal policeman within the city. A considerable amount of opposition has arisen to this type of state police on the part of organized labor, for it is feared that such police can be used as strikebreakers. Some states therefore confine the function of the police to the enforcement of particular matters. In Tennessee the principal duties of the highway patrol relate to the enforcement of the state's highway safety laws and the liquor laws. The Tennessee Bureau of Criminal Identification is available to assist local law enforcement agencies.

Most important in the machinery of law enforcement are the attorneys who act for the public. In most states the principal prosecutor at the local level is the district or county attorney. Throughout the United States the office is a political one, often plagued by problems of low pay and part-time status. Local election increases the chance, of course, of responsiveness to local standards of law enforcement, but it leaves the office open to the evils of political patronage. The discretion of the prosecutor is very great. He can, in effect and within limits, determine which laws he shall enforce, determine whether to prosecute particular individuals, negotiate with suspected persons, and otherwise influence the quality and scope of law enforcement in his area. Usually he is not subject to any system of statewide supervision.[18] Although the constitution says that the governor shall take care that the laws be faithfully executed, he does not, in fact, enjoy wide authority to enforce the statutes. He does not initiate ordinary enforcement processes in the courts, he exercises little or no authority over local enforcement officials, and he has no state prosecuting attorney under his orders. His military powers are used only in rare emergencies and then only reluctantly, for a governor who sends the highway patrol or the National Guard into a local area is mixing in controversy that is bound to cost him some votes. Occasionally governors bring pressure to bear on

[18]For extensive information on this office in the United States, see Task Force on the Administration of Justice, *The Courts,* 72 ff.

local enforcement officials, as Governor Clement did once in his early administrations when he thought sheriffs were lax on liquor matters, but normally governors feel they have enough trouble without dipping into such affairs. Senator Victor Ashe has long advocated the creation of an officer (either a popularly elected attorney general or a solicitor general) who could initiate statewide enforcement proceedings, but he has been unable so far to marshal much support for the idea. Tennesseans are strongly devoted to local independence.

In Tennessee in every judicial circuit or district having a judge with criminal jurisdiction, the voters elect for an eight-year term a district attorney general whose principal duty is the prosecution of cases in which the state is interested. He prepares cases for both the grand jury and the petit jury. Another official, the county attorney or solicitor, provides legal opinion to guide county officials.

The principal state attorney in Tennessee is the attorney general, who is appointed by the Supreme Court for a term of eight years. It has been a rather well-established tradition in the state that the Supreme Court (which has usually consisted of five Democrats, only one of whom is an East Tennessean) appoints an East Tennessee Democrat as attorney general, but this tradition seems likely to disappear as partisan election to the top court has become more open. In 1974 the Supreme Court, after hearing applications (in itself most unusual), elected a West Tennessean as attorney general, ignoring the claim of the incumbent to reelection. The attorney general attends to business before the Supreme Court, furnishes legal aid and advice to departments of the state government and sometimes to local governments, prosecutes and defends certain cases before the courts, and reports the decisions of the Supreme Court. As the system is structured the attorney general is independent of both the legislature and the governor, and some critics find this status objectionable on the ground that his discretion on prosecution is too unfettered. Indeed Tennessee is the only state in which this system of selecting the attorney general is employed, but so far attempts to change the method have aroused only small interest.

In the past, the attorney general has had little power in the enforcement of state law. As the 1980s begin, proposals are heard to increase his power and rivalry between the governor and the attorney general has developed, perhaps partly as the expression of party conflict. The attorney general's power to prosecute was slightly expanded in 1981.

12

☆ ☆
☆

BOUGHT AND PAID FOR

☆

Moral: Men of all degrees should form this prudent habit: never serve a rabbit stew before you catch the rabbit.

JAMES THURBER (1956)

THE LEVY AND COLLECTION OF TAXES BY STATES AND LOCAL GOVERNMENTS are surrounded by certain constitutional restrictions, some of them arising from the state constitution and others from the federal constitution. The constitution of Tennessee, until amended in 1972, mandated the taxation of all property "according to its value" and forbade the taxation of any "one species of property . . . higher than any other species of property of the same value." The legislature was required to exempt direct products of the soil (from any state, as construed by the Tennessee courts) in the hands of a producer or his immediate vendee and articles manufactured from the produce of the state, and was given permissive authority to exempt governmental property, as well as property held and used for "purposes purely religious, charitable, scientific, literary or educational" (these exemption provisions were not changed by the 1972 amendment).

The ad valorem tax provisions were substantially altered by the amendment proposed by the constitutional convention of 1971, which was heavily dominated by the Farm Bureau Federation. The amendment had powerful support from the farmers, the Tennessee Municipal League, and residential property owners, a combination that overwhelmed the opposition of the utility and commercial groups.

The new provisions, subsequently approved by the voters in 1972,[1] set

[1]Art. II, sec. 28.

173

up three classes of property: real property, tangible personal property, and intangible personal property. Real property is divided into three subclasses, to be assessed at percentages of appraised full value as follows: utility property at 55 percent; industrial and commercial property at 40 percent; and residential and farm property at 25 percent. House trailers, mobile homes, and other movable structures are assessed at the rates applied to the real property on which they stand. Three subclasses of tangible personal property were established: public utility property, to be assessed at 55 percent; industrial and commercial property at 30 percent; and "all other" at 5 percent. In the case of "all other" tangible property, the legislature is directed to exempt $7,500 of the value of such items as household goods, furnishings, wearing apparel, and so forth, in the hands of the taxpayer; the implementing legislation doubles this exemption for property owned jointly by husband and wife and increases it by $7,500 for each minor child living at home if "not used by him personally."[2] A 1977 act directs an assessor of property,[3] in the absence of a tax return or schedule to the contrary, to presume that household personal property, private passenger cars, and all intangible property do not exceed $7,500 per individual or $15,000 for property jointly owned by a husband and wife.

Other statutes attempt to exempt tangible personal property effectively from taxation, presumably because of the virtual impossibility of equitable administration; locating, viewing, and placing reasonable values on all movable personal property is indeed a formidable—and probably impossible—undertaking. TCA 67–5814 permits a credit against business taxes based on gross receipts for any tangible personal property taxes that may be assessed, and TCA 67–516 authorizes county and municipal governing bodies to declare that such property has no value for taxation purposes. TCA 67–616 states the ultimate: after dutifully expressing the constitutional requirement that "all other tangible personal property shall be assessed at five percent (5%) of its value," it states, "except that for the purpose of taxation under this statute, all other tangible personal property shall be deemed to have no value"!

The 1972 constitutional amendment adopted an approach to taxation of intangible property that is now generally used in other states. Intangible property is classified and taxed at a lower rate, or exempted entirely, because locating and assessing intangibles is also administratively very difficult and full taxation as other property would be confiscatory. The amendment vested in the legislature the "power to classify Intangible Personal Property into subclassifications and to establish a ratio of

²*TCA*, 67–516.
³*TCA*, 67–606.

assessment to value in each class or subclass," and further directed it to "provide fair and equitable methods of apportionment of the value of same to this State for purposes of taxation."

Legislation has been enacted[4] to implement the provision that "Banks, Insurance Companies, Loan and Investment Companies, Savings and Loan Associations, and all similar financial institutions, shall be assessed and taxed in such manner as the Legislature shall direct." A subsequent provision eliminates the problem of trying to assess taxes against the owners of intangible properties: "the taxes imposed upon such financial institutions, and paid by them, shall be in lieu of all taxes on the redeemable or cash value of all of their outstanding shares of capital stock, policies of insurance, customer savings and checking accounts, certificates of deposit, and certificates of investment, by whatever name called, including other intangible corporate property of such financial institutions."

The 1972 constitutional amendment also ordered relief from property taxes on not less than $5,000 of the full market value of residences of persons over sixty-five years of age who receive a total annual income of $4,800 or less. The legislature was also authorized to provide tax relief to home owners totally and permanently disabled, irrespective of age, in the same manner as provided for the elderly. Implementing legislation in 1973 granted the minimum relief to the elderly and to home owners who are totally and permanently disabled as determined under rules and regulations of the state board of equalization; a 1979 act increased the exempted amount to $12,000. Disabled veterans were granted relief from property taxes due on the first $25,000 (increased to $60,000 by a 1979 act) of full market value of their homes, irrespective of their total annual incomes.

A 1979 act authorizes a county or city to freeze property taxes at the 1979 level or at the level of a later year in which the property was acquired, on residential property of persons over sixty-five years of age whose combined annual income does not exceed $12,000; subsequent improvements to such property would result in a proportionate increase of the tax amount.[5]

Another provision of article II, section 28 preserved in the 1972 amendment empowers the legislature to tax "merchants, peddlers and privileges, in such manner as they may from time to time direct." To the foregoing, the 1972 amendment added "and the Legislature may levy a gross receipts tax on merchants and businesses in lieu of ad valorem taxes on the inventories of merchandise held by such merchants and businesses for sale or exchange." The latter provision validated the Business Tax Act of 1971[6] which placed a gross receipts tax on businesses in lieu of ad valorem taxes

[4]*TCA*, title 67, ch. 7.
[5]*TCA*, 67–670 to 67–674.
[6]Codified as *TCA*, title 67, ch. 58.

on inventories. The reference to privileges in this provision is of considerable significance, as it is the constitutional basis of all non-property taxes levied by the state (the Tennessee courts have held that taxes are of two types only: property and privilege).

The legislature has provided tax incentives for open space lands in urban areas.[7] Owners can petition the county assessor to classify lands as "agricultural," "forest," or "open space," and if so classified by the asessor the land is assessed on a basis of its current use; and a procedure is established for cumulative taxation if the land is subsequently converted to any other use.

The 1972 amendment is one of the most important to be added to the 1870 constitution. Its primary object was to substitute for the uniform property tax a classified property tax, which had the effect of burdening utility and business property more heavily than farm and residential property. While the classified property tax has often been justified on the ground that it permits favorable treatment, for reasons of public policy, for programs such as conservation and environmental projects—forests, parks, wildlife preserves, and so on—this amendment gives an advantage to farmers and homeowners at the expense of the commercial world and particularly of the utilities, except insofar as commercial firms may shift the tax burden through increased prices. It places in the constitution the long-established practice (declared illegal in 1966) of assessing utilities at levels higher than some other classes of property. An attack on the differential levels as being arbitrary and discriminatory was rejected by a federal district court.[8]

The amendment also severely limits the legislature, for it specifically sets the assessment ratios of the various classes, thus putting in the constitution matters that might better have been left to legislative discretion. Uniformity of assessment within each class of property is constitutionally required, but the proclivity of taxing authorities to overload the utilities apparently has not been curbed. In 1978 a federal district court ordered reductions in assessments of railroads and of the South Central Bell Company on grounds that the basis of applying the prescribed 55 percent was 100 percent of their properties' full value while the basis (statewide) for residential and farm property was about 60 percent of actual value (discrepancies in some counties were alleged to be even greater). Such discrepancies are no doubt largely the result of assessments of utilities by the Public Service Commission, aided by a professional staff, while residential and farm properties are assessed by locally elected assessors. Following this litigation the State Board of Equalization directed that railroads and utilities be assessed at the same level as other property in each county, as indicated by state-conducted sales ratio studies.

---

[7]*TCA*, 67–651 to 67–658.

[8]*Louisville & Nashville R. Co.* v. *Atkins*, 390 Fed. Supp. 576 (1975). However, the railroads gained some relief through federal legislation.

In 1923 the legislature of Tennessee enacted a 3 percent excise tax on the net earnings of corporations. Although legally an excise tax, this levy was frequently referred to as a corporate income tax, and its constitutionality was immediately challenged on the ground that the new law violated the uniformity clause of the constitution. The state Supreme Court sustained the act on the ground that the tax on corporations was not a property but a privilege tax, and it was therefore not necessary to observe the uniformity clause. After several increases, the last in 1971, the rate of this tax is now 6 percent.

In 1929 an act was passed exempting stocks and bonds from ad valorem taxes and taxing the income therefrom at a rate of 5 percent, based upon a recommendation of a special tax commission created in 1915 that such a tax be levied at 10 percent. A challenge to the act resulted in a Supreme Court ruling that the constitutional clause authorizing this type of tax permitted the legislature to tax stocks and bonds according to value, or if it preferred, to exempt them from ad valorem taxes and levy a tax on the income derived from such securities.[9]

The securities income decision did not, of course, touch on the question of a general personal and graduated income tax. The joining of that issue was delayed until 1931, when the strained financial condition of the state evoked an act levying a direct tax on individual and corporate incomes, the former on a progressive, the latter on a flat rate basis.[10] In a test case the state Supreme Court invalidated the act on the ground that it violated Article II, section 28 of the constitution, which states that property must be taxed uniformly and equally, according to value.[11] Critics have pointed out that this decision was inconsistent with the court's previous decision that had upheld the corporate income tax on the ground that it was a privilege tax and not a property tax.

Support for an income tax persists, however, and many groups and individuals over the years have endorsed the tax. The latest plea for the income tax came in early 1981 from Herbert Bingham of the Tennessee Municipal League, not exactly a surprising development, given the fiscal pressures on Tennessee cities and the long record of support by the league for broader taxing authority generally. Three approaches have been suggested to overcome the 1932 negative court decision: a constitutional amendment, another act and test case in hopes that a new court would reach a different decision, and a levy on the privilege of engaging in business and occupational activity measured by the amount of income

[9]*Shields et al.* v. *Williams*, 159 Tenn. 349 (1929).
[10]*Public and Private Acts of Tennessee*, 1931, 2d ex. sess., ch. 21.
[11]*Evans* v. *McCabe*, 164 Tenn. 672 (1932). For a critical review of this decision, see T. McN. Simpson, III, "The Tennessee Constitution and the Income Tax," *Tennessee Bar Journal* 10:1 (Feb. 1974), 27–31.

TABLE 12-1
STATE REVENUES BY SOURCE
ALL GOVERNMENTAL FUNDS[a]
FISCAL YEARS 1969, 1973, 1977, 1980

(Expressed in thousands)

Source	1969	1973	1977	1980
Tax Revenues				
Sales and Use	$208,290	$ 370,905	$ 690,079	$ 924,007
Gasoline	64,691	84,402	96,153	94,167
Motor Fuel	6,925	12,328	16,271	19,646
Gasoline Inspection	21,743	28,754	22,202	20,062
Motor Vehicle				
Registration	54,193	68,508	85,809	90,761
Income	7,923	10,665	15,791	21,403
Privilege	8,371	13,504	21,218	28,473
Gross Receipts	11,793	20,329	38,463	77,051
Alcoholic Beverage	13,719	18,393	21,294	23,217
Franchise	15,805	24,396	32,249	43,938
Excise	61,633	102,978	156,042	198,222
Inheritance and Estate	19,566	31,488	41,247	28,307
Tobacco	36,586	58,103	67,829	73,819

Table 12-1 (*cont.*)

Insurance Companies				
Premium	18,763	28,624	43,525	60,006
Unemployment				
Insurance	45,336	69,326	95,678	161,844
Other	8,043	14,530	22,557	26,818
Totals—Tax Revenues	$603,380	$ 957,233	$1,466,407	$1,891,741
Other Sources				
Licenses, Fees, and Permits	$ 16,242	$ 21,488	$ 29,095	$ 38,260
Interest on Investments	14,452	23,624	33,586	92,012
Federal	267,175	474,057	804,226	1,150,746
Departmental Services	34,851	86,083	131,167	170,570
Other	699	2,110	4,503	10,083
Totals—Other Sources	$333,419	$ 607,362	$1,002,577	$1,461,671
Total Revenues	$936,799	$1,564,595	$2,468,984	$3,353,412

[a]General Fund, Highway Fund, Employment Security Fund, Debt Service Fund, and Capital Projects Fund. Revisions in data reported in previous years have been made to conform with standards in *Governmental Accounting, Auditing and Financial Reporting*, prepared by the National Committee on Governmental Accounting in 1968.

Source: State of Tennessee, *Annual Financial Report*; for the year ended June 30, 1978, pp. 50–51; for the year ended June 30, 1980, pp. 62–63. (Nashville: Comptroller of the Treasury and Department of Finance and Administration).

received (so-called "payroll taxes" have been sustained on this basis on grounds they are not income taxes; such a levy, however, would not reach other types of income, such as from investments, rentals, and the like). The principal stumbling block, however, is the legislature. Several moves to initiate a constitutional amendment have drawn little support, and passage of a new act seems highly unlikely.

We have commented on the principal express restrictions on taxation in the Tennessee constitution. To provide a detailed discussion of the restrictions that can be inferred from the terms of the state and federal constitutions would take us considerably beyond the scope of this study. One or two cardinal points may be made. Taxation must be for a public purpose; this is equivalent to saying that the money collected from taxation must be spent for a public, not a private, goal. What constitutes a public purpose in a specific instance is for the courts to determine whenever a challenge to a tax or an expenditure reaches them. As a general principle, the state may not tax the federal government or its instrumentalities, and the reverse also holds true (although states and local units in practice pay many federal charges). But, again, the courts determine how far this principle may be carried. For example, it used to be considered unconstitutional for the federal government to levy an income tax on the salaries of state officials and employees, but this is no longer the view of the courts. Generally, too, when a state engages in a business for profit, it may be expected to pay federal taxes, although the same taxes would not be levied against the operations of the state in carrying on the functions of government. The widespread activities of the federal government in these days have made this question more important; several federal agencies, such as the Tennessee Valley Authority, although they do not pay state taxes, have received permission from Congress to make payments to the states and local governments in lieu of taxes.

Tennessee's tax structure has grown in a highly haphazard way. As the means of financing government have been debated over the years, no doubt rudimentary notions of fairness and equity have received some attention, but the main consideration has been how to secure revenue in substantial quantities from sources that will bear impositions without unduly sharp political or economic reactions. A prominent tax authority once expressed as a cardinal axiom that raising taxes is like plucking feathers—"pluck the most feathers with the least squawk."

The sales and use tax produced about 28 percent of the state's total revenue in 1979–80. Originally levied at a 2 percent rate in 1947, the rate is now 4.5 percent (consisting of a "permanent" rate of 3 percent and a "temporary" rate of 1.5 percent that has been levied on an annual basis since 1976). The "and use" in the designation reflects that part of the law which makes the tax apply to products imported into the state and used here, to the extent that this is permissible under federal strictures respecting taxation of interstate commerce.

The original sales tax applied only to retail sales and rentals of tangible personal property, but the base was broadened in 1963 to include most services and sales of electricity, water, and gas. In 1976 prescription drugs were exempted and the rate on energy fuels and electricity for residential use was reduced to 1.5 percent. A number of other minor exemptions have been added in recent years. The tax is fairly easy to administer and relatively painless on the taxpayer, as it is usually paid in small amounts. But it applies to products and services consumed daily and bears more heavily on low-income people.

Several taxes apply to the use of motor vehicles: gasoline, at the rate of 10 cents per gallon (8 cents prior to June 1, 1981); other motor fuel, at 13 cents per gallon (9 cents prior to June 1, 1981); and annual registration (license plates or decals). Together these sources provide about 7 percent of total revenue (revenue from drivers' licenses is reported under "licenses, fees, and permits," and from motor vehicle title fees as a part of "other" taxes). A proposal to shift the gasoline and other motor fuels taxes from a gallonage basis to a percentage of sales price, to offset declining consumption and to meet increasing costs of highway construction, had considerable support, but it failed largely because Governor Alexander would not give his approval to the measure.

A number of taxes are levied on business activities. Since 1923 corporations have paid an excise tax on net earnings from business done within the state; the present rate is 6 percent. A franchise tax on corporations, added in 1935, is levied at a rate of 15 cents per $100 of stock, surplus, and undivided profits or of the actual value of property owned or used in Tennessee, whichever is greater. An insurance companies premium tax is 2 percent on gross premiums of non-Tennessee companies and 1.75 percent on companies chartered in this state; included in the revenue reported from this source are also various fees and charges paid by insurance agents. The "gross receipts" tax source includes several rates applied to the gross receipts of certain businesses subject to taxation by the state only. The "privilege" tax source consists of taxes on court litigation, transfers of realty, and recording of mortgages. The "other taxes" category includes the 15 percent state share of local taxes (county and city) imposed at varying rates on certain businesses, vocations, and occupations, under the business tax act of 1971; a tax on building (savings) and loan associations of 3 percent of their gross profits; motor vehicle title fees; and corporation filing fees. Some of these taxes can be taken as credits against other taxes due, so the full amounts calculated by applying the foregoing rates are not paid by all businesses. Altogether these sources account for about 13 percent of total revenue.

Tennessee's taxes on the income from stocks and bonds and on inheritances and estates together produce less than 1.5 percent of total revenue. The income tax was enacted in 1929 to apply in lieu of the ad valorem property tax, at a rate of 5 percent on all such income; this was changed in 1937 to the present rates: 6 percent on dividends from stocks and interest on bonds, except that the rate is only 4 percent on stock dividends from companies that have more than 75 percent of their corporate property within the state. The inheritance and estate tax is an indirect privilege tax on the transfer of property by inheritance or by gift. Recipients are divided into two classes: Class A includes husband, wife, son, daughter, and lineal ancestors and descendants; and Class B includes all others. Variable rates apply, from 1.4 percent to 20 percent, graduated by amount and higher for Class B recipients. The state was encouraged to levy this tax by a federal law that would levy the federal estate tax if no state tax were collected.

The unemployment insurance tax, ranging from .4 to 4.0 percent of taxable wages (dependent on an employer's experience rating), produced about 5 percent of the total in 1979–80; all of this revenue is deposited in the Employment Security Fund. The tax on tobacco products brought in more than 2 percent (almost $74 million).

Federal aid is the largest of the nontax (at least non-state-tax) revenue sources, accounting for 34 percent of the state's total revenue in 1979–80. Charges made by state departments and agencies for current services (such as charges to private patients at state institutions and fees at state parks) produce 5 percent. Various licenses, fees, and permits bring in barely 1 percent. Interest on investments has ranged from 1.4 percent (1976–77) to over 3 percent (1974–75) in the twelve year period; the largest amount was collected in 1979–80. All other sources have produced negligible amounts.

The chief agency of the state in the assessment and collection of state taxes is the Department of Revenue which, like other operating departments, is headed by a commissioner appointed by the governor. This department collects directly from the taxpayers such taxes as the alcoholic beverage tax, beer tax, franchise and excise tax, income and inheritance tax, motor fuel tax, sales tax, and tobacco tax. The state uses county officials to collect certain taxes and fees, such as motor vehicle title and registration fees.

The distribution of responsibility for providing public services among the three levels of government . . . does not correspond at all well with their respective tax-raising capabilities.

DICK NETZER (1970)

WHERE WILL THE MONEY COME FROM to support present-day and future governmental requirements? At least three separate methods have been suggested to increase state revenues: (1) the imposition of new taxes, (2) the reimposition of repealed taxes, and (3) changes in existing tax laws with respect to such things as scope or coverage of individual taxes, tax rates, and credits and exemptions. To this we might add, of course, improving the effectiveness of tax administration. The principal problem here is in finding solutions to the revenue dilemma that will not only satisfy questions of legality and justice but will also be accepted by the public without undue protests.

Governor Ellington pledged himself, in his messages to the General Assembly in 1959 and again in 1961, to a program of continuation and improvement of state services without new or increased taxes. This would be possible, according to the governor, as a result of vigorous enforcement of existing tax laws, the continued promotion of a program of economy and efficiency within the government, and the continued expansion and growth of industry. When Governor Clement took office again in 1963, he found it necessary to ask for legislative authority for a broadened tax base. The needs of the state had become greater. Among other actions, the legislature expanded the coverage of the sales tax; this change, particularly the extension of the tax to utility bills, aroused considerable animosity. Increases in revenue from existing sources and in federal aid have enabled succeeding governors to maintain the state's programs, and to improve some (such as Governor Dunn's upgrading of mental health services), without imposing new taxes.

In 1947 the General Assembly created a tax revision commission to make a thorough study of the state tax system. The commission reported that, on the whole, the tax system was good. Its major inadequacies were found at the local levels, where growing needs for services have exceeded local tax resources. The commission recommended the introduction of improved local accounting systems, annual reports, better budget systems, and more speedy audits as possible improvements in administration at the local level. At the state level it recommended that appointments of personnel be made under the merit system and that more extensive use be made of statistical machinery and field audits, among other things. The commission also made specific recommendations pertaining to the improvement of tax legislation and amendment of the constitution to provide for a classified property tax. The recommendations of the commission bore little fruit (the classified property tax adopted by constitutional amendment in 1972 was the result of court cases won by the railroads— not of the commission's work).

A tax modernization and reform commission created in 1972 made important recommendations for changes in the tax structure of the state and local governments. The most important conclusion of the commission was that the tax structure was inadequate on two main counts: it is significantly regressive at low levels of income and it is relatively unresponsive to economic growth. The Tennessee structure, state and local, depends heavily on the property tax and on taxes on consumers. A number of recommendations were offered, the most controversial of which was the imposition of a personal income tax and the reduction of the property tax.[12] It is questionable whether the imposition of a personal income tax would result in the reduction of a local property tax; the immediately expressed dissatisfaction of Tennessee Municipal League officials with the idea of an enforced reduction of the local property tax illustrates how unlikely it is that such a substitution would occur. It seems more likely that an income tax would be only another added tax, a condition that accounts in great measure for the decided unpopularity of the income tax with the Tennessee voter, no matter how just and reasonable such a tax may be. The report of the reform commission brought the income tax out into the open again and generated much public discussion, but it failed completely to motivate the General Assembly to risk the imposition of such a tax.

The regressive character of the Tennessee tax structure is duplicated in most tax structures in the United States. The property tax falls heavily on the poor, and consumer taxes, which are widely used, are clearly regressive. Even the graduated personal income tax, which is supposed to be progressive, is partially regressive because of the numerous exemptions permitted under the tax. Regressivity is undesirable, but a high and stable yield is desirable, and that high and stable yield cannot be readily secured by progressive schedules. Tax relief for the poor is very likely to result in a higher burden for the middle classes, including the lower middle class, for there are not enough rich to assume all the burden. Beginning with the severe cutback in California's property taxes by a statewide referendum in 1978, the level of taxes in general and the amount of funds that should be committed to the public sector have been much discussed. Where all of this might lead, and the impact on public services, is currently problematical.

Tennessee like other states concentrates heavily on sales taxes and automobile taxes. Unlike most other states it has refused to use the progressive income tax; five states levy none, and two others, like Tennessee, tax only limited income and not salaries and wages. Comparatively few states emphasize the income tax. One study indicates that Tennesseans are required to pay less of their income in state and local taxes than are residents of other states; the percentage (9.56) of average

[12]*Summary Report on Tax Modernization and Reform: A Second Interim Report by the Tax Modernization and Reform Commission of the State of Tennessee* (Nashville, Sept. 1973); and *Final Report of the Tax Modernization and Reform Commission* (Nashville, March 1974).

resident personal income taxed in Tennessee in 1974 and 1975 placed the state forty-eight among the states in this respect.[13]

⊛

State-local expenditure is dominated by resource-allocation activities.

DICK NETZER (1970)

COMPLAINT ABOUT GOVERNMENTAL EXPENDITURES is an old story; some of the time that complaint has been mixed with a genuine measure of alarm. This is one of the areas, too, where statistics and loose talk have often been mixed without too careful regard for the complete picture. A typical propaganda statement is that the citizen worked so many days out of his year in order to support the government. The statement is misleading. The citizen worked a certain number of days in order to provide everything from military uniforms to missiles and then, added thereto, he secured schools and teachers for his children; streets and highways on which he could get from here to there for reasons no doubt appearing to him entirely reasonable and necessary; sewage disposal systems; a certain modicum of protection against epidemics and other threats to ill health; a variety of other services, some of which he probably didn't always want (but which his neighbors probably did want); and, finally, a fairly high degree of protection of life and property which we do not seem able to do without. Now, this is not to say that what he got was exactly what he wanted or that he shouldn't have had it in return for less effort, if government had been better managed. But the notion that the taxpayer gets nothing at all from governmental expenditures is thorough nonsense.

At the same time the dynamics of politics is such that new tasks, and fresh expenditures, are continually thrust on or assumed by government. More time is spent in trying to find money for new ventures than in trying to curb expenses or eliminate functions. There is a case for leaving as much to the private sector as possible, for it allows the private person to allocate his resources as he wishes; public expenditure does not offer that kind of choice to the individual.

The adoption of a state constitutional property tax limitation by the voters of California in 1978 sent shock waves into other states, generating much speculation as to the possibilities and consequences of a "tax revolt." Tennessee voters earlier in the same year adopted a constitutional limitation on state spending that is not nearly as rigid, but we may see still more action directed toward the objective of tax reduction. Some very

[13]*Measuring the Fiscal "Blood Pressure" of the States—1964–1975* (Washington: Advisory Commission on Intergovernmental Relations, Feb. 1977).

TABLE 12-2

STATE EXPENDITURES BY FUNCTION
ALL GOVERNMENTAL FUNDS[a]
SELECTED FISCAL YEARS 1969–79

(In thousands)

Function	1969	1973	1977	1980
Education	$371,256	$ 565,137	$ 856,288	$1,230,510
Health and Social Services	218,976	429,033	824,168	1,197,936
Transportation	205,758	236,181	329,844	479,599
General Government	24,630	53,242	141,814	174,117
Law, Justice, and Public Safety	31,693	52,846	99,592	145,516
Capital Outlay	48,633	37,261	110,395	89,383
Debt Service	26,456	41,243	76,566	78,104
Recreation and Resources Development	17,146	27,855	44,994	64,538
Regulation of Business and Professions	3,227	4,941	9,900	13,808
Totals	$947,775	$1,447,739	$2,493,561	$3,473,511

[a]General Fund, Highway Fund, Employment Security Fund, Debt Service Fund, and Capital Projects Fund.
Source: State of Tennessee, *Annual Financial Report*; for the year ended June 30, 1978, p. 49; for the year ended June 30, 1979, p. 64 (Nashville: Comptroller of the Treasury and Department of Finance and Administration).

serious problems will undoubtedly face future governors and legislators as they wrestle with the inflationary spiral, mounting costs of retirement systems as the rolls of retirees lengthen, and other seemingly inexorable forces demanding still more public expenditures (for example, united actions by public employees wanting pay increases, and court orders to upgrade the state's correctional and penal system).

Table 12-2 shows state expenditures for major functional areas. Education (universities, colleges, technical schools, the public school system, and the state department of education) ranked first, followed closely by health and social services; together these two areas accounted for 70 percent of the total in 1979-80. Transportation has ranked third.

How far [is it] right or expedient to raise money . . . not by laying on taxes . . . but by taking a portion of the capital of the country in the form of a loan?

JOHN STUART MILL (1848)

WE HAVE BECOME all too familiar with the phenomenon of government debt. State constitutions quite ordinarily contain provisions regulating the authority of the state to incur debt, and Tennessee is no exception. Thus, Article II, section 31 of our constitution states: "The credit of this State shall not be hereafter loaned or given to or in aid of any person, association, company, corporation or municipality; nor shall the State become the owner in whole or in part of any bank or a stockholder with others in any association, company, corporation or municipality." According to Article II, section 33, "No bonds of the State shall be issued to any Rail Road company which at the time of its application for the same shall be in default in paying the interest upon the State bonds previously loaned to it or that shall hereafter and before such application sell or absolutely dispose of any State bonds loaned to it for less than par." These restrictions are a reflection of that era of state government in this country when credit was freely extended to shaky enterprises concerned in the development of internal improvements. The sad experience of that period resulted in a constitutional resolve never to do it again. Actually the state constitution of Tennessee has far fewer debt restrictions than many of the states.

A debt retirement plan was designed in 1937, when Tennessee's general bonded debt was $129 million (principal only), and by 1958 the total actually declined to $114 million. Subsequent reports by the state have shown future interest amounts as well (as much of an obligation as the repayment of principal), and table 12–3 shows both principal and interest at two points since 1958; the total increased 672 percent from 1958 to

1978. From 1978 to 1980 the net debt declined by 16.5 percent to $809,175,000 (principal $603,020,000, interest $208,976,000, less funds on hand $2,821,000).

TABLE 12–3
STATE GENERAL BONDED DEBT
1963 AND 1978

	1963	1978
Principal	$142,050,000	$698,940,000
Interest	35,595,075	272,004,000
Totals	177,645,075	970,944,000
Funds on hand	3,003,528	1,800,000
Net debt totals	$174,641,547	$969,144,000

Sources: State of Tennessee, *Annual Financial Reports* (Nashville: Comptroller of the Treasury and Department of Finance and Administration).

Reports by the U.S. Bureau of the Census show principal amounts only and are the only data available for comparing Tennessee with other states, in three classifications: (1) long-term debt backed by the full faith and credit of the state, reported as "general bonded debt"; (2) long-term debt backed only by pledged revenues, reported as "nonguaranteed debt"; and (3) "short-term debt," which is not divided as to whether guaranteed or not. General bonded per capita debts in 1978 ranged from none in ten states to $1,981 in Alaska; twenty-two states had higher amounts than Tennessee's $185 per capita. All types of debt ranged from $38 per capita in Nebraska to $3,755 in Alaska; twenty-seven states were above Tennessee's figure of $352.[14]

[14]U.S. Department of Commerce, Bureau of the Census, *State Government Finances in 1978* (Nov. 1979), 55–58. Populations in 1970 were used for calculating per capita amounts. These are gross amounts and do not reflect funds on hand for retirement of debt.

13

☆ ☆
☆

URBAN GOVERNMENTS:
TASKS AND TECHNIQUES

As far back as one can look in recorded history, there appears to have been a steady trend of population increase on this planet—a trend that has accelerated in this century and will assume uncertain proportions in the future. Seemingly most of these people want to live in or near cities and towns. The pull of the amenities and conveniences of urban living and the location of jobs because of the industralization of our economy, and the push of large-scale, mechanized agriculture, have greatly increased the proportion of our population who reside in urbanized areas.

The data in table 13–1 indicate that Tennessee has lagged behind the national averages in this respect, but less so in recent decades as the industrialization of the state has accelerated. The national urban proportion in 1900 was 39.6 percent, which compared with 16.2 percent in Tennessee; in 1970 the national average was 73.5 percent, and in Tennessee the urban proportion was 58.8 percent (this includes residents of urbanized fringes around cities and is therefore higher than the 55.1 percent living inside cities, as shown in table 13–2). The 1970 proportion of Tennessee residents living in the census-defined four large metropolitan areas was 48.9 percent; in 1980 over half of the state's people were living in these four urbanized areas in and near Memphis, Nashville, Knoxville, and Chattanooga.

Since 1970 the federal government has recognized (in addition to the previous four big areas) an SMSA (Standard Metropolitan Statistical Area) consisting of Sullivan, Washington, Carter, Unicoi, and Hawkins counties and two counties in southwest Virginia, and another composed of Montgomery County, Tennessee, and Christian County, Kentucky.[1]

[1]The four original "metro" areas still have major political significance.

TABLE 13-1
URBAN AND RURAL POPULATION PERCENTAGES
UNITED STATES AND TENNESSEE
1900–70

| | United States | | Tennessee | |
	Urban	Rural	Urban	Rural
1900[a]	39.6	60.4	16.2	83.8
1910[a]	45.6	54.4	20.2	79.8
1920[a]	51.2	48.8	26.1	73.9
1930[a]	56.1	43.9	34.3	65.7
1940[a]	56.5	43.5	35.2	64.8
1950[a]	59.6	40.4	38.4	61.6
1960[a]	63.0	37.0	45.7	54.3
1950[b]	64.0	36.0	44.1	55.9
1960[b]	69.9	30.1	52.3	47.7
1970[b]	73.5	26.5	58.8	41.2

Source: U.S. Census, 1970.
[a]Based on previous definitions of urban and rural.
[b]Based on current definitions of urban and rural.

The problems arising from such congregations of people are myriad and complex. Municipal policymakers and administrators face insuperable odds in trying to cope, and citizens damn their efforts. Some would probably concur with Thomas Jefferson's comment: "I view great cities as pestilential to the morals, the health and the liberties of man."

(★★★)

Municipal corporations owe their origin to, and derive their powers . . . wholly from the legislature . . . unless there is some constitutional limitation.

DILLON, CHIEF JUSTICE (1868)

IN THE CONTEMPLATION of the law, the city is merely the creature of the state. The city is a corporation operating under a charter granted by the state; with this charter of incorporation the city is given its being, its structure, and its powers and duties. In the absence of constitutional restrictions (some of which do exist in Tennessee), the charter can be altered by the state; it can even be withdrawn and the city, as a government, abolished. Small communities have disappeared, in this way, from time to time. Large communities do not disappear, but the state by statutes both general and local controls the way in which their governmental lives shall

TABLE 13–2
NUMBERS OF TENNESSEE CITIES BY POPULATION RANGES
1950, 1960, 1970, AND 1980

Population Range	1950			1960			1970			1980		
	No. of Cities	Aggregate Population	% of Total	No. of Cities	Aggregate Population	% of Total	No. of Cities	Aggregate Population	% of Total	No. of Cities	Aggregate Population	% of Total
Over 100,000	4	826,117	58.5	4	910,234	53.4	4	1,168,086	54.0	4	1,352,117	51.5
50,000 - 100,000										1	54,777	2.1
25,000 - 50,000	2	58,071	4.1	4	119,046	7.0	6	192,102	8.9	8	260,161	10.0
10,000 - 25,000	9	123,814	8.8	16	234,853	13.8	20	304,317	14.1	24	362,206	13.8
5,000 - 10,000	23	160,678	11.4	22	152,701	8.9	26	181,429	8.4	32	226,704	8.6
2,500 - 5,000	26	95,479	6.8	33	122,870	7.2	38	137,361	6.4	45	164,200	6.2
1,000 - 2,500	60	94,187	6.7	65	103,730	6.1	65	106,387	4.9	86	136,416	5.2
Under 1,000	114	52,836	3.7	130	61,991	3.6	144	71,879	3.3	131	67,978	2.6
All cities	238	1,411,182	100.0	274	1,705,425	100.0	303	2,161,561	100.0	331	2,624,559	100.0
State total population		3,291,718			3,567,089			3,924,164			4,590,750	
Cities total pop. as % of state total		42.9			47.8			55.1			57.2	

Source: U.S. Census, except 1970 and 1980 for Nashville. The population of the urban services district of the Nashville metro government for these years, as certified for distributing state-shared taxes, was used instead of the U.S. census figure for all of Davidson County (this was the only census enumeration reported for the metro government). It should also be noted that the data in this table do not include urbanized areas around cities.

shall be passed. (Memphis for a while in the late 1800s lost its charter and existed as a taxing district, as a result of state legislation.)

The city exists for a dual purpose. Part of its existence is to be attributed to the need for the provision of certain services for the locality, many of which are made necessary by the gathering of large numbers in a limited space. For example, rural people can live with outdoor privies or, if they are fortunate, with septic tanks, but a large city that fails to provide a sewage disposal system is flirting with catastrophe. The city is like an organism; health depends upon the successful elimination of waste products.

But the city also exists as an agent of the state. Through it the state carries out, in great measure, its principal functions: the provision of education, the promotion of health, the protection of public morality, and, to some degree, the defense of the realm. Indeed, not a few of the services of the state (and indeed of the national government) reach its rural people through agencies housed in the central city.

When we say that the city is a creature of the state, we do not thereby imply that it is a creature of any particular state agency. Some state constitutions have elaborate provisions to govern the relationships between state agencies and the cities. Where these provisions are absent, however, it is the state legislature that, through its power to pass acts regulating city affairs, has complete authority over urban life. Until 1953 this was the situation in Tennessee, as there had been no significant state constitutional restrictions on the legislature's powers over Tennessee cities. The General Assembly was able to pass acts generally applicable to cities and towns (no distinction is made between these two terms) or local or private acts applicable to particular towns alone. Both types of legislation were in constant use.

This arrangement was changed with the revision of the state constitution in 1953. Local, or private, legislation that would remove incumbents from office, abridge terms of office, or alter salaries was outlawed by that revision, and any other private act will be considered void unless it requires the approval of the local governing body by a two-thirds vote, or by a majority of those voting in a referendum in the city or county affected. Moreover, the constitution, as amended, provides for optional home rule. If adopted by the voters of a municipality, home rule permits the municipality to frame, adopt, and amend its own charter without resort to the legislature and prohibits the legislature from adopting private acts applying to that municipality. Such a system permits the citizens of a municipality to frame a charter that is designed to meet community needs and, at the same time, frees the legislature for consideration of legislation of general concern to the state as a whole.

In addition to constitutional grants, cities have those powers that are granted to them by general or private acts of the state legislature. When a city operates entirely under the general law, we speak of it as being "chartered," or incorporated, under general law provisions. The more usual rule in Tennessee has been for each city to operate under a private or special act (frequently amended, in many cases), which is referred to as its "charter."[2] The practice of special legislation (private acts) permits considerable variety and experimentation, but as an indirect result the student of Tennessee government can make only broad generalizations about city governments in this state.

This pattern could change now that home-rule charters have been provided for by constitutional amendment, but so far comparatively few cities have adopted home rule, although those that have include some of the very large cities. The legislature can no longer pass special acts applicable to such cities, but, of course, state legislation on matters of general concern is still equally applicable to all cities, except on the subject of pay of municipal employees.[3] As of 1965, twelve years after adoption of the home-rule amendment, only twelve Tennessee cities had voted to assume home-rule status.[4] Chattanooga adopted home rule in 1972, bringing the total number to thirteen; two efforts to abandon home rule by referendums in 1976 and 1978 failed; abandonment has not been attempted in the other cities. It is clear that home rule is not a particularly lively issue. With the exception of Memphis, all home-rule cities are in East Tennessee.

From time to time when cities seek to exercise powers, questions are raised about their authority to do so. In order to be as fully protected as possible from adverse court decisions, the city charters granted by the legislature usually contain long lists of city powers, phrased in a variety of ways, so as to remove any question about the city's right to move ahead. The charter's statement of what the city may do in no way accurately reflects what the city does. Indeed there is nothing in the fact of incorporation as a city that of itself guarantees that the city will perform any functions at all. The powers of the city are mostly permissive; the city is not compelled to perform them. There have been in Tennessee a number of very small communities incorporated as cities which never became activated. In the past some towns had officers but no city functions and, happily, no debts and no taxes. This simply means that governmental functions in that area have been left to the county. Some small towns spend only what they receive from state-shared taxes; few such towns receive any federal grants.

[2]Of the 334 cities in existence on July 1, 1980, 105 were organized under general law charters, 228 had private act charters, and one (Nashville) had a locally drafted charter under a general law providing for a metro government (combined city and county).

[3]See Victor C. Hobday, *An Analysis of the 1953 Tennessee Home Rule Amendments,* 2d ed. (Knoxville: Bureau of Public Administration and MTAS, Univ. of Tennessee, 1976).

[4]Clinton, East Ridge, Etowah, Johnson City, Knoxville, Lenoir City, Memphis, Oak Ridge, Red Bank, Sevierville, Sweetwater, and Whitwell.

When a question is raised concerning the authority of a city to carry out a function, the answer will be sought in any special or private acts that have been passed by the General Assembly concerning that city, in its charter if it is a home-rule city, or in the general laws. If the power is not specifically granted by such authority, may it be implied from some other power? If a dispute over city powers lands in the courts, those courts will have the final word on this point, but, like all human institutions, the courts are not always completely consistent. The most that we can say is that the courts are inclined to allow some implication of powers from specifically granted authority, but they are cautious in drawing such an implication. Basically, power rests with the legislature, and cities are restricted to powers specifically granted or rather clearly inferred from specific grants. Hence the sweeping terms of many city charters.

Although the city is legally a subdivision of the state, recent events have brought city programs closely under the influence of the federal government. In the development of federal urban policies the state has at times been substantially bypassed, and its traditional power arrangements disregarded or deliberately avoided. Cities generally have promoted direct dealings with federal agencies to avoid dependence on state action, and Congress has usually acquiesced in their wishes. Federal–state–city relations were a major source of state–local political conflict in the 1960s and 1970s.

⊛

Only a half-truth is expressed in . . . Pope's famous couplet, "For forms of government let fools contest, Whate'er is best administered is best."

CHARLES M. KNEIER AND GUY FOX (1953)

THREE FORMS OF municipal government—the mayor-council, council–manager, and commission forms—are in use in Tennessee as well as in the United States generally. The use of these forms in Tennessee towns and cities is determined by legislative act, either general or special, or by home-rule charter. The statutes of the state contain three general acts, one permitting cities to adopt the mayor-council form (referred to in the statutes as the mayor-aldermen form),[5] the other two allowing the adoption of the council-manager plan. The older of the two general laws for council-manager government, enacted in 1921, refers to the council as a commission. The other law was passed in 1957 and was limited to the incorporation of hitherto unincorporated territory with at least 5,000 residents; it was

[5]The terminology has carried over from the nineteenth century.

designed for Oak Ridge and was limited to unincorporated places apparently because influential forces within the Tennessee Municipal League did not wish a modern manager plan to be available for adoption by existing cities.[6]

The most venerable form of municipal government is the mayor-council form. We inherited it from England, where its use is sanctioned by time, and we have continued to look upon it as the traditional scheme of things. The number of incorporated municipalities in Tennessee increased from 223 in 1938 to 334 on July 1, 1981; of these, about 230 used the mayor-council form. Essentially this form is based upon the principle of an elected legislative body, the council, and an elected executive, the mayor. The legislative body is often referred to as the board of aldermen.

Very often a distinction is made between the "strong mayor" and "weak mayor" forms. The executive under a "strong mayor" system may be known by his powers of participating in the legislative process, together with his possession of significant appointing, removal, and administrative powers. Thus the mayor of Knoxville appoints virtually all city employees, exercises substantial removal powers, approves purchases, and prepares and administers an executive budget. In a weak mayor form the executive holds a place subordinate to the council, which will have authority to control even his administrative powers. The Tennessee mayor-aldermen general law incorporates the "weak mayor" form.

Mayors are popularly elected in Tennessee mayor-council municipalities, with both the mayors and the council members being elected for two-year or four-year terms; the four-year term is now the rule in most cities. A large number do not have full-time executives. Many mayors possess insufficient authority to control their subordinates with any great degree of effectiveness, but they have considerable power in most of the larger cities.

The council in all Tennessee cities is unicameral in form. In most mayor-council cities, the number of members on the council ranges from five to seven, including the mayor. Council members are often paid only nominal salaries, but in the larger cities more substantial payments are becoming the rule.

The council is to be regarded as the principal policymaking body in the city. Insofar as the city exercises legislative powers, the council is the legislative body. In fact, however, a major portion of the council's duties relate not to legislation, but to administration, and the agenda of any

---

[6]Two cities (Union City and Elizabethton) ignored this limitation and adopted this general law charter; their actions were subsequently validated by general legislative acts. However, when Dyersburg tried the same tactic, a challenge in court resulted in a Tennessee Supreme Court decision that the law means what it says. *State ex rel. Rector et al.* v. *Wilkes et al.*, 222 Tenn. 384, 436 S.W. 2d 425 (1968).

council meeting will quickly indicate that the council is primarily concerned with granting contracts, issuing licenses, approving or making appointments, and the like, rather than adopting ordinances.[7] This activity is a reflection of the character of the city itself, which is more concerned with the provision of services than with the passage of rules. The council, therefore, is unlike the legislature, which is concerned primarily with the establishment of rules and regulations.

The Memphis city charter contains an unusual feature: the institution of a president of the city council, a position that offers the possibility of a center of power rivaling the mayor. In Nashville the council is headed by its own presiding officer, the vice-mayor elected by popular vote. The mayor does not participate in council meetings in those two cities, but in Knoxville he is the presiding officer and may vote to break a tie.

The mayor-council system is a model, with some variations, of the relationships between the executive and the legislature in the national government and in the states. The scheme has significant differences at these three levels, yet the general pattern is a familiar one. To many persons this scheme of affairs seems quite inappropriate for municipal affairs. These critics see nothing in the nature of municipal powers or problems that makes it necessary to divide municipal authority between two contestants, the mayor and the council. At the national or state level, such separation, it is thought, serves to protect the citizen from a too-powerful government, but such protection is not necessary in city affairs. The mayor and the council are thus set in a position that sometimes develops into rivalry; the public is treated to the unedifying and troublesome spectacle of divided leadership and petty bickering. For this state of affairs a remedy has been sought; the commission form of city government and the council-manager plan seemed to some to furnish answers.

In the mayor-council plan the executive and legislative branches were thrust asunder; in the commission plan man put them together again, with not entirely happy results. The essence of this form is that the members of the board of commissioners—normally three to five persons—are at once (as a body) the city council and, as individuals, the heads of the city's administrative agencies. One of the commissioners is the mayor, who serves for ceremonial and legal purposes, and may head a department, and the others control the departments of finance, public works, police and fire, and the like.[8]

Commission government was thought to be integrated government, but

---

[7]A city law is called an "ordinance," a term derived from the traditionally required initial enacting clause, "Be it ordained by. . . ."

[8]Because the old form of the council-manager system is called the commission-manager form in the Tennessee general statutes, a number of small places that use the term "commission" are actually under a manager scheme.

it disclosed a fatal defect. Unless the mayor is a forceful person who establishes strong personal leadership, no central direction is provided. Each department head is his own boss, for each is a commissioner elected directly by vote of the people. Coordination must be voluntary, and every politician knows that the will to such is not always forthcoming. The gradual abandonment of the commission plan goes on in Tennessee. Memphis went over to the mayor-council system in 1966. Maryville and Bristol changed to the council-manager form, the former in 1967 and the latter in 1973. Chattanooga, Cleveland, and Jackson are among the fifteen cities that still cling to this form.[9] In the early 1970s there was talk of change in these cities, but the issue never reached the ballot.

In many ways the best form of city government is the council-manager plan. It was first developed in this country almost contemporaneously with the commission plan, but it has shown greater vitality. As a form of government it is widely, although not universally, approved by students of administration, and its growth in popular favor has been steady and continuous.[10]

The essence of the council-manager plan is to be found in the integration of all municipal administration in the hands of a professional manager, appointed by an elected city council that makes city policy. Occasionally the manager is referred to by some other title, such as administrator. The plan assumes that the manager will follow this policy, that he will stay out of politics, and that the council will stay out of administration. The plan may not be useful for a very small town, for there must be enough business to keep a manager occupied full time if a professional is to be employed. Its adoption in very large cities has sometimes been hampered by the difficulty of keeping the manager out of the political limelight, and many informed persons feel that any attempt to separate politics and administration is bound to fail. Moreover, the council-manager city, like others, is usually plagued with independent boards and commissions.

The council-manager plan made its first appearance in Tennessee in the private act incorporating Kingsport in 1917. Alcoa followed in 1919, and the number has grown sporadically since then; currently eighty-six cities are under this plan or some semblance thereof.[11] Many of these cities are

---

[9]The hybrid forms in several cities make it difficult to fix an exact number using the commission plan.

[10]An extensive literature developed at one time around the operations of the council-manager plan, especially with reference to the political activities and leadership role of the manager. The plan does envision a distinction between the policymaking of the council and the administration of the manager, just as differences exist between the state and national legislatures and the bureaucracy, but no person acquainted with managers would expect them to be intellectual or administrative eunuchs.

[11]In January 1981 the International City Management Association recognized sixty-two of these cities as having established an appointed position of overall professional management; others no doubt would qualify but had not been processed by ICMA for formal recognition.

TABLE 13–3
RATES OF CRIME IN THE UNITED STATES AND TENNESSEE[a]
1958, 1968, AND 1978

	1958		1968		1978	
	U.S.	Tenn.	U.S.	Tenn.	U.S.	Tenn.
Murder	4.7	8.4	6.8	8.7	9.0	9.4
Robbery	43.5	26.2	131.0	71.2	191.3	152.4
Aggravated assault	65.5	59.2	141.3	129.0	255.9	190.2
Burglary	392.4	416.5	915.1	719.7	1,423.7	1,213.6
Larceny-theft	226.0[b]	142.1[b]	636.0[b]	390.3[b]	2,743.9	1,766.1
Motor vehicle theft	156.4	131.9	389.1	267.4	454.7	328.1
Forcible rape	8.4	7.4	15.5	11.6	30.8	30.6

[a]Rates per 100,000 population.
[b]Over $50 in value.
Source: FBI annual uniform crime reports "Crime in the United States in recent years).

Table 13–4
INDEX OF CRIME, BY MAJOR OFFENSES, IN SMSAS CENTERED ON FOUR LARGEST TENNESSEE CITIES[a]
1958, 1968 AND 1977

	1958[b]				1968				1978			
	Chatta-nooga	Knox-ville	Mem-phis	Nash-ville	Chatta-nooga	Knox-ville	Mem-phis	Nash-ville	Chatta-nooga	Knox-ville	Mem-phis	Nash-ville
Murder	16.9	5.5	7.8	18.1	12.2	7.3	10.6	14.9	10.3	6.6	13.6	12.9
Robbery	73.2	23.2	38.1	69.4	151.9	35.1	134.8	145.0	114.8	126.2	341.2	246.0
Aggravated assault	102.2	56.2	75.5	88.4	78.4	121.8	89.4	282.8	252.9	212.3	270.2	207.3
Burglary	750.4	492.3	579.3	803.7	1,267.4	724.6	1,258.9	1,106.3	1,039.7	1,344.9	1,981.8	1,464.5
Larceny-theft[c]	77.4	198.4	223.5	364.7	305.8	313.8	705.4	761.7	2,535.2	1,976.4	2,340.7	2,145.4
Auto theft	182.1	377.1	135.1	311.2	634.2	258.7	357.3	572.2	380.5	416.9	568.1	379.4
Forcible rape	7.9	4.4	4.8	13.7	9.6	8.5	17.3	18.0	15.2	24.9	79.7	33.3

[a]Based on number of offenses that became known to law enforcement agencies, taken from complaints of crime victims or other sources, or discovered by law enforcement officers.
[b]1958 was the first year for which crime index data were published for standard metropolitan areas.
[c]Over $50 in value for 1958 and 1968; no floor for 1978 (floor was removed, beginning in 1973).

small—only thirty-one have above 5,000 population; eighteen have populations in excess of 10,000.[12]

Fortunately Tennessee cities do not seem to be unduly worried by the dismal failure of the council-manager plan in Knoxville, where it was originally adopted in 1923 and, after many troubles, abandoned by legislative act in 1937, reestablished in 1939, and finally given up in 1947. Knoxville furnished a much publicized example of how not to run a manager city. Its managers, although often very able, were with a few notable exceptions nonprofessionals—often enough, hometown boys with local and state political connections and ambitions. Its councils either interfered in his business or were under the manager's thumb. Several vigorous attempts on the part of local citizens to improve the city management were frustrated by private acts of the legislature, which twice abolished the manager plan outright.[13]

The councils of council-manager cities tend to be small, containing from three to seven members. Four-year overlapping terms are common. Salaries are nominal. The managers can anticipate payment in accordance with respectable professional salaries. They serve at the pleasure of the councils instead of being hired for fixed terms of office. In most cities fairly active turnover is the rule, partly because professional managers are in demand and frequently move on to other posts either in Tennessee or in other states. The managers of Kingsport have enjoyed long tenure; unusual stability has been characteristic of this city.[14]

The council-manager plan has not always been acceptable to the large cities, and some political scientists feel that it is essentially inappropriate in the context of big-city politics. A variation has been developed in some cities (New York, New Orleans, Philadelphia, and elsewhere) by the invention of the CAO—the chief administrative officer—attached to the mayor as his principal administrative aide. In Tennessee the CAO was set up in the 1966 Memphis charter as an aide to the mayor; there the office has been occupied by trained and innovative administrators who have worked well with the chief executive.[15]

[12]Many small places used the manager law for initial incorporation as a matter of expediency because of a lower referendum requirement before 1959: adoption required only a majority of the votes cast. Until amended in 1959, the only other general law permitting incorporation had required an affirmative vote of two-thirds of all qualified voters. Some very small towns do not fill the office of manager.

[13]For an account of Knoxville's early experience under the manager plan, see Louis Brownlow, *A Passion for Anonymity* (Chicago: Univ. of Chicago Press, 1948), chs. XV––XVIII.

[14]For a comparative study of the three major forms, see *Forms of Municipal Government* (Knoxville: Bureau of Public Administration, Univ. of Tennessee, Oct. 1973).

[15]The Memphis charter was prepared by a group of outstanding citizens of Memphis, including Walter Armstrong, Lewis Donelson, Dan Kuykendall, and William Farris, under the chairmanship of Downing Pryor, who subsequently became president of the city council. Lee S. Greene and former city attorney Frank Gianotti served as consultants to the group.

Many . . . activities of government are directed to seeing that individuals are efficiently supplied with what . . . they want.

A. D. LINDSAY (1930)

THE CITY EXISTS PRINCIPALLY to provide services to its inhabitants, either on its own initiative or as an agent and instrumentality of the state or the national government. True, the city does impose some regulations on those within its jurisdiction, but the main business of the municipality is to provide utilities, run airports, collect and dispose of waste and sewage, build and maintain streets, and so on. All of these activities make urban life possible.

In some political systems police administration is a function of the central government. In Anglo-American systems, policing has been a tightly held power of local government, exercised primarily by the county and the city. In exceptional cases the police have been taken over by the state, usually in an attempt to combat municipal corruption, but the customary pattern of organization in the United States, and, of course, in Tennessee, is for the cities to maintain police forces. Counties maintain policing, as a general rule, through the constitutional office of sheriff.

Statistics gathered by the FBI give some indication of crime trends.[16] Their reports have consistently shown a higher level of crime in the larger cities. The most significant comparative measure is the "crime rate"— number of crimes per 100,000 of population. Table 13–3 shows the rates for major offenses at ten-year intervals from 1958 to 1978 in the country and in this state. From these data it appears that Tennessee has shown some improvement. Table 13–4 presents similar data for Tennessee's four major metropolitan areas.

The discontent of the 1960s in central cities and at universities focused more public attention on municipal police forces as they tried to cope with mounting rebellion. Many of the critics on the sidelines apparently thought that a police officer should be a paragon of virtue under conditions of great stress and provocation. Those circumstances generated a movement of widespread police reform that has touched nearly every city. The upgrading process in Tennessee has been helped along by the Tennessee Law Enforcement Planning Agency (TLEPA) and massive federal funding since 1969 for new equipment, training and technical assistance.[17] These programs have now ended.Through state action alone the Law Enforcement

[16]Published annually as *Uniform Crime Reports for the United States* or *Crime in the United States* (Washington: U.S. Department of Justice).

[17]Funds have been granted to the larger cities both directly and through development districts. The program also funded technical assistance by the Municipal Technical Advisory Service, an agency of the Univ. of Tennessee, until June 1981, when it was terminated.

Training Academy has provided training programs at a central facility in Donelson (suburb of Nashville) since 1966. TLEPA has funded regional training programs offered by the state's development districts and also monthly meetings of the police chiefs of cities. A state law encourages participation in training programs by providing salary supplements to police officers who meet minimum requirements. Significant advances have been made in the communications field and in the keeping of records and reports; in the latter area some 200 cities have installed a uniform records system. Unquestionably the quality of municipal police services has been considerably improved by these efforts, but no objective measures can tell us to what extent. Continuing problems include pay (strikes have occurred in a few cities) and conformity with federal guidelines (such as "affirmative action" hiring and validation of tests used in the recruitment process).

All but the very small cities make an effort to provide some protection against fire. Any Tennessee city above 500 population and probably most of the smaller cities are likely to have at least a volunteer fire-fighting force. Combined professional-volunteer forces are found in some medium-size cities, and full-time paid personnel are universal in the larger cities. Centralized training for firemen is provided at the Murfreesboro Area Vocational Technical School, and field personnel conduct training courses in cities—especially in those dependent on volunteers.

Fire and police departments are sometimes referred to as the "uniformed services," and in some of the larger cities they are combined in a department of public safety (with a police division and a fire division); Knoxville is formally organized in this manner, but several mayors have elected to leave vacant the headship of the department, thereby effectively eliminating it (the position was filled by Mayor Randy Tyree in late 1979). A few cities have effected some measure of consolidation of the two services—in Tennessee, Lookout Mountain is the only city that has gone this far.[18]

Cities are rated as to the effectiveness of various factors relating to fire protection, including adequacy of water supply, manpower, and equipment of the firefighting force; fire prevention programs; and control of hazardous conditions (primarily through city ordinances concerning building and electrical codes, storage of flammable materials, and so on). These ratings are made by the Insurance Services Office of Tennessee (formerly

[18]A survey in 1977 by ICMA included seventy-nine cities of over 10,000 identified in a previous nationwide survey as having some form of consolidation; fifty-six responded, of which only twenty-four actually had some degree of consolidation (eleven reported full consolidation). International City Management Association, *The Municipal Year Book, 1978*, p. 137. Johnson City in 1979 initiated a program to phase in gradually a consolidation by hiring "public service officers" trained for police and fire services to replace traditional police officers and firemen as attrition reduces their numbers.

the Tennessee Inspection Bureau), a nonprofit, unincorporated association supported by the insurance industry. Under a system in use nationwide, each city is assigned to one of ten classes (numbered one to ten), and this rating determines the level of premiums for fire insurance on all property in that city.[19] Memphis is the only Tennessee city in class 2 (the ISO home office reported that no cities are in class 1 (the highest rating) and only about seventy cities nationwide are in class 2). Nashville, Knoxville, Chattanooga, and Oak Ridge are in class 3. The numbers of Tennessee cities in other classes (as of February 1980) are as follows:

Class	Number of Cities
4	3
5	15
6	42
7	41
8	77
9	11
10	All Others

The improvement of public health that has been characteristic of Western countries in the past two hundred years is partly attributable to the development of hospitals. Hospitals have been created in Tennessee as the result of private enterprise, the charity activities of churches, or the initiative of governments. Generally governmental action looking to the construction and operation of hospitals has been started by cities, particularly in the development of hospitals serving indigents. States have tended to take over or to provide the specialized hospitals, such as those dealing with tuberculosis or mental health.

Indigent hospitalization has been widely considered a municipal function in the past. There is little reason, however, for a city to assume the responsibility for indigent hospitalization. A case can be made for state assumption of such costs, perhaps with federal aid, on the grounds of equalizing the burden over a larger population (the same argument is made for other welfare programs). Certainly, as between a city and its county, the latter is the appropriate unit because its taxes are collected from city residents as well as from non-city residents. This view has prevailed in Tennessee, and only one city is known to be making any appropriations for this purpose.[20]

[19]Memphis and Nashville are exceptions. Premium levels in those two cities reflect the loss experience in each city. Premium levels in all other Tennessee cities are determined by the loss experience in the remainder of the state and the class of a particular city.

[20]Johnson City, in the amount of $20,000 per year. A 1970 survey of twenty-eight Tennes-

Mountains of Garbage—Johnson City Landfill. Photograph courtesy UT Municipal Technical Advisory Service.

Wherever man goes, garbage follows. Every city administrator knows how troublesome this fact of life is. However useful the dumps of the world are to the archeologist, they are a constant source of expense and dismay to the urban areas. Waste disposal is a distasteful and mundane subject, but it is a matter of the most urgent concern which grows larger as people multiply and congregate in urban areas, especially when they consume more and throw more things away.

The disposal of solid waste is still accomplished in far too many places by dumping trash along the roadsides. The results are visible along the roads of Tennessee, in farm areas, in recreational and scenic spots, and in the cities, where the beer can tossed from the speeding car is as familiar as the dirtied side of a surburban road. The collection and disposal of garbage can be undertaken by the city, by the county, or by private persons. Combinations of these arrangements are common. Often the collection is undertaken by cities with the county maintaining a dumping or disposal ground. The operations may be financed either by taxation or by service charges.

Sanitary landfills are now the most used method of disposal in Tennessee, replacing the open dumps of yesteryear (outlawed by state law in 1972). Any disposal facility must first be approved by the state Department of Public Health and is subject to continuing state inspections. For approved disposal facilities the state makes annual operating grants that have ranged from 50 to 70 cents per capita (up to $1.00 per capita is authorized by law). The biggest problem is locating a sanitary fill site, as any site selected seems to arouse intense opposition from residents in its vicinity. Nashville has a plant that burns refuse to produce steam that is sold for heating and air conditioning in some of the state buildings in the downtown area. A few other cities are in various stages of planning similar facilities; Lewisburg began operating such a plant in 1981. Memphis is hoping to build a plant to burn sewage sludge and solid waste. Both the federal and state governments provide financial assistance, through loans and grants, for construction of facilities to recycle wastes for production of energy and recovery of useful materials, but the municipal response to such incentives has been slow—primarily because the development of such technology is still in the experimental stage and no single process has been demonstrated to be the most effective of those available.

The collection of waste is often accompanied by labor problems for the city administrator, for collectors are among the lower paid of city workers and are among those most ripe for union organization. Troubles in this sector were present in some Tennessee cities during the 1960s and early 1970s, notably in Memphis.

Tennessee has shared with other states the increasing pollution of its

---

see cities of over 10,000 disclosed that seven cities were paying all or part of such costs for their residents.

waters by the practice of cities (and industries) of dumping their sewage and industrial wastes, untreated, into streams, lakes, or even occasionally underground water. One need not dwell on the evident disadvantages, and ultimate unacceptability, of this practice. No one would argue that the practice should continue, but treatment plants are expensive, and cities were reluctant to undertake corrections. At last the state, under the pressure of national legislation, is firmly compelling cities and industries to build adequate treatment facilities. The Tennessee Department of Public Health through the division of water quality control has the job of compelling public and private agencies to cease the pollution of Tennessee waters. The basic authority for its operations is the Water Quality Control Act of 1971. The activities of the division include the study of water quality by various means, the inspection of private and public disposal and treatment systems, the provision of training for employees who operate disposal and treatment systems, and various kinds of enforcement actions to compel cities, counties, and private persons to avoid polluting the streams and other waters of the state. In a few cases substantial fines have been levied against cities for the killing of fish by the discharge of polluted waste.

Cities have received state loans and federal grants to assist them in building adequate sewage disposal plants, and although Tennessee streams are by no means cleaned up completely, they are in much better condition now than a few years back when some resembled open sewers, at once dangerous and distasteful. As minimum standards of effluents have been raised, more sophisticated plants are being required; under the impact of inflation many of these are imposing seriously high costs, even to the point where some cities are asserting that they cannot afford to operate the plants. The federal Environmental Protection Agency is now stressing the necessity of considering other methods of treatment (such as land application) and selecting the method that is most cost-effective. An alternative that has been utilized by many small cities is a sewage lagoon; the sewage is discharged into a body of water, and the natural forces of sunlight, bacteria, and acquatic plants provide the purification process.

Many of the functions that we now take for granted as city duties in the past were either not performed at all or were carried out by private organizations. Publicly owned and operated housing, on the scale now practiced, is something of a new function for American municipalities. Such housing has become a significant feature of European life, its origins extending back to the period before the First World War. In the United States the development of municipal housing began with the New Deal; the provision of such housing, supported by federal funds, has been a regular feature of municipal activity ever since.

The first federal support for housing appeared in the National Industrial Recovery Act of 1933, which authorized slum-clearance and low-rent housing; there soon followed creation of a housing division in the Public Works Administration which financed many projects in Tennessee cities. Since that time the legislative and executive branches of the federal government have expended a great deal of effort in trying various approaches; the story is far too extensive and complex to summarize in these pages. Most of these efforts have involved city governments in one way or another because the cities are where most low-income people live. Various programs have been undertaken, such as construction and operation of multiple-housing projects for low-income and elderly people, neighborhood conservation and property rehabilitation, model cities, and urban renewal, to name a few.

Housing for low-income people, and more recently for the elderly, has been the most extensive in terms of the number of cities involved and the number of people served; in 1980 there were ninety-nine housing agencies in Tennessee.[21] This program was halted by President Nixon in 1973, and no new projects were authorized for about five years, as the federal government decided to try rent-supplements and subsidized housing, working through the private sector. When results from those programs did not live up to expectations, in 1978 the older program of direct construction and operation by housing agencies was resumed on a much smaller scale (there are some indications that it might be expanded).

The "urban renewal" program, initiated by the federal Housing Act of 1949, was similar to the earlier programs in England that replaced huge run-down areas with completely new and better designed structures. It has been almost wholly financed by federal funds and has brought about extensive redevelopments, especially in the larger cities, that have completely changed the character of large areas. Thirty-six Tennessee cities have undertaken such projects. The program came under attack in the 1960s from low-income people (especially blacks) who objected to the destruction of their neighborhoods and from owners of small businesses who alleged that it was primarily for the benefit of big business interests. The urban renewal program was terminated in 1974 when a new program came on stage—the Community Development Block Grant program under the Housing and Community Development Act of 1974.

The federal government's efforts to improve housing and the character of our urban areas over the years have added up to astronomical expenditures. No doubt people's living conditions are better, in Tennessee and elsewhere, than they would have been in the absence of these programs.

---

[21]Organized under the Housing Authorities Law of 1935 (codified as *TCA* title 13, chapter 20). A few of these are county agencies. Some municipal agencies operate projects in other nearby cities. Some of these agencies have been given larger missions and new names, such as Knoxville's Community Development Corporation, Nashville's Metropolitan Development and Housing Agency, the Elizabethton Housing and Development Agency, and the Tullahoma Community Development and Housing Commission.

But their cost effectiveness, as compared with alternative approaches, is an unsolved and probably insoluble, problem. Estimates by the Tennessee Housing Development Agency indicate that much remains to be done in this state—in 1978 over 253,000 residential units (from a total of 1,459,000) were adjudged inadequate.[22]

The legislature in 1973 established the Tennessee Housing Development Agency for the purpose of providing financing for low-income housing developments.[23] The agency's financing activities have involved primarily the purchase and making, through lending institutions, of mortgage loans for single-family, owner-occupied housing; some loans are also made on multi-family developments for rental occupancy. By the end of 1979 the agency had made 7,657 single-family mortgage loans totaling $174,972,670 and had purchased from lending institutions an additional 1,446 such loans amounting to $41,023,330. The agency is governed by a fifteen-member board composed of five state officials as ex officio members and ten members appointed by the governor for four-year terms. It received $450,000 in appropriated funds in the first two years of 1973 and 1974 but has been self-sustaining since; its board has endorsed in principle repayment of the appropriated funds to the state.

The Tennessee Housing Rehabilitation Corporation is governed by a seven-member board composed of four ex officio state officials and three members appointed by the governor for staggered four-year terms (two must be "persons of low income").[24] This agency functions much like a private mortage insurance company, insuring loans for the rehabilitation of residential housing units that meet certain minimum requirements. The law also authorizes interest subsidies for loans to low-income borrowers if it can be shown that such subsidies will prevent default. The agency was slow in getting underway due to adverse market conditions and was placed in inactive status in 1979, subject to executive and legislative review as to whether it would be reactivated; at that time it had insured a total of about 250 loans.

As a part of the Tellico Dam project TVA had plans for a model city to be developed in an area adjoining the to-be-formed lake. The Boeing Company became involved, committing a considerable sum of money and staff effort toward planning such a development, in hopes that it would eventually be selected by TVA as the developer (the company withdrew after protracted delays caused by litigation). Extensive staff work by TVA and state planning office personnel produced a bill that was enacted by the

[22]*Report on the Need for Housing in Tennessee, 1978* (Nashville: THDA, July 1978), 67–70. The estimates were based on 1970 census reports and subsequent building data.
[23]*Public Acts*, 1973, ch. 241; codified as *TCA*, 13–23–101 et seq.
[24]Originally created by *Public Acts*, 1973, ch. 313; codified as TCA, 13–22–101 et seq.

Oliver Springs Housing. Photograph courtesy Tennessee Valley Authority.

legislature in 1974 as the New Community Development Act;[25] it was especially designed to make this project achievable. This act established a Tennessee Community Development Board and directed that staff assistance be given to it by the state planning office. All plans were "put on hold," however, by prolonged litigation initiated by environmentalists who eventually convinced the U.S. Supreme Court that the federal Endangered Species Act prevented closing of the dam (after TVA had expended over $100 million appropriated by Congress for this specific purpose) because it would destroy what was then thought to be the only known habitat of the snail darter.[26] The state board held a few meetings (the last one in March 1975) and then became inactive; it did not accomplish the statutory mandate of adopting "minimum standards for the development of new communities in this state on or before June 30, 1976." Whether this act will ever be used is unpredictable.

Cities also operate enterprises that are financed by the sale of products —water, electricity, and gas are the most common. These are sometimes referred to as "proprietary functions," to distinguish them from "governmental functions" such as police and fire protection, public health services, and solid waste collection and disposal. At one time the distinction was very important, because municipal governments were immune from liability in carrying out governmental functions but not in carrying out proprietary functions; in recent years this immunity has been removed in most states by judicial rulings or by legislation.[27] The water system in nearly every city is a municipal operation; the privately owned company that serves Chattanooga is a notable exception. Sewer systems, once financed from general funds, are now almost universally self-supporting from fees levied in proportion to quantities of water used. Natural gas is supplied to most cities in Tennessee by municipally owned systems or utility districts;[28] private companies supply a number, including Nashville, Chattanooga, Johnson City, Kingsport, and Cleveland.

Municipal electric systems have a long and honorable history. A former TVA board chairman, A. J. Wagner, noted that in the same year (1880) the first private electric distribution system and four publicly owned systems were established. In Tennessee the pre-TVA high point was forty-four in 1922; by 1927 private companies had acquired thirty-seven of these, and the total number of municipal systems was eighteen. In 1980 there were

[25]*Public Acts,* 1974, ch. 749; codified as TCA, 13–15–101 to 13–15–117.

[26]*TVA* v. *Hill,* 437 U.S. 153 (1978). Efforts by the Tennessee delegation to overcome this decision in Congress were eventually successful, and the dam was closed the latter part of 1979.

[27]Accomplished in this state by the Tennessee Governmental Tort Liability Act of 1973; codified as *TCA,* 29–20–101 et seq. It fixes maximum amounts of liability for governmental functions.

[28]Organized under the Utility District Law of 1937; codified as *TCA,* title 7, ch. 82.

sixty municipal systems in Tennessee serving most of the urban areas; some smaller cities and nonurban areas were served by three county-owned systems and twenty cooperatives. All of these systems were distributing power purchased from TVA under contracts that specify in considerable detail how they are to be operated.[29]

Some mass transit systems (such as New York's subways) have been municipally owned for a long time, but the numbers have greatly increased in the last twenty years or so as people have switched to private automobiles and cities have had to take over failing private companies. The number of systems publicly owned in the United States increased from 98 (9 percent of total) in 1967 to 463 (48 percent of total) in 1978; the operating revenue of these systems in 1978 ($2,145 million) and the vehicle miles operated (1,825 million) both constituted 90 percent of the industry totals.[30] Transit systems are municipally owned in Memphis, Nashville, Knoxville, Chattanooga, and Jackson. Until 1973 the decline in riders had been steady, leading to operating deficits that could only be covered by municipal funding; in recent years the federal government has provided considerable sums also. After ridership reached its lowest point in 1972 (5,253 million revenue-trips), each year since then has seen an increase, and in 1978 the total was 7,616 million revenue-trips; however, inflation has moved even faster and the need for public subsidies has continued to increase.[31] The rationale for such public subsidies has been that mass transit is an essential service to the life of a city, one that cannot be fully supported by the fares charged.

Varied additional functions are being performed by Tennessee urban units. Airports, river wharves, parks (a somewhat neglected function in some cities including, notably, Knoxville), recreation, market houses, public auditoriums, and even cemeteries are included in the services operated by some cities. Significant expansion of park and recreation activities have been noted in a number of localities.

Boards and commissions have been used for a variety of special functions. Utilities, education, libraries, parks, recreation, liquor control, hospital administration, juvenile court administration, and transportation have all been the recipients at times of this special recognition. Cities do not all follow the same detailed pattern of organization with respect to such

[29]For a careful study of the relations between TVA and Tennessee municipalities, see Victor C. Hobday, *Sparks at the Grassroots: Municipal Distribution of TVA Electricity in Tennessee* (Knoxville: Univ. of Tennessee Press, 1969).

[30]'78–'79 *Transit Fact Book* (Washington: American Public Transit Assn., 1979), 38–39. The 1967 data were obtained by phone from the APTA office.

[31]*Ibid.*, 24. Savings under municipal ownership are also realized, such as nominal fees for license plates and exemption from taxes on motor fuel and other products. For 1979–80 Memphis appropriated about $4.4 million to its bus system and Knoxville nearly $1 million. In 1978 the nationwide total subsidy from all levels of government was $2,231.7 million (local $977.8, state $564.3, and federal $689.5). *Ibid.*, 20.

bodies. The number of members, length and overlapping of terms, and method of appointment vary from one city to another. A few are chosen by popular election, others by the city council, by the chief executive, or by both. In some cases they are self-perpetuating. Generally board members serve with little or no compensation.

Some boards are administrative agencies, some hear appeals, others are limited to furnishing advisory services, and still others grant licenses. Examples in the above order of the various types would be a school board, a board of zoning appeals, a planning commission, and a beer license board. The council exercises some control over most of these groups through the power of appointment, the practice of reviewing board actions, and the dependence of the boards on the city governing body for funds. However, some charters require the council to provide funds for certain boards; in such cases, of course, the board is likely to be quite independent of council control.

Boards, particularly advisory boards, furnish a means of involving citizens in policymaking, building support for municipal administrators, and taking pressures off them (something the municipal reports would doubtless refer to as sharing responsibility). Various federal programs have required "citizen participation" in municipal programs, and the use of boards is one way to comply. In spite of the supposed virtues of integration and central responsibility, mayors and professional administrators often find boards useful; they like them—in reasonable doses.[32]

The quality of municipal administration depends on manpower and money. The manpower may be provided by some kind of formal or informal merit system or it may be provided by patronage. The same motives that lead state officials to bestow jobs and other favors upon friends and allies operate at the municipal level. Elected officials need means of attracting support at the polls and loyalty to issues will not suffice; often enough such issues do not exist. Also in small cities the number of jobs does not justify formality. It is no surprise, therefore, that formal and effective personnel systems have been slow to develop in Tennessee; patronage and merit programs compete. No doubt most urban personnel programs, whether formalized or not, are a mixture of the two, but it is reasonably certain that top-notch municipal performance will not be secured without some consideration for the qualifications of municipal workers. As of October 1979, the municipalities of Tennessee were employing the equivalent of 80,000 full-time workers, and the payrolls for that month amounted to almost $78 million. This was an increase of about 40,000 people since 1962, and more than a fivefold increase in payroll expenditures.[33] Even accounting for

[32]See Stanley T. Gabis, "Leadership in a Large Manager City: The Case of Kansas City," in Lee S. Greene, ed., *City Bosses and Political Machines, The Annals of the Academy of Political and Social Science,* 353 (May 1964), 52–63.

inflation, these figures indicate the continued importance and growth of urban government.

The same principles that operate in state personnel management—employment and promotion on the basis of competence, equal pay for equal work, planned promotion, on-the-job training, and so on—should function wherever possible at the municipal level. An increasing number of municipalities in Tennessee are using merit personnel programs; from 1972 to 1981, they were assisted in these programs by two personnel consultants of the Municipal Technical Advisory Service, funded partially by grants under the federal Intergovernmental Personnel Act before the act's 1981 termination.[34] In the larger cities such programs are administered by a personnel office or agency responsible for personnel administration as such, but in most Tennessee cities these duties are "add-ons" for existing officials. The first steps are adoption of a personnel ordinance and rules and regulations covering such matters as sick and annual leave, employment procedures, grievance procedures, disciplinary actions, and dismissal; in small cities all of these matters are generally incorporated into one ordinance. The final stages are classification of positions, based on detailed position descriptions, and development of a pay plan based on the classification.[35] Although a retirement plan is an integral part of a complete personnel program, only a handful of Tennessee cities have had long-standing municipal retirement systems. Practically all municipal employees are covered by the federal social security program. Cities can also participate in the statewide consolidated retirement system; at the end of 1979, eighty-two had chosen to do so for general government employees, and seven cities (including Memphis and Chattanooga) had enrolled for their schools only.

In-service training of municipal officials has attracted some interest in Tennessee, and various organizations have attempted to stimulate such operations from time to time. The establishment in 1967 of the Center for Government Training at the University of Tennessee (and the subsequent association of regional institutions in the program) has greatly increased the opportunities for training.

When the national government became seriously committed to the improvement of job opportunities for minority groups of various kinds, the so-called "affirmative action" program became a common feature of

---

[33]U.S. Dept. of Commerce, Bureau of Census, *Public Employment in 1979* (Washington: Government Printing Office, 1980), 18. These estimates were based on a sample that included all Tennessee cities over 25,000 in population.

[34]In 1979 the consultants reported that some eighty cities had substantially installed personnel systems. Many of these actions have been activated by requirements of the federal Equal Employment Opportunity program.

[35]Assistance to cities (and counties) in these stages has been provided by the state Department of Personnel, with partial funding under the federal Intergovernmental Personnel Act.

TABLE 13–5
Revenues of Selected Tennessee Cities[a]
Fiscal Year Ended June 30, 1977

Source	Memphis Amount	% of Total	Clarksville[b] Amount	% of Total	Tullahoma Amount	% of Total	Union City Amount	% of Total	Clinton Amount	% of Total
Taxes										
Property tax[c]	96,447,396	31.99	1,438,235	24.76	1,731,882	25.93	1,119,531	25.31	447,849	22.49
Local Sales	33,627,999	11.15	26,032[b]	.45	787,993	11.79	663,797	15.00	203,950	10.25
Beer sales[d]	5,214,008	1.73	417,374	7.18	121,917	1.82	82,759	1.87	10,354	.52
Other alcoholic beverages	2,987,956	.99	99,289	1.71	52,796	.79	76,212	1.72	19,647	.99
Cigarette	839,542	.28			51,846	.78				
Gross receipts[e]	1,980,690	.66	199,548	3.44						
Payment in lieu of taxes[f]	6,350,556	2.11	420,119	7.23	143,437	2.15	109,881	2.48	205,147	10.30
Coal severance									8,806	.44
Subtotals	147,448,147	48.91	2,600,597	44.77	2,889,871	43.26	2,052,180	46.38	895,753	44.99
State shared revenues										
Sales tax	10,805,072	3.58	838,268	14.43	252,283	3.77	193,136	4.37	78,712	3.95
Income tax (dividends & interest)	1,433,081	.47	48,972	.84	18,076	.27	22,589	.51	7,768	.39
Taxes on alcoholic beverages	484,319	.16	42,682	.74	11,059	.07	13,728	.31	1,816	.09
Appropriation for streets	4,037,127	1.34	317,891	5.47	94,930	1.42	72,674	1.65	30,618	1.54
Tax on gasoline & motor fuels	7,258,006	2.41	562,567	9.68	169,464	2.54	129,734	2.93	52,872	2.65
Appropr. for refuse disposal	420,000	.14	31,410	.54	9,288	.14	7,118	.16	14,556	.73
School equalization	37,617,684	12.48			1,362,810	20.40	815,973	18.44	328,877	16.52
Subtotals	62,055,289	20.58	1,841,790	31.70	1,917,910	28.71	1,254,952	28.37	515,219	25.87

Federal aid

	Amount	%	Amount	%	Amount	%	Amount	%	Amount	%
Community development grants	5,808,323	1.93	324,023	5.58	501,000	7.50	i		140,000	7.03
Anti-recession grants	1,051,110	.35	37,064	.64	28,764	.43	20,444	.46	11,574	.58
Subtotals	31,650,071	10.50	873,837	15.04	866,494	12.97	248,148	5.61	303,455	15.24
Other federal & state aid										
For school system	16,593,428	5.51			719,736	10.77	128,139	2.90	92,378	4.64
For other purposes	6,965,228	2.31			53,462	.80	18,589	.42	70,144	3.52
Subtotals	23,558,656	7.82			773,198	11.57	146,728	3.32	162,522	8.16
Other revenues										
Franchise fees	4,178,320[j]	1.39			250		72,046	1.63		
Auto license & inspection fees	8,231,404	2.73					53,507	1.21		
Refuse collection fees	10,174,212	3.38	186,959	3.22	26,586	.40	349,602	7.90		
Parks & recreation fees	4,144,816	1.37	196,455	3.38	44,013	.66	17,285	.39	43,495	2.19
Fines & forfeitures	2,926,297	.97	17,594	.30	46,302	.69	38,406	.87	8,249	.41
Building & other insp. fees	966,085	.32			9,050	.14	12,940	.29	4,783	.24
Parking fees	307,784	.10					26,904	.61	12,041	.61
Ambulance service fees	324,240	.11								
Interest on investments	2,386,396	.79	80,540	1.39	29,431	.44	22,138	.50	12,562	.63
Airport income	743,769	.25			40,458	.61	35,335	.80		
Miscellaneous-schools	286,952	.09			36,906	.55	93,942	2.12		
Miscellaneous-other	2,078,366	.69	11,505	.20					33,113	1.66
Subtotals	36,748,641	12.19	493,053	8.49	232,996	3.49	722,105	16.32	114,243	5.74
Totals	301,460,804	100.00	5,809,277	100.00	6,680,469	100.00	4,424,113	100.00	1,991,192	100.00

a Includes revenues for all purposes except for enterprise funds (utilities, parking facilities, etc.) that are self-sustaining.

b Clarksville is the only one of these cities that does not operate a city school system. The city waived its share of the original 1 percent local sales tax to the county school system indefinitely, and for 8 years its share of an added ½ percent; after this period the city will share in the ½ percent proceeds, by increasing amounts over a few years.

c Includes portion of county tax allocated to city school system.

d Levied on wholesalers at rate of 17 percent of their sales within the city.

e Privilege taxes on various businesses.

f From utilities and housing authorities.

g Comprehensive Employment and Training Act of 1973.

h All of CETA funds allocated to the county.

i No receipt of such funds occurred in this year, but in preceding 1975–76 fiscal year the city received $915,887.

j From the telephone company at a rate of 5 percent on billings to customers within the city. Memphis is the only city that receives such fees; any other city would have to secure approval of Public Service Commission.

SOURCE: Audit reports filed in State Comptroller's Office. Supplementary information obtained from finance officers of the cities.

TABLE 13–6
GENERAL REVENUES OF TENNESSEE CITIES[a]
Fiscal Years, 1956–57, 1976–77

	1956–57		1976–77	
	Amount	% of Total	Amount	% of Total
Property Taxes	44,143	30.4	256,909	21.0
Sales Taxes	7,231	5.0	68,873	5.6
Other Taxes	6,513	4.5	33,527	2.7
State Aid[b]	41,431	28.5	283,865	23.1
Federal Aid	370	.3	175,366	14.3
Other Intergovt. Revenue[c]	17,215	11.8	172,956	14.1
Charges & Misc.	28,425	19.5	234,920	19.2
Totals	145,328	100.0	1,226,416	100.0

[a]In thousands. Excludes utility revenues.
[b]Includes any federal funds channeled through state government.
[c]Principally cities' share of local sales taxes, collected by state and remitted through county governments.
Source: U.S. Census of Governments: 1957, vol. III, no. 5, p. 148; 1977, vol. 4, no. 4, pp. 16–18.

TABLE 13–7
1979 PROPERTY TAX RATES OF TENNESSEE CITIES

Actual Tax Rates		Effective Tax Rates	
Range	No. Cities	Range	No. Cities
$0.20–$0.50	23	$0.085–$0.500	47
0.51– 1.00	59	0.501– 1.000	79
1.01– 1.50	39	1.001– 1.500	81
1.51– 2.00	47	1.501– 2.000	19
2.01– 2.50	40	2.001– 2.500	13
2.51– 3.00	14	2.501– 3.000	5
3.01– 3.50	11	3.001– 3.500	1
3.51– 4.00	7	3.501– 3.550	1
4.01– 5.60	6		
Total	246		246

Source: *Tennessee County Local Motor Vehicle, Sales and Property Tax Rates—1979, and Municipal Property Tax Rates—1979* (Nashville: Division of Local Finance, Office of the Comptroller, Dec. 1979).

public employment. The program is intended to guarantee that minority groups—blacks, women, and others—receive equal treatment in the provision of job opportunities; in fact, the results are oftentimes preferential treatment for such groups. Federal grant requirements have spurred a number of Tennessee cities to adopt such programs in recent years—a trend most likely to continue.[36]

The Advisory Commission has strongly urged a more balanced revenue system.

ADVISORY COMMISSION ON INTERGOVERNMENTAL RELATIONS (1969)

PROBABLY THE MOST DIFFICULT PROBLEM faced by any government (at least in the United States) is how to finance its operations. Citizens (voters) are affected in their most sensitive areas—their pocketbooks. Unlike the federal government, which has a printing press at its disposal, the state and local governments must operate on balanced budgets; they must take in as much as they spend.

Historically the property tax has been the mainstay of municipal finance, but the situation has changed considerably in the last fifty years. Prior to the 1930s, the property tax provided three-fourths or more of the general revenue of American local governments and more than four-fifths of their locally raised general revenue (that is, excluding payments from other levels of government). Largely because of the greatly increased grants-in-aid for welfare and school purposes from state and federal governments, the property tax declined sharply as a proportion of total general revenue in the 1930s and 1940s. From the early 1950s to the early 1960s, the property tax stabilized at just under half of total general revenue. However, in the past few years, a slow decline in its relative role apparently has resumed, again largely due to increased grants-in-aid.[37]

According to a report of the U.S. Joint Economics Committee, in 1968 "the property tax continues to provide about two-thirds of locally raised general revenue, both within and outside the major urban concentrations."[38] These figures include revenues of counties, townships, and special districts; since these units of government have been and still are much more dependent than cities on property tax revenue, the property tax proportion of city revenues is somewhat less. Tennessee cities have been below national averages in their dependence on the property tax. Table 13–5 illustrates the revenue structures of Tennessee cities by presenting detailed data for a small sample of various-sized cities.

[36]More than forty have requested assistance from the Municipal Technical Advisory Service within the past several years.

[37]U.S. Congress, Joint Economics Committee, *Impact of the Property Tax: Its Economic Implications for Urban Problems* (Washington: Government Printing Office, 1968), 6.

[38]*Ibid.*, 8.

Table 13–6 shows amounts and relative percentages of taxes collected for all Tennessee cities from major sources in fiscal years, 1956–57 and 1976–77; in this period the property tax proportion dropped from 30.4 percent to 21 percent, although the dollar amount increased from $44,143,000 to $256,909,000. State aid, which since 1962 has exceeded revenue from the property tax and which accounted for 23.1 percent of total revenue in 1976–77, includes funds for city school systems, a portion (12.5 percent) of the original 2 cent state sales tax levied in 1947, the proceeds from 1 cent of the state tax on gasoline and other motor fuels, a small share of state taxes on beer and on income from stocks and bonds, and in recent years appropriations for maintenance of city streets; in lieu of such an appropriation in 1981 cities were allocated a share of the tax increase of 2 cents per gallon on gasoline and 4 cents per gallon on other motor fuels. There has been a steady upward trend in federal aid, from .3 percent in 1956–57 to 14.3 percent in 1976–77, reflecting a plethora of categorical programs and, since 1973, the general revenue-sharing program for all local governments in the country. "Other intergovernmental revenue" consists for the most part of sales taxes levied by counties (by referendum) as "piggyback" additions to the state sales tax which are shared with cities; counties must also share with city school systems property taxes levied for schools, on a basis of relative numbers of students in attendance. On July 1, 1981, all counties but one (Anderson) were levying sales taxes, at rates as follows: 7 counties at 1 percent; 47 at 1.5 percent; 7 at 1.75 percent; 10 at 2 percent; and 23 at 2.25 percent (the maximum permitted). Five cities had city-only sales taxes or were levying the tax at rates higher than the counties' rates. Only Oak Ridge had neither a county nor a city tax in effect. Revenue from the city-only sales taxes and gross receipts taxes on businesses have been reported in the "sales tax" category. "Other taxes" include wheel taxes on motor vehicles and various license taxes not on a gross receipts basis. The final classification, "charges and misc.," consists of various other sources such as sewer surcharges, solid waste collection fees, building inspection fees, parking meter receipts, fines and penalties, and interest earnings.

The most critical phase of property tax administration is the determination of assessed values, as these are the bases of applying the tax rates fixed by municipal governing bodies. Formerly most cities made their own assessments, duplicating the work of county assessors (some small cities exercised their option to use the county assessments), but legislation enacted in 1973 required cities to use county assessments after a county-wide reappraisal had been completed.[39] At the request of Oak Ridge, a 1976 act excepted cities lying in two or more counties from this requirement;[40]

[39]*Public Acts,* 1973, ch. 226; codified in *TCA,* 67–337.
[40]*Public Acts,* 1976, ch. 609; codified in *TCA,* 67–337.

Oak Ridge is the only city making its own assessments under this exception.

The assessment of a parcel of property is half of the formula that determines the amount of tax to be paid—the other half is the tax rate fixed by the municipal governing body. Many private act charters and the mayor-aldermen general law in the past specified maximum tax rates, but all of these were repealed by a 1973 general act,[41] to compensate for a drastic reduction in assessments mandated by the constitutional amendment that went into effect that year requiring all farm and residential property to be assessed at 25 percent of full value. A compilation by the state comptroller's office of the 1979 tax rates of nearly all Tennessee cities that use this tax (many very small cities levy no property tax) shows that tax rates ranged from 20 cents to $5.60 per $100 of assessment.[42] The seven highest cities were Norris ($5.60), Etowah ($5.25), Knoxville ($4.80), Morristown ($4.60), Tullahoma ($4.37), Lookout Mountain ($4.30), and McMinnville ($4.00). Table 13-7 shows the number of Tennessee cities in each tax-rate range. Generally, the small cities levy lower tax rates, but there are exceptions; Norris has a population of 1,359 and Lookout Mountain has 1,741 (both of these communities are primarily residential, and this class of property is assessed at 25 percent). The rates in other large cities were: Memphis, $3.74; Chattanooga, $3.65; and Nashville (urban services district), $1.56. As to estimated effective tax rates (rates that would produce the same revenue if all property had been assessed at 100 percent of value), the highest cities were Elizabethton ($3.55), Oak Ridge ($3.06), Lookout Mountain ($2.881), Bristol ($2.776), Knoxville ($2.774), Morristown ($2.659), Signal Mountain ($2.546), Memphis ($2.513), and Chattanooga ($2.446); in the urban services district of the Nashville metro government the rate was only $.952.

An analysis of the reasons for variations would be far too complex to undertake in these pages, but a word might be said about Nashville's unusually low rate. More of the urban services in that city are financed from the countywide tax rate (for example, most of the police service) because of the metro government that consolidated the city and county; as a result the tax rate in Davidson County was higher than the rates in Shelby, Knox, and Hamilton counties. The greater efficiency of the consolidated government is also probably a contributing factor.

The first step in sound fiscal administration is the provision of a city budget, a plan for the expenditure of city funds during the fiscal year, in line

[41]*Public Acts*, 1973, ch. 226; codified as TCA, 67–643. New maximum tax rates could subsequently be imposed; Red Bank is the only city known to have considered such action, by a home rule charter amendment referendum that failed in 1976.

[42]*Tennessee County Local Motor Vehicle, Sales and Property Tax Rates—1979, and Municipal Property Tax Rates—1979* (Nashville: Division of Local Finance, Office of the Comptroller of the Treasury, Dec. 1979).

with a definite program of action related to the city's income. The three Tennessee general laws under which many cities are incorporated, and most private act charters, require the preparation of annual budgets and of appropriations by the governing body to authorize expenditures pursuant to the budget. In the past, many small cities either ignored such requirements or went through the motions without subsequently using the budget as a controlling instrument. In recent years, however, virtually all cities have applied sound budgetary procedures (with varying degrees of sophistication, of course) in response to requirements of the federal general revenue sharing program and of the state comptroller. A 1975 act empowered the latter official to prescribe a uniform accounting system for municipalities,[43] and a manual was issued in January 1976 that included a section outlining and requiring a budget procedure. Accountants in making annual audits have called attention to these requirements, and the result has been a vast improvement in budgeting practices by small cities; the larger cities, by force of necessity, have for many years observed such procedures.

In most cities preparation of the budget is the responsibility of the chief executive officer, usually the mayor or city manager, with the assistance of various staff personnel (thus, a mayor may rely heavily on the city recorder to put the budget together). Wide variations exist in formats used, but generally the budget includes a comparison of at least expenditures and revenues for the previous, current, and next fiscal years. Public hearings on proposed budgets have become the general rule (this is required for use of federal general revenue sharing funds), but in most cases these are poorly attended and tend to attract persons with special interests, either for appropriations to support a favorite cause or against reductions in existing programs; representations by employees seeking higher pay and benefits have become fairly common in recent years. The budget, after approval (possibly modification) by the governing body, then becomes the basis for controlling all expenditures. Usually monthly reports are prepared to inform the chief executive and department heads of amounts expended as compared with amounts authorized, and to compare revenue collections with revenue estimates. Thus the budget process is a primary mechanism whereby a governing body and the executive officials can shape, direct, and control the various programs and services undertaken by a municipal government.

Proper budgeting is the first requisite of effective municipal fiscal administration. The second is an adequate system of accounting. Accounting serves the purpose of keeping the spending agency informed of the relation of its obligations to its resources; it keeps the chief executive informed of the operations of the departments under his supervision; and it provides

[43]*Public Acts*, 1975, ch. 173; codified in TCA, 9–2–102.

the basis on which the public can be informed of the expenditures of public money.

Some of the more common accounting pitfalls that Tennessee municipalities have not always been able to avoid include the failure to centralize responsibility for the accounting system under a single head, an unnecessary multiplicity of separate accounts, and inadequate expenditure controls.

States are increasingly tending to correct the faults of local fiscal administration by exercising greater supervision over accounting methods at the local levels of government. This supervision has usually taken the form of establishing uniform accounting systems, making it mandatory for local authorities to file annual financial reports and budgets on a uniform basis, providing for periodic audits of local accounts by state officials, and the like. Tennessee has only recently moved in this direction. An act of 1972 required each municipality to provide for an annual audit and made the comptroller of the treasury responsible for insuring that such audits are made in accordance with generally accepted standards, and the comptroller has taken steps for enforcement. The audits may be done by private firms or by the department of audit in the comptroller's office; in either case a copy of each audit must be filed with that office.

The uniform accounting manual for municipalities, prescribed by the comptroller in January 1976, has already been mentioned. This has provided the technical guidance needed for many cities and towns to upgrade their accounting systems. Many improvements have been effected as a result of technical consulting assistance provided by the Municipal Technical Advisory Service since the early 1950s. The availability of a computerized accounting service from the Local Government Data Processing Corporation,[44] which meets the comptroller's requirements, has also vastly improved municipal accounting; eighty-three cities were being served by this corporation in July, 1981 (as well as twenty-one utility systems and forty-seven counties).

Restrictions on the indebtedness of Tennessee municipalities have emanated almost entirely from the legislature, inasmuch as the state constitution deals with this matter only as it concerns the extension of public credit to private individuals or companies. General statutes and many private act charters specify the purposes for which bonds may be issued, limit the rate of interest, and specify means of repayment (from property taxes, revenues of enterprises, or a combination). The manner of approval is also prescribed—usually by ordinance subject to a referendum if a protesting petition is filed, but sometimes a referendum is required.

[44]Organized by the Tennessee Municipal League and the Tennessee County Services Association, with assistance from TVA and the Institute for Public Service, Univ. of Tennessee, to serve cities, counties, and other local agencies of Tennessee.

None of the three general law charters and few special charters fix limits on the amount of municipal debt. Formerly some municipalities relied upon special acts to authorize the issuance of bonds and to provide a special tax levy sufficient to retire the bonds, but in recent years most bond issues have been made under general laws. A former practice of validating bond issues by special acts of the legislature after the bonds had been voted or sold has been virtually discontinued.

In 1937 the state legislature created a division of local finance in the new Department of Administration with duties that included those of promulgating regulations with respect to bond issues of counties and cities, the refunding and retirement of their debts, and the handling of their defaults. This division was changed to a department in 1939, but was abolished in 1959, and the comptroller was given optional authority to create a division of local finance (which he did that same year). In 1937 a Cash Basis Act was passed authorizing all cities and counties to issue general obligation funding and refunding bonds, not subject to any limitations previously imposed on the amount of bonds or on the tax rate. The act was not made mandatory upon local governmental units, and enforcement of its provisions was not seriously undertaken. The act is now of no consequence. In November 1978 the State Funding Board proposed rules that would have made financing plans for all city and county bond issues subject to the approval of the director of local finance, but strong opposition from the securities industry and local governments blocked their final adoption. Many states have moved toward more administrative control of local governments; in Tennessee such proposals have been stoutly, and usually successfully, resisted by the municipalities.

Under a central purchasing scheme, the duty and responsibility of making all purchases is vested in a single department or officer. Such a system affords lower unit costs resulting from large purchases and competitive bidding; unauthorized expenditures are more readily prevented; standard bid specifications afford protection against inferior merchandise; and unnecessary purchases can be minimized. The very large cities and some of those of medium size—such as Oak Ridge, Kingsport, and Cleveland—use some form of centralized purchasing. In other cities the function is combined with the duties of another officer such as the mayor, the recorder, the city engineer, the finance officer, the manager, or the city clerk. Charter provisions frequently require sealed bids when a purchase or contract involves a cost above a stipulated figure, regardless of whether a central purchasing system is provided for. Moreover, it is not uncommon that the approval of the legislative body of the municipality is required for purchases or contract expenditures in excess of a stipulated amount.

14

☆ ☆
☆

Politics in an Urban Setting

DESPITE THE SIZE AND NUMBER OF TENNESSEE CITIES, THEY HAVE FIGURED in the political past less importantly than the counties. The county has the weight of tradition and practice on its side. The county has been the basis for apportionment of legislative seats (although this has suffered a change). The county is the agency to which the state has turned for localized aspects of state administration. The county has been, and still is, the basic local unit of party organization in both parties. The election machinery is county machinery. County politics has been the basis of state politics.

The city has been typically weak in comparison. State party machines are factional in character and somewhat temporary, for each political leader must build his own organization, but those machines, such as exist, seem to be constructed primarily on county organization rather than city, although some city contests reflect state factional fights. In the past the city's wishes were less tenderly cared for in the General Assembly than might have been expected on the basis of the size of the urban population (although this, too, is changing).

Even in earlier years, there were exceptions to county and rural dominance, of course. Memphis has been politically important to the state, as has Nashville. Memphis has long been identified politically with Shelby County, although coordination between the two is less close than when Crump ruled there. Nashville, on the other hand, once frequently at odds with Davidson County, is now a consolidated "metro" organization, appearing as a united organization before the legislature and the public. Generally, however, it is not true that either the big or small city dominates the fate of its surrounding county.

Trying to determine the lines of advancement to state and national political prominence is an intriguing exercise. Insofar as patterns can be discerned, municipal prominence is no guarantee of statewide political success, although some city leaders rise to national and state prominence. As urban life has become more important in Tennessee, urban political experience may be more significant in the future than it has seemed to be in the past. Mayor Edmund Orgill of Memphis was a candidate for governor in 1958, and Mayor Rudy Olgiati of Chattanooga ran for the office in 1962. Richard Fulton, mayor of Nashville-Davidson County, ran a weak third for nomination for governor in 1978. Mayor John Duncan of Knoxville captured the Congressional seat in the Second District, one of the safest seats in the country. Mayor William Baird of Lebanon served in the state Senate longer than any other member remembered in history (before his defeat in 1978), part of the time holding the office of mayor concurrently; he was speaker of the Senate from 1959 to 1962. Some councilmen have been prominent in state affairs; William Farris of Memphis was an unsuccessful but significant contender for the nomination for governor. But neither Governor Clement nor Governor Ellington, dominant in the executive branch, for eighteen important years in the middle of the century, ever held important municipal office. (Clement, indeed, never held any elective office except that of governor, on which he had beamed his ambition since boyhood.) Municipal officeholding is certainly no guarantee of state preferment.

⊛

Factions are found in both major parties in all parts of the nation.

CHARLES ADRIAN (1967)

THE TYPICAL MUNICIPAL ELECTION in Tennessee is fought on factional or nonparty lines. In the past, party divisions would have been impossible because of the single-party orientation of the Grand Divisions—Republican in the East, Democratic in the Middle and West. Partisan divisions in such a situation had to be factional. To some degree this dominance of the single party has eroded, but party lines are still not ordinary in municipal contests.

Then, too, many cities attempt to hold nonpartisan elections, where choice is supposedly on the basis of qualifications rather than party loyalty. It is difficult, however, to keep elections on such a plane of critical selection among aspirants to office, and factions and alignments, often very temporary, do form, even in officially nonpartisan elections. The factions that do arise are sometimes, in reality, groups that do represent the two parties, although often under temporary (and meaningless) names. But even this does not mean that the election will be fought along party lines. Many city elections show evidence of quiet alignments between Republicans and Democrats.[1]

[1]These alliances in the City of Knoxville, often between city and county officials, are

When factions inside parties develop in municipal politics, they are not likely to be durable. As is the case generally in Tennessee politics, the individual political figure may be more important than the party membership. Persons like George Dempster and John Duncan of Knoxville, Ben West, Beverly Briley, and Richard Fulton of Nashville and Davidson County, P.R. Olgiati of Chattanooga, and Walter Chandler and Henry Loeb of Memphis attained enough prominence to stay in the public eye and favor, off and on, for years, but the public is generally not aware of the alliances that may have been formed temporarily for the support of such figures. The shifting political peace treaties that furnish the framework for municipal politics form no easily understandable pattern for public inspection. More or less *sub rosa* alliances with state machines figure in city politics and help to determine state contests. In 1978, factional fights between Memphis blacks affected the gubernatorial contest between Jake Butcher and Bob Clement, and local contests had an effect on Democratic state affairs in the days of Clement and Ellington.

Personalities rather than issues constitute the major focus of urban politics, although occasionally subjects of dispute arise that attract voter attention and furnish bases for choice. Annexation can be a bitter issue. Prohibition has long been a municipal controversy (liquor by the drink was defeated in Jackson in 1978). Fiscal issues, such as taxes on automobiles or municipal sales taxes, sometimes arise, and the adoption or rejection of changes in the form of government, such as a shift from the commission plan to the mayor-council or council-manager form, has interested the voter, but even these concrete matters are often disposed of in special elections unconnected to the choice of officials.

Except for constitutional amendment, the referendum is not authorized in the constitutional scheme of state politics in Tennessee (although advisory referenda appear on the ballot), but its use at the local level is frequent, either because of the authorization or requirement of municipal charters or because of its inclusion in general state statutes. Referenda offer the cautious leader a chance of avoiding troublesome issues. Such appeals to the voter are often required when fundamental changes in the organization of government are made, and they are a regular feature of the scheme of home rule for cities. Voter participation, generally low in city elections, sometimes reaches substantial levels in referenda, particularly when an especially vital and emotional issue is at stake, such as an authorization for liquor, the expansion of the sales tax, or the consolidation of city and county governments.

---

described in Todd A. Baker, "The Politics of Innovation," diss., Univ. of Tennessee, Dec. 1968.

⊛

Getting a government that will normally obey the people is a matter of making it feasible for the people to put into public office the men they really want there.

RICHARD S. CHILDS (1952)

MUNICIPAL ELECTIONS ARE DIRECTED principally to the selection of city councilmen (or commissioners) and the mayor. The typical municipal ballot is therefore a short one; the voter is not called upon to fill a formidable battery of offices from a bewildering mass of candidates. At the same time the direct primary is generally not used in the city, although runoff elections are frequently used so that the voter does face the task of reducing a field of candidates often quite large. The voter must often choose, in addition to mayor and councilmen, a city judge, a city recorder, and, in some cases, a few other officials. At some elections he may be asked to vote on specific issues—authorization of bonds, purchase of utilities, and, for home-rule cities, changes in the city charter. In those cities that operate their own schools the city voters usually choose the school board.

Qualifications for officeholding vary from one charter to another, but in any case they are simple and easily fulfilled. Such qualifications usually include merely age and residence.

The dates of municipal elections vary greatly from city to city. Generally speaking they are not tied to state or national elections, and this factor weighs some against city politics becoming an important aspect of state and national politics. It also helps to account for low voter turnout in municipal elections.

Qualifications for voting in Tennessee vary in detail from city to city, but they are simple. The voting age of eighteen is now required, and a short period of residence is necessary. In the past the possession of a poll-tax receipt was necessary, and the wholesale purchase of blank poll-tax receipts used to be a factor in the corruption of urban politics, but the poll tax has long since been eliminated (the *coup de grâce* was administered by one of the constitutional amendments of 1953). The possession of property once figured in voting qualifications, and remnants of this qualification still exist in charters that either limit voting in certain special elections to property owners or permit property ownership as a qualification for voting aside from residence, but these qualifications are now principally oddities of interest only to the antiquarian of politics.

Municipal elections are administered by the county election organization, and the comments made earlier in this book on the administration of elections apply equally well to urban contests.

⊛

The boss had only seven principles, five loaves and two fishes.

ELMER E. CORNWELL (1964)

ALL OBSERVERS OF AMERICAN POLITICAL LIFE have noted, with discouragement or indignation, that urban elections fail to attract the percentage of eligible voters who turn out for the more dramatic and stirring contests at the state or national level. Tennessee behavior fits this pattern. Where a well-organized local political machine exists, whether or not allied with a state political party, the machine will be able to count on a small but fairly certain nucleus of voters. If the machine becomes very powerful, as the Crump machine was in the past, a sizable vote can be "delivered." U.S. Representative Harold Ford claims to have delivered the black vote to his favorites in the primary election of 1978. The technique of building the nucleus of power is the same everywhere—friendship, family connections, favors, employment, contracts for public works. The machine can count on a small number of persons willing to work in politics just for the fun of it. Others will work for power.

The machine cannot count on electoral success by its own organization and votes alone. It seeks, by various means, to win the support of other organized groups in the community. Some of these groups are tightly structured, but probably most of them are not. Some of them turn to political activity only occasionally, but as they can exercise some influence on voting, their views are heard and their wishes considered. Such organized groups, which can sometimes exert political pressures, will include the teachers. Tennessee teachers are organized for professional reasons into state and national associations and, in the larger cities, into local associations. Some of them are unionized, and even the professional associations have recently become more militant and more inclined to use tactics such as strikes. Together with their families and friends, backed up at times by parents, they wield a rather large bloc of votes. Their voice is heard in the land. The strength of their position is often demonstrated by opposition to "teachers in politics," because every pressure group draws fire when its influence begins to be felt. The teachers' organizations are likely to be especially significant in affairs of the larger cities. Negroes vote and increasingly hold public office in Tennessee (the first black sheriff in Tennessee was elected in Hardeman County in 1978), and in some large municipalities such as Memphis, Nashville, and Chattanooga they constitute enough of a bloc or blocs (since they are not always united) to wield considerable power.[2] The black vote in Shelby County was crucial in 1978,

[2]Cf. Bertil Hanson, *A Report on Politics in Nashville* (mimeo. report copyrighted by Edward C. Banfield, 1960); for a lengthy exploration of the activity of citizens in Nashville, see Charles A. Zuzak, Kenneth E. McNeil, and Frederic Bergerson, *Beyond the Ballot:*

both on a local and on a state basis. A white backlash was also evident in this election. Labor unions take a fairly active part in urban affairs, and sometimes labor personnel are members of city councils, but organized labor in the United States has not been able to deliver the labor vote as a bloc, particularly not in Tennessee. City employees, when numerous, form blocs of voters. The rapidly growing American Federation of State, County, and Municipal Employees was an important factor in the primary election in Shelby County in 1978. The "white-collar" employees are also organized, perhaps less effectively than the uniformed forces. Ministerial councils speak out on issues such as prohibition, drugs, and pornography.

Although the officeholder must accustom himself to the exertion of pressure from these various interest groups, he does resent it when the pressures conflict or when they push him in directions he is unwilling to take. Pressure also arouses resentment when it is directed toward the further imposition of taxes. Thus we find the city council or other municipal spokesmen hitting back at the pressure group when it seems possible to do so. Teachers and other city employees, particularly, arouse resentment when they resort to political activity, for the council finds it hard that the employees should unite to direct the employer under pain of the employer's political demise. In this resentment may be found the origins of ordinances or administrative rulings of the city attempting to limit the political activities of city employees to the mere casting of the ballot. The problem is a difficult one. There is some basis for disquiet if the city is unduly influenced by its own employees, and yet the employees, as well as others, have a legitimate case for being allowed to organize their voting strength.

It would be naive to suppose that pressure groups are always either in the right or in the wrong. It is very probable that Negroes, as well as certain other underprivileged groups in the community, would secure less than they do if their votes were not available to back up their requests. On the other hand, political pressure is not always exerted wisely and unselfishly. Whatever else the organized employees of Knoxville may have done, they have not exerted much pressure to improve the city's personnel practices, and, in some instances, notably in regard to job classification, their influence has apparently been cast against improvement. The influence of Knoxville employees was undoubtedly exerted against the "Metro" plan in 1959. The record of municipal policemen and firemen in the state legislature before the 1953 amendments was disquieting, not to say even sinister at times. But it must be said that city administrations have shown

Organized Citizen Participation in Metropolitan Nashville (Nashville: Urban Observatory of Metropolitan Nashville-University Centers and Bureau of Public Administration, Univ. of Tennessee, 1971). See also Mingo Scott, Jr., *The Negro in Tennessee Politics and Governmental Affairs 1865–1965: The Hundred Years Story* (Nashville: Rich Printing Co., 1965).

little vision in attempting to channel the political activities of employees in the direction of civic, as well as self-, improvement.

It would be inaccurate to assume that city politicians always go into political battle backed by well-organized troops of machines or pressure groups. Such is not the way of Tennessee politics. In the small cities and towns, individuals may attain enough stature to win office without much organization; such offices are often not highly valued, and offices have occasionally had to seek candidates rather than the other way around. Even in the larger cities an individual candidate has a chance. Where a city or county comes under strong machine control, as was the case in Memphis under Crump, an independent candidate has little hope of success, but by and large Tennessee cities are not held under this kind of control. Even Memphis has ceased to suppress the individualistic candidate. In the big cities, councilmanic races are free-for-all contests, often filled with interest and color, even if a little weak on issues.

The most intangible factor in the changing day-to-day of municipal politics is the independent voter. He is the unknown Mr. X. We don't know—and the professional politician doesn't know—who he is, where he stands, or how many of him there may be. He is a worry and a threat. By definition he is unorganized and he will vote according to his convictions if he is sufficiently aroused to vote at all. Not uncommonly the independent voter remains independent because he is too busy or indifferent to acquaint himself with municipal affairs and alignments. Then, too, the notion prevails that "politics" is an occupation of doubtful respectability. The independent voter is likely, therefore, to be a spasmodic voter, an unorganized voter, and seldom, if ever, a candidate.

Every now and then the independent voter becomes sufficiently aroused about political issues at the municipal level to seek out his fellows and to unite into reform groups. This, for the professional politician, increases the general uncertainty regarding the independent voter, and the professional politician therefore regards the freewheeling reform groups with passionate dislike. The independent voters who compose them are likely, under discouragement and opposition, to lapse back into independence and the organization to collapse. The staying power of the reformer is poor.

This should serve to emphasize the fact that political life, in any city of more than small size, cannot be carried on without organizations. Nor is a political organization necessarily corrupt and exclusively self-seeking merely because it is an organization. Day-to-day political life, the good as well as the bad, proceeds through organization of political groups, and the larger the political unit that is to be governed the more essential such organization is. To understand this is the beginning of political wisdom.

One figure remains to be considered. He is the nonvoter. He is, in city affairs, numerous. Why is he absent from the polls? He may be too busy, indifferent, or uninformed. In some respects he is asked for too much; there are too many elections, too many offices filled by popular vote, and too much confused information and misinformation thrown at his head. Nonvoters are so numerous that the city is usually run by an active minority of the eligible voters, but, of course, there is no guarantee that it would be better managed if more people went to the polls. Yet it is somehow offensive to our feelings regarding democratic government that after the municipal ballot has been made widely available, at great expenditure of effort, only comparatively few persons use it regularly.

[The boss and the machine] often were responsible for incredible corruption, but they also . . . helped incorporate new groups into American society and aided them up the social ladder.

FRED I. GREENSTEIN (1964)

STUDENTS OF AMERICAN POLITICS have been greatly intrigued by the municipal party boss. Some attention has been given to the state boss; comparatively little to the rural boss. The urban boss, or the "urban political leader"—if a nicer term is preferred—has been extensively described by writers both learned and popular. At various times he is viewed as a sinister force, an object of entertainment, a colorful character, and occasionally he is treated as a normal outgrowth of governmental organization and governmental service. It is difficult to generalize the American municipal boss. Some have been rough enough. One who shall be nameless here once said of a prominent Tennessee urban politician (likewise not to be mentioned by name), "I like old [name omitted]; of course, he is a liar, and a thief, and he chases women."[3] Other bosses have been urbane and sophisticated gentlemen. Some have acquired their education in the rough-and-tumble of the streets; others have been schooled with the best. Some are hearty types (like the late Mayor Richard Daley of Chicago); others, reserved, standoffish. Bosses are not necessarily loaded down with stolen booty. The boss has been associated with corruption in the minds of the public (who, quite frequently, consider "politics" another word for "graft"), but there are bosses who keep themselves as free from corruption as the average citizen and even restrain their henchmen in such matters.

[3]A statement well remembered by the senior author, to whom the remark was made.

Usually the boss has been a politician who developed urban services and urban building; one element of his strength has typically been the underprivileged to whom he provided governmental services.

The boss is less often a fixture of American urban politics now than he was in the past.[4] Powerful machines, and rival organizations have existed in Nashville, Chattanooga and in Hamilton County. In the thirties and forties the best-known local boss in Tennessee was Edward H. Crump of Memphis. His remarks contributed richly to the store of Tennessee political invective, and his battles were chronicled by songwriters, authors, newspapers, and the general public.

Crump was a kingmaker. After obtaining control of Memphis and Shelby County, he extended his political influence to the state. Whether he did so for the love of power or because he felt state control necessary for control of his city is uncertain, but state–local relationships in Tennessee were then such that no local boss could feel secure in his own satrapy if he disregarded state politics. In any event, during his heyday, Crump picked the principal officers of Memphis and of Shelby County and managed to back a number of statewide winners.

One of Crump's advantages (an advantage denied a rural leader) was the possession of a large voting population that would outweigh the margins of opposition candidates in other communities in the state. The Shelby machine produced some big votes for its favorites, and it is to be expected that the machine was accused of voting the dead as well as the quick.[5]

In no other large city of the state has any one man succeeded in establishing himself in the public imagination as the one dominant and supreme political leader. Political machines existed in other big cities, led by figures such as Hilary House, Tom Cummings, and, later, Beverly Briley in Nashville. The political picture in those cities was one of constant seesawing between factions, with the city and the legislature as the battleground. One result was an instability of elected officials; the turnover rate among Knoxville councilmen has been notably high. It must be admitted that, whatever may be the advantages of the sort of cantankerous independence that seems to characterize the Knoxville voter, it has not led to an outstanding city government. The harmonization of voter independence and municipal stability remains one of the unsolved problems of city government in Tennessee.

[4]Cf. Greene, ed., *City Bosses and Political Machines*.

[5]Cf. William D. Miller, *Mr. Crump of Memphis* (Baton Rouge: Louisana State Univ. Press, 1964). See also Gerald M. Capers, Jr., "Memphis: Satrapy of a Benevolent Despot," in Robert S. Allen, ed., *Our Fair City* (New York: Vanguard, 1947), rpt. in Capers, *The Biography of a River Town: Memphis: Its Heroic Age* (New Orleans: The Author, 1966).

The disappearance of Crump from power is characteristic of a general decline of the old-time municipal boss throughout the United States. The ethnic vote can no longer be relied on, immigration has fallen off, and various groups such as labor are more independent of the "boss." New "types" have appeared among municipal leaders. A new era of black politics has developed. In Memphis the blacks in 1978 were split between two factions, one dominated by the Ford brothers, and the other tied to local leadership in the American Federation of State, County, and Municipal Employees.

American political scientists and sociologists have been much concerned with the existence and characteristics of elites that may wield power in municipal affairs. Few studies of urban elites have been developed in Tennessee, but it seems unlikely that a rigidly defined and closely limited governing class can be identified in cities in the state. Groups shift from issue to issue, exerting power and influence spasmodically. In most cases, no single small group or clique determines the urban policy of the individual city,[6] although in some smaller towns essentially unopposed elites appear to govern.

⊛

Fair treatment for city streets has become the battle cry for municipal officials.

JOSEPH SWEAT (1974)

THE TENNESSEE MUNICIPAL LEAGUE, a counterpart of similar organizations spread throughout the United States on a model first developed, of all places, in Kansas, is an organization of the cities of the state dedicated, among other things, to the defense of the cities' interests before the central government of the state. In Tennessee, an earlier league existed for a short time before it collapsed because of the intrusion of partisan and personal politics.[7] The present league grew up shortly before the onset of World War II as a means of securing a share of state revenues, beginning with the gas tax. After some years of rather uphill work during the war, when its executive leadership was limited and not too effective, the league is now well established. It began to demonstrate a political clout with the first election of Governor Frank Clement in 1952. Clement had promised to aid the cities to realize their initial objective—a share of the state gasoline tax—and the league helped him to become governor. Clement's chief rivals were Governor Browning, who agreed to the cities' position with evident

---

[6]See Zuzak et al.

[7]Cf. Lyndon E. Abbott and Lee S. Greene, *Municipal Government and Administration in Tennessee,* Univ. of Tennessee *Record, Extension Series* 25:1 (Knoxville, 1939), 8.

reluctance, and Clifford Allen, who rebuffed them. The success of Clement was the sign of sharp change in the climate of Tennessee affairs, when the old rural bastions began to collapse before the attacks of urban power.

The league is an organization of cities; dues are paid by the cities, not by officials or private persons. Membership is voluntary, but most cities belong (some fifty small cities are not members). The smaller communities are well represented, but on the whole the league leadership seems to have been successful in avoiding major conflicts between the very large cities and the smaller communities, something not always true in other states. The league maintains a full-time staff, and the prolonged tenure (since 1946) of its executive director, Herbert Bingham, has made him a personality to be reckoned with in Tennessee affairs. Bingham has worked single-mindedly, aggressively, and often abrasively for the interests of his clients, whom he refers to (with some Biblical overtones) as "my people." Whatever animosities Bingham has called up (and they exist for him as for all fighting personalities) there can be no doubt of his hard and single-minded efforts.

The league's main interest was and is focused on finance. The league wants cities to have a substantial share of the fiscal resources of the state, and it has demanded a role in the state's budget procedure. It gained concessions in the constitutional revisions of 1953, 1972, and 1978. Since the cities' fiscal powers are granted by the state, the league must fight its primary battles in the state legislature. The league therefore is, first of all, a lobby. It cannot and should not be considered a nonpartisan, fact-finding organization. It is set up to protect urban interests, and its pronouncements and views must be considered in this light. From time to time the league's wishes clash with the governor's or with those of the legislature, and the relations of Bingham with some of the governors have been stormy. Also, the interests of the cities cannot always be harmonized with those of the counties, although by and large the league (under some pressure from state officials) has been quite successful in avoiding sharp conflicts with county interests. The league speaks for incorporated areas, and suburban interests give the league some opposition, particularly with respect to annexation law.

But legislative concerns of the cities go beyond the fiscal realm. The league was in the forefront in the campaign to alter the state constitution so as to limit special legislation of the "ripper" variety and to provide home rule. The constitutional changes of 1953 that secured these objectives also included, somewhat as an afterthought, the generalization and easing of annexation procedures, and the league has fought steadily and, on the whole, successfully to preserve the power of the municipalities to annex contiguous unincorporated territory. The league was never conspicuous in the battle to secure a more equitable apportionment of the state legislature;

on this matter its silence did not reflect fear of a politically troublesome issue so much as general content with the status quo. The league did reasonably well with the malapportioned legislature; it has not always done so well since, particularly as the move to single-member districts in the legislature left the league facing the political power of suburbs unfriendly to the central cities. The league has been a spokesman for the cities as the General Assembly has gradually extended the liability for tort that falls on the municipalities. And through all these controversies, the league has made its members thoroughly aware that legislative battles are won finally by pressure at the polls on candidates for the legislature and for the governorship.

The league's program, however, goes beyond lobbying and politics. It has a good, even excellent, record in promoting the improvement of municipal administration throughout the state. An outstanding feature of the league's activity in this sphere is presented in the establishment of the Municipal Technical Advisory Service. The service exists to provide technical advice and assistance to cities on their request; its staff consists of lawyers, engineers, management experts, accountants, and so on. Its services have been widely used, and there can be no doubt the organization has been highly effective. The organization is part of the University of Tennessee, a location highly advantageous from the cities' point of view because it guarantees the availability of advice and assistance without any suggestion, or even the possibility, of supervision and command. The same kind of technical assistance provided by a regular department of the state government could readily slip into control, which the cities emphatically do not want.[8] The one conspicuous failure of MTAS has been its inability (by reason of legal restrictions) to provide service to counties; this lack was met by the creation in 1973 of a similar service for counties, also housed in the University of Tennessee.

The creation of MTAS was motivated in part by a desire to keep technical advice from developing into technical control and supervision. In a number of states specialized units have been set up at the state level to aid the local governments; the idea of doing this was probably given a push by the creation under the Johnson administration of the federal Department of Housing and Urban Development. The league has considered this kind of arrangement at the state level to be suspect. Governor Ellington nevertheless made a move in this direction by creating and staffing as a unit in the governor's staff an office of urban and federal affairs; this development seems to have taken place, some-

[8]The organization of MTAS was originally worked out by Herbert Bingham and Lee S. Greene in a pattern that drew on the knowledge and cooperation of the academic disciplines of the university.

what surprisingly, without consultation with league officials. In Governor Lamar Alexander's administration, the unit, after it had become relatively inactive, was abolished.

The league has evidenced some commitment to the training of municipal officials, principally through the promotion of various kinds of in-service training. Here again the services of the state's educational institutions have been employed, through the development of the Center for Government Training.

15

☆ ☆
☆

Counties—Reformed and Unreformed

THE COUNTY IS AN ANCIENT INSTITUTION, A DIRECT DESCENDANT OF THE Anglo-Saxon shire. Over a period of more than a thousand years it has been slowly transformed to fit in some fashion the changing currents of the times through which it has survived. Transplanted from the mother country during colonial days, the county has persisted down to the present with its structure and its officialdom remarkably unaltered, and now, faced with new tasks and functions, it seems as vital, and basically as unreformed, as any hardened old-timer.

Tennessee county government is based upon a pattern inherited from Virginia and, more directly, from North Carolina. In this scheme of affairs the county is the basic unit of local government. In Tennessee the county is particularly important, not only because it is the principal local government for much of the state, but also because there are relatively few county subdivisions or taxing districts such as are commonly found in other parts of the United States.[1]

Washington County, the state's oldest, was formed by the General Assembly of North Carolina in 1777 to include all of what is now Tennessee. All the remaining Tennessee counties have been carved from this one. The most active period of county formation occurred between 1800 and 1840. The last new county was formed in 1879, but minor boundary adjustments continue to be made from time to time. Constitutional requirements make it virtually impossible to form new counties,[2] these aside, time and tradition have assuredly frozen the present county pattern.

Present-day Tennessee consists of ninety-five counties ranging in area

[1]The Tennessee courts have held that the power of taxation can be delegated only to counties and cities. *Keesee* v. *Board of Education,* 46 Tenn. 127 (1868), and a long line of subsequent cases.

[2]Art. X, sec. 4. One requirement is that two-thirds of the qualified voters in any part of a county must assent to its detachment.

from Shelby's 769 square miles to Trousdale's 116. Three counties are more than 700 square miles in area; six less than 200 square miles. The average size is 445 square miles, and the median county is Claiborne, with 455 square miles. Sixteen counties are smaller than the constitutionally mandated minimum size of 275 square miles for a new county.

County consolidation—beloved reform of an older generation of political improvers—is a lost ball in the high weeds. It is still true, and perhaps more true than ever, that many counties are too small, in population or assessed valuation, to serve as adequate bases for administration or service. Even though Tennessee does not suffer from a surplus of small counties, as is the case in Georgia, for example, it is still true that the number of counties could be reduced in Tennessee to some advantage. But such action is quite unlikely.

If the Tennessee county is, in fact, too small, why should counties not be consolidated? The idea has appeal, but it requires examination. First of all, would such consolidation save money? Well, yes, some—but not as much as some people seem to think. A major portion of county expenditure goes for services to people—measures against hepatitis; teachers' salaries; schoolbooks; sand, gravel, and asphalt for roads; 4-H club meetings; and so on. These expenses cannot be cut much by county consolidation; they can be cut only by cutting the service, by a decline in the number of people served, or a decline in prices, assuming that the service is efficient. Some savings might be secured by combining offices. Would a consolidated county be more efficient? Perhaps. A county with a sufficiently large volume of business can use various labor-saving devices and could afford better management. And if the poorer sections of the state could be united with the wealthier, some equalization of opportunities would thus take place. But distance prevents the union of the Cumberland Plateau with the Nashville Basin, and so there are limits to equalization.

Over 3,000 counties have been created in the United States, and during our history relatively few cases of geographic consolidation have occurred,[3] one of which was, indeed, in Tennessee. The existing counties of Tennessee are now quite old; each one has become an established and remembered part of state life, and people do not welcome change. Furthermore, the counties have been bailed out of their difficulties by state aid. A legislature made up of senators and representatives elected by counties is not likely to be disposed to undertake any significant county consolida-

[3]A comparison of 1957 and 1977 U.S. census reports and correspondence with several states reveals that six counties were eliminated during this period (one in Nevada and five in Virginia). A lower number of counties was reported in several other states, based on city-county consolidations, but the states involved still consider the counties to be in existence. Wisconsin reported an increase of one as the result of federal classification of an Indian reservation as a county (since 1977 it has again been classified as a reservation instead of as a county).

tions. Again, political machines are based on the established counties; politics, like nonpolitical endeavors, is suspicious of upheaval.

We have said that one case of consolidation has occurred in Tennessee. That was the union of James County with Hamilton in 1919. A first effort had failed in 1890 when the Tennessee Supreme Court invalidated a legislative act that would have accomplished the deed by its own terms;[4] the court held that the constitutional requirement of affirmative approval by two-thirds of all qualified voters in that part of a county being taken off for a new county applied equally to all of a county being merged with another county. (The constitution is silent on consolidation—the framers thought only of new county formation!) A 1919 private act included the election requirement, and 953 of the county's 1,100 voters actually cast ballots for the merger (only 78 voted against it), a turnout of 94 percent of all voters. One observer saw this consolidation as a case of poor folks moving in on their rich relatives. Following the James County merger, an effort to merge Meigs County with Hamilton failed for want of legislative action.

A 1939 legislative act established a procedure of consolidation on petition of voters (25 percent of the total vote in the last governor's election) in a county to be abolished;[5] the act has never been used. An attempt was made to merge Union County with Knox, using this act, after a considerable portion of Union had been covered by Norris Lake, but the whole movement fell apart, it is said, on the feeling of Knox County Democrats that the addition of Union County Republicans to those already in Knox County would only increase the troubles of the Democrats. Some personal political ties may also have been involved.

⊛

Counties are nothing more than certain portions . . . into which the state is divided for the more convenient exercise of the powers of government.

CHIEF JUSTICE ROGER TANEY (1845)

THE COUNTY IS A BASIC UNIT in the organization of government in Tennessee. The structure of political parties is built on the county. An executive committee in each county elects a county chairman, determines local policies, and plays an important role in the statewide organization and operations of the party. The county executive committee of a party determines how its nominees for county offices will be selected—usually at a convention or by a primary election (in Knox County a private act requires the use of primaries). The county is also the unit for administration

---

[4]*James County v. Hamilton County*, 89 Tenn. 237 (1890).
[5]*TCA*, 5–3–101 *et seq.*

of election laws. All elections, both general and primary, for congressional, statewide, county, and municipal offices, and all referenda, must be held under the direction of the county election commission.

The county is the unit generally used for representation in the state legislature. Until 1966 the Tennessee constitution prohibited any division of counties in forming senatorial districts only; an amendment in that year required single-member districts in counties having two or more senators or two or more representatives and also required that counties be kept whole (not divided) if two or more were combined to form a district. As adherence to county lines would produce districts in violation of the federal court decisions requiring observance of the "one man, one vote" rule, the apportionment act of 1972 included a principal plan along these lines and an alternative plan to become effective if the principal plan should be invalidated. Such invalidation did occur,[6] and a federal district court ordered use of the alternative plan (with minor modifications); this plan crossed county lines for eighteen senatorial districts and forty-six house districts. The General Assembly adopted another plan in the 1973 session, which crossed county lines freely in forming house and senatorial districts, and almost all districts now either split counties or cross county lines. The constitutional prohibition against crossing county lines seems now to be a dead letter.

The county is an administrative subdivision of the state government for programs such as public health, welfare, public schools, the court system, licensing (automobile, marriage, hunting, and fishing), settlement of estates, and the preservation of all sorts of legal papers. In these areas, policies, procedures, taxes, and fees are fixed by state law and county officials act as agents of the state. In recent years there has been a trend toward multicounty regional administration of some statewide programs, particularly those in the fields of public health and welfare (human services).

The county is also a major supplier of services to its own citizens, although even here basic policies are largely established by state laws. For example, police protection outside cities is provided by the sheriff and his deputies (who are limited to enforcement of state laws because the county governing body cannot adopt local laws comparable to the ordinances of a city council). In the larger counties the sheriff neglects enforcement inside cities, although city dwellers contribute heavily to the maintenance of the office, but most city administrators are well pleased to have the sheriff out of their hair.

[6]*Kopald* v. *Carr*, 343 Fed. Supp. 51 (1972).

⁂

*It is ridiculous that a surveyor, or a health officer, or even a collector
of rates, should be appointed by popular suffrage.*

JOHN STUART MILL (1861)

THE COURTS HAVE HELD that offices named in the Tennessee constitution
can be abolished only by constitutional amendments. The legislature's
power to remove from these offices all but their constitutionally mandated
powers, however, has been sustained. Other county offices and agencies
created from time to time by state legislation are, of course, subject to
legislative control.

Until recently the quarterly county court was the governing body in all
but a few counties (Shelby, Davidson, Knox, Hamilton, and McMinn). Its
forerunner was North Carolina's "county court of pleas and quarter
sessions," which was continued as one of the established courts under
Tennessee's first constitution of 1796. It met regularly once a quarter, as
the name implies, and early legislation fixed the time as the first Mondays
in January, April, July, and October—dates that persisted until the court's
demise in 1978.

The 1834 constitution empowered the legislature to establish inferior
courts, and an 1835 act created the "county court," composed of the
justices of the peace, to meet monthly but without the former function of
presiding over jury trials. In the 1837–38 session, continuing earlier practices, provision was made for a "quorum court" composed of only three
justices to meet monthly,[7] and distinctions were made between its functions, mainly judicial, and those of the entire court meeting quarterly,
which came to be principally administrative.

All of Tennessee's constitutions have provided, by implication, for the
quarterly county court; the only reference to it in the 1870 constitution was
in Article II, section 17: "No County office created by the Legislature shall
be filled otherwise than by the people or the County Court." The Tennessee Supreme Court held in 1871 that the "ancient institution of the State,
known as the Quarterly Court . . . [was] simply recognized and treated as
one of the existing institutions of the State," and that the justices of the
peace assembled constituted the quarterly county court with all the powers
of its predecessors.[8] Subsequent courts held that the county court could be
stripped of all but its constitutionally specified powers, namely, to appoint
notaries public, the coroner, and the ranger; to fill vacancies in offices of
sheriff, register, and trustee; and to fill any other legislatively created
offices not filled by the people (for example, in some counties the county
court named county school superintendents, but in these instances the

[7]This court had been established in several counties by private acts in the 1820s.
[8]*Pope* v. *Phifer*, 50 Tenn. 682 (1871).

legislature could negate the court's power by providing for popular election).

The county lacks power to enact local ordinances comparable to those that a municipality may adopt within broad powers conferred by charter or general law; the county's capacity for independent action is thus severely restricted. Although the quarterly county court was often referred to as a county's "legislative body," the Tennessee Supreme Court imposed limits such as "pursuance of a specific enabling Act"[9] and "the authority and jurisdiction of county courts will not be extended by implication, but must be conferred expressly by the Legislature."[10] Explicitly delegated powers that have been upheld include levy of taxes, appropriation of funds, issuance of bonds, construction of roads and courthouses, and election of a school superintendent. When Loudon County attempted to implement a general law empowering counties to "regulate and license the maintenance of automobile graveyards . . . and prescribe fines and other punishment for violation," the Tennessee Supreme Court declared the law to be unconstitutional on dual grounds: only the state legislature can prescribe fines or other punishment, and empowering a county to define conduct to be criminal that would not be so defined in other counties contravenes Article I, section 8 of the Tennessee constitution, which requires that "the law of the land be general."[11] Thus, effectively, the General Assembly is each county's lawmaking agency, and the county legislative body is empowered to exercise discretion only within the narrowly defined limits of the statutes. This may be changed for "chartered county governments."

The Tennessee constitution and statutes, prior to 1978, required that two justices of the peace be elected in each district other than the district that included a "County town" (the county seat), where three were elected. ("County town" was construed by the courts to mean in the larger cities

[9]*Davidson County* v. *Rogers,* 184 Tenn. 327 (1947), sustaining the power of Davidson County to zone land under an explicit private act.

[10]*State* v. *Wilson,* 194 Tenn. 140 (1952).

[11]*State* v. *Toole,* 224 Tenn. 491 (1970). *TCA,* 5–9–101, lists twenty-five purposes for which county courts may appropriate funds, and the Tennessee Supreme Court, in *Maury County* v. *Whithorne,* 174 Tenn. 384 (1939), held that the court has no authority to appropriate money for any other purposes than those enumerated by statute. Several other cases hailed such laws as salutary regulations and limitations on the power of the court. An unchallenged 1951 private act (ch. 401) prescribed a procedure whereby Coffee County could enact ordinances to establish speed limits on county roads, to fix times for county offices to be open, and to control zoning and regulate public health outside cities, with power to make a violation thereof a misdemeanor. The legislature passed an act in 1974 empowering Sequatchie County to set speed limits in unincorporated areas but made no provision for assessing fines. Other 1974 private acts authorized Smith and Fayette counties to adopt by reference standard codes regulating building construction, housing quality, electrical wiring, and plumbing and gas installation; one objection in *State* v. *Toole,* was met by prescribing a fine ($50 for each day of violation) in the acts—whether the other requirement that "the law of the land be general" can be overcome remains to be seen. Often, of course, the purposes of such acts are accomplished because they go unchallenged.

the district in which the courthouse was located.) The first deviation from this pattern was ordered by a federal three-judge court (by a two-to-one decision) in the twin cases of *Hyden* v. *Baker* (involving Shelby County) and *Bennett* v. *Elliott*[12] (Washington County); the decision implied that the Tennessee constitutional provisions were invalid because they did not conform to the federal court rule of "one man, one vote." Other federal district courts followed suit, and several counties, thus encouraged to ignore state law, did likewise; by 1973 at least sixteen counties were not conforming to the constitutional pattern. A curious bit of logic was evident in these cases: because some counties had fallen into the sin of malapportionment, the state had lost the power to determine the composition of quarterly county courts![13] In mid-1974, however, the Tennessee Supreme Court held that the state's requirements must be observed and ruled invalid a contrary plan that had been adopted by the Washington County quarterly court.[14]

Tennessee's county government is based on the "long ballot" principle, with power dispersed among many officials put in office by the electorate. In exceptional cases an aggressive county judge or chairman could parlay his political support and limited budgetary and fiscal powers into a position of leadership, but he could not exercise realistic executive power. The long ballot for counties is in reality an abuse of democratic theory, for there is little sense in entrusting the choice of officials such as court clerks or registers of deeds to popular vote. The average voter neither knows nor cares about such officeholders.

Prior to 1978 in fourteen counties the county court elected one of its members as chairman for a one-year term, as provided by general law, and the office of county judge, established by private acts, was found in seventy-four counties (the office carried only judicial duties in Davidson County).[15] In seven counties the voters elected an executive officer

[12]286 F. Supp. 475 (1968).

[13]See Lee S. Greene and Victor C. Hobday, "A Short Inquiry into Tennessee County Court Apportionment by the Federal Judiciary," *Tennessee Law Review* 37 (Spring 1970), 528–37.

[14]*Jones et al.* v. *Washington County,* 514 S.W. 2d 57 (1974), affirming an opinion by the Tennessee Court of Appeals, 514 S.W. 2d 51 (1973). Subsequently the federal courts accepted this decision as finally determinative of the matter. *Seals* v. *Quarterly County Court of Madison County,* 526 F 2d 216 (U.S. Court of Appeals, Sixth Circuit, 1975).

[15]An 1856 act created the office of county judge in every county, abolished the quorum court, and vested all of the county court's judicial powers in this office. On Nov. 4, 1857, the legislature repealed that act; on Feb. 18, 1858, this legislature adopted an act almost the same as the one repealed but applicable only to Davidson, Shelby, Knox, Montgomery, and Williamson counties; the only significant difference was to change the term from four to eight years. The 1858 act was attacked in Knox County, and upheld *(Moore* v. *State,* 37 Tenn. 510), the court saying that the office of county judge was "an anomalous tribunal, and its construction and jurisdiction are unique." Other private acts subsequently extended the institution.

(various titles were used) for a four-year term, and a general law of 1974 provided that in any county where the judge was relieved of judicial duties his term was to be changed to four years. In the assignment of judicial and administrative duties the statutes generally treated the offices of county judge and chairman as the same. Judicial duties included the probate of wills and other actions to settle estates, legitimation of children, the changing of names, "inquisitions of unsoundness of mind," domestic-relations matters, and, except in a few counties with juvenile judges, original and exclusive jurisdiction over juvenile cases. Most of these powers, except in juvenile and probate cases, were also vested in chancery and/or circuit courts. The typical county judge or chairman had to devote considerable time to such duties at the expense of attention to administrative matters.

The constitutional convention that met in 1977 proposed an amendment dealing with the organization of county governments, which was subsequently approved by the voters in March 1978. This amendment and the implementing legislation[16] enacted by the 1978 General Assembly made some changes in the structure of county government (the 1979 General Assembly amended the legislation in some minor respects).

The amendment itself prescribed a number of structural details. Every county, except a county that has consolidated with a city under Article XI, section 9 (presently only Davidson County), must have a "legislative body" and a "county executive." The implementing legislation abolished all quarterly county courts, county commissions, county councils, or other county governing bodies upon termination of the terms of office of incumbent members (September 1, 1978, in most counties),[17] and vested their powers in the new county legislative body. The law also declares every county to be a "corporation" and authorizes the legislative body to act for the county. Private acts not in conflict are not affected by this law.

The constitutional amendment sets an upper limit of twenty-five members for the county legislative body and requires election from districts apportioned by this body pursuant to state statutes and reapportioned at least every ten years based on the most recent federal census; a maximum of three members per district is also fixed. The implementing legislation establishes a minimum of nine members (and requires at least nine districts

---

[16]*Public Acts*, 1978, ch. 934.

[17]County councils in McMinn and Polk were declared to be county legislative bodies and extended until Sept. 1, 1982, unless a new form is adopted earlier. (McMinn County voters rejected continuation of the county council form in an election on May 6, 1980, and the general law will govern election of a county executive and county commissioners to take office on Sept. 1, 1982.) Knox County's government was extended to Sept. 1, 1980, when the general law became effective. A provision in *TCA* 5–6–101, that "the county executive may be otherwise appropriately entitled by private act" preserved the "county mayor" title used in Shelby County.

in Knox and Hamilton counties) and directs that "members of the county legislative body shall be known individually as county commissioners and collectively as the board of county commissioners."[18] The body must elect from its membership a chairman and a chairman pro tem; a county executive can be elected as chairman until September 1, 1982. All quarterly county courts were redesignated as county legislative bodies and, with a few exceptions, were directed to bring their respective counties into conformity with the constitutional amendment by May 20, 1978. Changes were made in several counties that had county courts with more than twenty-five members, but in most counties the existing pattern of representation was continued (supported by an opinion of the attorney general that the old pattern of three JPs from the county seat district, with 50 percent more population, and two JPs from each of the other districts, is acceptable under the new constitutional provision). The implementing legislation vests discretion in each legislative body to determine the number of members from each district up to the constitutional maximum of three; special provisions require that, if multimember districts are used in Bledsoe and Wayne counties, candidates must run for separately designated offices, but this is discretionary with the legislative body in other counties.

The office of county executive was invested with the administrative powers and duties of a county judge or chairman of the county court (implementing legislation simply substituted "county executive" in appropriate statutes), but the term of office is four years instead of the previous eight for a county judge and one for a county chairman.[19] As "accounting officer, general agent, or financial agent," the county executive has custody of some county buildings, audits claims against the county, approves warrants (orders to make payment for services rendered or materials purchased), audits and settles accounts of the trustee and of others who handle county funds, supervises the maintenance of financial records, participates in the budget process, and prepares semiannual statements of the county's financial condition. The most significant additional power is a veto over resolutions of the county legislative body, which can be overridden by a majority of all of its members; this power does not extend to resolutions "exercising administrative or appellate authority," and veto of budget items is denied (the budget as a whole is subject to veto). Unless otherwise provided by general or private acts, the county executive is empowered to appoint department heads and members of boards and commissions, subject to approval by the legislative body. The office of

---

[18]*TCA*, 5–5–102(a). In general usage the term "county commission" is frequent.

[19]Except for a few counties the implementing legislation also vested judicial powers in the county executive, but this was held unconstitutional by the Tennessee Supreme Court in *Waters* v. *Schmutzer and Ogle*, 583 S.W. 2d 756 (1979), primarily because the constitutionally

county judge was abolished at the end of terms of office of incumbents or when a vacancy occurred, except in Hamilton County where a special provision continues the office as a court of record.

Although the 1978 constitutional amendment was hailed as a reform of county government, it was far from being a sweeping change. It failed to integrate all of a county's operations under a single executive. It explicitly required election of a sheriff, trustee, register, a county executive, county clerk, and assessor of property (the last three officers were added to those previously named in the constitution). It did not order any changes in a county's school system or highway administration. Much of a county's work is performed in these offices, and the county executive cannot exercise any effective control over their operations. All the same, the amendment did establish executive direction for the other operations that formerly were subject to control by the county court, and this at least must be viewed as some improvement. A proposal was made to a legislative committee prior to the 1979 session of the General Assembly that the elective offices should be under the executive budget process instead of the traditional "salary suits" before judges; this would have made possible a degree of executive control, but it was not recommended by the committee.[20] Other changes may be accomplished by private acts. Knox County, for example, obtained enactment of a private act in the 1980 legislative session that authorized changes by the county commission and established three administrative departments under directors responsible to the county executive for the discharge of functions not under the elective offices or otherwise covered by general law; the act also establishes procedures and standards for budgeting, accounting, and purchasing for all county departments, agencies, and offices.[21]

A 1979 act was enacted pursuant to a provision in the 1978 constitutional amendment empowering the General Assembly to "provide alternate forms of county government including the right to charter."[22] Much of this act is patterned after the legislation authorizing a city and county to consolidate and form a "metropolitan government." An existing county government can be replaced if a charter proposed by a charter commission is approved by a majority of votes cast in a referendum. But, in order to overcome opposition to the new act, a provision was added that "the duties of the constitutional county officers as prescribed by the General Assembly shall not be diminished under a county charter form of government."

mandated four year term conflicts with the older constitutionally mandated eight year term for all judicial officers.

[20]A committee member remarked that sponsorship of this proposal would have to come from legislators wishing to end their legislative careers. This illustrates a principal difficulty in attempting to reform county government—all of these elected officials have many supporters.

[21]*Public Acts,* 1980, ch. 286.

[22]*Public Acts,* 1979, ch. 402.

(The Lord giveth, and the Lord taketh away.) This will effectively bar any significant changes in the structure of county government unless the General Assembly cooperates by diminishing the duties of constitutional officers (and even then the offices must be continued, as in the Nashville–Davidson County metro government where the sheriff has the limited role of jail custodian).

An innovation in the 1979 act is authority for the legislative body of a chartered county government to "pass ordinances relating to purely county affairs." The enabling language is similar to that usually included in the charters of cities. In hailing this as a great accomplishment, the executive director of the Tennessee County Services Association commented, "For years, county government officials have argued that county legislative bodies should be given the same opportunity that city councils have in Tennessee to determine the best solution to problems at the local level. Now that this bill is passed, counties will be able to do just that.[23]

A question might be raised as to whether this authorization, founded on only the constitutional words "right to charter" in the 1978 amendment, would stand up under attack based on the court's previous interpretations barring legislative delegation of such authority to county courts. An adverse decision in this respect would probably frustrate the general objective of the act, which was to create a corporate structure that could function in the manner of a municipal corporation.

The 1978 constitutional changes included repeal of the section that required election of those ancient offices—justices of the peace and constables. The former office no longer exists, being replaced by the office of county commissioner (member of the county legislative body). The office of constable—that pitiful remnant of the past—though not now required by the constitution, continues as a statutory office with a two-year term in all but Davidson, Hamilton, Knox, Perry, and Shelby counties, where it has been abolished. Special provisions are made for the election of constables in five counties;[24] in eighty-five counties they are elected from "constable districts" established by a county's legislative body, and their total number cannot exceed one-half the number of county commissioners. In forty-nine counties a constable is invested with police powers by statute as well as having the common-law powers of the office; in forty-one counties the duties are limited to process serving.[25]

---

[23]*Tennessee County News* 3:3 (Sept. 1979), 8.
[24]*TCA*, 8–10–101.
[25]*TCA*, 8–10–108.

⊛

County governments have gradually been acquiring functions and powers of a municipal character. . .

EISENHOWER COMMISSION ON INTERGOVERNMENTAL RELATIONS (1955)

WE HAVE SAID THAT MUCH of a county's work is performed in the offices of a number of elected officials. Under the 1978 constitutional amendment all of these are elected for four-year terms.[26] The trustee collects taxes and other revenues, is the official custodian of county funds, and disburses funds on properly drawn warrants. The register is custodian of deeds, mortgages, and other legal papers relating to land and personal property. The county clerk serves as the recording officer of the county legislative body (board of county commissioners) and of special courts in some counties. In addition to being a county's chief law enforcement officer, the sheriff is responsible for a long list of statutory duties, including supervising the county jail, serving all sorts of legal papers, and "attending upon" all courts while in session.

The county assessor of property (formerly called the tax assessor) assesses all property except public utilities assessed by the state public service commission. State law requires that all assessing for both county and municipal taxes is to be the responsibility of this officer after the reappraisal of property has been completed and an adequate maintenance plan has been approved by the state board of equalization.[27] No county adopted the option of an appointive assessor made available by a 1967 act, and this act was overruled by the 1978 constitutional amendment that required election of an assessor in every county. The 1978 arrangement destroyed the chance of improvement that nobody had used anyway. Still, assessment procedures have been considerably improved in recent years under state laws requiring the training and certification of county assessors and the use of standards prescribed by the state board of equalization. Updating assessments to keep up with inflation continues to be a troublesome problem.

Each county has a public school system as a unit of the statewide system, administered by a county school board and a full-time administrator (titled "county school superintendent" in nearly all counties) who is selected by the county commission in sixteen counties, by the county board of education in three (including Anderson), and by popular election in the remaining counties. Anderson voted in 1980 to change to election, but this was invalidated by the Tennessee Supreme Court because it would have

[26]Formerly the sheriff was elected for a two-year term, with a further limitation that he could serve no more than six years in any eight-year period.

[27]The law was amended in 1976 to authorize a municipality in two or more counties to maintain its own assessment office; to date only Oak Ridge has elected to do so.

removed the incumbent; another referendum will be held in May 1982, to determine the method after the incumbent's term ends. In counties where a large proportion of the students are in city or special district school systems (partially supported by their taxes) proportionately less of a county's budget is spent for this purpose—for example, 18, 24 and 31 percent, in 1977–78, in Crockett, Shelby, and Carroll counties, as compared with 65, 67 and 69 percent, in Montgomery, Warren, and Hardeman counties, where only county systems exist. Occasionally controversy arises over whether city school systems should be consolidated with county systems, as a means of increasing administrative efficiency, equalizing funding and programs, and the like. Such moves have been successful in Bedford, Montgomery, Warren, and White counties (Davidson also has one school system, as an integral part of the "metro" package approved in that county); efforts in Hamblen and Knox counties have failed.

Tennessee by general law provides for county highway commissions and chief administrative officials, but private acts apply to some degree in ninety-three counties and introduce a variety of organizational arrangements: forty-five counties have no highway commissions and forty-eight have such commissions composed of two to eleven members, who are elected in twenty-five counties and appointed or ex officio in the other counties; nearly all counties have chief administrative officials (with titles such as road superintendent, road supervisor, commissioner, engineer, and director of public works), elected in sixty-five counties and appointed or employed in the other counties.

Records systems are generally of poor quality; in recent years the state comptroller's office has attempted to institute better accounting practices, with some success. Financial reporting is accomplished mainly through quarterly and annual reports to the board of county commissioners. Purchasing procedures are often below standard. Little administrative control is exercised by the state, even though most of the funds expended come from the state or from the federal government channelled through the state; the principal means of state control has been through the post-audit function exercised by the state comptroller's office.[28] A 1980 act directs withholding of a county's share of state gasoline tax proceeds if it fails to file inventory reports required by state law.[29]

The proceeds from two cents of the state gasoline tax are distributed to counties by a three-part formula: one-half equally to each county, one-fourth proportionate to land area, and one-fourth on a basis of population. Efforts of legislators from urban counties to change this formula have

[28]See *Report of the House Transportation Committee Subcommittee on Local Government Highway, Street and Road Department Administration to the 1980 Session of the Ninety-first General Assembly,* March 1980, 63 pp.
[29]*Public Acts,* 1980, ch. 473.

failed, but in recent years a small measure of success has been attained in giving greater weight to population for distribution of special appropriations for county roads.[30] However, the traditional formula was used for distributing the counties' share of the 1981 tax increase on gasoline and other motor fuels.

The quality of highway work has been mediocre, largely as the result of political administration of units too small to be efficient. Districts within counties certainly are undesirable; multicounty districts would make more sense. Many county highway departments have suffered from below-par engineering; assistance from the state highway department when requested has partially remedied this deficiency in some counties. In the late 1960s some state legislators advocated state assumption of the highway function, an action taken in North Carolina years ago, but the idea made no progress against the solid opposition of county highway officials.

The Tennessee County Uniform Road Law, enacted in 1974,[31] was designed to correct some of the deficiencies in county highway administration. This act sets minimum requirements of education and experience for the "chief administrative officer," prescribes a minimum annual salary equal to the county clerk's salary (effective September 1, 1980, the minimums ranged from $9,789 to $22,410 according to the class of the county), requires preparation and annual revision of a three-year plan and conformity with annual budgets, and directs an annual inventory of all equipment, tools, materials, and the like. Following a time-honored Tennessee practice, seven counties were completely exempted from the act's application. Through the 1980 session of the legislature, four additional counties had been exempted and the exemption of two had been removed, leaving the number of exempted counties standing at nine. Several counties are also exempted from various other provisions of the law. The law continued in effect those "provisions of private acts not in conflict." Although it is deficient in some respects—a result of compromises to get a bill passed —this legislation is still a significant step forward, and it could become the foundation for an improved system of county highway administration.

A few of the larger counties are fairly self-sufficient in administering public health programs, but for most of the state this is a responsibility of the state Department of Public Health through a division of local health

---

[30]The total distributed from the two cent tax in the year ending June 30, 1979, was $58,358,799 and ranged from $362,049 for Moore County to $3,234,244 for Shelby County. For the 1980 fiscal year $6,000,000 was appropriated for distribution on a population basis, with a minimum of $20,000 to any county, and in addition thereto $6,438,000, half for per capita distribution and half for distribution on a basis of road mileage. For the 1981 fiscal year, $9,480,000 was appropriated, 75 percent to be distributed on a basis of population and 25 percent on a basis of road mileage, with a minimum of $20,000 to any county (each county must allocate for the same purposes 20 percent of its amount from locally levied taxes).

[31]*TCA*, 54–7–101 *et seq.*

administration and nine regional offices. State law provides for a county board of health made up of the county executive, superintendent of schools, county health officer or county physician, two doctors of medicine or osteopathy, a dentist, a registered nurse, and a graduate pharmacist; a county optionally may add a doctor of veterinary medicine and a consumer representative. The involvement of these boards varies widely —they seldom meet in some counties, while in others a close oversight of the program is exercised.

Welfare programs are administered by the state Department of Human Services, using the geographic boundaries of counties as administrative units. Before July 1, 1973, counties were required to participate in the cost of the public assistance, Medicaid, and food-stamp programs; subsequently the only county financial support has been for foster-home care of children—all counties have participated even though not required to do so by law.

As unincorporated areas of counties have become more urbanized in recent years, and as suburbanites and country folks have viewed with increasing envy services such as fire protection enjoyed by city residents, more demands have been made on county governments for urban-type services. A 1961 act empowered counties to construct and operate revenue-financed "urban type public facilities," such as water and sewerage systems, incinerators, landfills, and docks;[32] fire protection was authorized in three counties (Hardin, Shelby, and Wayne). A 1965 act as amended authorized the establishment of countywide fire departments and of fire tax districts,[33] the tax levy in each district to be sufficient to pay the district's allocated share of total costs. The special taxing authority of this act has not been utilized by any county, but Knox County secured an amendment authorizing such expenditures from the general fund and established a county fire department that served a county-owned industrial park and nearby areas. The department was abolished in 1981.

In 1969 the legislature authorized counties to provide "garbage and rubbish disposal services."[34] Financing can be provided by a special property tax levy within a defined district (another act prohibits superimposing a levy on property within a city or town not receiving such services[35]) or by fees collected from persons served. In the past decade this has become an area of considerable activity by counties. Bulk collection systems (from strategically located large containers) exist in forty-two counties (including two joint systems in Bledsoe-Sequatchie and Montgomery-Stewart counties), and house-to-house collection is provided in

[32]*TCA*, 5–16–101.
[33]*TCA*, 5–17–101.
[34]*TCA*, 5–19–101.
[35]*TCA*, 5–19–108.

Dyer and Hamblen counties (in the former the county pays a contractor $1.25 of the monthly charge of $4.25 per customer, and in the latter a property tax levy, excluding Morristown, finances the service). In 1979, landfills were operated by forty-six counties (one jointly with a city), which were also used by many cities, and four counties were responsible for delivery of the wastes to other landfills.

The functions of the county, like the county's structure, have been inherited from the past. As many of these once-localized functions have become increasingly important to the state as a whole, a move has developed to bring them increasingly under state control or even operation. This we see happening in highways, welfare, health, and schools—even, to some degree, in law enforcement. If carried to its final conclusion, this trend would not necessarily cause the disappearance of the county, but it might well transform it from a partly local agency into a merely administrative subdistrict of the state. That the county has been saved from this development is partly attributable, no doubt, to the fact that new functions have been added to the county's tasks. Thus the county, which is the only local unit available to rural people, may become the unit for county parks and recreational activities, libraries, county forests, and for the provision of utilities, ambulance services, public housing, airports, and so on. The South has seen much development of this sort, and so has Tennessee, but, on the whole, the development of new functions outside the traditional fields has been slow. Nevertheless, the county is still an important unit of Tennessee government and seems certain to remain so for a long time to come.

⊛

Local governments, which derive seven-eighths of their tax revenue from property taxes, need to reform that workhorse. . . .
    ADVISORY COMMISSION ON INTERGOVERNMENTAL RELATIONS (1969)

THE PRIMARY ROLE of the county judge (chairman) as "accounting officer, general agent, or financial agent" of the typical county has been noted, and in many counties his leadership brought about significant improvements (the "county executive" now performs such functions). The state comptroller, through his power to prescribe auditing standards for private auditors, through audits of counties by his staff (who performs the audit is determined by each county),[36] and through promotion of improved fiscal systems, has also been a major factor in improving the quality of county financial administration. The 1957 General Assembly enacted three model

---

[36]The comptroller reported that for the 1979–80 fiscal year eighty-four counties were audited by his staff and eleven counties by independent certified public accountants.

laws which may be adopted by any county (the number of adopting counties at mid-1979 is indicated after each): the county budgeting act (twelve), the county fiscal procedure act (twelve), and the county purchasing act (eleven). Similar modernized systems are in operation in a number of other counties, including the largest counties, under the provisions of private acts (nine had central accounting acts and twenty-seven had purchasing acts). Rudimentary fiscal systems and an independent status of the elective offices still characterize most county governments.

A 1959 act requires annual submission of budget estimates by all officers and agencies to the county executive,[37] but fee-financed offices and boards or commissions that file such estimates directly with the county legislative body are excepted. This act falls far short of providing for an executive budget; it simply directs filing of the estimates with the county executive for study and submission to the county legislative body or to an appropriate committee. Usually the county executive submits his recommendations to a committee of the legislative body, and he is influential in working with the committee in formulating a budget for presentation to the full body.

The laws governing compensation for county officers who collect fees (clerks of various courts, county trustee, register of deeds, and sheriff) are somewhat complicated.[38] In general they require an accounting for and deposit of all fees into a county's treasury, with minimum and maximum salaries fixed for counties in various population groupings. Since 1921,[39] salaries of deputies and other employees in their offices have been determined annually by "salary suits" filed in designated courts by the officer against the county judge or chairman (now county executive) as defendant; orders of the court fix the number of personnel and the salaries to be paid. Funds for other expenses to operate these offices are obtained through the budget process as appropriations from general funds.[40] All such expenditures are related to fees collected, and if the latter exceed the former the "excess fees" become revenue to a county's general fund; if the reverse is true the deficiency must be covered by an appropriation. Since 1974 a quarterly county court (now the board of county commissioners)[41] may elect to pay all such salaries and expenses from the general fund through the regular budget and appropriation process, in which event all fees are

[37]*TCA*, 5–9–401.

[38]*TCA*, Title 8, chs. 20 and 24, and parts of ch. 22.

[39]*Public Acts*, 1921, ch. 101. See *Hunter* v. *Conner*, 152 Tenn. 258 (1925), for an interesting summary of prior unsuccessful efforts, which began in 1879, to shift such officers from fee compensation to salaries.

[40]Most sheriffs in the state elect to use this process instead of the salary suit procedure for all of their operating funds.

[41]Counties under a metropolitan form of government (Davidson) and five other counties (Hamilton, Houston, Knox, Montgomery, and Stewart) are excepted from this law and instead are required to follow a prescribed reporting procedure to determine deficiencies or excess fees (*TCA*, 8–22–104).

handled as revenue to the general fund; a large number of counties have chosen this option, and a trend in this direction is evident.

Additional service demands and erosion of the dollar's value by inflation have combined to increase the amount of revenue collected by Tennessee's counties more than elevenfold in thirty years—from $112 million in 1947–48 to $1,283 million in 1977–78. Table 15–1 analyzes their revenues by five major categories in 1947–48, 1967–68 and 1977–78 (not available for 1957–58). These figures show a shift away from state aid as a proportion of the total: from 59 percent in 1947–48 to 33 percent in 1977–78. There was also a slight decline in the property tax portion, from 33 to 29 percent. Federal aid moved from zero to 15 percent (the 1947–48 "other" category may have included a small amount of federal aid), the local sales tax accounted for 9 percent in 1977–78 as compared with none in 1947–48, and the "other" category increased from 8 to 14 percent.

Table 15–1
Major Sources of County Revenues
Fiscal Tears 1948,[a] 1968, 1978

Source	1948		1968		1978	
	Amount	%	Amount	%	Amount	%
Property tax	$ 36,956,864	33	$166,579,088	35	$ 365,065,803	29
State aid	66,374,546	59	171,273,703	36	424,888,110	33
Federal aid			41,236,658	9	196,267,520[b]	15
Local sales tax			35,022,597	7	115,294,882	9
Other	8,656,243	8	62,782,556	13	181,559,421	14
Totals	$111,987,653[c]	100	$476,894,602	100	$1,283,075,736	100

[a]Not reported by the source breakdown in the latter 1950s or early 1960s.
[b]Includes $44,723,678 from general revenue sharing account, which started in 1973.
[c]Excludes reported amounts of bond proceeds.
Source: Annual Surveys of County, City and Town Government in Tennessee (Nashville: Tennessee Taxpayers Assn., for years indicated).

Counties are still heavily dependent on the property tax, though somewhat less so than in former years. The 1980 actual tax rates ranged from Coffee's $1.27 (per $100 of assessed valuation) to Anderson's $7.91; nine counties had rates under $2.00, twenty-four from $2.00 to $3.00, twenty-eight from $3.00 to $4.00, eighteen from $4.00 to $5.00, thirteen from $5.00 to $6.00, and three had rates of $6.00 or more. Effective tax rates in 1980 (equivalent rates that would have produced the same revenue if all property had been assessed at full value) ranged from Wayne's 93 cents to Morgan's $4.20; only Wayne was under a dollar, forty-five counties were over $1.00 and under $2.00, forty-two ranged from $2.00 to $3.00, six were between $3.00 and $4.00, and one was over $4.00. The tax rates were

TABLE 15–2

ANALYSIS OF OPERATING EXPENSES

ALL COUNTIES AND THREE SELECTED COUNTIES

Fiscal Year 1977–78

Purposes	All counties		Shelby		Hardeman[a]		Van Buren[b]	
	Amount	%	Amount	%	Amount	%	Amount	%
General county	$ 298,979,118	23	$ 67,111,368	56	$ 856,749	12	$ 271,772	16
Public schools	657,436,882	51	29,046,574	24	5,045,550	69	866,840	49
Roads and bridges	115,773,340	9	4,011,381	3	952,135	13	516,774	29
Debt service	111,348,837	9	7,916,299	7	244,260	3	76,382	4
Other	100,840,934	8	11,972,852	10	221,745	3	36,540	2
Totals	$1,284,379,111	100	$120,058,474	100	$7,320,439	100	$1,768,308	100

[a]County with median total expenses.
[b]County with lowest total expenses.
Source: 1978 Annual Survey of County, City and Town Government in Tennessee (Nashville: Tennessee Taxpayers Assn., Nov. 1, 1979), 48–49.

broken down by funds, more so in some counties than in others. All counties made levies for their general funds; only Pickett reported no levy for a school fund; all but eight counties made levies for debt service funds; seventy-seven counties made levies for road and bridge funds; and several counties made levies for special purposes, such as ambulance service, refuse disposal, and fire protection.[42]

State aid, primarily for schools and roads, has provided more funds than the other sources. It can, of course, be argued that these are not strictly local functions and are more truly matters of statewide concern, to justify this degree of support from the state government. Such assistance has a long history.[43] The first assistance, for schools, began in 1854 and did not exceed $200,000 in any one year until 1904, when $407,299 was distributed. Payment of certain county highway bonds began in 1927; the distribution of a portion of gasoline tax proceeds commenced in 1929, increased to two cents in 1931, and increased again in 1981. Sharing a portion of the state tax on income from stocks and bonds began in 1931, and distribution of a part of beer tax proceeds was initiated in 1933. Substantial increases occurred in the 1930s (a 63 percent increase, or $6,485,913, from FY 1934–35 to FY 1937–38), but in the 1937–38 fiscal year state aid was only 36 percent of total county expenditures (as contrasted with 59 percent of total revenues in 1947–48).

In July, 1981, all counties but one (Anderson) were levying local sales taxes; seven at 1 percent; forty-seven at 1.5 percent; seven at 1.75 percent; ten at 2 percent; twenty-three at 2.25 percent (statutory maximum). Under special legislation twelve counties in 1980 were imposing taxes on hotel and motel services, at rates of 3 to 5 percent. Robertson County was the first county (1947) to levy a "wheel tax" ($5.00) on motor vehicles; its rate was raised to $35.00 in 1979. Twenty-seven other counties have followed suit, generally by private acts enacted by the legislature, but several counties have utilized a 1976 general law to levy the tax by local referendum.[44] In 1980 the rates varied from $5.00 (Lake) to $50.00 (Cheatham); the rate was $10.00 in twelve counties, $15.00 in seven, $20.00 in one, $25.00 in five, and $35.00 in one. These taxes are payable concurrently with renewal of state auto licenses, except in Davidson County.[45] This rash of county wheel taxes focused attention on a common practice of registering vehicles in counties other than those in which the owners reside (a tactic that has been

---

[42]*Tennessee County Tax Statistics* (County Technical Assistance Service, Univ. of Tennessee, Technical Report No. 22, Oct. 1980). Several counties levy variable rates in cities and special school districts; in making this tabulation the rates outside cities and such districts were used.

[43]The remainder of this paragraph is based on material in *The Third Annual Statewide Survey of County, City and Town Government in Tennessee* (Nashville: Tennessee Taxpayers Assn., Dec. 1, 1938), 9–10.

[44]*TCA*, 5-8-102.

[45]*Tennessee County Tax Statistics*, 26–31.

used for many years to evade city wheel taxes). A 1980 act prohibits this practice for noncommercial vehicles and declares a violation to be a misdemeanor, punishable by a fine of $50 to $100 (only $5 to $10 if a county wheel tax has been paid or is not due).[46]

A constitutional amendment requiring the classified assessment of property, effective in 1973, was designed to reverse victories in 1966 by the railroads in federal and state courts invalidating the *de facto* classification that had placed public utilities' property on the tax rolls at 50 to 100 percent of value and locally assessed property at 7 to 48 percent. The new situation in 1973 was summarized as follows:

> Now that 1973 tax rates have been set in most counties, trends are becoming apparent, generally along property class lines. The tax burden has increased considerably for business taxpayers and at an even greater rate for the public utilities. Farmers and home owners, who were the strongest supporters of [the amendment], received significant property tax reductions in some counties but many counties show no appreciable change and some counties even increased taxes on homes and farms. The ability of the counties to shift the burden of the property tax from farms and homes to business and utility taxpayers depends upon the amount of business and utility property within a county. Predominantly rural counties, having little business and utility property, have no opportunity to shift taxes, so the burden must remain on farms and residences.[47]

It appears that the railroads will be successful in partially reversing this shift in tax burden. They have won a case upholding a federal statute that requires railroad property to be assessed at a level no higher than other commercial and industrial property;[48] under this decision, beginning in 1979, railroad property must be assessed at the same ratio of actual value as is applied to other commercial and industrial property in a particular taxing jurisdiction (county). This reduced the 1979 total assessments of all railroads by more than $96 million, with a resulting tax loss for all cities and counties in the range of $4 to $6 million.

In recognition of the fact that assessments by county assessors have not reflected increases in actual market values, beginning in 1978 the ratio of such assessments to actual value in each county, as indicated by state-conducted sales ratio studies, is applied to the estimated full value of all public utilities, and the resulting figure is multiplied by 55 percent (40 percent for railroads beginning in 1979) to arrive at assessed values.

A legislatively mandated reassessment program for all counties, initiated in 1967, was completed when reappraisals were placed on the assessment rolls of Carter and Monroe counties in 1978. Another program to update

---

[46]*Public Acts,* 1980, ch. 744.

[47]*1972 Annual Survey of County, Town and City Government* (Nashville: Tennessee Taxpayers Assn., Oct. 1, 1973), 2.

[48]*State of Tennessee* v. *L. & N. Railroad Co. et al.,* U.S. District Court for Middle District of Tennessee, Nashville Division, No. 79–3025, August 15, 1979 (not a reported case); affirmed by the federal Court of Appeals in Cincinnati on April 14, 1981.

property assessments was initiated by the state division of property assessments in 1976, utilizing a computer-assisted appraisal system. A 1980 act provides for a continuing reassessment program on a mandatory basis, to begin in 1981.[49] In the first seven years (ending December 31, 1987) the real property in all counties must be reappraised and reassessed unless the State Board of Equalization determines that such action is unnecessary in a particular county; thereafter this must be accomplished in five-year cycles. In the event that a county assessor of property fails to place such reappraisals on the assessment rolls, the State Board of Equalization is directed to do so as a part of the annual review and equalization process. It is evident that the state intends to haul the reluctant counties into a modern administrative system.

All counties spent over $1,284 million in fiscal year 1977–78; $299 million for general county purposes, $657 million for schools, $116 million for roads and bridges, $111 million for debt service, and $101 million for other purposes. Davidson County (metro general services district) spent the most (over $262 million), primarily because more functions are funded from the county budget in relation to the city (urban services district). Nine counties spent less than $2 million. Table 15–2 shows the amounts spent by five major categories, for all counties, for the largest county (Shelby), and for the counties that spent the median (Hardeman) and lowest (Van Buren) amounts. Public schools accounted for more expenditures in every county but two; they were second place in Shelby and third place in Crockett. Roads and bridges were in second place in forty-two counties (first place in Crockett), and ranked third in thirty-three; this was the lowest category in the counties containing the four largest cities (Shelby, Davidson, Knox, and Hamilton). Second place was taken by "general county purposes" in thirty-six counties, by "debt service" in twelve, and by the "other" category in three.

The total net direct debt of all counties in 1978 was $874.5 million, an increase of 60 percent from the 1970 total of $546.4 million. The three largest counties had the most debt: Davidson (Metro General Services District), $162.5 million; Shelby, $56.5 million; and Knox, $49.5 million (excluding $29 million of Public Building Authority bonds secured by rentals and payable by Knox County). Changes from 1970 ranged from a decrease of 80 percent in Lake to an increase of 2,435 percent in Rhea. Expressed as percentages of total property assessments in 1978, the net debt was between 15 and 30 percent in eighteen counties, between 10 and 15 percent in nineteen, from 5 to 10 percent in thirty-four, and less than 5 percent in twenty-four (Fayette, Haywood, and Lake counties were under 1 percent).[50]

[49]*Public Acts*, 1980, ch. 820.

[50]The statistics in these two paragraphs are taken from the *1978 Annual Survey of County, City and Town Government*(Nashville: Tennessee Taxpayers Assn., Nov. 1, 1979).

⊛

. . . political parties . . . in the majority of the states look on county jobs . . . as necessary patronage for building campaign organizations.

G. THEODORE MITAU (1966)

WE HAVE REPEATEDLY STRESSED the importance of the county as the basic unit of party politics in the state of Tennessee. The party is the unit at the bottom of whatever political party organization exists in the state. Typically the party organization is a rather loose affair that operates on mutual hopes and interests rather than on discipline. Candidates form their own organizations, but in these organizations, too, the county is the fundamental unit.

The county organizations function without programs or issues. Most county elections come and go without any detectable issue of importance. Political contests are concerned with the dispensing of jobs, contracts, and favors, where competition is often keen. Party contests, contrary to those in cities, are openly and frankly partisan; elections are based on party designations. In many sections of the state, one or the other party is dominant (even though this is slowly changing), and the real struggles are carried on between factions of the same party. In all these county contests there are few differences in policy between the parties or factions, and fewer still that can be made evident to voters. The outs want in, and the ins want to stay in, and appeals are made to the voter, not on issues, but on personal qualifications, friendships, and purely partisan attachment. Lip service to improved services and more efficient management are common, but few informed voters can believe all the promises any more than the candidates themselves. The foolishness has been compounded by the all-encompassing cheapening of everything by the television commercial, which lends an aura of complete "phoniness" to the entire performance.

In this intricate and shifting pattern of county politics, the local county boss rises and falls. For the most part he is not widely known to the general public, although he has his share of influence in state and national affairs. Burch Biggs in Polk County and his protégé, Paul Cantrell of McMinn, rose to dominate and hold their counties for some years until driven out by GI's returning from World War II, and it is safe to say that they are now pretty much forgotten. Commissioner of Education Howard Warf was a powerful leader in Lewis County before and after he joined the administration of Governor Frank Clement. His power disappeared in the years following the Clement–Ellington period. The political life of the average county leader is often obscure, short, and full of problems. He "is of few days, and full of trouble; he cometh forth like a flower and is cut down. He fleeth also as a shadow, and continueth not."

16

☆ ☆
☆

Diversity and Union: The Search for Balance

THE FEDERATION THAT MAKES UP THE UNITED STATES OF AMERICA COMPRISES fifty individual states, each with its own scheme of local government, the fifty joined together into a national organization. The national government has powers delegated to it in the written constitution, either expressly or by implication; the states have powers by reason of being states, that is to say, inherent powers; and the localities have powers delegated to them by the state. But this simple and logical scheme does no more than introduce us to the complicated and confusing apparatus that functions in the government of the United States and the individual states. The actual situation has been summed up in these words:

> The history of the United States reveals an increasingly powerful national government. Although the states and localities have also become more powerful and active, the national government has, in comparison, gained more power, and the states and the localities are relatively less powerful and independent than they were in the past. The triumph of nationalism at the close of the Civil War finally confirmed the national authority and sovereignty, and the twentieth century has seen the steady sweep forward of national power.[1]

In present-day government the different components of the system—the nation, the states, and the local units—function through a wide range of relationships with each other, relationships that enable the federal system to work, at least after a fashion.

The component units of the American system are much the same as those of other governments—a geographical area of great or small extent, inhabited by a number of persons living under political arrangements of some kind. In the United States these units consist of the whole national

---

[1]Thomas R. Dye, Lee S. Greene, and George S. Parthemos, *American Government: Theory, Structure, and Process* (Belmont, Calif.: Duxbury Press, 1972) 77.

government, the individual states, and a bewildering collection of local governments that display a great variety of names but that are essentially cities, counties, and special districts. The names do not tell us too much about the characteristics of the local units. Very roughly speaking, the cities are urbanized units, but these units show great variation in size, and many such areas are not organized as cities. In many ways the county is the basic subunit of the state; in most states the area of the county includes the area of the city, but this is not everywhere the case, and in a few places the county has virtually disappeared. Variety among the special districts is so great that it is difficult to say what a special district is, but we may describe the city and the county as units that have a variety of functions—multi-purpose units—and a special district as a unit that has a single function or a limited number of functions.

The pattern of intergovernmental relations among the nation, the states, and the local units that surround, and doubtless bewilder, the citizen can be described within the following scheme:

national (or federal)—state relations
federal—local relations
state—local relations
state—state relations
local—local relations.

The relationships among these units involve the divison of power between units; fiscal interactions of various sorts, including grants and loans; exchange of information, particularly when that information includes expert technical advice and assistance; administrative supervision; and contracts. Often these actions overlap: a contract may be the basis for giving technical advice; a grant may flow from a contract; and so on. The variety of relationships can become evident only by the examination of details.

TVA is a good thing and let's have no more of them.

PARAPHRASE OF 1948 CAMPAIGN REMARKS OF THOMAS E. DEWEY

ALL OF THE ARRANGEMENTS INVOLVED in the relations between governments can be found readily enough in Tennessee. An example—a prime one for Tennesseans—is provided by the Tennessee Valley Authority, an agency in most ways unique in the United States. TVA was created by an act of Congress in 1933; its statute has been subsequently amended as to certain details. The years between 1933 and 1949 were years of struggle for the Authority, filled with political controversy and contested issues of constitutionality. Most of the issues were decided favorably for TVA. The

Authority is a government corporation, headed by a board of directors consisting of three persons appointed to nine-year staggered terms by the president, with Senate approval. The agency's program must be authorized by Congress, and certainly the agency will heed the president's directions; thus it appears that TVA, like many other federal agencies, has two bosses, an uncomfortable arrangement that most federal administrators would find familiar enough. The president designates one of the members of the board as chairman, but he is no more than the presiding officer among his equals. The board names a general manager who serves as executive head of the Authority, directing, through several thousand employees, the translation of the board's orders into the reality of reservoirs, river transport, power, flood control, and other aspects of river development.

The Tennessee Valley Authority was established, in the words of its enabling act, "to improve the navigability and provide for the flood control of the Tennessee River; to provide for reforestation and the proper use of marginal lands in the Tennessee Valley; to provide for the agricultural and industrial development of said Valley; to provide for the national defense. . . ." The aims set forth in this act have been followed with a degree of success that may well be considered unusual for a governmental agency. The periods of flood alternating with low water on the Tennessee have been eliminated. Floods on tributary streams still take place, but the main stream is now under control. Navigation has been promoted, although here as elsewhere the amount of river navigation induced by federal public works never comes up to the sometimes rosy predictions of the navigation engineers. National defense has been aided. Improved agriculture and forestry have been supported, although in a period of urban development they do not attract the interest manifested in the early days of the New Deal.

It is the power program of TVA that has attracted the most attention. In a legal sense power is a byproduct of the navigation and flood control programs of TVA. There is a basis for this, too, in the care taken by the Authority to see that the interests of flood control come first in the management of the reservoirs, but from the point of view of benefits to the Valley and the recovery of funds for the national government, power is a very important byproduct indeed. To the original hydroelectric program of TVA has been added a larger steam power program (now being supplemented by nuclear power), so that over the years Tennessee has become the scene of one of the major public power developments of the world. All but a few spots of Tennessee are now served by public power.

Does the power program pay its way? This is a question open to complex argument, but the situation may be briefly described as follows. When the Authority constructs a dam, it is building to serve three purposes. That portion of the construction attributable to power is charged to this purpose, and by far the largest portion, over 85 percent, of the investment of TVA is charged to power. The amount charged to power is reasonably in line with the division of charges on other federal projects. After payment of the costs of power production, tax equivalents, and charges for depreciation, the Authority normally shows annual earnings of between 3 and 5 percent on its power investment. (Before 1961, interest-free capital was available to the Authority.) This rate of return is not as large as that earned by some businesses and would not at present be considered satisfactory for a private power firm. TVA is required now to make some return to the federal treasury. TVA has the right to issue bonds to pay for further power development; it has used this authority, and its bonds (before the drastic rise of interest rates in 1979–80) usually yielded interest of from 4 to over 9 percent, well within the range available on industrial bonds generally. Interest charges are now a very heavy burden on the Authority, and charges are passed on, necessarily, to the increasingly dissatisfied consumer.

Like other federal agencies TVA receives annual appropriations for soil and forestry work and similar programs, and these, of course, are not charged as expenses to power, nor should they be. Flood control and navigation involve expenditures that do not yield a large direct return to the federal treasury, however beneficial they may be to the public at large, but here again Congress has followed a policy for TVA that it has consistently applied, although not always wisely, to the rest of the country.

There can be no doubt that TVA has had massive support in the state of Tennessee. Candidates for office, whether of Democratic or Republican persuasion, have generally found it advisable to support the agency. But as the interest in the preservation of natural conditions has grown in the 1960s and 1970s, the continuing program of dam construction that has seemed to many to be TVA's main stock in trade has begun to arouse the opposition of "environmentalists." The proposed construction of Tellico Dam in East Tennessee was met by a long, drawn-out litigation that culminated in 1978 in preventing the closing of the dam for a time. Opposition to certain other projects has developed as well.

The Authority has made a point of working through state and local agencies in many respects, although on some important questions it has pursued its own policy, independently of state or local concerns.[2] The power program functions primarily through local units, for the Authority, when selling power, is directed by its act to give "preference to States, counties, municipalities, and cooperative organizations of citizens or

[2]For a criticism of some of TVA's policies with respect to state cooperation, see Elliott Roberts, *One River—Seven States: TVA—State Relations in the Development of the Tennessee River* (Knoxville: Bureau of Public Administration, Univ. of Tennessee, 1955).

farmers, not organized or doing business for profit, but primarily for the purpose of supplying electricity to its own citizens or members." This expression of policy is a familiar one in the operation of federally owned power-producing systems. As of 1980 the Authority had entered into contracts with 107 cities, 3 counties, and 50 cooperatives in and near the Valley for the retail distribution of electric power. The contracts between the Authority and these agencies exert a firm control over maximum retail prices for power and over the disposition of the funds realized from power sales, the intent of such controls being to keep power rates down and to prevent power revenues from being used to support the general functions of the towns and cities that sell TVA electricity.

The costs of coal, rising wages, costs of protecting the environment, and rising interest costs—all aspects of inflation—have contributed to a steady increase in the costs of TVA power to the consumer, and, as a result, the Authority has encountered a growing barrage of public criticism, including attacks from some members of Congress. The Authority is no longer quite the sacred object it once was in local politics.

The relationship between TVA and the contracting cities has been described as follows:

> TVA, because of its expertise, prestige, and aggressive defense of its power interests, has played a dominant role in shaping Tennessee laws respecting power distribution. These laws make each municipality virtually a free agent in the process of contract negotiations, subject only to statutes largely reflecting TVA policies. In this process TVA has a great advantage over a single municipality, and observers have noted a need for more concerted action by the cities. Sporadically, on special issues, such as levels and disposition of tax equivalents, the Tennessee Municipal League has performed such a role. The Tennessee Valley Public Power Association, an organization made up of managerial personnel of the municipal and cooperative power systems, also has represented distributors on such issues as rates and direct service by TVA to large industries. The league is generally inclined to take an independent stance and to represent the interests of municipal governments, but TVPPA is strongly oriented toward TVA. . . .
>
> Although some of TVA's activities may be viewed as intervention in local affairs, another view is that TVA personnel are simply following through to make sure that the Authority's mission is accomplished. In this perspective, the extent of local irritation might be regarded as a rough measure of the persistence and thoroughness practiced by TVA in enforcing contractual provisions. It can be argued that its distributors know what these provisions are before signing the contracts, that they should expect to hew to the letter of the contract, and that restrictions are to be expected along with the benefits of such contracts. However, this line of argument may oversimplify the situation. It presumes that cities are free agents and voluntarily assume the burdens of the contracts, when as a matter of fact they have no real choice, because their only source of power is

TVA—they must take the power on TVA's terms, and there is no practicable alternative. . . . The ideal that TVA and the municipalities are partners tends to break down under scrutiny.[3]

A second facet of TVA's relationship with local units is its connection with the agricultural extension services of the Valley states. This cooperation, designed to coordinate research and extension activities of the services and TVA, has been a cornerstone of TVA policy. It has not escaped criticism,[4] but the criticism has made no change in TVA attitudes. TVA agricultural methods have run into opposition from another federal agency, the Soil Conservation Service, and the conflicts between the two must be considered to have been a draw, for both are now in operation in the same territory.[5] Other TVA interests are pursued through cooperative efforts between TVA and state or local units, as in the case, for example, with forestry, park development, public health, and higher education.[6]

What can be said of TVA's philosophy of working through existing state and local agencies? It can certainly be said that this approach is likely to be pleasing to the people of the Valley. It undergirds existing institutions and their political supports. This is not to say that the Authority's benefits were everywhere considered to be such. One school, probably small, resented the Authority's role in promoting industrialization in an area it considered to be happily rural.[7] Perhaps the aroused environmentalist is a new and more valid manifestation of this view. Those who see in TVA an attack on private enterprise possibly remain numerous, although much less vocal than formerly. And academic critics often considered TVA's support of the establishment to be somehow reprehensible. But nonetheless the Authority has withstood all the criticism, which it could hardly have done without substantial local support.[8]

[3]Hobday, *Sparks at the Grassroots*, 232–34.

[4]See Philip Selznick, *TVA and the Grassroots: A Study in the Sociology of Formal Organization* (Berkeley: Univ. of California Press, 1949).

[5]See Norman I. Wengert, *Valley of Tomorrow: the TVA and Agriculture* (Knoxville: Bureau of Public Administration, Univ. of Tennessee, 1952).

[6]For example, the development of the College of Engineering and the creation of the Department of Political Science at the University of Tennessee are traceable, in part, to early support from TVA. The cooperative relationships of TVA are described in Roscoe C. Martin, ed., *TVA: The First Twenty Years: A Staff Report* (University and Knoxville: Univ. of Alabama Press and Univ. of Tennessee Press, 1956).

[7]An outstanding example of this somewhat sentimental point of view is presented in Donald Davidson, *The Tennessee* (vol. I, 1946, rpt. Knoxville: Univ. of Tenn. Press, 1980; Vol. II, New York: Rinehart, 1948). The contrary view is expressed in a review of Davidson's book by Lee S. Greene, "Götterdämmerung in the Knoxville Twilight," *Public Administration Review* 9:4 (Autumn 1949), 294–97.

[8]Examples of local support of and some opposition to TVA can be found in the activities of the Eisenhower administration as described in Aaron Wildavsky, *Dixon-Yates: A Study in Power Politics* (New York: Yale Univ. Press, 1962).

⊛

This intergovernmental fiscal imbalance is the product of many factors . . . including a lopsided Federal aid system.

ADVISORY COMMISSION ON INTERGOVERNMENTAL RELATIONS (1969)

THE TENNESSEE VALLEY AUTHORITY is an excellent example of the influence of the federal government exerted through contracts with the local units. But an equally important phase of federal–state and federal–local relations is furnished by the grants and loans made available from the national government either to states or to municipalities. This method of aiding or persuading states and localities to engage in activities is not new; signs of its use could be detected early in our history as a united country.[9] The grants available from the federal government now cover such a range of functions that a sizable catalog is required merely to furnish a list of subjects for which grants may be made.

Grants are of four kinds. One is the categorical grant for specific purposes. Categorical grants are sometimes grouped into block grants. Or grants may be made either by special revenue sharing or by general revenue sharing. The categorical grant limits the discretion of the unit that receives the money; the block grant preserves or extends that discretion. During American history federal grants to the states and localities have been principally categorical, but in the Nixon administration a system of block grants was instituted. Revenue sharing may be something of a misnomer, for it does not imply in any way that the federal government allows the states or the local units to determine whether the money is to be raised. As with the categorical and block grants, the federal government determines whether the money is to be raised and how much is to be provided.

The bulk of the federal grants coming to the state are for education, highways, and public welfare, which throughout the United States are the three most costly functions of the state governments. Health and hospitals, employment security, and natural resources also receive substantial sums. The following table indicates the relative use of these funds in Tennessee by functions:

---

[9]See Daniel J. Elazar, *The American Partnership: Intergovernmental Cooperation in the Nineteenth Century United States* (Chicago: Univ. of Chicago Press, 1962), 24. Apologists for national policy tend to take the view that grantsmanship is a long-established feature of the federal system, but see Lee S. Greene, "The Condition of the States," in Lee S. Greene, Malcolm E. Jewell, and Daniel R. Grant, *The States and the Metropolis* (University: Univ. of Alabama Press, 1968), 11–35.

TABLE 16–1
INTERGOVERNMENTAL REVENUE FROM THE FEDERAL
GOVERNMENT TO THE STATE OF TENNESSEE BY FUNCTION,
1978 (in thousands)

Education	$196,660
Highways	155,146
Public Welfare	307,416
Health and Hospitals	37,645
Employment Security	39,413
Natural Resources	17,192
Other	115,109

Source: Table 15.5, *Tennessee Statistical Abstract,* 1980, p. 523.

From the point of view of the federal government, the grant-in-aid can be useful as a means of decentralizing the administration of a program in which the central government is interested. Were it not for the state and local governments, the national government would be compelled to devise means of administering these programs locally. But whether or not this means of decentralization is a good one, it is politically necessary. The states and the localities would certainly resent being bypassed by all federal programs, particularly if highly localized federal offices were set up everywhere. But at the same time the grants have been much criticized. They leave final policy decisions in the hands of the central government even though organizations of states and local units are quite vocal as pressure groups in the national capital. And the categorical grants are confusing and complicated, so much so that the states and the larger cities and counties have created administrative units that specialize in keeping track of federal opportunities. Categorical grants often demand matching state or local expenditures in directions the state or local governments would not otherwise have chosen, at the expense of other possible functions. Grants of funds from the federal government usually carry requirements regarding expenditure, the kinds of persons to be employed, and other restrictions on the discretion of the receiving governments, restrictions that are often distasteful to local administrators. In short, the whole system brings into focus the natural enmities that everywhere seem to exist between a controlling central office and the field agencies. To some extent these animosities may be diminished by the development of the shared revenue system.

Revenue sharing is a new experience for the United States, and it is full of pitfalls. On what basis are the funds to be doled out? If the funds are distributed on the basis of population only, wealthier states may be at a disadvantage. If the funds are to be given without regard to the efforts made by the states to help themselves, then those states that elect to get along on a limited range of services will be able to shift more of their burdens to the national taxpayer than some of those taxpayers would like. And the truth of the matter is that the national policymakers are not really prepared to turn over full powers to the states to do what they want with their shares. The central government gives up power with about the same amount of alacrity that any group of politicians exhibits in such matters. So some complex formulas have been developed to control the distribution of the shared funds.

We see no reason for stating the details of these formulas here, particularly as they will be changed from time to time. But the outlines of those formulas can be indicated as a measure of the character of the problem and the ways in which a solution may be sought. Some of the revenues have gone to the state governments, although there is considerable pressure to limit or cut out the states' share. For a time, indeed, that share was dropped from the program. The states were not to use the existence of the shared revenues as a basis for decreasing their former contributions to local governments, although it is also possible for a state that assumes functions that were formerly local to secure a greater share of the revenues. Shared revenues may not be used as matching funds to secure some of the categorical grants that the national government still hands out.

Supposedly, block grants, or shared revenues, should be free of attached strings that tell the recipient how to spend the money. But the central government is not willing to go all the way, so local governments may use their shared revenues only for priority expenditures, such as maintenance and operating expenditures for public safety, environmental protection, transportation, health, recreation, libraries, services for the poor and aged, and financial administration, plus ordinary and necessary capital expenditures. This is a wide list and should take care of most local expenditures, but the restriction leaves an additional channel of federal supervision, for the act empowers the secretary of the treasury of the United States to withhold payments after hearings to determine whether violations of the law by state or local governments have occurred.

The basis of the allocation to the states and the localities has included population, income, and tax effort of the unit securing the funds. The determination of the total amount to be shared rests with the Congress. Other strings were attached, notably requirements for prevailing wage payments.

President Nixon attempted to extend the concept of shared revenues to other grants by eliminating categorical grants in part and substituting block grants covering general areas now reached by categorical items. One sort of opposition to this move came from classes in the community such as blacks and the poor, who felt themselves disadvantaged in the political arena. Such groups feel they have a greater leverage with the national government. This is precisely the view of labor organizations who seek the extension of public safety, minimum wages, and collective bargaining by national decision. Among the groups that may feel some reluctance to accept revenue sharing are the local units, who react unfavorably to any scheme that increases the power of state administrators over local officials.

Revenue sharing, which began in 1972, was extended in 1976 and again in 1980. In the early days of the Reagan administration, federal grants were under review, but it seemed clear that the president would seek to reduce the flow of federal funds to other units of government.[10]

⊛

Local governments are the children of the state. The state has been most unwilling to allow its children to grow up.

CHARLES R. ADRIAN (1972)

ALTHOUGH BY VARIOUS DEVICES the national government is steadily increasing its influence and control over the states, the legal relationship of the federal government to the states is fundamentally different from the relations of the states to their local units. On paper, at least, the states have a sphere of activity different from that of the national government, and in that sphere the states are independent. This was the theory on which the federal system was founded, and it is the theory implied by any reasonable interpretation of the word "federal." In fact the states still do exercise a good bit of autonomy, but their right to this autonomy becomes more and more illusory and remote. The states themselves contribute to their declining position by their unwillingness to proceed on their own and their constant acceptance of or search for national surveillance.

The legal theory of the relationship between the states and the local units is quite different from actual state–local relations. In our system the local units are the creations and the creatures of the state; the state may supervise, supersede, or abolish these units. In other words, the state of Tennessee, like all the other states in our system, is a unitary state, rather than a federal unit. Of course, the political actuality is a little different. The state cannot function without some kind of local units, and local units will not accept complete domination by the central state government. And state constitutional restrictions of various sorts limit the power of executive and legislative branches over local units, so that, even though the "state" in

[10]For a discussion of grants, see Dye, Greene, and Parthemos, *Governing the American Democracy*, 113–17, 120–21.

theory has complete power over the local units, in practice the organs of the state do not enjoy or exercise this degree of authority.

State agencies exercise some supervisory power over local units through inspection and the issuance of orders. Inspection takes place, for example, when the comptroller of the treasury audits the books of county officials. Orders may be exemplified by the state's action in requiring the construction of adequate sewage-disposal plants, an area of considerable activity in the 1970s. But in addition to direct supervision, the state actively provides advice and technical assistance to local units. An outstanding example has been the aid and advice provided by the Tennessee State Planning Office.

The intergovernmental fiscal relations of the national government and states find some duplication in the relations of the state to the cities. In Tennessee various state grants are made to local units in support of particular programs. These are in effect categorical grants; they are especially important in the field of education. In addition the state shares portions of various taxes with the local units, a form of shared revenue that differs slightly from the pattern of federal revenue sharing. Tennessee shares with its local units the taxes on gasoline, on income from stocks and bonds, on beer, on alcoholic beverages, and other motor fuels, on sales and use, as well as payments in lieu of taxes made by TVA. The shares received by the local units from sales and gasoline taxes are particularly significant in their budgets; the local units received them only after decisive political battles, and they would put up sharp fights to retain what they have or to increase their shares.

⊛

It was not until the twentieth century that the congestion and mobility of people began to raise . . . the general question of subnational interstate arrangements.

HARVEY C. MANSFIELD (1955)

IN THE AMERICAN FEDERAL SYSTEM, relations between the states are governed by the national constitution. States are forbidden to conduct relations with foreign countries, but they are permitted to establish compacts among themselves with the consent of Congress. Consent is not required where compacts do not affect national power. The use of interstate compacts has greatly expanded in recent years; Tennessee is now a party to compacts covering drivers' licenses, juveniles, libraries, mental health, forest fire protection, energy, and other matters. It has long been a member of the Interstate Oil Compact and of the Southern Regional Education Board.

The other provision of the constitution governing state–state relations is the "full faith and credit" clause, which requires a state to credit acts and documents of other states, without requiring a state to enforce the policies of other states within its own borders.

TABLE 16–2
STATE TAXES DISBURSED TO LOCAL UNITS, FY 1979–80
(by 1000)

Tax	Counties	Cities
Income	$ 1,522	$ 6,329
Beer	1,041	1,041
Alcoholic beverage	4,872	7,511
Mixed drinks	2,153	3,718
Gasoline and motor fuel	54,235	27,132
TVA in lieu payments	9,590	2,809
Coal severance	1,980	
Sales		$54,436

Source: *State of Tennessee Annual Financial Report,* for year ended June 30, 1980 (Nashville: Comptroller of the Treasury and Department of Finance and Administration), 176–89.

⊛

The most intricate aspect of State–local relations is the problem created by the modern metropolitan area.

COMMISSION ON INTERGOVERNMENTAL RELATIONS (1955)

AT ONE TIME, presumably, the distribution of the population was in some harmony with the areas over which local governments exercised jurisdiction. Urban populations were within cities; rural folk were governed by rural units. The demarcation between the two was fairly clear, although usually in the United States the urban people were subject to the county along with the rural, a "fact of life" far less well known than the sexual matters usually covered by that term. But with the sharp upward trend of urban population in the United States (and elsewhere too) in the last half-century, these demarcations of the urban from the nonurban have become confused and bewildering. Some urban population clusters became so large that they could not be included in a single manageable urban government. Some could have been put into one municipality, but for one reason or another were not. Large numbers of people moved to the suburban areas, beyond the taxes, politics, and other undesirable features of the original central city. Special districts were created to provide for these suburbanites some of the services available in cities; other services were provided by townships and counties, generally ill-adapted administratively to their new chores; and as for the rest of the services, the suburban dwellers simply did without.

And so we have the "metropolitan problem." What is it exactly? Metropolitan problems are of two kinds. One set consists of situations induced by urban and suburban living—housing, sanitation and health, certain types of crime, and so on. These problems are affected by, but are not produced by, the kind of local governmental organization that exists in the area. With these we are not concerned here. The other set of problems that plagues the metropolitan area has to do with the lack of rational organization of the governmental units in those areas. There are three basic reasons for readjusting the local governmental boundaries in the metropolitan area. First, without reorganization, the distribution of services within the area is uneven. Second, the burden of providing those services is inequitably distributed. Third, the whole scheme of local government in such areas is nonrational.

The Tennessee metropolitan area shares these characteristics with such areas in other states, but for various reasons the metropolitan area in this state is far less heavily burdened with this form of bad organization than are the great cities of the North and West. Tennessee has no Chicago, New York, or Los Angeles. Compared to these monstrosities the problems of Memphis, Nashville, Chattanooga, and Knoxville are pale indeed. Whether this comparatively happy state of affairs can continue is not so certain.

The troubled relationship between local units that comes to the fore in metropolitan areas is present to a degree in smaller communities, for the small town, such as Sparta, Morristown, and Elizabethton, has suburbs that bring city–county relationships into question in the same way as in the large city.

The services that are missing in the suburbs include such important matters as sewerage, fire protection, and adequate police protection. Roads are likely to be poor; sidewalks and street lighting, unknown. The maldistribution of burden for public services shows up when suburban taxpayers fail to pay properly for services for the indigent or when they pay once for a service for which the city taxpayers pay twice, since the city dweller pays both city and county taxes. The nonrationality appears when the total organization is confused, hard to understand, erratically based on the chance decisions of the past, and altogether illogical and unreasonable.

The reorganization of metropolitan areas can take the following forms: annexation, city–county consolidation, city–county separation, federation, functional transfers and joint efforts, and metropolitan special districts.

Most of these adjustments are represented in the governmental activity of Tennessee.

Before the constitutional amendments of 1953, municipal boundaries were set by local legislation passed by the General Assembly; such local acts were normally passed whenever approved by the local delegations. This procedure was highly flexible, and it was capable of being adjusted to the wishes of the local people, including the local city councils. In fact, however, annexation came to a virtual standstill in most communities because the local delegations were unwilling to alienate the growing numbers of suburban voters. There were few exceptions to this situation; Memphis grew more steadily than most. But it must be remembered that Memphis, Shelby County, and the legislative representatives from that area were all under the direction of a boss, the "Red Snapper" Ed Crump, and evidently Mr. Crump saw to it that Memphis had a sensible annexation policy. In terms of this program, Memphis was far ahead of Nashville, Knoxville, and Chattanooga, where annexation had virtually ceased, but even in Memphis, annexations did not keep up with growth.[11] The home-rule amendment of 1953 contained a "sleeper" providing that the General Assembly should provide for annexations and deannexations only by *general* law.[12] The legislature in 1955 provided by general law that annexation of contiguous unincorporated territory could be achieved by ordinance; in almost all cities this means an ordinance passed by the city council. The law did not provide for a vote either by the persons to be annexed or by the voters of the annexing city, although if an ordinance can be passed by the voters of a city, apparently annexations could be so undertaken. Annexations undertaken in this way can be challenged in the trial courts, and in fact considerable litigation has since arisen over changes in city boundaries. Generally speaking, however, in cases where there was a reasonable difference of opinion as to the wisdom of the annexation, the courts refused for some years to interfere on the ground that such differences of opinion can be resolved only by legislative action on the part of the city council, with which the judiciary cannot appropriately interfere. Since 1955 annexations have been extensive. All the big cities of the state have taken in substantial areas, and many of the smaller towns and cities have had similar programs. The central cities have received further protection against the creation of neighboring incorporations (as a means of stopping

[11]See Abbott and Greene, 42; David M. Tucker, *Memphis Since Crump: Bossism, Blacks, and Civic Reformers, 1948–1968* (Knoxville: Univ. of Tennessee Press, 1980), 69.

[12]The home-rule amendment was based on a draft prepared by Dr. Wallace Mendelson of the Univ. of Tennessee, Department of Political Science, working for the Tennessee Municipal League. Dr. Mendelson included the provision for general law on annexations, and this version was accepted, but there is reason to believe that league officials paid little attention to the annexation clause in the process of adopting the draft amendment. See also Hobday, *Analysis of Home Rule Amendments.*

annexations) by a provision added later to the basic act, permitting a central city to take over a neighboring area that is seeking to incorporate.

In the big cities annexations have not kept up with the ever spreading population. In spite of the big chunks added to the cities, builders have continued to place the usual sprawling and often substandard subdivisions beyond the new boundaries. The cities have had to fight continuing attempts to emasculate the annexation law, and some additions to it have made the process more difficult. Some attempts have been made to stop annexations in specific counties by special legislation, but such acts have been declared unconstitutional in two cases.[13]

In 1974 the burden of proof was placed on the city[14] for showing an annexation ordinance to be reasonable and in the interests of both annexer and annexed. In 1979, a severe blow was given to annexation by a ruling of the Tennessee Supreme Court that in annexation suits reasonableness is a question for jury determination when a jury is demanded. The court held that the earlier procedure allowing reasonableness to be determined by the city, when there was a difference of opinion, had been abrogated.[15]

When cities take in additional territory they have an ethical, and probably a legal, obligation to extend services to the areas annexed. By and large, Tennessee cities have performed reasonably well on this point. They have moved to sewer the urban areas—a very large and expensive job; they have improved the street and traffic situation, extended fire and police protection, and undertaken garbage collection. On the whole they have given better service than the counties have given, for the Tennessee county has a well-deserved reputation for being lax in these matters. It is, for example, a notorious fact that the typical county sheriff does not and cannot extend adequate policing to the suburban areas. The cities have at times annexed and provided services when it is far from certain that the new residential areas will pay their own way in taxes. It can be generally said (although each individual situation must be studied before a precise statement can be made) that residential areas will not pay for their new services in new property taxes, particularly if the very expensive services, such as sewering, are made chargeable to city taxes.

Some of the maladjustments of the large metropolitan area, and even some of those in smaller communities, may be cured by transferring functions from the city to the county. In other words, the county taxpayer rather than the city taxpayer is made to pay for the function transferred. It

[13]*Frost* v. *City of Chattanooga*, 488 S.W. 2d 370 (1970); *Pirtle* v. *City of Jackson*, 560 S.W. 2d 400 (1977). Examples of the kinds of attack made on the annexation act are disclosed in *Study on the Adjustment of Municipal Boundaries* (Nashville: Legislative Council Committee, 1973).

[14]*Public Acts*, 1974, ch. 753.

[15]*State of Tenn. ex rel. Moretz* v. *Johnson City*, 581 S.W. 2d 628 (1979). Some annexations have received unanimous jury approval.

must be reemphasized that the city taxpayer in Tennessee is also a county taxpayer. What happens in these transfers is that the burden of the service or function is spread over a larger jurisdiction and a larger number of taxpayers, and the general effect of the move is to lower the city tax rate and to raise that of the county. These transfers are appropriate where a function is either provided for everyone in the whole county or where the burden is one that ethically should be shared by every taxpayer in the whole county. The first case is illustrated by the abandonment of the public health function by the city and its assumption by the county, a practice that has become general in Tennessee. The second is illustrated by the provision of hospitalization for the destitute; if providing this kind of care is an obligation of the public, there is no reason it should be regarded as an obligation of the city taxpayer alone. A good bit of action has taken place in this sector also.

Another kind of transfer is possible, and that is the transfer of the function to the state (or to the national government). This allows everybody's pocketbook to be tapped, without regard to residence, but it also transfers the control over decisions to some central agency less amenable to local influence.

The transfer of schools and streets and roads to a larger jurisdiction presents serious difficulties. For one thing, it is extraordinarily difficult to say who should pay for streets and roads, for all citizens benefit to some unmeasurable degree. The transfer of the function of schools to county control would be a rationalizing move and would simplify fiscal and other relationships, but it would also bring a larger unit of government into being in precisely the area where local citizens would like to have a maximum say-so, and it raises the spectre of court-ordered busing of children for racial reasons.

One word of caution: if the transfer leaves the city still paying a part of the cost of the jointly operated function, it is not a real transfer. All this means is that the city taxpayer continues to pay twice, once as city taxpayer and again as county taxpayer. This is a fact that seems unusually hard for the public to assimilate, probably because to so many people "county" denotes the area outside the city and that alone, a notion quite far from the truth.

To some degree consolidations can correct the maladjustments of metropolitan areas. Such consolidations could take place—they rarely do— between two or more cities, or they could occur by putting a city and county together. A city–city consolidation would be appropriate in a number of cases where small incorporations border—or are inside—large ones, such as in the case of Red Bank and Chattanooga. Very occasionally the small cities could be appropriately combined, as in the case of Alcoa and Maryville. But city–city consolidations involve putting together entities that have been created for purposes of separation, and here not even God can put together what man has put asunder. City–county consolidations have a better chance, but, even so, Tennessee can boast of only one such, albeit one that has received national attention. That is the consolidation of Davidson County and Nashville. This union was consecrated on the basis of a statute passed following the 1953 constitutional amendments. Under the Davidson–Nashville arrangement, one government covers the entire area; the structure provides for a single mayor and a large—too large—council. Two taxing districts are provided: the general services district covers the entire county; the urban services district covers the old city area plus anything annexed to it subsequently. A general tax rate is levied on the whole area, and this area gets all the basic services of a general sort; another and added tax rate is levied for the urban services district, to pay for added services of an urban character that only this district gets. "Metro," as this government is called, has been in existence for nearly two decades. It seems well established and may be an improvement on the old system's long rivalry between city and county, but it has exhibited three major faults. First, annexation to the urban services district has moved very slowly, far more slowly than is demanded by the enormous growth of urban building in the county. A second flaw is found in the spread of the metropolitan area into the neighboring counties—Sumner, Cheatham, and Williamson—that cannot be reached by unification through the mere consolidation of one county with one city. The third failure is that the consolidation does not include several independent incorporations within the county (Belle Meade, Berry Hill, Oak Hill, Forest Hills, Goodlettsville, Lakewood, and a portion of Ridgetop).

The consolidation of city and county can be achieved in Tennessee only by concurrent majorities in the city and in the area outside the city. Such an arrangement is as effective in blocking action as is the free veto in the United Nations Security Council; the consolidation in Davidson–Nashville was achieved (on the second try) because the voters inside and outside were "sore" at then Mayor Ben West. Consolidation was a neat way of doing him in, and the voters availed themselves of the opportunity. Municipal reformers owe Nashville a monument commemorating the martyrdom of Mayor West, whose return to private life was thus accompanied by a contribution denied the average city politician.[16] Racism is a

---

[16] A fairly extensive literature exists on "metro" in Nashville-Davidson. Discussions of the subject include Daniel R. Grant, "Metropolitics and Professional Political Leadership: The Case of Nashville," in Greene, ed., *City Bosses and Political Machines*, 72–83; also by Grant, "Urban and Suburban Nashville: A Case Study in Metropolitanism," *Journal of Politics* 17:1 (Feb. 1955), 83–98; David A. Booth, *Metropolitics: The Nashville Consolidation* (East Lansing: Michigan State Univ. Institute for Community Development and Services, 1963); and Daniel R. Grant and Lee S. Greene, "Surveys, Dust, Action," *National Civic Review* 50:9

factor in these consolidations. Although black leadership is split, some central-city blacks fear submergence in a consolidated government, and doubtless many suburban whites would prefer to maintain a distance from the central-city blacks and their growing political power. City–county consolidation has been attempted in Hamilton, Hamblen, Knox, Montgomery and Shelby counties, but all such attempts have been defeated, sometimes in both city and county. The concurrent majorities have always been a formidable—perhaps almost always an insurmountable—obstacle.

A favorite (although not the best) way of attacking metropolitan problems has been the creation of special districts, large and small. They abound in most metropolitan complexes, particularly in the bewildering giant urban areas of the North, East, and Far West. Tennessee has comparatively few of them. The most important such district in the Tennessee metropolitan area is the utility district, which may be created for a variety of purposes but is principally used to supply water. The utility districts have no taxing authority. Their source of financing is revenue bonds, generally sold at higher rates of interest than cities obtain, for the districts serve areas that are relatively thinly populated and where costs are higher on the whole than in the more densely settled municipalities. The districts have served some purpose in that they supply water, but their frequent inability to provide full sewerage has meant in effect that a substantial amount of urban development has been allowed only by use of the temporary expedient of septic tanks. The districts have been run by self-perpetuating boards not responsible to ratepayers or subject to regulation by the state's Public Service Commission; these highly independent conditions have been subject to attack,[17] and some limited controls by county judges and the Public Service Commission were set up by a 1973 statute. Still, the independence, backed by a lobby in the state house, continues to exist.

Metropolitan federation has developed in some of the large areas of the country; such federation divides the local functions between a central government that provides areawide services and the component units of the federation that provide highly localized services. Tennessee affords no examples of metropolitan federation.

(Oct. 1961), 446–71. See also David H. Grubbs, "Legal Aspects of City-County Consolidation in Tennessee," *Tennessee Law Review* 30, (Summer 1963), 499–516.

[17]These districts have been thoroughly described in Community Services Commission, *A Future for Nashville: Report of the Community Services Commission* (Nashville: The Commission, 1952), prepared by Lee S. Greene and Daniel R. Grant; Arthur Bruce Winter, *The Tennessee Utility District* (Knoxville: Univ. of Tennessee Press, 1958); and Nelson M. Robinson and John R. Petty, *Public Utility Services in Tennessee: A Study for Subcommittee 1 of the Tennessee Legislative Council Committee* (Knoxville: Bureau of Public Administration, Univ. of Tennessee, 1966).

County consolidation is a reform of local units that could affect either a metropolitan area or rural sections. The people of the United States have managed to create over 3,000 counties and have even abolished a few, but only two instances of county consolidation have so far occurred, one in Georgia and one in Tennessee. The Tennessee consolidation took place in 1919 when James County was joined to Hamilton by special act of the legislature. James County thus disappeared. County consolidation is possible under state law, but no one is much interested.

⊛

We have inadequate regional governmental machinery and therefore rely too heavily on relatively small-area local governments.

DICK NETZER (1970)

CITIES AND COUNTIES were invented in the far distant past when communications were slower and populations smaller and more scattered. They have served two purposes in America: they have been agents of the state (this is particularly true of the county), and they have served as the action organization of local communities. They continue to serve those purposes, but in some ways they are not large enough. The Tennessee county is not especially small (with some exceptions); Georgia has, on the whole, much smaller counties. And yet one can easily drive across the usual county in a half-hour, without particularly pressing the upper reaches of the legal speed limit. Some of the cities are large enough to take in the urbanized area and even some developing fringes, but even with annexations the big cities are not keeping pace with the spreading development. And the cities and the counties need to get together for some purposes. Hence proposals have been frequently made in recent years that some kind of regional organization be set up, smaller than the states and larger than the counties. Tennessee has been affected by these notions, especially as the federal grant-givers have conditioned their largesse on the acceptance of the coordination that might be achieved by regional organization. We can spot three types of such regional agencies that operate—or try to—in this state.

One such type of organization represented an attempt, by the Tennessee Valley Authority in cooperation with (and sometimes under the pressure of) some kind of local group, to use the area of a stream tributary to the main river as a basis for resource development. These attempts date back to 1951, when TVA developed some demonstrations in the Chestuee area south of Knoxville. Most of the tributary organizations created in the 1960s operate under such names as development associations, watershed development associations, and development agencies. Some of them were active achievers; others have never really gone beyond the talking stage, and TVA seems to be allowing this program to decline.[18]

A second kind of regional organization was the Council of Governments—the COG. The COGs were created in response to pressure, through grants-in-aid, from the federal Department of Housing and Urban Development, which wanted local coordination in housing and land-use planning. COGs were made up of representatives of the local governments in the areas concerned; four of them covering the four major metropolitan areas were created in Tennessee. They had objectives related to the improvement of local building code enforcement, the improvement of local land-use plans, and the provision of assistance to local governments in making use of federal and state aids for housing.[19] The four COGs have consolidated in various ways with the development districts and no longer can be considered highly significant.

The third regional organization now operating in Tennessee is the development district, established by the state's Development District Act of 1965. The creation of the development districts is a response to another federal scheme, that of regional economic development. This program is embodied in two federal statutes, the Public Works and Economic Development Act of 1965 and the Appalachian Regional Development Act of that same year. The development districts, like the councils of governments, represent the local governments of the area through the chief executives of those governments.[20] Tennessee boasts nine of these organizations; two of the COGs (one centered in Johnson City and the other centered in Memphis) cross state lines.

All of these developments arose partly from federal pressures, from programs and departments inadequately coordinated at the national level. The state government of Tennessee, acting through the office of urban and federal affairs (now abolished) and the State Planning Office, managed to effect some union of the COGs and the development districts by compelling them to use the same staffs. And Governor Dunn required the state departments to use the development district areas for their regional operations. The tributary associations do not fit into this pattern of cooperation and appear to be dying.

Some persons profess to see in these regional units a pattern destined to become permanent and significant. But nagging doubts remain. The agencies were induced by the federal cornucopia and are supported by that

[18]See Ralph F. Garn, "Tributary Area Development in Tennessee: TVA's Changing Perspective," diss., Univ. of Tennessee, 1974.

[19]See Keith J. Ward, *Metropolitan Cooperation and Coordination: Tennessee Councils of Governments* (Knoxville: Bureau of Public Administration, Univ. of Tennessee, 1972).

[20]See James J. Glass, *Regional Planning and Politics: Development Districts in Tennessee* (Knoxville: Bureau of Public Administration, Univ. of Tennessee, 1973). We are indebted to Robert Freeman for information on these districts.

"fount of every blessing." It is far from certain that, if the national government were to taper off or abandon that support, the local governments would cling to agencies that coordinate and perhaps inhibit them. The reform may be no more than budget-deep. But if these districts stay around long enough and gradually assume powers of independent action, we may develop larger local agencies that will supplement and, who knows, gradually replace the cities and the counties. Such an eventuality seems, at the moment, far away.

17

☆ ☆
☆

Consent and Force

★★
★

*Mere legal enactments, enforced, or left unenforced, by paid officials
or the police, to be effective must themselves become taboos, printed
on the fleshy tablets of the individual citizen's heart.*

HAVELOCK ELLIS (1922)

IT IS ALL VERY WELL FOR GOVERNMENTAL AGENCIES TO EXPRESS THEIR WILL
by means of the constitution, a statute, a regulation, an order, a judicial
decision, or even a pious wish, but it is quite another matter to devise
means to see that such will is translated into action. Even in the crassest
dictatorship a government is not in a position to secure absolute obedience,
and in the face of determined opposition such a dictatorship may fall. When
individuals feel that governmental control should reach the behavior of
other individuals, the idea that "there ought to be a law" still exerts an
attraction for the naïve and the uninformed, and in absolute desperation
the thought is given utterance at times that "there ought to be a law to see
that people don't break the law." Those that pass only slightly beyond the
state of naïveté quickly realize that the mere statement of policy in the
form of a statute or regulation will provide no guarantee of obedience. A
way must be found to compel or induce observance. To discover effective
means of compulsion or inducement is one of the principal tasks of the
legislator or regulator.

One of the prime means of persuading people to acquiesce in public goals
is found in educational activity of various kinds. It is a basic feature of the
education of the young that they are taught to observe the customs and
laws of their society. But governmental education of the public goes far
beyond this elementary and almost universal activity. Modern governments at all levels make extensive use of education and information to
persuade and influence the private citizen. All kinds of examples leap at

once to the attention: the TV program that promotes the sale of government bonds (often at comparatively disadvantageous interest rates); the spot announcements on social security benefits or equal employment opportunities; the governmental reports on commodity markets; the weather; the crime reports of the FBI. The list is long.

Educational efforts of various sorts are sometimes used in place of more vigorous enforcement in wasteful or misguided ways; Americans are devoted to advertising and frequently let it get out of hand. In recent years, as people have become disturbed by rising crime—robberies, burglaries, muggings, rapes—the harassed police have responded by trying to enlist public support for crime prevention. Some of this takes the form of educating the public on preventive measures—burglar alarms, better locks, marking of property, creation of neighborhood patrols—that show some promise, but when metal signs advising the public to "think crime prevention" are plastered all over residential areas it seems probable that public funds are being wasted.

These educational efforts are often elaborately coupled with research activities designed to discover and disseminate information and techniques useful to private persons. Perhaps the outstanding example of this type of activity is furnished by federal-state-local programs in the field of agriculture, where for a century a combination of research, education, and extension has created in the United States a great reservoir of agricultural production now of the most vital concern to a world already overpopulated. This great program has fully involved the individual states and counties, although to a large extent initiative lies with the national government. A comparable example is that of forest conservation, a field in which mere regulatory activity could not have achieved the results obtained when private owners have come to realize that their true interests, as well as those of the whole public, lie in correct forest management. It seems clear enough that, if we are to exercise a wise control over our environment, we must rely in considerable measure on an educated and informed public willing to give cooperation to measures for the general good. Mere suppression will not be enough.

From time to time governments have attempted to use publicity to regulate the activities of private persons, the idea apparently being that bringing the activities of private groups to public attention will serve to keep them within proper bounds. This is the device used when legislative lobbyists are required to register. Supposedly the loss of secrecy will force these representatives to follow acceptable modes of behavior. This is a technique often tried in the early stages of a regulatory activity. Publicity for rates was the first requirement used to prevent railroads from excessive charges and from favoritism. That particular use of publicity did not achieve much, and this stage of railroad governance was soon followed by more extreme forms of control. But publicity is still the principal device used for regulation of the sale of securities to the public, perhaps because to go beyond this would involve government in more details of management than it could possibly handle.

Technical advice and financial aid to various private interests are a common feature of governmental policy. All levels of government are involved in such activities to some degree, but the financial aid of the national government looms larger than state and federal activity because of its sweeping and complicated character. Nonetheless state and local examples can be noted. When a locality subsidizes mass transport, as is happening increasingly often, it provides us with a prime example of this sort of governmental policy enforcement.

But eventually in surveying governmental enforcement mechanisms we come to measures of a repressive or retaliatory nature. A very considerable portion of such measures are exercised, through the authority of the law, by one private person on another. Notably an injured person may use the governmental judicial process to establish and enforce his rights as against another person. When a private person sues another for damages for an injury, or sues to compel another to observe a contract, or obtains an injunction from a court to stop or prevent an injury by another party, the action of the plaintiff is exercised according to the law and policy established and preserved by the state. Here the state provides a forum for the peaceful resolution of disputes, but relies upon private initiative to secure the enforcement of the state's policy. If these private suits are not instituted, the policy may remain unenforced. We have an excellent example of this situation in Tennessee in the state's antitrust or antimonopoly statutes. These statutes state a policy, but they are almost a dead letter (as indeed they are in most states) because few suits are ever brought.

Suits between private parties are civil suits. Governments may also be involved in civil suits, either as plaintiff or defendant, and enforcement may follow from governmental action in civil suits.

The courts may also be used for the punishment of crimes and misdemeanors. Here government is the plaintiff, but oftentimes it does not or cannot act without an initial complaint by a private person. A typical example of this situation is afforded in the way in which garbage is treated in rural or suburban areas. Throwing garbage along the road is illegal, but any side road (and some main ones) can demonstrate that such illegal disposal is quite customary. Suits against the practice are highly unusual, not only because enforcement is difficult, but because private persons do not complain.

The punishment exacted for a crime or a misdemeanor can be either fine or imprisonment, or both, when the offense is committed by an individual; when the offense is committed by a corporation or other type of business firm, imprisonment, of course, is not available. Other types of punishment can be devised. A corporation might, for example, lose its right to do business if it fails to obey the law, and the same punishment may be applied to an individual.

One of the ways used by government to control professional or business activity is to require a license to engage in the activity. This is a commonly used method for regulating the entrance of persons into an occupation. Such entrance is, in theory, justified on the right of the state to care for the public morals, health, and safety—in other words, the police power. In fact entrance into a profession is often used to limit competition in the trade or profession being followed, and as the courts have grown reluctant to limit the power of the state with respect to the police power, the freedom to enter occupations is increasingly restricted. The list of occupations requiring a license in Tennessee is a long and gradually growing one.

The regulations imposed on a person or firm by state statute or by administrative regulation are enforced very often by periodic inspections, perhaps accompanied by a system of reporting. Safety regulations are enforced in this way. The inspections become means whereby the law can be enforced, but they also serve to keep the firm informed of its obligations.

Courts may secure enforcement of the law by various orders, such as injunctions; violation of such orders may incur a penalty of fine or imprisonment for contempt of the court. Administrative agencies are also often given the power to issue orders—for example, an order to cease and desist from a particular practice. It is not usual in American practice for the administrative agency to be given the power to enforce its orders by contempt procedures such as the courts use. For enforcement the administrative agency usually must turn to a court; this procedure automatically assures a degree of judicial review of the validity of the administrative order. It is not impossible or necessarily improper for the administrative agency to be given enforcement powers, but the American legislator has been uncommonly reluctant to extend the administrative power this broadly.

Tennessee makes less use of the administrative agency and the administrative order than do many of the states, but probably this use will increase as the state becomes more urbanized and makes greater use of governmental regulatory power. In 1974 the administrative procedure of Tennessee was consolidated under a general state administrative procedure act such as has been enacted by the national government and a number of other states.[1]

_____

[1]*Public Acts,* 1974, ch. 725.

The governmental techniques here briefly outlined are the means by which the State of Tennessee and its subordinate local units seek to secure observance of the policies that form the subject of the succeeding chapters.

18

☆ ☆
☆

The Ills We Have

DISEASE AND DISASTER HAVE PROVIDED THE BACKDROP FOR HUMAN DRAMA.
Governments have long concerned themselves with the condition of public
health and, as ignorance of the causes of disease has diminished, public
efforts to conquer or combat illness have often been dramatically effective.
The woeful sanitary conditions of the cramped medieval city and its
successor, the nineteenth-century industrial town, have been greatly
altered in advanced countries. Memphis need no longer live in fear of
yellow-fever epidemics; the thousands of Tennesseans once threatened by
tuberculosis or typhoid have been liberated. But, though these dangers
have gone, others have developed. Public health is as urgently required as
ever.

⊛

*Migration from rural areas to metropolitan areas has altered the
nature of health problems in both settings.*

Health in Tennessee (1973)

THE STATE OF TENNESSEE through various central and local agencies is
concerned with preventing disease, where this can be done, providing
maternal and infant care, and providing and supervising sanitary engineering. Laboratory services of various kinds are provided and vital statistics
are maintained. The treatment of mental disease and mental retardation
has become a major state service.

Disease continues to be a persistent problem for mankind, but the kind of
disease that must be fought changes. The plagues of the past have yielded
in part to treatment of changing conditions, only to be succeeded by other

285

enemies. Tuberculosis was once a major concern in Tennessee. In 1927 it was the major cause of death in the state. Death from tuberculosis in Tennessee had been sharply reduced by the use of drugs by 1953, and by 1980 most of the big tuberculosis hospitals of the state were closed down. Syphilis and gonorrhea continue to receive the close attention of the department and had reached serious proportions by 1974; in 1979 the number of cases was over 32,000. Malaria must be watched, but a high degree of control has been achieved. Tennessee likewise has very few cases of typhus. Outbreaks of rabies have occurred and danger still threatens. Hepatitis cases reached a peak in 1961, but have now declined. On the other hand some diseases that were the source of dread to our fathers and mothers, such as diphtheria, are declining. Smallpox is gone—perhaps forever—and measles is increasingly rare. Typhoid fever, once widespread, has become a little-known disease in our state. The major killers in Tennessee are now heart disease, cancer, stroke, accidents, influenza and pneumonia, diabetes, suicide, and arteriosclerosis.

Perhaps one of the principal health problems faced in Tennessee from the point of view of the administrator was the unequal distribution of our health services. Some areas of the state, generally the poorer counties, were relatively underprivileged and unprotected in health matters. Fortunately county and district health offices are now located in practically all areas of the state, but still, the major portion of full-time health personnel will be found in wealthy counties. The maldistribution of doctors and nurses continues to be a problem.

In the past, Tennessee suffered from lack of hospital service. The Hospital Survey and Construction Act (the Hill-Burton Act) passed by Congress in 1946 set a maximum allowance of 4.5 general hospital beds per 1,000 population; Tennessee at that time was considerably below the standard set. Furthermore Tennessee had fewer hospital beds in proportion to its population than the nation as a whole. The hospital situation in Tennessee showed roughly the same pattern of maldistribution of facilities as existed with respect to other phases of public health. Many of the counties on the Cumberland Plateau and the Highland Rim had no hospitals at all. In these counties hospital service, if supplied at all, was supplied by private hospitals.

Under the encouragement of federal money the state Department of Public Health prepared a comprehensive plan for a statewide, coordinated system of general hospitals, topped by regional centers in Memphis, Nashville, Chattanooga, and Knoxville. The plan was revised in 1963.

This survey, plus federal and state financing, produced results. In 1946, Tennessee possessed 145 general, mental, chronic, and tuberculosis and other special hospitals, with 15,087 beds. By 1971 the state possessed facilities with about 26,500 beds. Hospitals tend to be concentrated, of course, in the centers of population. Tennessee in 1981 had more than the nationally-set minimum of hospital beds, and the state health plan proposes a reduction in the number of beds. In most areas in the state quick access to hospitals is provided, although some of the poorer counties are less well supplied than others.

In 1969 Tennessee started its participation in the Medicaid program, under which hospitalization and medical care of other kinds are provided for the indigent. The expense of this program is borne by the national government and the state, with a very slight assistance from local budgets. The major burden is carried by federal appropriations.

The mental health movement began early in Tennessee's history with the creation of asylums and hospitals. But for many years treatment of the problems of mental disease and retardation lagged badly. The Tennessee Lunatic Asylum opened in Nashville in 1840—the first mental health care the state offered. In 1852 the Tennessee Hospital for the Insane was opened; this remained the mental health program for over thirty years. The East Tennessee Hospital for the Insane was established in 1886 in Knoxville and a similar institution was opened in 1889 in Bolivar.[1] The creation of the separate Department of Mental Health and improved funding of mental health are widely regarded as among the major achievements of Governor Frank Clement. The promotion of the mental health program is given honored place in the list of accomplishments in the memorial plaque to Clement attached to the wall of the Dickson hotel where he was born. Before Clement's time, institutions for mental health were managed in various departmental arrangements that combined such hospitals with other facilities such as prisons.

With the creation of the new department an upgrading of the personnel of the program was made possible. The commissioner of the Department of Mental Health and Mental Retardation (so named by a 1975 act) is likely to be a physician ordinarily divorced from the political life of the state, as has been the case for a long time with the commissioner of public health, unlike the great bulk of the remainder of the cabinet, most of whom are, and are expected to be, active in party affairs. It is true that Commissioner Nat Winston became a significant political figure, but this is unlikely to be a continuing pattern. The pressures of the mental health program, like those of public health, are almost sure to produce an administration somewhat divorced from political patronage, but individual institutions have not been entirely free from such considerations.

To the concern for treatment of the insane that has been so closely associated with Governor Clement has been added in subsequent administrations an expanded program for the mentally retarded. The treatment of

[1]Tennessee Department of Mental Health and Mental Retardation, *The Needs We Met in 1979* (Nashville: Spring, 1980).

the insane and of the retarded emphasizes the reduction of the number of persons confined in institutions and their return to family and community life, and recent departmental reports emphasize the progress of this policy.

How does the State of Tennessee attack its public health problems? A principal state agency for this purpose is the Department of Public Health, one of the major departments of the state administrative machinery. The structure of this department follows the usual hierarchical pattern. Health organization was made more complex by the Tennessee Health Planning and Resources Development Act of 1979, passed in part to implement in the state the federal Health Planning and Resources Development Act of 1974. The state statute creates a Health Planning Authority, a Statewide Health Coordinating Council, and a Health Facilities Commission, multi-member bodies that represent existing agencies and the public. The intent of the legislation is to plan, coordinate, and regulate health facilities, but whether an elaborate set of commissions is the best administrative means for the purpose is open to some doubt.

The sources of operating funds for public health purposes consist of state appropriations and state fees, revenue raised from local governmental and medical units, aid from the federal government including the TVA, and assistance from other agencies such as foundations. The federal government has a heavy stake in public health. There is every warrant for thinking, too, that if the federal government were not as heavily concerned as it is, we might have a greater maldistribution of health services than we actually have.

The basic local public health units of the state are the county health departments, ninety-five in number. The independent city health department has disappeared in Tennessee, except for the city of Oak Ridge, a center of atomic operations, which tends to be different from the ordinary Tennessee city in many respects. Of the ninety-five county health units, seventy-two are supported by state, federal, and county funds, without direct appropriations from any city, although it is possible that in some of these areas cities contribute in kind, through buildings or other facilities. In twenty-two counties, cities contribute some monetary support to the county departments, the sums ranging down to very small amounts of aid. In Nashville–Davidson, health is a charge on the general services district that covers the whole county. It is clear that public health still remains as a charge on some municipal budgets; it should not, for this is one function that clearly belongs entirely on the county budget, although it could be that some small charges are for services limited to urban residents.

Service to the public is the keynote for much of the work of local public health agencies. For one thing, this is the place to which the public can turn for information and advice on many problems of health. There, also, the public may receive inoculations against the principal communicable diseases. Foodhandlers may be examined for infectious diseases. It is worth remembering that these local activities are generally aided by state and federal funds and subjected to a certain degree of state supervision.

Local agencies receive the aid and support of the state department in various ways. To begin with, technical consultation is provided for local health personnel by specialists on the state staff, working in fields such as industrial hygiene, tuberculosis, and maternal and child hygiene. Demonstrations are provided for local doctors and public health personnel; the dental demonstration program is a good case in point. Special education courses are provided; drug use has recently occupied the attention of health educators.

But if a reading of the annual reports of the state Department of Public Health and those of local public health agencies discloses a strong emphasis on the use of educational and service techniques, there is nevertheless a coercive side to public health at both state and local levels. Most cities, for example, have passed ordinances directed to the preservation of the public health. Such ordinances provide for the inspection of eating places, foodstuffs, dairies, markets, and so on. Foodhandlers are often required to pass physical examinations. Statutes, ordinances, and regulations governing the quarantine of persons suffering from communicable disease are passed and enforced. Some of this coercive work is performed by public health agencies, some by other divisions of the administrative machinery.

We have already observed the fact that the federal government takes a big hand in public health. Primarily the central government makes its influence felt through the provision of funds. Moreover, a major portion of such funds is earmarked for certain types of expenditure. In this way the national government is able to bring about attacks along specific lines which it has selected. An examination of health funds available in Tennessee will indicate the federal government's interest in the control of venereal disease, tuberculosis, mental disease, and cancer, and its concern for the development of hospitals and special care for mothers and children.

The mental health program has been considerably decentralized; it operates partly through institutional care and partly through outpatient care, through hospitals and mental health centers widely distributed in the state, and the department has the ideal, a realistic one, of bringing mental health care within close reach of every patient in the state. That care includes psychiatric treatment and care of various kinds for the mentally retarded. The department also works with drug and alcoholic addicts.

Although the national government makes grants for mental health and the department is aggressively pursuing this source, the major portion of this burden is carried by the state budget. In 1973 the state appropriation exceeded $50 million, as compared to federal support of slightly over $2 million.

How properly to alleviate the troubles of the poor is one of the greatest troubles of the rich.

O. HENRY (1925)

MISINTERPRETATION OF A REMARK OF Jesus has often been used to justify or to support the continued existence of poverty as the foreordained lot of some of mankind. Theology aside, poverty has persisted, in spite of hope aroused from time to time that it might be limited. Poverty is, however, a relative concept; the poor in one age and place will be better off than the affluent of another time and locality. The definition of poverty differs with the definer. The causes of poverty are equally elusive. For some, poverty is the outcome of sin; for others, poverty is the result of the ingrained nature or outlook of the poor; for still others, poverty is the result of an inadequate or malfunctioning economic and social structure. Poverty as the outcome of the sinfulness of man carries little conviction in these times. But whether poverty is the result of economic troubles or the result of the character and nature of the poor can excite impassioned argument.

Poverty has been defined by the Bureau of the Census for the purposes of securing information on the number of poor families. In 1969 the threshold of poverty was defined for farm and nonfarm families of various sizes. That threshold, as averaged for all families, was at an income level of slightly under $3,400 annually, a figure now clearly unrealistic after the severe inflation of recent years. On the basis of the census definitions, which differ for size of family, of course, almost 22 percent of the population of Tennessee in 1970 were below the poverty level. This figure included almost 20 percent of those persons under sixty-five years of age, and a staggering 42.3 percent of those above sixty-five.

It is evident that poverty, widespread as it is, is a particular problem of old age. Poverty and unemployment also hit the blacks hard; while 17.8 percent of the whites were below the poverty line, 43.3 percent of the blacks were in this condition.

Poverty is found throughout the state, but it is most heavily concentrated in the four major cities and the most rural counties. In 1973, the counties, aside from the four large ones, where the poor families constituted from 30 to 55 percent of the total number of families were primarily in East Tennessee and on the Cumberland Plateau, although a few were found in the west. Hancock County was the worst. The poor in these counties numbered over 120,000 persons. But the heaviest concentration of the poor was in the four major cities, which accounted for close to 250,000 poor people. The condition of poverty in these and other areas of the state was accompanied by low educational achievement, poor housing, heavy unemployment, and social and economic isolation, often in the center of the highly urbanized areas.[2] In these respects Tennessee was very much a counterpart of other states. Poverty figures from the 1980 census are not yet available, but there is little reason to suppose that conditions have greatly altered from 1970. In 1975, despite improvement over 12 percent of all Tennesseans were below the poverty level. The aged and the blacks still are hard hit. Poverty is probably still concentrated in particular counties. The problem of poverty is stubborn and puzzling.

Public health in a rudimentary way has long been a political and governmental concern but only when it was clear at last that germs carried sickness and death did health become a major public matter. On the other hand, some sort of public care for the poor has been provided for hundreds of years. The aged, the handicapped, and the poor, once the charge solely of the family, later looked to the church for help. Very likely such aid was often sufficiently unsystematic to be a clear reflection of the disorganization of the times. During a number of decades of American history, social welfare furnished the basis for political machines and political bosses. The church (or, in these days, better said, the churches) has never relinquished completely to the state the field of aiding the unfortunate, but it has declined in importance, yielding to a secular welfare machine that is at once wealthier, better organized, and more powerful. As federal and state administrative machinery has developed, the power of the political boss has declined.

The beginnings of our own welfare system date back to 1601 when the Elizabethan Poor Law was passed.[3] This act became the model for Tennessee, as for the American colonies and states in general. The Elizabethan Poor Law, with its sister statute, the Settlement Act, firmly established several poor-law principles in our jurisprudence; those principles were not shaken until the Great Depression and the Roosevelt New Deal. First of all, the principle was established that the family must assume the care of its

[2]See *Extent of Poverty and the Public Welfare System,* (Nashville: Legislative Council Committee, 1973). See also Ray Marshall and Virgil L. Christian, Jr., eds., *Employment of Blacks in the South: A Perspective in the 1960s* (Austin, Univ. of Texas Press, 1978).

[3]The major portion of the history of welfare legislation was taken from Ashcraft, *Public Care.*

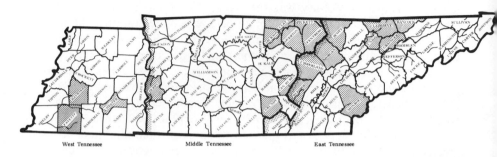

West Tennessee   Middle Tennessee   East Tennessee

Map 3. Poverty in Tennessee

COUNTIES WHERE THE PER CAPITA ANNUAL INCOME IN 1978 WAS LESS THAN $4500
SOURCE: *Tenn. Stat. Abs.*, 1980, 64.

unfortunates. If the family is unable to respond, the local community must provide aid. No central bureaucracy provided either service or supervision; the care of the poor was placed upon the local community in 1601 and there it stayed for over 300 years. We can imagine, without being far from the truth, that such local aid was kept as low as possible. We know, too, that poverty carried a stigma. "Over the hill to the poorhouse" was a fear thoroughly based on reality. These were the means used to provide some care for the poor and, it was hoped, to keep their numbers within reasonable bounds.

On the "other side of the hill" in Tennessee in the early days stood the almshouse, maintained by the county, as provided by an act of 1827. This historic institution housed the indigents without regard to individual problems; here would be found the aged, the poverty-hounded (of all ages), the feebleminded, the insane, the physically handicapped, and the sick. Under early legislation, these abodes of hopelessness might mix their inmates together without regard to the character of their troubles, their sex, or their age. Some of them must have been fairly grim centers of human misery. Some counties could not, or would not, maintain almshouses; in such instances the county's responsibility could be discharged by contracting with other counties. The whole system was under the county courts; no central state supervision existed. There was little, if any, rehabilitation of broken people.

Of course, the almshouse, even in those days, could not be used as the sole answer. The "furiously insane" could be bound over to keepers under county contracts. In 1891 counties were authorized to build asylums or hospitals for the indigent insane and the chronically ill. Nevertheless the almshouse remained the backbone of poor relief in Tennessee until the 1930s. It has been replaced by various forms of social insurance and poor relief.

Child welfare was not separated from the general provision of social legislation in the early history of the state. Efforts were made in the early years, however, to keep illegitimate, orphaned, or abandoned children from becoming public charges by appointing guardians or by "binding out" children of this type under the authority of the county court. The state's first orphan asylum wes established in 1855. Other provisions for destitute children slowly developed.

The highly localized system of public relief of poverty collapsed amid the distress of the Great Depression of the thirties. The national government assumed the burden of providing relief to the needy through the creation of several programs under the general rubric of "social security." Originally most of these programs were administered by the states with the aid and under the supervision of the national government, but most of these programs have now been transferred to national administration. A basic feature of the social security system was an insurance scheme to prevent destitute old age; this was the old age and survivors insurance program, which from the start was administered by the national government on nationwide standards, financed by charges made on the employer and the employee. It has the basic characteristics of a retirement system, although in some particulars it resembles a system of poor relief. The states have nothing to do with this program, its financing, or its administration.

The states were left with the administration and some of the policymaking in other aspects of poor relief, although federal support both pushed the states into and aided them by providing most of the funds of such relief. These so-called "state" programs included assistance for the aged, a program of straight-out poor relief based on need, aid for dependent children, aid for the blind, and aid for the disabled. Only aid for dependent children now remains under state administration.

Aid for dependent children is administered by the Department of Human Services. This agency also operates programs of foster care for children and provides care or foster homes for disadvantaged adults. It provides adoption services, dealing mostly with black children, white children over six years old, and sets of brothers and sisters who should go into the same home. These are the problem cases. The department also provides day care service and aids in the prevention of blindness. It administers Medicaid, the program of medical aid for indigents, a program whose increasing costs have proved a serious burden to a state whose 1982 projected income is falling short of threatened outgo.

Welfare is extraordinarily expensive. The field accounts for one of the major objects of state expenditure, even though the states are heavily reimbursed by federal funds. Aid for dependent children has become especially controversial, for it has been charged with promoting the procreation of illegitimate children, with breaking up families, and with encouraging laziness, lack of ambition, and other ills that the poor are supposed to exhibit.

Expenditures to aid dependent children support what we have noted with respect to the location of poverty. The figures for such aid, distributed by counties, show heavy expenditures in the metropolitan areas where poor whites and blacks abound, in certain other counties where black population is heavy, and in certain counties where mountain coal mining is a characteristic feature of the area. By far the heaviest fiscal burden is in Shelby County.

The expenditures of the states for welfare purposes have by no means been uniform. Tennessee, as might be expected with its limited wealth, is classed as a state with low benefits that accrue to a medium number of recipients, as compared to some states that give to very many or very few. Federalization of welfare programs has been urgently suggested throughout the United States. Proponents of federalization argued that welfare should be administered by national standards of eligibility and benefits. They charged that state administrators were too much concerned with the chiseler and with the state budget. Under legislation passed by Congress in 1972, the national government assumed full responsibility for old-age assistance, aid to the blind, and aid to the disabled. The state was left with the program of aid for dependent children, the most significant of the state's programs in terms of the expenditures made. It is also one of the most controversial since it involves the question of "welfare mothers" and the possibility that the requirements are inimical to family relationships.

A number of other federal welfare programs have been operated by the national government through or with the cooperation of the states and the localities. An important example was the federal Comprehensive Employment and Training Act of 1973, which was designed to provide training opportunities for the unemployed. The Johnson administration, with its push to cure the ills of American society, was particularly prolific in the introduction of antipoverty programs. Tennessee shared in those programs, notably those conducted through the office of economic opportunity and in the program to aid the Appalachian region. These efforts, federal in inspiration and financing, were a bitter disappointment, partly because the problems they were dealing with are unusually stubborn and persistent, and the attempts of the Reagan administration to reduce federal spending include cuts in appropriations for CETA and the abolition of the Appalachian Regional Commission.

19

☆ ☆
☆

Schoolhouse and University

IN A WORLD WHERE THE DEMOCRATIC WAY OF LIVING IS THREATENED BY enemies and beset with problems, the education of the public—children, young people, and adults—is a compelling necessity, and a major expense. The provision of public education is a function shared by the nation, the states, and the localities. Everywhere demands for service increase; expenditures already large are constantly mounting. Teachers are organized into powerful lobbies. In the states as a whole, the three most costly functions are education, highways, and public welfare.

⊛

Opportunities for education were much less available during the pioneer period than they were to become later, after the use of public land revenue and state and local taxes had provided greater support.

FOLMSBEE, CORLEW, AND MITCHELL (1969)

EDUCATION HAS NOT always been considered a public responsibility.[1] Many of the early colonies shared the medieval view that education was primarily the concern of the church. Not until 1860 was the principle of state responsibility for public education generally established. In early Tennessee history, education was looked upon mostly as a matter of private

---

[1]This section is based largely upon ch. 2 of Rhey Boyd Parsons, *Teacher Education in Tennessee* (Chicago: Univ. of Chicago Libraries, 1935); the slow development of rural schools in Tennessee is described in J. Leonard Raulston and James W. Livingood, *Sequatchie: A Story of the Southern Cumberlands* (Knoxville: Univ. of Tennessee Press, 1974), 213–15. See also *Development of the Tennessee State Educational Organization, 1769–1929* (Kingsport: Southern Publishers, 1929), 10; and Andrew David Holt, *The Struggle for a State System of Public Schools in Tennessee, 1903–1936* (New York: Teachers College, Columbia Univ., 1938).

concern. The Tennessee constitution of 1796 made no mention of education; however, the period from this time until the constitution of 1870 reflects a slowly emerging concept of education as a public responsibility.

One factor retarding the development of public schools in Tennessee was the notion that education at public expense should be restricted to children of the poor, an idea prevalent in legislation passed in 1815 and 1823. The beginning of the theory of public education at public expense may be traced to an act of 1829, but even in this act may be found a vestige of the "pauper school" idea. Nine years later the state's first general school law was passed, but the act made clear that public funds might have to be supplemented by tuition fees from the parents of the children benefiting from the schools.

The state's concern with education was clearly set forth in Tennessee's constitution of 1870. The broad language of the constitution enjoined the legislature to foster education without giving it specific direction. Article XI, section 12 reads in part:

> Knowledge, learning, and virtue, being essential to the preservation of republican institutions, and the diffusion of the opportunities and advantages of education throughout the different portions of the State, being highly conducive to the promotion of this end, it shall be the duty of the General Assembly in all future periods of this Government, to cherish literature and science.

Three years following the writing of the new constitution, the General Assembly passed the law that forms the basis of the state's public education system. The act of 1873, while a far cry from our present basic law, was a significant step forward. Schools were made free to persons between the ages of six and twenty-one. A permanent school fund was provided, to be supplemented by the proceeds from a levy of a poll tax of $1.00 on male inhabitants and a property tax of one and one-half mills on the dollar on all property subject to taxation. The county courts were authorized to supplement the state fund when the latter was insufficient to provide a school term of five months.

The period from 1873 to the present has been one of hard struggle to provide an adequate system of public education. An act of the legislature of 1899 authorized the county courts to establish and maintain public high schools. As late as 1916 only forty-two of the ninety-six counties in the state had four-year high schools. By this time the school system presented a rather confusing picture inasmuch as so-called "secondary schools" consisting of grades one through eight had been established by a law passed in 1891. The elementary schools at this time provided for only five grades, these overlapping the first five grades of the secondary schools. These secondary schools continued in operation until 1917, and for a period of almost twenty years conflicted in function with the public high schools.

The confusion was ended in 1917 when the legislature abolished the secondary schools and established an eight-year elementary system supplemented by a two-, three-, and four-year high school system. The permissive feature of this school legislation was made mandatory in 1921 when the legislature provided that at least one four-year high school be provided by each county.[2] Finally, in 1931, the junior high system was introduced.

⊛

State supervision of public education is more highly developed than in any other field of local administration.

JOHN A. FAIRLIE AND CHARLES M. KNEIER (1930)

ALTHOUGH PUBLIC EDUCATION is looked upon as a state function in all fifty states, it has been traditional in America to leave some control to local units of school administration. Local interest in schools is strong, and the school is in small communities very much the community center. The quality of the education program is directly related to the size, composition, and functions of these units.

Before 1923 the local district system for school administration presented a confused pattern. In 1838 an attempt was made to establish a degree of local uniformity by making school districts coterminous with civil districts.[3] Until the Civil War the basic unit of school administration was either the civil district or specially drawn school districts; the counties, in true Tennessee style, showed considerable variation in practice.[4] Finally in 1873 the General Assembly passed the so-called "parent act" of the state's educational system, which established the county and the civil districts as the basic units of control.[5]

In 1907 control of school administration passed to the county,[6] and in 1921 a more closely integrated county unit plan was created under which a single board of education for each county was established.[7]

The general county plan is subject to local modification, however, either by reason of nonconforming practices in individual counties or because of the special legislation that has been so characteristic a feature of Tennessee government.

Although the county is the basic unit for school administration in Tennessee, the General Assembly has provided for the establishment of separate municipal and special district systems. Municipalities have re-

[2]Some counties have managed to escape this compulsory requirement through private acts.
[3]*Public Acts*, 1837–38, ch. 148.
[4]Parsons, 22, 26.
[5]*Public Acts*, 1873, ch. 25.
[6]*Public Acts*, 1907, ch. 236.
[7]*Public Acts*, 1921, ch. 120.

ceived authority to operate their own schools either from their charters or from general laws. They are independent of the county systems, electing their own boards of education, hiring their own superintendents and teachers, and handling their own financing. They receive their allocations of state and county funds through county officers and report their activities to the state Department of Education, but are otherwise operated as independent systems except as they may enter into voluntary cooperative arrangements with the county schools.

In addition to the municipal school systems the legislature has from time to time established special district systems. In 1977–78, in addition to the ninety-five county systems in Tennessee, fifty-three city and special district systems were in operation.

When cities in Tennessee have seen fit to operate their own schools or to contribute to the operation of the county schools in order to provide better educational opportunities for their children, a complex web of fiscal and administrative arrangements, involving such matters as city support for county schools, joint provision of physical facilities, pupil transfer relationships, and joint operation of schools by the two systems, characterizes city-county school relationships in the state. A number of statutes permit various forms of cooperation between cities and counties. Laws passed in 1947 and 1949 permit the transfer of city schools to the county upon the holding of a referendum. A 1957 statute permits contracts for joint operation of schools. Finally, a 1963 statute authorizes the complete consolidation of city and county systems, also subject to referendum. Contracts for joint operation of vocational schools are also authorized by the statute. But all these statutes are permissive, and not much outright consolidation has been produced.[8] In Knoxville, for example, the consolidation of the city schools with those of Knox County has been studied repeatedly. City-county consolidation has been effected in some places, as, for example, in Davidson and Montgomery counties.

The basis for the pattern of administrative machinery that now exists was enacted into law in 1925.[9] A county board of education was provided for each county, composed of seven members elected by the county court (after 1978 by the county commission) for staggered terms. But it must be remembered that, in Tennessee, general law is much altered by local acts. The general law itself has been changed to provide that the board may have three, five, seven, or nine members. The general law now provides for six-year or seven-year terms so as to make an effective system of staggered terms.[10] In actuality board membership has ranged from three to twelve,

[8]*Study of Joint Operation by Local Public School Systems, 1970: Final Report of the Legislative Council Committee* (Nashville: Legislative Council Committee, 1970), 31–39.
[9]*TCA*, Title 49.
[10]*TCA*, 49–208.

with terms of from four to seven years.[11] Powers of the county boards of education include the selection and dismissal of all principals, teachers, and other school employees; the fixing of salaries for all authorized positions; the purchase of supplies; the suspension and dismissal of pupils —in short, the management and control of all county public schools.

Far-reaching as the boards' powers may seem, it is apparent that the county court (now the commission) exercises considerable influence over the educational program. The election of the county superintendent is vested in the county court, except in those counties where he is elected by the people. Moreover, the county court is authorized to review and adopt the school budget, levy school taxes, review and examine the accounts of the board of education, and issue bonds authorized by the voters. In sum it can be said that the general trend in the evolutionary growth of school administration has been away from direct participation by the people in school affairs, together with a significant measure of domination of the boards of education by the county courts (now commissions).

Not uncommonly board members have in the past assumed personal charge of school supervision in their respective areas, a practice considerably diminished in recent years. Although the law intended the election of the seven board members to be "at large," they have been, in actuality, often elected by the commission or voters from seven different parts of the county, providing an unofficial district for each member to supervise.

⊛

Where . . . the method of election shall not be fixed differently by special legislation, the quarterly county courts . . . elect some person . . . as county superintendent of public instruction.

TCA, 49–222

A COUNTY SUPERINTENDENT is elected in almost all counties either by the county commission (before 1978 the county court) or by popular vote. In a few county systems a director (not a superintendent) is chosen by the board of education, or a superintendent is elected by the board of education and approved by the county commission. In most counties the superintendent is elected by popular vote.

According to state law the county superintendent must be a person of literary attainment and experience in the art of teaching and school administration and in possession of a certificate issued by the State Board of Education. To secure such a certificate an applicant must have teaching experience, a teacher's certificate, and must have completed a master's

[11]*Study on the Governance of Education,* (Nashville: Legislative Council Committee, 1973), 41ff.

degree with adequate specialized training in school administration. City systems are governed by city charters, and the means of selection of city superintendents can vary. Selection by the city school board is normal.

The duties and powers of the county superintendent are enumerated in a law passed in 1925 that provides the legal framework within which the office presently operates. These duties include, among others, the following: general supervision of the schools to see that laws relating to education are enforced; maintenance of fiscal records relating to public school funds and the issuance of authorized warrants for the expenditure of such funds; making recommendations to the county board of education concerning teacher salaries and appointments; reporting as required to the state commissioner of education, the county trustee, and the county court on matters concerning average daily attendance and the expenditure of school funds; and preparation of the annual budget for county schools for submission to the county board of education and the county commission.[12] The superintendent's powers as set forth by the legislature indicate that considerable leeway is provided for the board of education to act as a restricting influence reducing the superintendent, if it so desires, to a mere figurehead. The importance of the position varies, therefore, depending upon the board of education in the particular county concerned.

The present system splits responsibility, for the county school teachers are elected by the county board of education, while the county superintendent is elected either by the county commission or by direct vote of the people. Such a system violates sound administrative principles and has furnished the impetus for a movement in some quarters to provide for election of the superintendent by the board of education. The state constitution specifically states that no county office created by the legislature shall be filled other than by the people or the county court, and this has resulted in invalidation of attempts to provide for election of the superintendent by the board of education. This provision was not changed by the 1978 amendment that substituted a county legislative body (the board of county commissioners) for the county court, but presumably the legislative body succeeds to the court's powers under this clause. In a few counties a director of education or schools is appointed by the school board, and no superintendent is named.

⊛

The public school system is a matter of State, and not local, concern.
State v, Meador, 153 TENN. 634, 637 1925)

THE EVOLUTIONARY TREND of control of education in Tennessee had its beginnings in strong local school districts. Gradually control shifted to the

[12]*TCA*, 49–224.

county and, although the county remains today the basic unit for school administration, a strong measure of centralization has gradually developed at the state level in the form of a state board of education and a state Department of Education. Indeed, Tennessee is one of the states where state support of education is high as compared to local support; a strong measure of state central control has been achieved, as might be expected.

The key administrative figure at the state level is the commissioner of education. This office dates back to 1836, The office subsequently underwent various changes. The school law of 1873 provided for a state superintendent of education appointed by the governor and confirmed by the Senate to serve a two-year term. In 1915 an act was passed by the legislature providing for election of the state superintendent by the state board of education, but under the reorganization act of 1923 the office (with title changed to commissioner of education) was again made appointive by the governor but without Senate confirmation. The same act established a state Department of Education with the commissioner of education at its head.[13]

The Department of Education, as it is now constituted, consists of the commissioner's office and several specialized divisions. The commissioner of education is responsible for seeing that the school laws of the state and the regulations of the state board of education are properly executed. He appoints all heads and subordinates in the department and its divisions, except those concerned with vocational education, subject only to the governor's approval. He is responsible, moreover, for the revocation of teachers' certificates and collects data on matters pertaining to average daily attendance and the receipt and disbursement of public school funds for use in reporting to the governor and the state board of education. The supervision of the county high schools comes within his authority, and he recommends courses of study for the rural elementary schools. Moreover, he serves as chairman of the state board of education.

Since the governorship of Tennessee was captured by a Republican in 1970, some have suggested that the commissioner of education should not be appointed by the governor or that the powers of the board of education should be increased. This is an old and familiar gambit for "taking the schools out of politics." Such a change would not, of course, take the schools out of politics, because that cannot be done as long as public schools exist.

The office of commissioner of education is one of the cabinet posts that

[13]Some would argue that appointment by the governor without Senate confirmation opens the way for the exercise of political pressure on the Department of Education. However, students of public administration would very likely take the view that executive appointment of department heads is indispensable to strong executive leadership, and that any advantages which might ensue from "hamstringing" the executive in this regard would be outweighed by the disadvantages inherent in weakened executive control.

requires specialized training, but appointments to it have never been entirely free from partisan considerations. When Governor Clement first came to the governorship, he offered the post to Andrew Holt, then vice-president of the University of Tennessee. Holt declined the position, but suggested that Clement appoint Quill Cope, UT associate professor of education. Clement did appoint Cope, who served a number of years. But in Clement's final term as governor, he named Howard Warf, a former school official in Lewis County, who was a powerful political figure. For the most part, the recent commissioners of education have had experience as teachers and administrators in the public schools and, often, in universities. They are drawn from Tennessee residents and some of them have graduated from the commissioner's office to Tennessee college presidencies.

A state board of education has been in existence in Tennessee since 1875. Although it possessed little power during its early years, it became an important agency in 1909 and has since witnessed an increasing concentration of power and authority. The board now consists of twelve members, four from each of the Grand Divisions of the state, appointed by the governor for nine-year staggered terms, plus the governor and the commissioner. The board must contain at least three members from each of the two leading political parties. The far-reaching powers of the board may be noted by the fact that among its functions are the control of the examination and certification of county superintendents, control of elementary and high schools by prescribing their curricula and making regulations for their government, and the adoption of a minimum uniform salary schedule to be used as a basis for the distribution of the state's Equalizing Fund.[14] The regulation of pupil transportation was brought within the scope of the board's powers in 1947, along with the power to select textbooks for use in public schools.[15] In 1951, however, a state textbook commission was created that took over the board's powers in connection with the selection of texts. The state board of education serves as the state board for vocational education with broad powers to create and operate a statewide system of vocational schools.

⊛

Most State aid is provided to help finance particular programs . . . education tops the list. . . .
ADVISORY COMMISSION ON INTERGOVERNMENTAL RELATIONS (1969)

THE TENNESSEE GENERAL ASSEMBLY in 1945 provided for a comprehensive study of the state's program of public education in order to pave the way for "as nearly an ideal program of public education as possible."[16]

[14]See *Public Acts,* 1925, ch. 115; *TCA,* 49–106ff.
[15]A state textbook authority had been responsible for this previously.
[16]*Public Acts,* 1945, ch. 121.

The survey found deficiencies in a number of areas,[17] and recommendations were advanced that led to the adoption of a law in 1947 providing the basis for a new minimum program for elementary and secondary public school education.

The Tennessee General Education Act of 1947 provided for an equalization program for grades one through twelve for a nine-month school term. This plan as amended was revised in 1977.

The purpose of the state equalization program is to provide sufficient aid to support an annual minimum expenditure. In order to participate in this aid the county must raise a proportionate share of its own local revenue based upon an index of relative financial ability. The school program includes aid for salaries, transportation, capital outlay, and textbooks.[18]

A new source of revenue in the form of a state retail sales and use tax was tapped in 1947 to support the state's revamped school program. Originally the sales tax was set at the rate of 2 percent and 80 percent of the yield went for education. The General Assembly, in 1955, increased the rate of the sales tax to 3 percent, and 98 percent of this third cent is earmarked for education. Other sources of state school revenue include interest on the Permanent School Fund and the proceeds of a state tobacco tax (except 4 percent used to cover collection costs).

⚑

That pattern [of university governance] is best which most effectively facilitates the accomplishment of the primary mission of the university . . . learning and inquiry.

HERMAN E. SPIVEY (1974)

IN THE LATTER PART of the 1960s Tennessee went through a burst of building development in higher education, particularly in the field of community colleges. The already existing institutions of higher education continued their expansion, although the onset of the 1970s witnessed some stabilization of enrollment and even perhaps foretold some decline.

Seven public institutions of higher learning, not including the community colleges and technical schools, are maintained in Tennessee today: the University of Tennessee, Tennessee Technological University at Cookeville, East Tennessee State University at Johnson City, Austin Peay State University at Clarksville, Middle Tennessee State University at Murfreesboro, Memphis State University at Memphis, and Tennessee State University in Nashville.

[17]For a complete analysis of the study, see *Public Education in Tennessee, A Report Prepared in Accordance with Chapter 121—Public Acts of Tennessee, 1945* (Nashville: Tennessee State Dept. of Education, 1946).
[18]*TCA,* 49–602ff.

The University of Tennessee is the oldest and the largest college institution maintained by the state. Its origins are found in Blount College, started in a log building on what is now Gay Street in Knoxville in 1794, two years before Tennessee entered the union. It has become a multicampus institution. The principal campus is at Knoxville, where the central administration is located, and the principal graduate programs and the largest enrollment, both graduate and undergraduate, are found. The medical units of the University are located in Memphis. At Nashville a center for extension teaching became a full-fledged campus of the University in 1970 (since merged with Tennessee State University under federal court order). The University of Chattanooga, an institution that had existed for many years as a private organization with some municipal support, became a part of the University of Tennessee in 1969. The campus at Martin has been in existence for many years, but now offers four years of undergraduate work instead of the two year program that originally existed there.

The state universities in Johnson City and Murfreesboro and the Memphis State University were formerly colleges and, before that, normal schools. They were converted into teachers' colleges following passage of the General Education Law of 1925, which authorized the maintenance of such colleges in the three Grand Divisions of the state. Austin Peay State University in Clarksville was also formerly a normal school established in 1927 to train elementary school teachers. Its original two-year program had been expanded in 1941 into a four-year program, and in 1943 it was made a state college. Tennessee Polytechnic Institute (now Tennessee Technological University) was established in 1915 and, during the first eight years of its existence, offered work only at the high school and junior college level. It has since discontinued high school subjects and has been authorized to grant the bachelor of science and graduate degrees. While primary emphasis is placed upon technical and engineering training, its curriculum provides for a general cultural program of studies as well. Tennessee State University (a land-grant institution formerly called Tennessee Agricultural and Industrial State University), originally a segregated institution for Negroes, started as a normal school under a 1909 act. It became a college in 1922; in 1941 its educational program was broadened, and it was made a university in 1951.

After 1965, the state embarked on a program of building community colleges; ten such were in some degree of operation by 1977, their campuses scattered across the state, mostly in communities where other colleges are not available, although there are exceptions. These colleges are designed to provide two years of collegiate work that may be transferred to the universities, to provide technical training short of degrees, and to provide adult extension courses. They are designed for residents of the area who can commute to the school, but some of the institutions have shown a determination to expand. The enrollment in these institutions has grown; some of them claim enrollments of several thousand. The largest enrollment in state institutions, that of the University of Tennessee system, is about 45,000 on all campuses; at the Knoxville campus the enrollment is about 30,000. Memphis State stands next with an enrollment in the neighborhood of 21,000.

As the number of persons of college age declined relative to the total population, the higher educational institutions looked with envy and hope on the field of adult education. Rivalry and duplication between the institutions developed. The University of Tennessee had a monopoly on the agricultural extension field, and it had a long-established general Extension Division that furnished a springboard for further activity. Under the presidency of "Andy" Holt, it took especial steps to capture the field of in-service training of public employees and has managed to remain preeminent in that area, but it does not enjoy a complete monopoly and is not immune from attempted competition.

Institutions of higher learning—a clumsy phrase often more indicative of aim than achievement—all itch to give advanced degrees. The result is that all the four-year institutions offer the master's, although the University of Tennessee gives more than any of the others. The University also gives the great bulk of the doctorates. The decision as to which institutions should give what is by no means free from the politics of regionalism; sources of institutional strength in the legislature can be identified without much trouble. Both the University of Tennessee and Memphis State give law degrees, degrees formerly called bachelors' degrees, but now—following a nationwide pattern—called doctorates in jurisprudence.

The rivalries of institutions also lead to competition among university presses. The leading university press in the state is the University of Tennessee Press, which has experienced a remarkable growth in the past twenty-five years, but Memphis State developed a university press (recently abandoned), and East Tennessee State University has published a few items.

The fight in the 1970s over the location of a new medical school in Johnson City is illustrative of the political struggle that surrounds the creation and development of institutions of higher learning. Colleges are important to communities for the cultural opportunities they bring and the payrolls they add locally. A college once established seeks usually to extend its activities, to engage in graduate programs and adult education. It rivals the programs already established. In Tennessee this type of struggle, apparent in almost all American states, takes place in a state historically divided into sections, each interested in its "fair" share of whatever is going. The governance of the educational institutions themselves furnishes further occasion for political maneuvering, typically between the hosts of "coordination" and the armies of "independence." Tennessee has its educational struggles, familiar enough to the historian of state higher education everywhere. In 1979 proposals were made to absorb Peabody College and King College into the state system of universities and community colleges, but the trial balloons were shot down.

At present the governance of Tennessee's institutions is divided among two major boards, both subject in certain important particulars to a third—the Higher Education Commission. The University of Tennessee is directed by a board of trustees, consisting now of seventeen members appointed by the governor subject to Senate confirmation, plus five ex officio members—the governor, the commissioner of agriculture, the commissioner of education, the executive director of the Higher Education Commission, and the president of the University. Those not ex officio members originally had terms of fourteen years, but the terms were reduced in 1967 to nine, although members originally appointed for fourteen years served out their full terms. In any case, no one governor can appoint all the members. The appointed members must be residents of the various Congressional districts; some of them must be residents of Shelby County, Weakley County, and Hamilton County; and one must be from a combination of counties, on the Cumberland Plateau and lower Middle Tennessee. They must also be representative of the alumni and of the two political parties, and at least one must be a woman. The legislature in 1974 placed a student representative on the board. Membership on the board carries prestige, and the pressure on the governor for appointment is intense.

The State University and Community College Board of Regents, created in 1972, governs the community colleges and the universities not part of the UT system; it consists of the governor, the commissioners of agriculture and education, the executive director of the Higher Education Commission, and eleven public members appointed by the governor, subject to Senate approval, for nine-year terms, and representative of various sections of the state. One member must be the immediate past commissioner of education. The Higher Education Commission, created in 1967, consists of nine members appointed by the governor for nine-year terms, three from each Grand Division. At least one-third of the commission must be members of the minority party.

A deeply troublesome problem of university administration is that of determining the role of faculties. In the 1930s and early 1940s there can be little doubt that, in many respects, faculty members were considered by the governing boards and the presidents as employees. Even then, of course, the faculties exercised substantial power over curricula, and, in the nature of things, some power over appointments and promotions. As the state's institutions grew to the large enrollments of the 1960s and 1970s, faculty authority was expanded, particularly over appointments and promotions. The faculties exerted less influence on budgets, and they have never been able to acquire substantial power over the selection of the chief administrators in the systems, although they have tried repeatedly to make their influence felt. At the same time, the faculties have acquired some power, even if not formalized, in the selection of middle administrators, at least in some institutions.

During the unrest of the 1960s, attempts were made by some students, aided by some administrators, to provide means of representing students in university decisions. Students were placed on committees and faculty governing bodies. Actually, students never succeeded in gaining much power, and the attempts to give them authority must be regarded as a failure. Students lack the tenure and experience essential for influencing educational decisions. The whole movement was contrary to the traditions and experience of American institutions, and quite understandably died.

The top administrators—the presidents and the chancellors—have not been lame-duck politicians, although there have been a few exceptions. Burgin Dossett, one-time candidate for governor, became president of East Tennessee College. But, generally, the oft-repeated rumors that an ex-governor, such as Governor Cooper or Governor Clement, would succeed to a presidency have been unfounded. Top politicians do not, in Tennessee, become top university administrators. On the other hand, top state administrators sometimes do, and it is significant that some of the leading administrators in the Tennessee system of higher education, such as Edward Boling, Roy Nicks, and Joseph Johnson, were key administrators of the Clement–Ellington years. And some commissioners of education, such as Quill Cope and Sam Ingram, have become university presidents. But, as administrators last rather well in Tennessee, this pattern of selection may turn out to be an exception rather than a rule.

The teachers of Tennessee (the University faculties aside because they wield little power) constitute what many consider to be the state's most powerful pressure group; they speak through the Tennessee Education Association and affiliated regional associations. Affiliated unions have made little headway in the state or in localities, although local unaffiliated organizations exist. The TEA concerns itself with professional development, but one of its primary objectives is to raise tax support for the schools and for the teachers. According to measurements used by TEA and by the parent organization, the National Education Association, such as per capita expenditures for education, amount spent per pupil, and similar measures, Tennessee now stands and has always stood in the lower ranks among the fifty states, along with most of its sister Southern states (a grouping sometimes joined by certain Western states). It is a striking fact that the ranking of the states on educational expenditures and educational relationships is remarkably durable over a long period of time. In short, things do not change much in spite of the optimistic promises of candidates for the governorship. Tennessee is one of the states where state expenditures are high in relation to local expenditures. It is also one of the states where school expenditure is proportionate to total expenditures, being neither unusually high nor unusually low. Furthermore it is one of the states where expenditure is highly related to income, a group that includes most of the low-income states and several of the very wealthy. It is also one of the states in which the expenditure for higher education is proportionate to the expenditures for the elementary and secondary schools. One of the innovations of the Dunn administration was the introduction of publicly supported kindergarten, an addition of some consequence to the school budget, and an even larger cost may be involved in the expansion of vocational education.

Taking the states as a whole, the most important factor in determining state expenditure for schools is income, but historical tradition plays a considerable part. The political structure of the state and the nature of its party competition have little to do with the pattern of state expenditure or the relationships between the central and the local school system.

Like other states, Tennessee has felt the impact of the greatly expanded federal expenditures for education that have characterized the last fifteen years. These expenditures are directed now toward education at all levels and through a number of different programs, and while they increase the resources available for schools and school programs, they are somewhat uncoordinated and spotty, and, in some instances, justified more by current prejudgments than by thoughtful long-term policy. The states and localities suffer from lack of coordination at the federal level, for the pressure of federal funds is difficult to resist.

⊛

Does segregation . . . solely on the basis of race . . . deprive the children of the minority group of equal educational opportunities? We believe that it does.

Brown v. Board of Education 347 U.S. 483, 493 (1954)

THE EDUCATION OF NEGROES was undertaken in Tennessee in accordance with a constitutional ban against the mixing of white and black schoolchildren. The state constitution specifically provided that "no school . . . shall allow white and negro children to be received as scholars together in the same schools."[19] Thus it had become necessary for the city and county

[19]Art. XI, sec. 12.

school systems to provide about 600 separate schools for some 140,000 Negro boys and girls (grades one through twelve) in Tennessee. Some counties did not have school facilities for Negro children extending through the twelfth grade. Some of these counties had attempted to provide such facilities by paying tuition, transportation expenses, or room and board for Negro children so that they might attend school in neighboring counties. A new feature was added to black education and the segregation issue in 1954 when the United States Supreme Court held segregation to be unconstitutional.

Tennessee's response to the two Brown cases, the first finding that segregation was unconstitutional, the second laying down steps for desegregation, was cautious. Certain fire-breathing elements in the state called for bitter-end resistance, but Governor Clement and the two United States senators, Kefauver and Gore, declined to be pressured into the assumption of an untenable position. In the middle 1950s, no one was certain how far the courts would go to enforce desegregation, and a "wait-and-see" attitude was widely adopted. Governor Clement was determined to prevent precipitate action by the General Assembly, and he vetoed or otherwise discouraged extremist response in the legislature, even alienating, at least temporarily, some of his fellow governors in the South. In the subsequent political campaigns in the state, segregation did not become a red-hot issue, although, on the other hand, no gubernatorial candidate adopted a strong desegregationist attitude. Such a stance was unlikely to be productive in Tennessee. Governor Clement's attitude was based on the premise that desegregation was a local problem, a position comfortable for the governor and appropriate to the political culture of the state. It was a position that at least occasionally found backing among black leaders.

The first desegregation of a school system took place in Oak Ridge, where the city and the schools were under direct federal control. The first serious violence occurred at nearby Clinton, which desegregated under federal court order. Rioting in this community began with the opening of school in late August 1955, aided by outside agitators and a plethora of sensation-hungry newsmen. Reluctantly, Governor Clement called in the highway patrol and the National Guard, not to desegregate, he always insisted, but to establish law and order.

In the autumn of 1957, violence was visited upon Nashville, as the city schools started desegregation. One school was dynamited at night, but vigorous action by the police ended illegal resistance.

In the quarter-century since the outburst at Clinton, Tennessee schools, both urban and rural, have been officially desegregated, either voluntarily or by court order. Violent resistance has never been characteristic of the behavior of the public during this period, but this does not mean that desegregation has been readily accepted. Legal battles have been fought over methods and degrees of desegregation, and whites have withdrawn in rather substantial numbers from integrated schools in some localities, either by turning to private schools or by moving to residential areas in the suburbs (the white flight). On the whole, however, the public schools have not lost enrollment because of desegregation. Statistics for private school enrollment are inadequate, but it appears that, as of 1975–76, some 71,000 students were enrolled in private and parochial schools, as against about 874,000 in public institutions. But white flight of one kind or another has adversely affected a few school districts, including Memphis, Chattanooga, Nashville–Davidson, and Jackson. Here the percentage of blacks in the public schools has risen sharply, from 1953 to 1978, most notably in Memphis, whose school system was about 73 percent black in 1977–78.[20] Private schools are not required to report their existence to state agencies, and the number of such schools appears to be on the increase in other metropolitan areas. Desegregation and busing are activities that make for such schools, but a wish for a religious orientation or for higher academic standards also pushes parents in this direction. Some observers fear the growth of private schools will seriously hurt the American public school system.

The four systems mentioned are the only ones in the state that operate under court orders requiring the busing of students to maximize desegregation. The increased proportion of blacks in the schools is out of line with the population ratio in several large cities in the state, indicating that white resistance to busing goes on quietly by nonviolent means. In some of the western counties, where blacks are in the majority, there may be no schools where whites are in the majority, and those families who can afford the burden may simply desert the public school system. Fayette County is an example. In some places the housing pattern of the city dictates the pattern of schools. In Knoxville the schools on the east are likely to be black, those on the west, white; substantial segregation still exists, even in the public sector. The outstanding private school, Webb, is overwhelmingly white. Black families simply cannot afford the tuition.

The segregation practiced at the elementary and secondary school level had been the rule in Tennessee at the college level, and the order in the second Brown case in 1955 was quickly followed by moves to open the almost all-white institutions to the blacks. We say "almost all-white" because a limited enrollment of blacks had been allowed at the graduate level at the University of Tennessee, even before the Brown case, in programs that did not exist elsewhere. Earlier decisions of the United States Supreme Court had begun to put a halt to transport of Negroes outside the state for advanced education. As the consequence of the

[20]Connie Pat Mauney, *Evolving Equality: The Courts and Desegregation in Tennessee* (Knoxville: Bureau of Public Administration, the Univ. of Tennessee, n.d.), chs. 4, 5, 9.

gradual opening of the white schools to blacks, some Negroes appeared among the student bodies throughout the state; they were especially numerous at Memphis State, located in that section of the state where the black population was heaviest.

But Tennessee had long maintained a black institution in Nashville —originally called Tennessee Agricultural and Mechanical College, eventually to become Tennessee State University. This was a land grant school, like the University of Tennessee at Knoxville, and the state's leaders claimed at times that it was the equal in treatment of the white university, but, of course, this was never true. Whites did not go there originally, for segregation was the law of the state. At one time, the black school, located in the north, and black, section of Nashville, was the only state institution of higher education in that city.

In the 1960s, the situation changed. The adult education program of the University of Tennessee had been caught up in a wave of expansion. Night classes were made available in various centers in the state, including Nashville and Memphis. Buildings were acquired, and a permanent resident staff was built up. In the 1960s plans were made to develop a more elaborate campus for what was to become UTN—the University of Tennessee at Nashville—and a building was constructed on Charlotte Avenue, just two blocks from the state capitol. Teaching programs were expanded, undergraduate and graduate degrees were authorized, and enrollments burgeoned. Blacks were admitted along with whites, and they took advantage of their opportunities in considerable numbers. In the meantime, TSU remained overwhelmingly black.

The situation in Nashville was quite similar to situations in certain other Southern cities where the states maintained or were developing institutions, desegregated but predominantly white as to faculty and students, in localities where state-supported black institutions still existed.

In the meantime the desegregation movement, starting as a move to open up white institutions to Negro entrants, had shifted ground to demands for positive action to require mixes of white and black students. It no longer appeared enough to civil rights proponents that blacks could choose to go where they wanted; some kind of action was required to see that whites and blacks had to go to the same places.

The issue surfaced in the federal district court of Judge Frank Gray in 1968. (Gray was a former mayor of Franklin, Tennessee, and a campaign worker for Kefauver; it was through this connection that he landed on the federal bench.) Black plaintiffs sought to enjoin the proposed construction of the UTN building at 10th and Charlotte. Judge Gray refused that injunction, but he did say that the state had to act to suppress the operation of a dual system of higher education in Nashville (UTN and TSU), which he held to be contrary to the much-invoked Fourteenth Amendment of the federal constitution. Thus began a long process of litigation that extended from 1968 to 1977, in which the United States Department of Justice was allowed to intervene on the side opposed to the "dual system."

As the case dragged on through the years, it became increasingly evident that nothing would content the black plaintiffs short of the elimination of UT in Nashville and the transfer of UT's programs to TSU. This aim had the support of the Department of Justice, and in the end that is what Judge Gray ordered in 1977, an order subsequently backed by the Court of Appeals and the United States Supreme Court. Judge Gray said that the two institutions were in competition, with TSU losing. He objected to the lack of whites on the TSU campus; the fact that blacks could enter UTN freely failed to move him. The attempts of the two institutions to run joint programs had not increased white presence on the TSU campus. He rejected the idea that TSU should be turned over to the UT board, for that, he thought, would signify the end of TSU. So his solution was to turn UTN over to TSU and the Board of Regents.

What this decision portends is not clear, as yet. In particular, whether whites will now start to attend the former all-black campus in north Nashville is not certain. The immediate effect was a sharp drop in enrollment at the former UTN campus and the termination of a number of white professors and administrators. It is possible that enrollment will climb again. It is too early to make a judgment as to the effect of the merger on the quality of the programs, but one can hazard a guess that a residue of considerable white resentment and suspicion will last for some time.

20

☆ ☆
☆

Air, Earth, Fire, Water

There is a pleasure in the pathless woods,
There is a rapture on the lonely shore.

BYRON (1818)

WHEN THE WHITE MAN MOVED FROM THE EASTERN COAST OF THE UNITED States into the land which is now the State of Tennessee, he found what appeared to him an inexhaustible abundance of natural resources. The state was blanketed in forest, game and fish were plentiful, and farmland was available when the forest could be cleared away. The early history of the use of natural resources in the state is a history of unlimited exploitations of the materials at hand without thought of the future. After the Civil War the hitherto unchecked and largely unnoticed drain on the natural resources of Tennessee gradually changed. This change was felt first with respect to land and later appeared in other fields as well.

The history of state activity in conservation in Tennessee may be said to have started with the establishment of the Tennessee State Agricultural Bureau in 1854. This agency was replaced in 1875 by a bureau of agriculture, statistics, and mines. In the 1870s the first beginnings were made in the state to protect lands against floods. The 1870 constitution of the state authorized the General Assembly to enact statutes to protect game and fish, and after 1870 legislation concerning game and fish conservation gradually began to appear.

A full-fledged conservation movement did not appear in the United States until the twentieth century. The conservation movement in this country was sparked by several national conferences, one of the most important being the conference called by President Theodore Roosevelt in

1908. Under the impulse of nationwide interest in such matters, Tennessee commenced to explore in various ways the possibility of adequate protection of the great natural resources of the commonwealth. For example, the first comprehensive forest fire statute was enacted in Tennessee in 1907. A uniform national park system was established in 1916. Tennessee started its active program of state parks as late as 1934, although a state park and forestry commission had been created in 1925. The present state park system dates from legislative authorization of 1937. Responsibility for flood control in the State of Tennessee was originally considered to be a local one. Thus counties were authorized to construct levees as early as 1871. By 1901 the policy had changed so that a major portion of the burden of levee costs was transferred to the state at large.

The first steps toward conservation in Tennessee were hesitant and incomplete. Roughly speaking, the state can be said to have begun an approach to a progressive and coordinated conservation policy only within the last quarter-century. Now we can point to an active and informed conservation program, although, as the conservationists themselves would be the first to admit, a great many tasks still lie unfinished.

The interest in conservation in Tennessee extends to the protection of the soil, the development and preservation of the state's extensive forests, both public and private, the development and use of state parks, the wise use of mineral resources, and the conservation and utilization of water, both surface water and ground supplies.

Soil conservation in the State of Tennessee has been a major interest of federal agencies, including the Soil Conservation Service and the Tennessee Valley Authority. In addition, the University of Tennessee, through its College of Agriculture, its Extension Service, and its experiment stations, has maintained a strong interest in soil conservation. Aside from these agencies, however, the state has not taken a major role in soil conservation. The state does have agencies active in the field of forest conservation, state parks, minerals, and water control and use.

Roughly half of Tennessee is covered by forests and woodlots. Forests are an important resource for the state, commercially and aesthetically. The vast stretches of wooded hills and mountains lend the state its always pleasing and often spectacular beauty, but it must be admitted that a forested state is likely to be a poor state. Forests are essential to human life, but they do not provide the basis for the local abundance provided by intensive agriculture or urban development. Yet in the economy of Tennessee the forest is a major element, and its preservation and nurture require public concern. The prevention of fire, the promotion of effective forest management on state and private lands, the control of disease and insects, the improvement in the quality of trees, and the promotion of effective utilization and marketing of forest products are all important parts of the forest program.

Between the years 1961 and 1971, the area of forestland in the state actually declined by about 5 percent, but during the period between the two surveys, the volume of both soft and hard wood growing stock very sharply increased. Some 80 percent of the state's commercial forestland is much less than fully stocked with sound trees of kinds that are commonly marketed, but the quality of the timber is steadily improving. Much of this improvement is attributable to the increasingly effective fire prevention and control program. The forest-fire record of the state has improved from year to year, and competent observers think the burned areas have been pushed about as low as possible. Forest fires are caused by a mixture of accident and incendiarism, neither of which can be precisely predicted. Fire protection is conducted in cooperation with the counties; ninety-two counties have entered cooperative agreements with the state.

Forest management is a major project for the division of forestry of the Department of Conservation. Management must take place primarily on privately owned land, for over 80 percent of the forestland is under the ownership and control of about 180,000 owners. Many ownerships are small. The division gives advice and aid to owners of both large and small tracts, under a program started in 1941. Demand for management assistance and advice is still greater than can be met with existing personnel. The state owns fourteen state forests, protected and managed as timber farms and used as demonstration projects to show the results obtainable from proper management.

Both the TVA and the state division of forestry operate nurseries that produce seedling trees to be used for reforestation. The state's forestry nursery produces millions of seedling trees. Federal cost-sharing programs, such as the Forest Incentive Program, assist the state by providing funds for planting on idle lands and in converting from unproductive to productive stands.

The change to a policy of conservation in the interest either of preservation or of prudent use, after a century or more of reckless and ignorant spoliation, was to affect forestry interests first, but disastrous wind storms and heavy rainfall eventually forced attention on soil conservation. The development of TVA and related projects on the Cumberland and the tributary rivers added water control to the list of objectives of conservation policy, and forest and water control led to the ever-increasing attention to recreation made both necessary and possible by an expanding population with more leisure.

In recent years, though, the public and its governments have been moved increasingly to a concern for the environment. It must be admitted that this concern has been translated into action only under the pressure of the national government. Aside from a long-time and necessary consideration of minimum sanitation requirements, all indications are that Tennessee shares with most of the other states a demonstrated inability to act effectively to protect the environment. The inability (or unwillingness) is a severe, but just, criticism of the states as effective units in the federal system.

Federal pressure has been applied in the last decade or so by monetary assistance, the customary carrot, and by national legislation that warns quite clearly that the states must take action or the national government will. That pressure has been applied by such legislation as the Federal Clean Air Act of 1970, the Federal Clean Air Act Amendments of 1977, the national Solid Waste Disposal Act of 1965, and various federal water quality acts. Federal interest has been manifested with respect particularly to the improvement of the quality of water and air, and the disposal of wastes, both liquid and solid. Strip-mining has come in for special attention in those areas especially affected by this practice, areas that include the Cumberland Plateau in Tennessee. Some state action, including some in Tennessee, has anticipated federal legislation.

Sanitation has been an established task of government, particularly of urban units. Indeed the origins of the modern city are closely bound up with the development of the germ theory of disease and the spreading knowledge of the fundamental connection between waste disposal and public health. A measure of achievement of such disposal goes far to explain the differences in life expectancy between the developed countries and those in backward areas (areas called, in the colorless language of diplomacy, the underdeveloped or, now, the "developing," whether they are or not). But that is not to say that waste disposal, either of liquids or of solids, is exactly satisfactory in Tennessee. One has only to take a drive along the sideroads to see how far we still are from cleaning up.

The urban governments of Tennessee have long provided sewer systems that collected liquid waste from some of the urbanized area. But those systems never kept up with urban growth in the fringe areas, where the septic tank or the privy was the rule, whether adequate or not.[1] Even where sewer systems existed, they were collection systems only; disposal of sorts was achieved by dumping raw sewage in the streams. The vigorous and candid language of Tennesseans laid clear the nature of things in such terms as "Stinky Point," "Pugsley's Gut," and "Cumberland cocktail," the latter an apt description of a draught from Nashville's main waterway in the days before the cleanup. But the state is changing. The basic legislation in Tennessee is the Water Quality Control Act of 1971; the basic enforcement agency is the division of water quality control of the state Department of

---

[1]For an example of the predicament of the fringe areas in the past, still true for many sections, cf. Commission on Community Services, *A Future for Nashville*.

Public Health. This agency, backed by federal legislation and federal aid, is compelling the cities and private interests to cease the destruction of the streams of the state. Such a cleanup cannot be achieved overnight, but progress is evident. The pressure on the cities is troublesome, not only financially but technically. The difficulties that Knoxville experienced in finding a site for a sewage disposal plant (and the opposition the city gets from urban fringe residents) or in locating landfill sites for garbage illustrate the problems the cities have faced, problems partly created by pussyfooting and lack of foresight in the past. And the septic tank remains with us, its existence aided by the continued opposition to effective and timely annexation to municipalities, the sloth and incompetence of county governments, and the pressure for relatively inexpensive housing and poorly planned suburban developments. Sanitation is expensive; the opposition to good planning is understandable, but short-sighted.

But the cleanup of the streams and the extension of sewage collection systems leave solid waste to be collected and treated; such waste constitutes one of the most serious obstacles to a clean environment. Tennessee's basic legislation on this subject is the Solid Waste Disposal Act, passed in 1969 under pressure of federal law and administration; the basic state agency for administration of this legislation is the division of environmental sanitation of the Department of Public Health. This division prepared a solid waste management plan, published in 1971, aptly describing the waste disposal situation in the state: "The current conditions which prevail in the disposal of solid waste in Tennessee are, for the majority, unacceptable."[2] Cities are the primary public agencies for providing for solid waste disposal in the state. Counties have been largely uninvolved in waste disposal, although some counties are now beginning to provide disposal sites open to public and private collectors, or even to undertake limited collection programs. Inasmuch as the counties take on this service reluctantly, some of the failure to collect and dispose of waste must be laid to the failure of the annexation program to keep up with the expansion of urban fringe development. (It must be remembered that the cities and the Tennessee Municipal League have had to fight a continuous battle against annexation opponents). The 1971 plan noted that about 90 percent of the urban people of Tennessee were served by some kind of solid waste collection system, but that only 57 percent of the total population were so served. The state is trying to improve this situation by assisting local governments to enable them to meet standards of state regulations imposed in 1972.

The nature of the problems that beset the division of environmental sanitation is disclosed by an internal report of the division made in the late 1970s. The division is plagued by a shortage of personnel. A constantly

[2]Tennessee Department of Public Health, *Solid Waste Management Plan* (Jan. 1, 1971), 12.

recurring complaint is lax enforcement in some of the counties; this was the case, for example, with the subsurface sewage disposal program, the organized camp program, and the mobile home park program. The school sanitation program was made difficult by lack of discipline in the use of restrooms. Clearly, it takes a lot of effort to force human beings to keep clean.

In the chapter on planning, we note the all-pervading influence of builders and developers. These gentry are a problem for the sanitation force; the division of environmental sanitation evaluates some 25,000 new subdivision lots annually, and their efforts to protect the homebuyer and the general public have resulted, at times "in attempted dismissal of personnel, appeals to the Commissioner, appeals to the Legislators to use their influence and to get weakening changes in the law."[3] It is part of the normal cross the civil servant bears, but the agency and its programs survive.

In 1980 the federal General Accounting Office was critical of the effort to clean up streams, charging that many projects were unnecessary, too costly, or unsuccessful. But no specific projects were pinpointed for attack.

Inadequate solid-waste disposal is a pox on both water and air. But the low quality, at times dangerously low quality, of the air is caused by the other pollutants as well. This problem has been around for a long time. Those who lived in Tennessee thirty years ago will remember the pervading soot in the big cities when particles fell like heavy snowdrops all day long on anything and anybody in the open. The character of the pollution has changed since then, for, with the disappearance of the steam locomotive and the decline of coal furnaces, the falling black drops are no longer evident, but the haze that hangs over considerable areas of Tennessee is sign enough that all is not well. On a bad morning, downtown Chattanooga disappears from the view of the observer on Missionary Ridge. From Knoxville to Nashville the driver and the passenger, whether in the Great Valley or on the Plateau, are seldom out of sight of streaks of dirt across the sky.

All of Tennessee is subject to air pollution, but the danger differs from one section to another because of both the concentration of population and the differing geographic conditions. The Great Valley of the Tennessee in the East, with its concentration of population and industry, is potentially the most endangered section of the state. The Highland Rim around the Nashville Basin is less endangered, particularly on the west of Nashville, but the growth of industry to the west of Nashville may change this. The potential for pollution of West Tennessee is generally light, and the

[3]From an internal report, undated but cited in 1980, from the Division of Environmental Sanitation.

Cumberland Plateau can tolerate some pollution because of its low population density, but pollution in the Central Basin can reach unacceptable levels. The kinds of pollution vary, depending upon the polluting agent. Fuel combustion is a heavy factor in producing pollution by suspended particulates, or sulfur dioxide, but transportation is the chief source of pollution by carbon monoxide and hydrocarbons.

Smoke control ordinances have been in existence in Tennessee cities for many years, and although officials were designated to secure enforcement, little enforcement ever took place; the official positions were probably largely obscure sinecures. A Tennessee Air Quality Act was passed in 1967, creating a Tennessee Air Pollution Control Board with some control powers, including the power to make rules and regulations, to issue permits and emergency stop orders, and to go into court to secure compliance. The metropolitan counties are exempted from the act on the theory that they will carry out their own air pollution control programs but they may turn the function over to the state. The power to go to court to secure compliance is an old administrative device, characteristic of boards with weak powers, but in the past such powers have gradually developed into agency-enforcing powers in many instances. Whether that development comes about in Tennessee will probably be determined by the gravity of the pollution problem in the future and the depth of national commitment to its cure. To begin with, Tennessee efforts were devoted to education and the securing of voluntary compliance, a good technique if it works. The division of air pollution control, the administrative arm of the Air Pollution Control Board, now operates a construction-permit system to insure that proper air pollution controls are built into new plants, and an operating-permit system to review already existing facilities. In 1979 power was given the Air Pollution Control Board or the courts to assess civil penalties for noncompliance with regulations, and it is apparent that teeth have been added to the machinery. The division feels that progress is being made, but it notes that in 1978 the federal Environmental Protection Agency designated all or part of seventeen counties as areas where air pollution control was still not completely attained. These areas include certain sections affected by TVA operations, and by copper facilities in Polk County, as well as substantial portions of the metropolitan cities.[4] Tennessee must meet the requirements of the 1971 Federal Ambient Air Quality Standards promulgated by the national Environmental Protection Agency under the authority of the amended Federal Clean Air Act of 1970.

[4]*Annual Report,* Tennessee Division of Air Pollution Control, July 1978–June 1979. See also *Air Pollution Control Implementation Plan for the State of Tennessee,* as revised Feb. 9, 1977.

Above: One View of Strip Mining. Sandy Campbell in the *Tennessean.*
Below: Interstate Roulette. Sandy Campbell in the *Tennessean.*

Few problems of environmental control occasion more impassioned argument than strip-mining. Coal is a major product of the state. That coal is increasingly important as an energy source, that it is significant to our economy and to our comfort, is clearly evident to anyone who looks at the huge pile of coal ready for consumption at the Kingston steam plant of TVA. From this site a few minutes of travel will provide a wide choice of views of the effects on the Cumberland Plateau and in the Cumberland Mountains of the strip-mining that supplies that coal pile. The pressures to protect the mountains from devastation or disfigurement, with the accompanying damages to streams, wildlife, and eventually the human population, have grown continually greater. Before the enactment of the Strip Mine Law of 1967 some 100,000 acres of Tennessee had been damaged in some way by this practice. The law of 1967 was superseded by a new statute passed in 1972. The latest legislation is the Tennessee Coal Surface Mining Law of 1980, which, following the scheme of earlier legislation, empowers the Commissioner of Conservation or his designees to conduct investigations, issue regulations, issue cease orders, and require plans for the reclamation of land by mining companies. The law covers the recovery of materials other than coal, but coal is most affected. The state's program is at least an improvement on old practices, but it will not restore the shape of the mountains and it will probably not satisfy the ardent conservationists. Since coal is still an essential ingredient of our industrial activity, we may expect the controversy to continue.[5]

There is no doubt that one of Tennessee's greatest assets, measured economically or otherwise, is the natural beauty of the region; millions of tourists bear witness. This beauty, like natural beauty everywhere, is endangered by man, his presence, his development, his use of the resource. Here again accommodation between use and preservation must be reached, and the state has been taking some steps in that direction, again too often waiting upon the inspiration and encouragement of the national government. The state owns and operates forty-five parks, or recreation areas in various stages of development, distributed throughout the state, and heavily patronized. The system is undergoing further expansion. Under the pressure of politically powerful sportsmen, the state has for a long time promoted the preservation and propagation of wildlife, and its well-established programs furnish a basis for a broadened concern for the natural environment that is always endangered by the pressures of human population. Beginning with statutes enacted in 1968, the code now contains a range of legislation creating and authorizing the administration of various areas of especial scenic value, such as the Scenic Rivers Act, the Tennessee Trails System Act, and the Natural Areas Preservation Act. The

---

[5]For a study of TVA's relation to strip mining, see Bruce D. Rogers, "Public Policy and Pollution Abatement: TVA and Strip Mining," diss., Indiana University, Feb. 1973.

purpose of this legislation is to keep reserved areas from spoilage through restrictions on development and in some cases through transferring areas to public ownership. Administration of the acts is generally lodged in the Department of Conservation. Legislation of this sort can become involved in sharp political argument between the "preservers" and the "developers." Policy here is likely to be the focus of continuing contention in the years ahead, not only in the State of Tennessee, but also throughout the entire country.

$$\odot$$

What I shall have to say will doubtless prove dull and prosy to most persons. A man cannot get up and make a speech on agriculture as on most other subjects.

ANDREW JOHNSON (1857)

THREE-QUARTERS OF A CENTURY AGO, devoted singers of popular songs were warbling one with the words, "How you gonna keep 'em down on the farm, after they've seen Paree?" It was an expression of the idea that farm life was dull and unenterprising—that the action was in the cities. Since then, not only in this country, but all through the world, the burgeoning population has flocked to overpopulated and overburdened cities. Farm life is still supposed to be dull.

But unenterprising it is not. The extent of agricultural production in the state of Tennessee makes for astonishing reading—57 million bushels of soybeans; 210,000 milk cows, 137 million pounds of tobacco, almost 1,300,000 hogs, 235,000 bales of cotton, and millions of chickens and eggs. Tennessee helps to feed the world. It is twentieth among the fifty states in the value of its agricultural exports, eighth in tobacco, cotton, and cottonseed oil, and tenth in soybeans, soybean oil, and protein meal. "It ain't hay."

Tennessee agriculture shows great diversity. King Cotton has been dethroned—even in the middle and western counties—to be replaced by soybean production, but cotton is still a significant product, sixth in value among the state's products. But it accounts for only five percent of the total value of the state's agricultural products, compared to 22 percent for oil crops. Beef and dairy cattle, tobacco, and swine outrank cotton as income producers. The state is by no means bound to one crop and the ups and downs of a one-crop market, nor is it wholly committed to the crops that deplete the soil or promote erosion, although the color of any rain-swollen river bears witness to the continued running away of the soil. (Indeed, there are signs of a re-emerging soil erosion problem of significant proportions.)

All of the weapons of state activity are brought to bear in one way or another on the problems of agriculture. They include: education, research, information, inspection, regulation (particularly by licensing), various forms of technical aid, demonstration, and a limited amount of public ownership. Subsidies are a major feature of American agricultural policy (although they have been largely inoperative at the high price levels of recent years) but they are conducted under federal programs principally, and the state has little to say about them.

Indeed agricultural programs of the state generally are heavily involved with and influenced by federal statutes, standards, and money. In one field after another the state acts with federal encouragement, leadership, and cooperation, often backed by the threat of more compulsive methods if ordinary persuasion fails. Since the programs of the state and of the federal government are administered by the technicians to a considerable degree and since technicians tend to form their own standards, there is good reason to believe that state and federal bureaucrats pursue the same general ends, even though federal supervision may be irksome at times. Agriculture furnishes an outstanding example of "marble-cake" federalism where state and federal activities are thoroughly intermingled.

America—and Tennessee—has ceased to have a primarily agricultural economy. Tennessee has shared in the industrial development of the United States, but agriculture is still significant in the state, as in the country as a whole. Agricultural well-being is still a principal concern of state government, and agricultural interests are still politically potent. It is no mere happenstance that Buford Ellington was commissioner of agriculture before he was governor, even though this line of succession was unusual. The first chief administrator of the state's agricultural program was Governor Andrew Johnson.

Significant changes are taking place in Tennessee's agriculture, changes like those in the country at large. The farm population in the state, which was 1,271,708 in 1920, numbered only 1,275,582 in 1940. This was a slight growth, but so slight that we could say that farming was barely holding its own in terms of population. By 1970, farm population had declined to 392,503. In the years between 1920 and 1950, the number of farms declined slightly, from 252,774 to 231,631. (There had been 77,741 farms in 1860.) In 1974, the number was down to 94,000. From 1920 to 1979 the land in farms declined from 19,511,000 acres to 13,700,000. The peak figure for land in farms between 1860 and 1945 was in 1860 itself, when 20,669,165 acres were in cultivation. The change in the area under farming is not so great or so rapid that it need occasion any alarm for the future of agriculture. More significant as a reflection of the changed way of farm life is the decline of the average size of farm in Tennessee from 250.9 acres in 1860 to 146 acres in 1979. Yet in 1935 that average size was down to 69.7 acres and, if trends in the size of farms in Tennessee follow patterns found in some states, we have passed from the plantation to the small farm and are developing again, under the impact of farm mechanization, a larger farm unit. The larger farms are developing in Middle and West Tennessee, whereas those in East Tennessee are smaller, perhaps a reflection of the growth of small farm operations in the industrial sections. Another great change has occurred in Tennessee agriculture. In 1940 over 40 percent of the farm operators were tenants; in 1974 the figure was 6 percent. Mechanization and migration are disposing of the tenant farmer; Tennessee's farms are overwhelmingly owned and operated by families.[6]

Man shares the world with other forms of life, some friendly, some inimical. Some of these forms are inimical to animals on which man is dependent. Dog-lovers are aware that their pets suffer from disease, but the average urban human must be taken aback at the wide range of ailments to which the animal world is subject. Cattle, hogs, and horses get pneumonia; pigs have gastric ulcers; arthritis attacks animals; cattle can acquire tuberculosis; encephalitis of various types occurs; and so the bewildering catalog goes on. Some of these diseases can be transferred to humans, and human society must aid the animals in order to protect man himself against contagion as well as to insure his food supply. As these diseases are often either contagious or are carried by insects or spread by transported products, individual efforts to eradicate them would be largely unavailing. Furthermore, the average farmer cannot be expected to know enough to combat disease unaided. The state has been compelled to take these matters in hand.

The regulatory authority of the state is also required to protect both the public and the honest and scrupulous seller of agricultural products against a two-legged pest—the human who in the pursuit of a dishonest dollar (or out of pure but perilous ignorance) will cheat the customer by selling spoiled meat or larding the all-beef wiener with a wee bit of pork. Hence the state has passed acts of various types to secure honest labeling of commodities, to authorize dealers to sell various products, and to grade goods, according to preestablished standards; and in 1977 the state legislature passed a Consumer Protection Act, administered by the Department of Agriculture. The division of consumer affairs investigates complaints of misrepresentation in a wide variety of modern "bunco" activities in a

⁶These figures are taken from *Farming and Progress: Thirty-Seventh Biennial Report of the Department of Agriculture of the State of Tennessee*, July 1, 1946–June 30, 1948, pp. 314, 315; *Farming and Living: Biennial Report of the Department of Agriculture of the State of Tennessee*, July 1, 1944–June 30, 1946, pp. 138, 139; and U.S. Dept. of Commerce, Bureau of the Census, *United States Census of Agriculture: 1950, Tennessee*, vol. I, pt. 20 (Washington: Government Printing Office, 1950), 3; *1969 Census of Agriculture*, pt. 31, *Tennessee*, vol. I, sec. I, ch. 1, *Summary Data*, tables 3, 4; ch. 2, table 1. Tennessee Department of Agriculture, *Annual Report, 1977–78*.

number of industries and facilities otherwise legitimate—health spas, auto repair shops, restaurant menus, insulation, and the music industry. The division's reports furnish interesting commentary on modern means of cheating.

Much of the total effort of state agencies, too, is directed toward making rural life pleasant and wholesome, as well as profitable. School programs include features directed toward improved rural living: rural electrification is fostered (largely through federal instrumentalities in this case), and adult educational work of various sorts is carried on, all with the view to enriching the lives of the people of the state. In many of these enterprises the state is merely a partner in the efforts of private persons and groups.

Agricultural development in the State of Tennessee is the concern of federal, state, and local agencies. The work of the state touching farmers and farm life is carried on through a variety of agencies. Rural health is a concern of the state and local health departments. Railway and other utility charges are the responsibility, when within the state, of the Public Service Commission, and so on. But some of the agencies of the state have been designed to have the farm as their particular care. The most important of these are the state Department of Agriculture and the University of Tennessee through its Institute of Agriculture.

The bureau of agriculture, statistics, and mines was established by the legislature in 1875. In 1854 the legislature had set up a single unit for agriculture alone, the Tennessee state agricultural bureau, reorganized later under a commission appointed by the governor.[7] In the reorganization of the state's administrative machinery in 1923, the Department of Agriculture took its place as one of the principal cabinet departments under the governor. It is headed by a commissioner appointed by the governor for an indefinite term. The commissioner serves as a member of a number of committees. On some of these his membership is a means of tying in his department with some function with which agricultural interests need coordination. Thus he is a member of the Board of Trustees of the University of Tennessee, and of the state Soil Conservation Commission. These positions, too, serve to recognize the particular concern of agricultural interests in certain state activities. Then, too, the commissioner often serves as a member of boards or committees through which the state and private interests together foster some branch of rural improvement.

The University of Tennessee's Institute of Agriculture is divided into four principal operating units: the College of Agriculture, the College of Veterinary Medicine, the Agricultural Experiment Station, and the Agricultural Extension Service. The Colleges of Agriculture and Veterinary

[7]Lee S. Greene, Virginia Holmes Brown, and Evan A. Iverson, *Rescued Earth: A Study of the Public Administration of Natural Resources in Tennessee* (Knoxville: Univ. of Tennessee Press, 1948), 11.

Medicine offer academic work at both the undergraduate and graduate level. The Agricultural Experiment Station undertakes fundamental and applied research in such areas as crop and livestock production, disease and insect control, and nutrition and food safety. In addition to the principal experiment station located in Knoxville, substations are maintained in West Tennessee, the Central Basin of Middle Tennessee, the Highland Rim, the Cumberland Plateau, and the East Tennessee Valley, these areas representing the principal physiographic and soil-type areas of the state.

The Agricultural Extension Service administers a program of agricultural and home economics extension instruction, demonstration, and guidance, through county agricultural and home demonstration agents. The Agricultural Extension Service has employees in every Tennessee county, supported by federal, state, and local funds. The College of Home Economics is also concerned with teaching and research activities of interest to farm as well as urban people.

Until the years immediately following the second World War, the University was dominated by the agricultural units, but this has long since ceased to be the case. Still, the units are highly significant components of the total university program.

The control of plant and animal disease is one of the most important functions of the state, a control exercised in great measure through the state Department of Agriculture, although with the help of other state and federal agencies. The fight against some diseases can be carried on by educational methods—training private persons to fight the disease, conducting schools for inspectors, and the like. But some diseases have required a more drastic remedy. In the years since 1916 the state, county, and federal governments have succeeded in reducing the incidence of bovine tuberculosis to a very low point, but this was done only through the purchase and slaughter of infected stock by governmental agencies. At the present time continual testing for the disease, reinforced by quarantine regulations, is necessary to prevent its reappearance. Equally drastic methods were applied against the foot-and-mouth disease, where international cooperation was a necessity, since the disease had ravaged herds far and wide in Mexico. Plant disease control relies on education for growers, testing and surveys to determine the presence of disease, the inspection of nurseries and seeds, and the development by research and experimentation of disease-resistant plants.

The regulatory laws of the state enforced by the division of marketing and other divisions of the department indicate a kind of activity that has the double function of protecting the consuming public (including the farmer) against inferior or misadvertised products or unhealthy stock and of protecting the dealer who complies with regulations against the noncomplying seller. Legislation of this sort has its dangers because it may become a tool for protecting established business from the inroads of unwanted competition. Statutes designed to suppress unfair and fraudulent practices usually define grades and provide regulations for packing and selling. Grading laws like these, besides being some protection to the customer, are useful in aiding the grower to find a readier market, for buyers will wish to purchase products of a guaranteed quality when they can.

Inspection is a basic technique used in the enforcement of marketing regulations. In the case of fruit and vegetable inspection, a federal-state cooperative agreement serves as the basis for inspection service operations. Inspection costs are financed by fees assessed and collected on a package or contract basis, and the actual inspections are conducted either at shipping points or at terminal markets. The issuance of certificates of inspection constitutes a significant aspect of the inspection process and is frequently used as a basis for settling claims. The certificate of inspection frees the buyer from exclusive reliance upon the seller's recommendations, thus aiding in the development of confidence in market transactions.

Even though Tennessee has become a heavily urbanized state, agricultural concerns are still important and agricultural interests continue to be powerful. The state shares with its sister commonwealths the agricultural expertise and capacity that make this country a major food source not only for itself but also for much of the rest of the world. This expertise has been developed over a century by the joint efforts of the national government, the states, and the counties, under the leadership in this state, as in the others, of the land-grant colleges and their programs of teaching, research, and extension. The political significance of agriculture is symbolized by such items as the presence of the commissioner of agriculture on the governing bodies of higher educational institutions, the significant status of agricultural educational leaders, and the power exhibited by the Farm Bureau Federation in various ways, most notably in the recent adoption of the classified property tax. Agricultural groups must now share power with other interests, but they remain forces to be reckoned with and to lean on.

21

☆ ☆
☆

The Public Economy

AT THE TIME THE AMERICANS SEPARATED FROM BRITISH RULE THE FULL powers of government devolved upon the individual colonies, now, in their own eyes, individual states. In order to maintain their newly declared independence they were forced into a degree of cooperation in foreign and military affairs, a cooperation grudgingly accepted with reluctance and backsliding. After the new country was recognized the initial union under the Articles of Confederation gave limited power to a national government in foreign and military affairs, with a restricted degree of national economic authority. The national power in economic, foreign, and military matters was sharply strengthened by the terms of the national constitution of 1787, but the states were left with great authority in internal economic affairs, and with some military power. The states still retain extensive power in economic matters. They can enact legislation and exercise regulatory authority over business, labor, agriculture, the professions, education, and a host of other matters, and they do act in these fields. Nevertheless, through the medium of the national power over interstate commerce, aided by the taxing and spending powers, the war powers, and the treatymaking power, the national government can supersede (and thus lead or control) the policies of the individual states in practically any sector of policymaking, including the activities of the states and their subdivisions—the local governments—with respect to their own governments and their own employees. It is clear that no sector of public life is now guaranteed freedom from national policymaking.

Although the individual states are still highly important in the scheme of things, they are becoming steadily less so as their policies are supplemented or replaced by the much more dramatic and forceful actions of the national government. Often the individual states have chosen, through neglect or deliberate wish, to refrain from policymaking in various areas, but this does not mean that such a decision is allowed to stand. Tennessee, for example, has so far next to no labor relations law. But this choice is not as significant as it might be because labor relations in the state, for large numbers of workers, are governed by federal law, enacted under the sweeping powers confirmed in Congress by judicial interpretation of the scope of the interstate commerce clause. The individual states, including Tennessee, have long had safety and health legislation covering workers, but this legislation has been overridden in interest, if not necessarily in complete effect, by the controversial Occupational Safety and Health Act of 1970.[1] The food and drug acts of the states are overshadowed by national food and drug regulation; the blue-sky laws of the states have been widely superseded by national securities and exchange regulation; the antimonopoly statutes of the states made obsolete and uninteresting by a long line of federal economic legislation.

This development downgrades the states as partners in the alliance. The state legislatures become less important as arenas of political conflict and decisionmaking. Perhaps the pride of the states is diminished.

The pace of nationalization shows little sign of diminishing, in spite of sporadic attempts to decentralize authority. Pressure groups—business, labor, the professions, even the local governments—seem to find it easier to fight their battles on a single national front than in the fifty individual states or the thousands of local governments; success in the national arena means success everywhere that national regulation can reach. For some of this development the states may take the blame, since they have often been slow to move in meeting the challenges that the contemporary world presents.[2] The Carter administration took steps at the national level to deregulate certain industries, particularly in transportation, and the succeeding Reagan administration is committed to pursuing a similar policy. Whether or not this will induce similar state action is by no means certain.

⊛

The state Constitution is not the source of legislative authority, but is the inclusive embodiment of such prerogatives of sovereignty as may be therein expressly or impliedly contained. . . .

Foster v. Roberts, 142 Tenn. 350, 355 (1919)

THE MOST IMPORTANT SOURCE of state authority over business and industrial activities is the power known as the police power. This is not something that can be defined with absolute precision. It is a concept of power

---

[1]Some provision was made for the protection of state control, if the state wished to exercise it.

[2]For a discussion of this attitude, see Greene, "The Condition of the States."

developed in relatively recent times, and it includes principally the power to protect the public health, the public safety, and the public morals; to suppress public nuisances; and to prevent fraud. The state has this power inherently; that is to say, the state constitution need not—and probably will not—either mention or grant this power, yet the power is recognized as essential to the existence and functioning of the state, and the legislature can use it to establish regulations governing the business and professional life of the community. The police power is of the utmost importance for such regulation. This is the basis on which states and their subdivisions can control the prices and services of public utilities, place restrictions on dangerous machinery, require pure food and drugs, destroy impure commodities, and otherwise protect the public interest.

Because the state can tax and spend, it can, by the choices exercised, exert a decided influence on the economy. Generally speaking the principal purpose of taxing is not to influence the economy, but rather to secure funds, and yet the way in which this is done will affect the business world. Thus if the state taxes sales, a different effect will be produced than if incomes were taxed. Sometimes, under cover of the taxing power, the state may lay extra burdens on businesses it considers undesirable, such as the liquor traffic. By the use of heavy amounts of taxation, the state may slow up the exhaustion of natural resources such as coal and oil. Activities thought desirable may be encouraged by light taxation or freedom from tax burdens. There is little evidence, however, that Tennessee policymakers are influenced in their choice of taxes by any motive other than the need for money.

Expenditure has even more direct influence on business. We spend heavily for roads, and this expenditure is undertaken to promote commerce, among other things. Vocational education and professional education feed skilled persons into the economic life of the community. The spending power is a weapon that can be used to attack a particular problem in the community directly and deliberately.

The state's power over corporations is particularly significant. Ordinarily the corporation is the creature of the state; that is to say, the corporation exists because the state says that it may. A corporation is nothing more than a collection of individuals who are treated by the state as though, for certain purposes, they constituted one person, and, because the state has allowed this situation to exist, it obtains certain rights over corporations that it may not have over actual individual persons. For example, the state has extensive powers of investigating corporations and inspecting their books. Numerous other regulations may be laid on the corporation as a condition of its existence.

The state owns property and enjoys property rights, and it can make contracts. Many relationships of this sort are entered into between states and private business firms, and states often require that certain conditions be met by those private business firms with which they do business. Furthermore, there is nothing to prevent the state from entering business on its own, and states have frequently done so. For example, some states operate their own liquor stores rather than, as in Tennessee, permitting such operation to remain in private hands.

Tennessee has been a poor state, economically, compared to many others. It has always been heavily forested, and still is, and a forest economy is not a rich one. Industrial development has therefore always beckoned Tennessee policymakers as the way to more people, more employment, higher wages, and a broader tax base. The problems that such development brings have not kept the governors and the legislators of Tennessee from attempts to entice industry by whatever legitimate means are available, and that with considerable success. Tennessee shares in the national phenomenon known as the "shift to the Sun Belt."

⭐

Any and all lawful business . . . may be . . . carried on by . . . corporations in this state.

TCA, 48–116

ALTHOUGH INDUSTRY has been and is growing in Tennessee and gives promise of similar growth in the future, this development is comparatively recent. Consequently we do not find in Tennessee the elaborate state regulation of industrial activity that would exist in New York and California, nor do we find a wide range of agencies concerned with the enforcement and elaboration of such regulation.

Very few agencies have been created in Tennessee specifically devoted to the regulation of business activity. When an act is passed regulating a branch of business or industry, the legislature has attempted to provide enforcement of policy by providing for criminal penalties or civil action, or both. If the penalty for violation of a statute is fine or imprisonment, the statute must be enforced by the ordinary processes of government; charges must be made and trials held. Whether this will be done will depend on the enforcing officers, locally elected, who are generally busy enforcing the law as a whole. If violation of a statute lays the violator open to civil action, then enforcement must await the action of the private person. The chances are that, if a special agency is not set up and charged with the enforcement of special types of business regulation, the enforcement of such special regulation will be spasmodic and uncertain.

In Tennessee, ordinary corporations are governed by extensive provisions on the statute books, but no special agency exists to control or supervise them. The statutes indicate that any lawful business may employ this form.[3] Any one or more natural persons having the power to contract may form a corporation by filing the required information with the secretary of state and with the register of the county in which the corporation's principal office is located. The secretary of state subsequently issues the certificate of incorporation.

A corporation has the power to sue and be sued in the courts under its own name; it may make contracts; it may purchase, hold, and sell property, borrow money, acquire and dispose of patents and copyrights, licenses, and other rights and interests; and it has a number of other powers similar to those enjoyed by a private person.

The law of the state governs the way in which stock may be issued and paid for. Such regulations are designed to prevent practices regarded as fraudulent or corrupt. The law contains provisions governing meetings of the stockholders, the number of votes to which each stockholder is entitled, the use of proxies, the selection of directors and officers, and their powers. Procedures are provided for the consolidation and dissolution of corporations. The books to be kept by the corporation are set forth in a general way.

Elsewhere in the statute books may be found a detailed list of provisions regarding particular kinds of corporations such as abstract companies and mining corporations.

No purpose would be served by describing in detail the regulations surrounding corporations in the State of Tennessee. What is noteworthy is that no special agency is provided to see that the law is obeyed. Reliance is placed upon the ordinary enforcement machinery of the state, a machinery decentralized to the local level. Thus directors, officers, agents, or stockholders intentionally guilty of fraud are liable for damages, and are guilty of misdemeanors, but enforcement depends once more upon action in the courts, at the suit of injured persons or public officials. It is difficult to judge the effectiveness of enforcement of this sort.

Foreign corporations, that is, corporations not set up in the state, may do business in the state by filing certain required information with the secretary of state and designating an agent within the state. Again there is no special agency of the state to inspect or regulate the foreign corporations.

Industry and monopoly cannot live together.

HENRY D. LLOYD (1894)

FOR A LONG TIME there has existed in the United States extreme animosity toward monopolies and trusts, a suspicion of "big business," and a general

[3]Reference here is made to *TCA*, Title 48.

friendliness toward the idea of preserving free competition. This approach
to the problem of business organization is inherited in some measure from
long-standing English attitudes, but it has received refinements and twists
peculiar to the American experience. The American view of monopoly was
embodied in state and federal court decisions even before the passage of
the basic federal act on the subject, the 1890 Sherman Antitrust Act, and
before the passage of this notable legislation many of the individual states
had already proceeded to establish policies against monopoly in business
life. Tennessee was one of those states. A statement on this matter may be
found in the Tennessee constitution: "perpetuities and monopolies are
contrary to the genius of a free State and shall not be allowed." This
constitutional provision is made specific by certain provisions of the
Tennessee code. The sections of the code relating to trusts and combinations in restraint of trade are based principally upon statutes passed
between 1891 and 1927, but little attention is given to their enforcement and
no special agency has been created to suppress or control monopolies.

Antitrust policy furnishes a fine example of an area that, although
subject to state activity, has been allowed to pass entirely, or almost so, to
national control. Economists pay next to no attention to state legislation in
this field, except to note in passing that state antitrust statutes are practically never enforced. Tennessee experience justifies the observation.

The devotion of state and national legislators to the idea of full and free
competition has not been without its episodes of backsliding. We have
groups in the community who, at times, want free competition even if it
goes to the point of becoming "cut-throat" in character. And so we have
swung back and forth from one attitude to the other. In 1937 the Tennessee
General Assembly placed on the statute books a fair trade act, designed to
limit competition. In this, Tennessee was following the lead of other states.
The first provision of this short but interesting piece of legislation stated
that no contract relating to the sale or resale of a trademarked or branded
article should be deemed to be a violation of any Tennessee law by reason
of provisions in that contract that the buyer would not resell such commodity except at the price stipulated by the seller or that the seller made such a
condition a part of his sale. The next clause, more sweeping and more
devastating to unrestrained competition, stated that it was unfair competition for a person, whether or not he personally was a party to the sort of
contract noted above, willfully and knowingly to advertise such a product
for sale or to sell it at less than the price stipulated in such a contract
between other parties. Such action, being unfair competition, laid the
responsible individual open to suit for damages. These two clauses, the
sum and substance of this act, indicated that if we wished to sell a bottle of
XYZ tonic, but the manufacturer of XYZ tonic had agreed with someone
else that the price should not be below a certain figure, then we had to

maintain a price of at least that amount, even though we had nothing to do with the contract, or else our sale or the advertising of our sale would lay us open to a damage suit. This was price-fixing by some parties, effective on all parties.

In the same legislature that passed the so-called Fair Trade Act, a second piece of legislation, called the Unfair Sales Act, was placed upon the statute books. This act made it a misdemeanor, punishable by fine or preventable by injunction, for retailers or wholesalers to advertise, offer for sale, or sell articles at less than cost with the intent of unfairly diverting trade away from a competitor or otherwise injuring a competitor.[4] An unfair cigarette sales law was passed in 1949. The "fair trade" laws covering milk and alcoholic beverages, passed in 1957 and 1959 and later amended, have aroused great controversy.[5] In particular, the milk control legislation is of doubtful constitutionality.

This type of legislation restricting the cutting of prices started with California legislation in 1931 sponsored by the druggists.[6] Subsequently other states adopted the same type of legislation. Congress by passing the Miller-Tydings Act exempted certain types of activity of this kind from the Sherman Act and later reinforced this with the McGuire-Keogh Act. The number of states having resale price maintenance laws reached as high as forty-six but by 1967 had so declined that the laws were repealed or unenforceable in all but sixteen states.[7]

Some of these acts, like Tennessee's antitrust act, provided no special system of enforcement. Because of this fact and because of the vagueness of the act itself, it is unlikely that the act dealing with sales below costs is of any particular force. On the other hand, the act limiting price-lowering of trademarked articles was possibly more effective. But the legislation became unpopular and in 1975 the Fair Trade Act and the "fair trade" law for liquor were repealed. Governor Blanton had advocated repeal of all "fair trade" laws.

Never give a sucker an even break.

REMARK OFTEN ATTRIBUTED TO W. C. FIELDS

WHEN HE IS ABLE TO DO SO, the American seeks to protect himself against "the slings and arrows of outrageous fortune" by insurance payable in

---

[4]For these various acts, see *TCA*, Title 69.

[5]Compare *Study on Regulatory Legislation Concerning Milk and Milk Products, 1968* (Nashville: Legislative Council Committee, 1968).

[6]Clair Wilcox, *Public Policies Toward Business*, 4th ed. (Homewood, Ill.: Richard D. Irwin, 1971), 700.

[7]*Ibid.*, 705.

event of death, accident, or ill health. Under the guise of insurance he may purchase an old-age annuity. Companies insure themselves against accidents to their workers. In some states automobile drivers are required to insure against accidents. The business of insurance has grown so phenomenally that it would be surprising indeed if it had not come under state regulation.

In the country as a whole the growth of the insurance business was attended with various sorts of abuses and, since the national government did not attempt federal regulation, the individual states did so. Early state regulation was very frequently colored by discrimination against foreign or out-of-state businesses. In various ways state supervision became chaotic and unsatisfactory. Some pressure for federal action in the interest of uniformity was exerted, but in the case of *Paul* v. *Virginia* in 1869 the United States Supreme Court held that insurance policies were not articles of interstate commerce. This ruling seemed to make federal supervision impossible and made it desirable that the states themselves seek uniformity. Shortly thereafter the National Association of Insurance Commissioners was formed; its present constitution sets as one of its tasks the development of uniformity among the states in insurance regulation. The association furnishes an interesting example of the influence of professional groups on public policy. The reform of state regulation proceeded rapidly after the Armstrong committee investigation in New York at the beginning of the century. In spite of regulatory reform, insurance company failures are common and regulation by the states is still lax.

Over 400 pages of the annotated edition of the Tennessee code are given over to detailed statutory regulation of the insurance business. It would be beyond the scope of our interest here to examine this statutory material in detail, but some appreciation of the sort of state regulation under which this business works is important for the average citizen. In the first place the insurance business is honored by the establishment in the state of a special agency of regulation. This is the Department of Insurance headed by a commissioner appointed by the governor, who enforces the state's insurance acts, as well as those relating to investment companies, building associations, and so on. We may obtain a notion of the commissioner's functions by examining some of his powers and duties. Companies must have certificates of authority granted by the commissioner, who must be satisfied that the company is qualified to do business under the law of the state. The commissioner or his deputies are required to examine the affairs of each company at stated intervals to determine its financial condition and its compliance with the law. The examiner is to have free access to all the company's books and papers relating to its business. The commissioner has several powers to prevent a company from engaging in further business activities if it appears that the firm is in unsound financial condition, or to stop the issuance of policies by a domestic company if its assets are insufficient to cover its liabilities. Insurance companies must furnish annual statements of their financial condition to the commissioner.

Various details of the insurance business are governed by statute. Such provisions cover the payment of dividends, the prevention of discrimination between customers, and the rates charged. Insurance agents must obtain licenses from the commissioner before doing business in the state; these may be revoked by the commissioner in the event the agent violates certain provisions of the law.

The state is concerned to provide, first, a means of determining what companies and agents may do business; second, it attempts to insure the financial soundness of insurance companies by requiring reports and permitting official inspections to the end that unsound companies may be prevented from doing further business; third, the law attempts to prevent companies from discriminating between customers. The means of enforcement involve a mixture of controls by the commissioner and the use of ordinary court procedure to enforce penalties for violation of the law.[8]

Insurance is under the control in Tennessee of the commissioner of insurance, and, often enough, the commissioner has been in the insurance business. Of course this makes some sense, but it also gives rise to the kind of conflicting interest that plagues Tennessee politics.

Another branch of business that has been subjected to detailed state regulation is banking. Banks are likewise subject to federal regulation, and such regulation continues, based upon a long experience with this field of economic activity. A primary purpose of banking regulation is to protect the public against unsound institutions. Thus a bank is not allowed to deal in its own stock; it is not to engage in trade or commerce; it is permitted to invest only in certain types of securities. Its internal management is closely regulated. Other regulations are designed to prevent discrimination between customers.

In the last few years, a number of banks in Tennessee have surrendered their federal charters, to become state banks, obviously to escape some of the more stringent regulations of the national banking system.

Banks are regulated by the Department of Banking. The law provides, as the chief officer conerned with banking, a commissioner of banking, appointed by the governor from nominees presented by the Tennessee Banking Board, an advisory body, appointed by the governor, representing banks and the general public. The commissioner is entitled to employ examiners to assist him in discharging his duties. Every banking business operating under the laws of the state is subject to the supervision of the

---

[8]*TCA*, Title 56 is devoted to regulation of the insurance business. The responsible state agency was the Department of Insurance and Banking until 1973, when separate departments of Insurance and Banking were established.

banking commissioner. Each bank is visited and examined twice each year for the purpose of seeing that it is solvent and its management prudent. In case of danger of improper use of state bank funds, the commissioner may take possession of such funds. The commissioner has extensive powers over liquidation and reorganization of state banks. As in the case of insurance companies, the enforcement of regulations regarding banks is secured by a mixture of actions by the Department of Banking and enforcement through regular court action. Various sections of the state code authorize cooperation with federal agencies engaged in banking regulation.[9]

The regulation of banks and insurance companies does not afford the investor complete protection against the sale of worthless stocks and bonds. As a means of protecting the general public against the sale of securities without value, most states have undertaken a certain degree of regulation under what is known as "blue-sky laws." Tennessee enacted a new statute on this subject in 1980. The principal means used for the protection of the public is the requirement that companies selling securities register those securities, giving extensive details about them. Salesmen of securities must also be registered under the control of the commissioner. A company or an agent that does business without complying may be punished by fine or imprisonment; defrauded purchasers of securities may sue for damages; and violations may be prevented by administrative stop orders.

✪

Law contemplates justice whether it is granted as a privilege or recognized as a vested right.

Fascination, Inc. v. *Hoover*, 39 CAL. 2d 260, 270 (1952)

THE STATE HAS ALWAYS EVIDENCED especial interest in the practice of certain professions that have seemed to offer peculiar dangers to, as well as advantages for, human life. As our technology grows more complex this interest deepens and broadens; the public control of professional life becomes greater. The customary method of control exercised over these professions is by the requirement of a license for the practitioner, backed by some sort of guarantee of his competence.

Professions that require licenses include medicine and surgery, dentistry, osteopathy, chiropractic work, pharmacy, optometry, nursing, veterinary medicine and surgery, accountancy, architecture, engineering, chiropody, barbering, cosmetology, embalming, plumbing, law, general

---

[9]See *Study on State Banking Laws, 1968* (Nashville: Legislative Council Committee, 1968). Banking statutes were extensively revised in 1969 and 1973.

contracting, dealing in real estate, and the eradication of insect pests, plant diseases, and rodents. One of the most recent additions to this group are the electrologists.[10] An attempt to require the licensing of photographers was ruled unconstitutional. The practice of naturopathy is now forbidden outright.

The requirement of licensing means more sometimes than the mere protection of public health, safety, and morals. It may mean that the respectable members of a profession are protected against charlatans and fly-by-night quacks. It may thus add respectability to professions once low in the social scheme. Furthermore, it is a means of cutting down on the numbers in the profession; a limit is thus provided to "cut-throat" competition. Most, but not all, of the professions listed above are important enough to public well-being that the licensing requirement, if carefully enforced, seems fully justified; some licensing seems principally designed to limit entrance into the occupation, and, hence, to limit competition.

Licensing, as generally required, is principally an instrument for guarding entry into an activity; it is not, as ordinarily used in the professions, a means of continuing regulatory control. Generally speaking, the rates charged and the service given by professional persons are of no concern to the state.

✪

Trade is a social act. Whoever undertakes to sell any description of goods to the public, does what affects the interests of other persons.
JOHN STUART MILL (1848)

AMONG THE BUSINESSES especially prone to invite public attention and, eventually, public regulation, those that furnish transportation, light, heat, and similar facilities to the public are especially significant. Both the states and the federal government have set up special agencies to deal with these so-called public utilities. Wisconsin and New York pioneered in the modern development of the public utility commission as a means of regulating gas companies, electric power companies, the railroads, and similar activities. In Tennessee the only commission of this type is the Public Service Commission, established as the Railroad Commission by an act of the General Assembly of 1897 and changed in 1955 to its present title.

The commissioners are three in number, each one representing one of the state's three Grand Divisions. Such regional representation, perhaps significant in the past, is losing any force it may have had, for potential candidates can establish residency anywhere. Commissioner Robert Cle-

---

[10]*Public Acts,* 1974, ch. 662.

ment, for example, who came from a Middle Tennessee family and was educated at the University of Tennessee and Memphis State, moved to East Tennessee long enough to qualify as a representative from that region. For all practical purposes, the division requirement might as well be dropped, but is unlikely to be.

The commissioners are elected by popular vote throughout the whole state for six-year, staggered terms. Compared to the race for the governorship, the contest for commissioner ordinarily attracts less attention, and people who occupy the office rarely move on to higher office. But this is not to say that they do not try. Aside from the judicial and legislative posts, this is the only job, other than the governorship, open to popular election, and commissioners often think of themselves as potential governors. This was the case, for example, with Hammond Fowler. The voters rarely acquiesce in such ambitions. The election of Robert N. Clement to the commission in 1972 was an exception, because it was widely recognized that Clement intended to run for the office of governor, once brilliantly held by his father, as, in fact, he did in 1978. Jane Eskind, having failed in her bid to become United States senator, ran successfully in 1980 for the commission, and it can well be assumed that her political ambitions will not be slaked by this one office. Frank Cochran was a candidate for governor in 1982. Sometimes the commissioners could be identified with particular factions within the Democratic party, but generally they enjoy the benefits and endure the hardships of low visibility. The commissioners have all been Democrats; no Republican has made it—so far.

Campaign funds for aspirants' campaigns are likely to come from potential litigants in commission proceedings; the system of election provides a built-in conflict of interest, a situation on which the general public is both uninformed and indifferent. Temporarily, this arrangement was highlighted in the winter of 1980–81 when the newly elected Jane Eskind openly solicited contributions from businesses subject to the commission as a means of lifting the sizable debt she had acquired in running for her new office. The solicitation was not productive, which indicates that the conflict of interest is not as serious as it might be.

The functions of the commission involve intrastate business. (Interstate activities come under federal jurisdiction.) With respect to these businesses the state has the following powers:

1. to fix just and reasonable rates for services performed;
2. to require the utility to furnish safe, adequate, and proper service and to permit abandonment of service;
3. to prescribe uniform accounting systems and to require the utility to make financial and other reports;
4. to fix proper and adequate rates of depreciation;
5. to make appraisals of the value of the property of a utility;

6. to fix standards for measuring service; and
7. to investigate any matter concerning any utility, on its own motion or on complaint of someone else.

In practice not all utilities have been subjected to a uniform degree of commission control.

The commission is responsible for evaluating and assessing for *ad valorem* purposes the properties of all railroads and other public utilities operating in the state. The practice of assessing utility property at a higher level than local assessment of other property has been successfully attacked in both federal and state courts by railroads. As a result the property assessment system was substantially altered by the adoption in 1972 of a constitutional amendment requiring the classified property tax.[11]

The coming of TVA to the State of Tennessee has had some effect on the Public Service Commission. TVA's expansion was accompanied by a growth of local publicly owned electric distribution systems. State law took these out of the jurisdiction of the commission. Some municipalities also acquired gas systems, and these were exempted from commission control. Independently of these developments, the state legislature removed city bus systems, even though privately owned, from commission jurisdiction and placed them under the city councils, even though it could scarcely be thought that councils are well equipped to deal with the technical problems of utility regulation.

It has been generally assumed that the regulatory commissions tend to become the captives of the industries they regulate. Recent studies indicate that this is not the case with the Tennessee commission, which is rather aggressive, consumer-oriented, and inclined to give the regulated industries a fairly hard time, at least from their point of view. The candidates for the commission frequently take a rather stiff line against the regulated industries and make campaign promises that would tend to cast considerable doubt on their impartiality as regulators, but if such doubt exists it appears not to get into the courts as one might expect. Seemingly the industries have learned to live with campaign verbiage.[12]

[11]Cf. Edward S. Overman, *Taxation of Public Utilities in Tennessee* (Knoxville: Univ. of Tennessee Press for Bureau of Public Administration and Bureau of Business and Economic Research, 1962).

[12]See David M. Welborn and Anthony E. Brown, *Regulatory Policy and Processes: The Public Service Commissions in Tennessee, Kentucky, and Georgia* (Knoxville: Bureau of Public Administration, Univ. of Tennessee, 1980).

⊛

The automobile and the American public are locked in a life and death struggle.

KENNETH P. CANTOR (1970)

TRANSPORT IS THE LIFE-BLOOD of a political structure. From the earliest days Tennessee's transportation needs have been the very stuff of politics. The town without transport dies. In the railroad-building era, communities struggled to get railroad service. When the automobile came, roads were essential, and governors sought office by promising roadbuilding. Now, in the air age, communities seek air service, but in this area the state can be of little help.

But transport policy calls for more than struggle between localities —political contestants battled on the mode of transport. Improvement of river transport has been principally a federal activity, except for local development of port facilities. But the prolonged battle between the railroads and the truckers affected political campaigns and campaign funds, as the truckers have constantly pressed for bigger and longer trucks and higher speeds. The battle played a major role in the contests between Governor Browning and Governor Clement.

Getting the farmer out of the mud has been one of the great services of the state and local units, increasingly with the assistance and, naturally, the direction of the national government. The importance of the highway is well underlined by the farmer who commented on the difficulty of marketing his corn over the then impassable roads, "They ain't no chanct to git hit out that way, but when we git hit made into likker, hit's plumb easy to fight it out."

Many of Tennessee's main highways follow the trails laid out by the Indians and early explorers. The "old Walton Road" extended from Kingston, Tennessee, into Middle Tennessee, and the old Natchez Trace followed a trail blazed by the Chickasaw Indians from Nashville to Natchez on the Mississippi. As early as 1801 the need for roadbuilding was called to the legislature's attention by Governor John Sevier, and the General Assembly responded by appointing commissioners for roadbuilding purposes. In 1821 the legislature became interested in highway planning and established a threefold classification of roads as a basis for the apportionment of taxes of state roads, roads that would support loaded wagons, and roads that would permit travel by a single horse and rider.

The advent of travel by rail in 1820 made long-distance highway transportation temporarily obsolete, and the legislature turned the highway problem over to counties and local officials. As a means of improving the condition of roads, counties were authorized to charter private turnpike companies to operate from revenues obtained from tolls.

What has been called railroad fever made its appearance in Tennessee in the late 1820s. The pre–Civil War attempt to construct railways in Tennessee, which took attention away from the roads to a degree, was attended by virulent sectional and local rivalries. East and West Tennessee united in competition with the Nashville Basin, for the attempts of Memphis interests to connect with Charleston, South Carolina, and of Knoxville and Chattanooga interests to markets in Kentucky, Georgia, and South Carolina aroused the jealousy and fears of Nashville, whose business concerns could envisage the decline of Nashville as a Cumberland River port. Financing was always a serious problem. State and local governmental credit was made available to railway companies, often with unsatisfactory if not disastrous results; later constitutional provisions attempted to prevent the recurrence of such extensions of credit. By the time the Civil War opened, the beginnings of today's network of railroads had been established.

With the coming of the automobile in the early part of the century the need for more adequate highways was once again recognized, and in 1909 the governor was authorized by the legislature to establish a state commission on public roads to study the need for improved highway facilities. In 1913 the legislature authorized the county courts to issue bonds for the construction and improvement of roads.

The first state administrative agency to deal with the highway problem was created in 1915 when the legislature established the State Highway Commission with authority to organize a state highway department to gather data, to set standards of road construction and maintenance, to advise county highway officials, and to execute contracts with the federal government in the designation of a connected highway system. An act of the legislature two years later authorized counties to purchase privately owned turnpikes, thereby removing an obstacle to an integrated highway system.

In 1919 the six-man commission was replaced by a three-man salaried commission, and funds were provided for an expanded highway program. With the state Reorganization Act of 1923 the commission was replaced by a single commissioner of highways and public works, thus setting the organizational pattern for what is now called the Department of Transportation.

A historical view of the pattern of highway administration in Tennessee reflects essentially the same situation as that found in the nation generally. What was once regarded as a function of local government had become, by the first decade of the present century, a matter in which the state exercised considerable concern. Although as late as 1890 no state had a highway agency, by 1917 every state had established some form of organization for highway administration. Many miles of roads still remain under county control, but local participation in the state highway function has suffered some decline.

The pattern of state highway administration varies from state to state. In some instances the highway function is under a commission or board appointed by the governor, and in others it is controlled by a single commissioner, director, or superintendent. In Tennessee the function is part of a recently renamed and enlarged Department of Transportation, under a single commissioner appointed by the governor.

Over the country the highway agency has been typically a principal hunting ground for patronage; this is the case in Tennessee as well as in many other states, but, since technical competence in highway engineering is essential, a highway personnel system completely dominated by patronage considerations is impossible.

County road administrators are selected in a multiplicity of ways in Tennessee. Some are elected by the voters and some have been chosen by the county courts (now boards of commissioners). Others are appointed by a commission or a commissioner who is either elected by the voters or chosen by the county board of commissioners. The varied pattern of county road administration that exists in Tennessee has been made possible by Tennessee's system of private bill legislation which permits separate laws for individual counties. The 1974 County Uniform Road Law attempts to set some minimum standards for county road administration.

At the municipal level in Tennessee the pattern for street administration is again varied. The larger cities have their own street or public works departments (with separate street divisions) headed, except in cities with the commission form of government, by appointive officials. In the smaller cities the street function is frequently handled in conjunction with that of water and sewer maintenance and construction.

The increasing centralization of the highway function has provided an administrative network of intergovernmental relationships. A pattern of these relationships has been evolving, but is by no means set firmly as yet. A forward step was taken by the Tennessee legislature in 1949 in the passage of the Rural Road Act. The objective of the act was to place, eventually, an all-weather road in reach of every farm home in Tennessee. Thus the law provided for the use of federal-aid secondary funds in addition to state-aid funds specifically assigned for county-aid purposes under the rural road program.

Tennessee's rural road program was further modified by legislation enacted in 1955 which established a rural roads program administered by a rural roads division in the Department of Highways. The commissioner of transportation, under this law as amended, designates the roads in the various counties that are to be included in the state's rural road system. The various county authorities prepare annual programs of road improvement applicable to such roads, which are subject to approval by the commissioner of transportation, and which must not exceed the funds allocated to each county for improvement purposes. It is the responsibility of the counties to obtain rights-of-way and to maintain all roads that have been improved under the rural roads program.

As a final note to state-county relations mention should be made of the fact that the legislature, by acts passed in 1927 and 1931, provided that the state assume the obligation of reimbursing counties for construction costs of highways acquired from the counties for inclusion in the state's primary system. Final payments on these obligations were made in June 1949.

Before 1947 the state was required by law to contribute to the construction and maintenance of all city streets over which traffic from the state highways was routed, but the state was not held responsible for the construction and upkeep of more than an eighteen-foot-wide pavement. This law was revised in the 1947 session of the legislature to provide for resurfacing and maintenance of the entire road surface from curb to curb or, in the absence of curbs, for the full width of the roadway.

Federal aid to highways goes back to the Federal Aid Road Act of 1916, which authorized the federal government to apportion matching funds to the states on the basis of area, population, and rural road mileage. The act was amended in 1921 to require the states to present a planned system of primary and secondary highways on which federal money would be spent. The Federal-Aid Highway Act of 1944 provided funds for the states for each of the first three postwar years on a matching basis. Subsequent federal-aid highway acts have continued authorizations of large sums which, in general, must be matched by state funds. Only a relatively small proportion of the county and urban systems is covered by the federal-aid program.

An important present-day feature of the federal-aid program is the construction of a national system of interstate and defense highways. Although authorized by the Federal-Aid Highway Act of 1944, on a 50-50 matching basis (later 60-40), relatively limited funds were made available to the program before 1956. In that year provisions were made for completion of the interstate system over a thirteen-to-sixteen-year period on the basis of a 90 percent federal, 10 percent state matching ratio. Tennessee has over a thousand miles of this system. The routes of these superhighways through cities have always aroused controversy. The most notable of such conflicts involved the proposal to put I-40 through Overton Park in Memphis. This was successfully stopped, and it now appears doubtful that this portion of I-40 will ever be built in that spot. During the period of railroad building, the passenger stations became a focus for urban development. The virtual disappearance of railway passenger traffic has eliminated the passenger stations; some of them have been torn down, others have been converted to other uses, such as Chattanooga Choo-Choo restaurant in the old Southern Railway station there. Attempts are being made to preserve the station in Nashville, long a landmark (its tower forms the leading picture on one of O.Henry's famous stories, "A Municipal Report") and the L and N station in Knoxville is being restored as part of the world fair set there for 1982. The bus stations never attained the architectural significance that the railway "depots" acquired; they are at best overworked generally dingy affairs. The airports, on the other hand, have offered architectural opportunities, but they have contributed nothing to the central city areas, of course, except to assist in their decline. The building of the interstates through cities brings architectural problems and opportunities. Older business and residential areas have sometimes been damaged, especially by elevated highways (duplicating the damage once wrought by elevated railroads in great cities like New York), but there are signs of adjustment as new structures gradually accumulate around the new highways, as in downtown Chattanooga.

The highway system of Tennessee as of 1979 consisted of the following mileage:

Interstate system	1,023 miles
State highway system	9,007
Local county roads	60,069
City streets	11,094
State and federal reservations	1,446
Total	82,639

Highway expenditures constitute a major burden on state and local budgets, not only in Tennessee but elsewhere. In Tennessee sources of funds for highway expense come from gasoline and other motor-fuel taxes, registration fees, and federal aid. The gasoline tax started at two cents per gallon in 1923 and has since climbed to ten cents. Two cents of the gas tax go to the counties, one cent to cities, (increased by the legislation of 1981) and the remainder to the state highway fund (less small percentages for the general fund, for administrative purposes). Supplements to these basic allocations to local units have been provided at various times. Highway expenditures are tied to the geographic character of a state. A state with a wide area and a limited number of wealth-producing cities will spend more of its wealth proportionately in providing highways than a small state with many cities.

(✪)

A stable and permanent union movement emerges when workers
recognize that their status as workers is not a temporary phenome-
non. . . . BENJAMIN J. TAYLOR AND FRED WITNEY (1971)

AS IN OTHER FIELDS, major interest in labor legislation covering labor conditions and labor relations has shifted from states to the national government. Originally the laws governing labor organizations, collective bargaining and representation, wages, hours, and safety were to be found principally in the state codes, and such laws are still on the books and still being enforced. But labor organizations now find it more productive to fight their legislative battles in the national arena, where success means nationwide compliance, rather than to struggle on fifty different fronts. Still, much of the history of labor legislation was developed at the level of the statehouse, where patterns for national activity were slowly established.

Labor legislation has been concerned with the safety and health of workers, starting with the well-being of special classes—women, children, workers in hazardous occupations—with wages and hours (minimum wages and maximum hours), again starting with the women and children, with compensation for injured workers, and finally with the right of workers to associate, to be represented, and to bargain collectively.

Tennessee is not one of the highly industrialized states, although industry is growing rapidly. Its labor law is therefore less highly developed than in the industrial states, such as New York and Illinois. One of the reasons for the comparative paucity of labor law in Tennessee is, of course, the relative weakness of organized labor in the state. Unions are active in the state and union tactics are a familiar feature of Tennessee life, but labor exerts comparatively little power in the General Assembly. This long-established situation shows little sign of change. Labor organizations are active in political affairs, and the friendship of organized labor is no doubt useful to the candidate, but it is not essential; labor does not appear to vote in a monolithic fashion, and few if any officeholders can be identified as labor-oriented. A very few members of the General Assembly are labor organizers or labor officials, and a limited number can be identified as blue-collar workers. The labor legislation on the books must therefore have been placed there because of support from outside the unions themselves; humanitarian sympathies and understanding must be considered contributors to the development of this area of social legislation.

State regulation of industrial health and safety goes back to the years before 1900. Regulations in Tennessee in the field of safety and sanitation include such matters as safeguards for dangerous machinery, the provision of adequate fire protection and ventilation, and adequate and decent sanitation. As the code has been built up over the years by piecemeal methods, Tennessee law seems sketchy and in need of overhauling. Enforcement of this type of legislation is shared between the Department of Labor and the Department of Public Health, carried out by inspections, administrative orders, and prosecutions in the courts. Voluntary compliance with regulations is sought where possible. The new federal Occupational Safety and Health Act provides that states may assume responsibility for enforcement of occupational safety and health by submitting plans for federal approval. In 1972 the General Assembly enacted a statute designed to meet federal approval, and the statute was submitted to the federal secretary of labor. The procedure is an interesting example of a further extension of federal control over state policymaking.

Compensation for the injured workman (known as workers' compensation) is governed by state law in all the states. The compensation laws are interesting illustrations of the change from the common law to modern social legislation. Under common law doctrine affecting the master-servant relationship, the employee was unable to recover damages for injuries sustained in the course of his employment so long as it could be determined that those injuries arose out of pure accident or were caused by his own negligence, the negligence of a fellow worker, or were the outgrowth of the necessary risks of the occupation in which he was engaged. Damages were secured by the slow and expensive operations of ordinary suits in court. To correct this situation, workers' compensation laws were passed in several states in the early years of the twentieth century and have since been enacted by all states and by the national government.

Tennessee first enacted workers' compensation legislation in 1919. The Tennessee law provides for an elective system of compensation (not all classes of workers are covered), but stipulates that an employer who has not come under the act may not resort to common-law defenses against damage suits (certain exceptions are provided). The system now covers specified occupational diseases as well as accidents. Employers may protect themselves by insurance, and the vast majority of Tennessee employers carry workers' compensation insurance.

Most states administer their compensation laws through special commissions that eliminate the courts, except for appeals. Tennessee still uses the courts as administrative agents, a system that would appear to be more expensive for the worker than the commission system. In 1972 the Legislative Council Committee recommended the widening of the coverage of the workers' compensation law, including its extension to all state and local public employees (some are already covered), and the establishment of the commission form of administration.[13] It seems odd and quite unjustifiable

[13]*Study on Workmen's Compensation Laws: Final Report of the Legislative Council Committee* (Nashville: Legislative Council Committee, 1972), 99–101.

for Tennessee to stick to court administration long after most states have abandoned this expensive system of procedure.

Forty-one states have their own general minimum wage laws.[14] Tennessee has not, and so far attempts to get such legislation enacted have been defeated, often decisively. Since the passage of the federal Fair Labor Standards Act in 1938 and its subsequent broadening, the pressure to enact state legislation is perhaps less significant. Furthermore, the criticism by economists of the concept of the minimum wage, particularly at the levels demanded by organized labor, has raised doubts about the wisdom of this type of regulation.[15]

Tennessee has enacted legislation covering the hours of women workers, and the state has controlled child labor for some time. Child labor is now regulated under the Child Labor Act of 1976. The legislation covering women workers has been criticized as defective by national standards, although child labor legislation and regulation generally meet standards considered adequate by experts in the field.[16] A 1974 act prohibits wage discrimination on account of sex.[17]

Labor relations—organization, representation, collective bargaining, unfair labor practices, and the regulation of the internal affairs of unions—are extensively governed by federal law, notably the Taft-Hartley Act and the Landrum-Griffin Act. Similar legislation has been passed by many states authorizing association, representation, and collective bargaining; providing arbitration or mediation; and governing union and management tactics. Not much of this exists in Tennessee. The state has no legislation authorizing or promoting collective relationships between management and organized labor, or governing specifically the internal affairs and conduct of labor unions. Tennessee has followed the practice of some states that have restricted the imposition of the closed or union shop either by statute or by constitutional provision. Tennessee's anticlosed-shop law, bitterly but vainly fought by organized labor, makes it illegal to refuse employment to a person because of membership or nonmembership in a union. The act is protected by a provision of the Taft-Hartley Act that authorizes state right-to-work laws.

A new issue faces the Tennessee policymaker in the field of labor relations: shall public employees, state and local, be authorized to organize and bargain collectively? Such employee activity is widely practiced in many states and localities, and in some instances the powers of the unions

---

[14]Bureau of National Affairs, *Labor Policy and Practice,* 100:41 (Washington, 1981).

[15]See, for example, Robert J. Gaston, "Some Minimum Wage Law Effects," in *Tennessee Survey of Business* (Knoxville: Center for Business and Economic Research, Univ. of Tennessee, April 1973), 16; for a more cautious view, see Wilcox, 715–16.

[16]J. Fred Holly and Bevars D. Mabry, *Protective Labor Legislation and Its Administration in Tennessee* (Knoxville: Univ. of Tennessee Press, 1955), 31ff.

[17]*Public Acts,* 1974, ch. 757.

have become so great as to threaten an unhealthy domination of public policymakers. What the rights and duties of Tennessee public employees should be has become a matter of dispute and division at recent sessions of the legislature.[18] So far Tennessee has not enacted a general statute on this subject, and practice varies from one city to another. There is a state employees' association; it lobbies, but is not recognized as a bargaining agent. Teachers were given collective bargaining rights by the 1978 legislature. Some unionization has developed, and some collective agreements have been made. Strikes are becoming more commonplace; it was during one of these in Memphis that Martin Luther King, Jr., was assassinated in 1967. In 1978, Memphis suffered severely from a strike of firemen and from hundreds of fires, some of them deliberately set. Knoxville was hit by a police slowdown and fictitious illness among firemen. Nashville was struck by firemen in 1980. Obviously, Tennessee is about to face some major policy questions in the management of public employee relations.

[18]See *Study on Public Employer-Employee Relations: Final Report of the Legislative Council Committee* (Nashville: Legislative Council Committee, 1970); see also Michael Brookshire and Michael Rogers, "The Status of Public Sector Labor Relations," *Tennessee Survey of Business* (April 1974), 3–7.

22

☆ ☆
☆

The City, the State, and Land-Use Planning

THE TIME WHEN MOST TENNESSEANS LIVED ON MORE OR LESS REMOTE
farms is now gone. Small towns, metropolitan centers, and suburban life
have replaced the rural environment of the past. Our towns and cities have
been shaped by private enterprise with some governmental control and
some public building in areas supplied with water lines and streets, sometimes privately built, and much of their development has been the result of
piecemeal action without whatever benefits long-range planning might
have conferred.

"Planning" is a word of many uses. When employed in government it
has more often than not referred to local efforts to encourage an orderly
development of a community through a land-use plan. But the word can
have wider significance. It can refer to state efforts to prepare a long-range
scheme for highway building. Or it can refer to the planning that nearly
every agency undertakes when thinking through its programs in preparation for subsequent action. In this chapter we are concerned primarily with
land-use planning and development, chiefly of an urban character.

Urban planning, if it is to cover more than schemes for transportation
and public buildings, must take account of the paramount role and influence of the private land speculators and builders who have come to be
known as "developers." These are the entrepreneurs—single persons,
partners, or corporations—who build suburbs, malls, shopping centers,
and at times rebuild or rehabilitate older areas of existing cities. Their
activities are highly visible in the metropolitan areas of the state, but they
are busy as well in medium-sized cities and even in small towns. And they
are deeply concerned with planning, for not only must they plan their own
enterprises, but they must also work in the framework imposed by governmental regulations. Like all businesses subject to regulation they seek
to control, or at least to influence strongly, the regulating authorities.

Planning in Tennessee is very much subject to the activities of the "developers."

Planning of cities in this country has proceeded by spurts. Some of Tennessee's cities were influenced by one of these periods of activity in the years following the First World War. The earliest planning commission in Tennessee was established in Memphis in 1920 by ordinance. The following year, the state legislature authorized the creation of such a commission and the adoption of zoning regulations. Chattanooga and Knoxville established planning commissions in 1923 and Johnson City followed in 1927. In 1932 Nashville, the last of the metropolitan cities to do so, set up a city planning commission. The Shelby County Planning Commission was established in 1931 by the state legislature.

These early efforts were not always marked by good fortune. Artists and architects have always had a deep concern with planning and they often concentrated on the creation of beauty in limited sections of the city. In the 1920s, cities had the rather futile habit of hiring outside planning consultants to draw somewhat grandiose plans—street development plans, zoning regulations, civic centers, railroad relocations, and so on—and while the proposals were usually impressive and not unreasonable, they often much exceeded the willingness or financial ability of the city fathers. This happened, for example, in Knoxville and Chattanooga. Some of the suggestions made in the Knoxville plan for street changes were subsequently carried out, but on the whole this early plan became a forgotten and unused document. In some other cities, as, for example, Johnson City, Murfreesboro, and Jackson, zoning regulations were adopted but not enforced. By 1933 the only active planning commissions operating in Tennessee were those of Memphis, Nashville, and Shelby County.[1] In the meantime most of the cities grew on, in their customary somewhat helter-skelter, absent-minded fashion.

Here and there in the state some attempts were made, principally by private action, to carry through planned developments. If one drives through certain sections of Erwin, Tennessee, for example, he may observe in the street layout a reflection of street planning different from the old-fashioned rectangular schemes. This could also be said of Alcoa. South Pittsburg was a planned town.[2] The outstanding example of a completely

---

[1]For material in this chapter we are heavily indebted to Eleanor Keeble Guess, *The First Fifteen Years: A History of the Tennessee State Planning Commission,* University of Tennessee *Record, Extension Series* 25:5 (Knoxville: Bureau of Public Administration, 1949). See also Abbott and Greene, 35–37. See also Aelred J. Gray and Mrs. Susan F. Adams, "Government," in Lucile Deaderick, ed., *Heart of the Valley: A History of Knoxville, Tennessee* (Knoxville: East Tenn. Historical Society, 1976), 117–19. See also Marion Clawson, *New Deal Planning: The National Resources Planning Board* (Baltimore: Johns Hopkins Univ. Press., 1981)

[2]Raulston and Livingood, 189.

planned city was Kingsport, founded in 1917, and designed from the beginning to be an industrial city. A plan was drawn by John Nolen, who made plans for a small manufacturing community, with an axis running from an arc of churches to the railroad station. Time, growth, and change have wiped out most vestiges of his scheme. The city has grown into one of the great sprawling urban areas of the state; the railroad station is deserted and half-derelict; the axis can no longer be readily perceived, although the churches and the street patterns are still there. The city is significant and well-governed, but the notion of a small, compact, and elegant small town has been lost. There is little architecture of any significance.

⊛

Thus in the final analysis, it will not depend on the "Battle of the Potomac." After the "last hurrah," it will not be the bird watchers, the little old ladies in tennis shoes or the growing ecoindustrial complex that will insure a better environment through land use reform, but state government.

RICHARD H. SLAVIN (1974)

THOUGH SOME CITIES AND COUNTIES in Tennessee undertook planning programs in the 1920s, it was not until the next decade that the State of Tennessee became actively involved in the planning process. In the early 1930s, the Roosevelt New Deal lent a new euphoria to the notion of planning in a very wide sense. The country was to be rebuilt and developed rationally—or so many hopeful souls thought. Under the influence of TVA and the National Planning Board (known under various later names as the National Resources Board, the National Resources Committee, and the National Resources Planning Board) a planning organization was developed. To begin with, in 1933, at TVA's suggestion, the state formed the Tennessee Valley Commission, consisting of six citizens. When later in the same year the National Planning Board set out to encourage state planning, particularly with regard to resources, the Tennessee Valley Commission was made the Tennessee State Planning Board. The duties of this agency were to include cooperation with the federal government in the improvement of the Tennessee Valley, surveying the possibility of obtaining cheaper electric power in Tennessee, and coordinating state agencies with TVA. The transition of the state planning agency from a position of impermanent and temporary idealism to a more humdrum but solid permanency was the product of national initiative. When President Roosevelt substituted the National Resources Board for the National Planning Board, the federal government offered assistance to the State of Tennessee for planning functions, provided the governor would sponsor legislation to put the planning commission on a continuing basis. This the governor agreed to do, and the necessary legislation was passed by the General Assembly in 1935.

The General Assembly of 1935 not only passed the State and Regional Planning Act, to give the State Planning Commission a base, but it also passed as companion legislation the County Zoning Act, the Municipal Planning Act, the Municipal Zoning Act, and the Municipal Subdivision Control Act; subsequent legislatures added the Community Planning Act, the Airport Zoning Act, and the Urban Redevelopment Act.

Under the powers granted the Tennessee State Planning Commission by the State and Regional Planning Act, that agency came to enjoy a national reputation based on its local planning assistance program rather than its statewide planning efforts. Through regional offices around the state its planners have served as planning consultants to small and medium-size cities that lacked professional planners of their own. In a number of instances cities that were so served by state planners came to see the value of programs staffed by municipal personnel.

The State and Regional Planning Act provided for the creation of the Tennessee State Planning Commission of nine members, the governor and eight citizens appointed by him, for four-year terms. This commission was retained until 1972, although its actual involvement in the operation of the planning work had been minimal for a number of prior years. The reorganization act of 1959 had placed the administration of planning under the commissioner of finance and administration; thereafter the commission, made up of prominent laymen, contented itself for the most part with an annual session where it heard a report from the executive director of what was now the division of planning in the Department of Finance and Administration.

Although local planning assistance was a successful feature of the planning program, planning for the state itself was not. An obligation had been established by law to develop a statewide "general state plan for the physical development of the state."[3] The Planning Commission was given far-reaching powers and responsibilities for obtaining information about proposed physcial developments in the state; it could review such proposals and report its views to the operating agencies. The powers were too broad; they were ignored. For example, the statute provided that every state commissioner was to keep the state planning commission informed

on all projects, improvements, and plans under contemplation or in preparation in their respective departments which relate to . . . buildings, structures or uses on, upon, under, over or of any land or water within the state, and make available to the [commission] for its information and examination any and all data, sketches, plans and specifications relating to . . . buildings, structures and uses,

[3]TCA, 13-1-103.

so that the [commission] may, before the location, character or extent of any such building, structure, or use comes to be decided, have an adequate opportunity for the study of and report upon the same.[4]

This idealized role was simply not attained.

Students of planning in the United States have long continued a dispute on the location of the planning function in the bureaucracy. One school thought planning a professional function, to be isolated as far as possible from the political pressures of normal governmental operations. To achieve this separation, independent commissions were seen as an appropriate device. A counterview held planning to be little different from most other governmental functions; all were part of the political process. Independent commissions might achieve some isolation from political pressures, but only at the expense of being cut off from policymaking. This group advocates placing the planning function directly in the chief executive's office, whether at the national, state, or local level. The 1959 reorganization was a victory for the latter view; the power of the commission was reduced, and in 1972 the Planning Commission was abolished. The State Planning Office was created in its place, but it appears to have had little impact on state policy; its two divisions have operated without an overall director since 1971.

From 1935 to 1972, governors tended to call on the planners infrequently. Governors during that period were political leaders who had succeeded in getting to the top without help from planners; perhaps they did not fully understand the nature of the planning function. During some of that period, planning was, for some people, un-American by definition.

The concept of planning now makes sense to both conservatives and liberals. Governor Dunn related planning directly to policymaking by securing legislation moving some state planning activities directly into the executive office of the governor, but some planning functions were exercised by the Office of Urban and Federal Affairs (now abolished) and others by the Department of Economic and Community Development. In addition, he urged the creation of planning units in those departments that did not already provide them.

As a substitute for the former commission, 1972 legislation provided for a local government planning advisory committee, composed of seven officers of local government appointed by the governor for staggered terms of four years. Even though organizational arrangements were changed decisively in 1972, the basic state powers in the field of planning were left essentially undisturbed. The idea was reaffirmed that some type of statewide plan should be developed. The statutes continue to include authority to make a state plan, but the notion that a general state plan can be made

[4]*Ibid.*, 13–1–108, as before amendment of 1972.

effective is dead; most planners no longer believe in it, and recent governors have recommended dropping the idea.

After World War II, the connection between planning, whether state or
local, was recognized by a nationwide trend to link industrial development
offices to existing planning agencies, but the emphasis was on attracting
industry. In Tennessee an industrial development division was created in
1945 in the state planning agency; the new agency concentrated on research and publication and on responding to inquiries from industries
seeking locations or from localities trying to attract industries. The division
was without authority to acquire industrial sites or to control industrial
location; the state considered industrial location to be primarily a local
function. To give more impetus to this effort, a separate agricultural and
industrial development commission was created by the legislature in 1953.
In 1959 the Department of Conservation and Commerce was given the
industrial recruitment responsibility. From 1963 to 1972 the industrial
development effort was headed by a staff director housed in the governor's
office. A major change occurred in 1972 when an entirely new department
was created by the legislature at the initiative of Governor Dunn. A
Department of Economic and Community Development, with an Industrial and Agricultural Development Commission serving in an advisory
capacity, was provided broad powers to improve the state's economic
position. The advisory commission was given authority (quite unusual in
Tennessee practice) to assist in the appointment of the commissioner of the
department, but because the governor appoints twelve of the fifteen
commissioners, the nomination of candidates for commissioner by the
advisory commission is not likely to limit the governor significantly. Since
there is a relationship between the community's planning program and its
industrial recruitment, moves have been made in recent years to coordinate state activity in local planning and development affairs. But in 1973
and 1974, efforts made to shift the local planning assistance effort from the
State Planning Office to the new Department of Economic and Community
Development were successfully resisted by opponents of the move.

Planning for state functions (as distinguished from land-use planning in a
narrow sense) is routinely carried on by major departments. Probably
highway planning is the best-known form of what can be called functional
planning since it has been in use for a long time and has been used to
prepare for enormous expenditures. The Bureau of Planning and Programming of the Department of Transportation (originally the Highway Commission) appears to be the oldest of the departmental planning units. Most
functional departments have now developed some ability to plan for their
future activities. In the process the activities of the State Planning Office
have been downgraded. Governor Dunn showed more interest in effective
planning in the departments than did his predecessors, and in response to

his pressures and to those from the national government new planning units were created in several agencies and existing agencies were strengthened.

Planning at the local and regional level in Tennessee has developed a variety of approaches. Cities and counties have three major options for carrying out planning activities within their jurisdictions: they can develop their own planning staffs; they can contract with the State Planning Office for staff services; or they can employ private firms. In any case, under Tennessee law they must establish planning commissions if they wish to enter into a program of zoning or regulating the platting of subdivisions. Some local jurisdictions initially contract with the state and then, as the demands for planning services increase to a certain point, they develop their own staffs. A rapidly developing community will generally feel the need for planning services more than will a quiescent area. All metropolitan areas have long maintained their own staffs, as have most medium-sized cities.

Some cooperative city-county planning efforts have been maintained over many years in the metropolitan areas and even in some medium-sized cities and counties. The logic of such cooperation is almost self-evident; developments that take place anywhere in a city will affect the county within which the city is located. County operations are equally important to the city. City and county planning operations tend to be preoccupied with zoning and subdivision regulation matters and spend relatively little time on what would generally pass as planning in the "true" sense, that is, long-range developmental planning. Zoning ordinances and subdivision regulations are major tools used to implement land-use plans adopted by the jurisdiction, although the most significant determinants of land use are decisions on the location of facilities such as highways and water service.[5]

Serious abuses of authority have occurred in zoning decisions by planning commissions and city councilmen who must approve changes in zoning ordinances. Ethical problems arise rather easily in zoning. In the first place, a built-in conflict-of-interest condition is created when building contractors, real estate investors, and subdivision developers serve on or (as often happens) dominate local planning commissions. A member with plans of his own for apartment buildings cannot be expected to view a rival's proposals with calm detachment. A conflict of interest is inevitable. The conflict is difficult to deal with, for the abuse can be characterized as "victimless" activity. If a city councilman takes a bribe for voting to change an area from residential to commercial, he can claim that he has

[5]We are indebted for some material in this chapter to Robert Freeman, Deputy Director of the East Tennessee Development District. For types of statewide land use plans that could be developed for Tennessee see Council of State Governments, *The Land Use Puzzle* (Lexington, Ky., 1974), Appendix.

harmed no one. Residents can complain at any change that adversely affects the neighborhood, but others in the area may see the zoning change as a potential increase in property values.

In 1974 a number of city councilmen in Nashville came under investigation because of their actions on zoning and related matters. In that situation the normal power of the councilmen was magnified by the development of the practice of "councilman's courtesy" whereby a councilman would enjoy virtually total control over what ordinances were passed for his district. Councilmen would defer completely to a colleague when he wanted to block a rezoning ordinance or when he wanted to have one adopted for his district. The scandal caused by abuses from this practice led to a change in procedures—at least temporarily. In any case Nashville has suffered for many years from spot zoning.[6]

Urban redevelopment has remade the central areas of the four big cities, but the process offers opportunities for private gain with public help and has given rise to sharp controversy. It also displaces old community structures, particularly those of central city blacks and small businesses, both white and black.

Urban development almost always spills beyond the city boundaries, and often beyond city control. When annexation subsequently occurs, as is frequently the case, the annexing city takes over substandard areas. As a remedy for this kind of situation, state law permits the State Planning Office to allow cities to exercise some control over development within a five-mile radius of the city's limits. Such control has been routinely authorized by the State Planning Office on request of a city for municipal-regional status, a status permissible in the absence of a county planning commission. Now, however, practically all counties have planning commissions, and the establishment of new municipal-regional commissions is seldom granted. Counties have shown some interest in seceding from regional commissions and, since the State Planning Office will not approve, some secessions have been accomplished by private act (that ancient Tennessee means of evading general standards).

County planning commissions were originally established to deal with subdivisions and zoning, but where such commissions were established in the 1960s and 1970s it was because they were required by federal law if the county wished to qualify for grants or loans for water and sewer systems; now such qualification can be secured by other means. County commissions often adopt subdivision regulations, partly because local developers have wished to eliminate fly-by-night housing promoters who might otherwise raid the communities.

Multicounty planning has normally been difficult to achieve. A definite

<hr>

[6] *A Future for Nashville*, 27–37.

body of theory, law, and experience has grown up around city planning, but those elements are less well developed with respect to affairs involving several counties. It is debatable, for example, whether multicounty planning is to be viewed as a local affair or as a segment of state or even federal planning. A flurry of such planning efforts based on multicounty activity began in Tennessee in the middle 1960s and was promoted by various federal agencies. For example, nearly one-half of the state was included within the jurisdiction of the Appalachian Regional Commission, a multistate regional planning and development operation; the ARC encouraged "local development districts." At about the same time TVA was vigorously encouraging multicounty planning based on the territories delineated as watershed tributaries to the Tennessee River. Watershed lines conform neither to county nor to state lines. Nevertheless they served as planning units for citizen associations and for several watershed development authorities established by state law. A number of planning documents were prepared, primarily by TVA planning specialists. When the state decided to establish planning regions of its own, it chose to disregard watersheds in favor of county lines based on the influence of major urban centers, and the watershed concept has mostly disappeared. TVA watershed districts have declined in number. At the governor's request the State Planning Office proposed eight planning districts, subsequently altered to form nine. Called economic development districts at first, they are now known simply as development districts. They are primarily organizations of local public officials, but they also serve as vehicles for coordination and cooperation between local government officials, as well as, by state action, administrative districts and planning regions for state purposes. All state agencies are obliged, by executive order of the governor, in effect, to adjust their administrative district lines to conform to the district boundaries. Though considerable foot-dragging was noted initially in adapting to the new lines, compliance now appears to be general. The creation of the development districts has tended to stimulate regional thinking and planning. Although the federal Economic Development Administration did much to "encourage" their creation, forces in the local political environment seem strong enough to make their continuation likely at least for some purposes. A principal task of these districts at present is to stimulate development of an economic and governmental nature. A statewide land-use planning effort originally undertaken on a district basis has apparently been abandoned. Still the status of development districts is ambiguous; in some ways they appear to be basically a form of local government, without the power to tax but with a very limited ability to raise revenue; in other ways, they serve as state agencies.

Memphis Urban Renewal—The Mall Construction. Photograph courtesy UT Municipal Technical Advisory Service.

⊛

*The best-laid schemes 'o mice an' men
gang aft a-gley.*

ROBERT BURNS (1785)

LONDON WAS ONCE DESCRIBED in the eighteenth century as "inconvenient, inelegant, and without the least pretension to magnificence or grandeur." At least some of this criticism could be applied to Tennessee's four big cities in the late twentieth century. Knoxville and Chattanooga are framed in a setting of magnificent mountains; Nashville occupies the beautiful Nashville Basin, and Memphis rears its skyscrapers along the broad sweep of Ole Man River. Buildings of architectural interest, beauty, and even grandeur can be found there, most notably the Greek revival structure of the state capitol. Urban redevelopment has given us more monuments of steel and glass in accordance with the taste of the times. Memphis and Nashville have developed civic centers that are open and attractive.

But these cities are flawed. They are approached and breeched by clogged interstates and main highways cluttered with crowded shopping centers and garish commercial developments. Housing ranges from the palatial down to the ramshackle; racial segregation is still a basic pattern. The downtown centers struggle for survival within the total urban sprawl. Nashville's skyscrapers tower over the sleazy enterprises of lower Broadway.

By and large Tennessee cities are no better and no worse than the rest of American cities. They spread beyond their boundaries without let or hindrance. Subdivisions, individual houses, and commercial buildings are scattered about where developers see fit to put them, without too much thought for the planning of services. Large undeveloped land areas held for speculation are often bypassed for development farther out in the countryside; increased costs for the extension of municipal services are thus made inevitable. The main highways into cities become long avenues of "visual chaos." Little can be done to correct such practices under current laws and traditions. Even though it is now well accepted in Tennessee that cities can be landlords and real estate developers, it is still not feasible for a city to become the sole or a principal land developer. Some European cities have gone this route but an approach of that sort in the United States seems remote.

The growth of Tennessee cities follows the generally familiar patterns of American development. The central cities have declined—often drastically. Vacant and derelict buildings offer dramatic evidence of change. Professional people—such as doctors and dentists—move out. Stores close. Even in the smaller towns, such as Cookeville, the change is evident in the neglect of the once-important central courthouse square. (Television has replaced the old-style campaign speaking in front of the courthouse.) The central cities become the financial and governmental centers, a process most visible in the rebuilding of central Nashville. In the rebuilding of the capital city thé new skyscrapers sometimes overshadow the earlier Greek revival buildings, but the axis between the city-county building and the World War I Memorial building, tucked in between the new glass towers, still offers a pleasing vista.

Generally Tennessee cities are not very beautiful (except in spots), a particularly distressing failure in view of the magnificence and charm of their natural settings. Age and surrounding countryside lend attractiveness to some small cities such as Rogersville and Fayetteville. Cities such as Franklin, Greeneville, and Jonesboro exhibit a strong interest in historical and architectural preservation, and renewed interest in historical preservation is now evident in some of the large cities (as in the case of the restoration of the Bijou Theater in Knoxville) and in the activities of the development districts. There are spots of architectural grandeur, such as the State Capitol, now emphasized by redevelopment projects but in some danger of being partially obscured by high-rise structures. The extensive downtown redevelopment projects in all four major cities and in many smaller ones have greatly altered and generally improved their appearance, even though individual structures of architectural interest have been lost in the change. Beautification of waterfront areas is underway in some areas, but opportunities were lost in some sections. In Knoxville, for example, the sewage disposal plant, a sand and gravel operation, and oil installations were placed along the Tennessee River where beautification projects would have been welcome. Unfortunately, there is not enough river to go around. But for the most part, our cities, although alive and interesting, are needlessly ugly.

Some of this must be attributed to the fact that city planning authority generally stops short of architectural control. In recent years planning commissions have been able to take a somewhat more active role in this area as they have begun to examine the architectural features of planned unit developments before approving them. Generally speaking, every private builder may put up what he pleases, from pseudo-Egyptian to the banality of aluminum and glass, using whatever material he chooses so long as he conforms to local fire control ordinances. Architectural control by government planners could result in deadening uniformity or a slavish devotion to conservative styles. Yet such control and uniformity are welcomed in small areas of the city. College campus buildings, for example, are frequently built in a uniform style, and the results usually are more pleasing than the miscellaneous architecture of our principal business streets. Some of the unattractiveness of our cities is attributable to the inferior housing in which too much of our population lives. The slum clearance efforts of our cities have led to some improvement but often at the expense of forcing families from single-family dwellings into multistoried massive public housing projects.

One could pick out a variety of factors that help to spoil both the city and the countryside, but most city planners would agree that outdoor advertising is one of the chief offenders. The principal business streets of our cities have become rashes of garish neon signs, many of them probably not especially useful for advertising and all of them, taken as a whole, dangerous to traffic control. Billboards, thickly scattered over the Tennessee countryside, have cluttered up the approaches to cities and towns and have in some areas diminished the quality of the natural scenery, one of Tennessee's principal assets. So far efforts to control outdoor advertising along the interstate highways have been sharply disappointing in Tennessee. In the 1981 session of the General Assembly proposals were made to allow sign owners to cut trees in front of their signs to preserve their visibility.

Control of land use has been at the core of city planning from its inception but outside the cities relatively little has been done in this connection. During the depression of the 1930s some work was done in rural land-use planning as part of the overall drive to improve the economy, but opposition to land-use controls was too strong to permit its implementation to any appreciable extent. County and regional zoning in Tennessee has not involved measures of control of agricultural use of land. Some states, most notably Wisconsin (which pioneered in this field) and Hawaii, have used zoning as a means of setting aside certain types of land for restricted use, principally as a means of preventing farming of land suited only to forestry. Great pressure is being exerted for conversion of farmlands into urban developments—subdivisions, apartment complexes, shopping centers. Here tax policy is as crucial, if not more so, than zoning policy, for the family farmer may be confronted with property taxes based on assessments set at potential urban value rather than farm use. The Agricultural, Forest, and Open Spaces Land Act of 1976 does attempt to protect agricultural land and open spaces from being taxed as urban land, but whether this policy can be made to work is uncertain.

"To Be Continued"—An Epilogue

THE FIRST EDITION OF THIS BOOK APPEARED TWENTY YEARS AGO. IT SEEMS logical to inquire how Tennessee government today differs from that of 1962. Differences there are, but the most noteworthy feature of those two decades is the remarkable stability of the government of this state and its subdivisions. Most that was written or implied in the 1962 volume is still valid in 1982, for the basic organization, philosophy, and functions of government remain now what they were then. It is the detail that differs.

Still, one can point to some changes that go deeper than mere detail. In the last twenty years Tennessee has ceased to be a state that the Democratic party can count on controlling. During this period, leaving presidential elections aside (for Tennessee has been a national apostate to the Democrats a number of times) the state's voters have twice indicated that they are willing to have a Republican in the governor's office. And, in 1982, Democrats are again running scared, wondering who can put up the best fight against Governor Alexander. To be sure, the Assembly, although now reapportioned—several times, indeed—remains in Democratic hands, but the threat of a Republican legislature is taken more seriously now than a generation ago, and party control and partisan politics are a bit more pronounced as a result. The farm population continues to decline; the urban and particularly the suburban voter is more influential than in the past. Metropolitan numbers are greater; it is not so clear that metropolitan power is. Twenty years ago Frank Clement was making his last bid for the governorship; he was beginning to pay more attention to the demands of the Negro voter, sometimes with obvious reluctance. In his third term the legislature began to reassert its independence. He and Governor Ellington promoted the employment and retention of young technicians in administration—a trend that has endured.

Even with these changes some things have remained the same—an unreconstructed court system, the tax structure, powerful and largely obscure lobbies, low voter turnout, and a Tweedledum-Tweedledee party system.

In the early 1980s surface ripples show signs of shoals ahead. A budget squeeze is on. Financial stringency is the dominating aspect of city and county governments in Tennessee (as well as elsewhere) as 1982 begins. The response of Congress in approving nearly all budget reductions proposed by the Reagan administration has reduced the flow of federal funds, and more cuts are in the offing; even the general revenue sharing program, which brings about $50 million annually to Tennessee's counties and $35.5 million to the state's cities, is threatened (it must be renewed by congressional authorization to extend beyond September 30, 1983), but some leaders—including one of its original sponsors, Senator Howard Baker—have promised to resist cuts in this program. Phasing out of federal grants for operating mass transit systems is planned over a three-year period (by 1985); without this subsidy local bus systems will probably be forced to charge prohibitively high fares, unless the unlikely provision of increased local funding occurs.

The Reagan program also proposes that many categorical programs be merged into "block grants" to the states (no doubt at much lower levels), which would be given discretion within broad limits as to how such funds would be spent. Such previous proposals have been resisted in Congress —many of its members prefer to control such funds to assure their use in pursuing specific objectives—but a renewed effort in 1982 may see some success, as the National League of Cities is supporting most of the proposed block grants (except for small city community development).

Incorporated in the Reagan approach is the notion that states and local governments should pick up some of the programs being abandoned by the federal government. This would, of course, place an added burden on their tax resources or result in loss of the programs. The budgets of the state and its county and city governments are already severely strained, and state legislators, county commissioners, and city councilmen are under strong pressure from taxpayers to avoid raising taxes.

Nevertheless, hope springs eternal. The 1981 Local Government Platform formulated by the Tennessee County Services Association and the Tennessee Municipal League, called for (1) delegation of power to counties and cities to tax any privilege that is subject to state taxation; (2) an increase in the state gasoline tax, half of the proceeds to be distributed to counties and cities; (3) removal of the $7.50 maximum local sales tax on a single item sale (a perennial legislative objective); (4) doubling the rates in the Business Tax Act and extending its coverage to the professions; and (5) authorization of a local option gasoline tax to fund mass transit systems. Governor Alexander's administration supported the first objective, but it failed in the Democratically-controlled legislature. Only the second objective was partially realized, with imposition of an added two cents per gallon on gasoline and four cents on diesel fuel; counties receive 28.6 percent of the proceeds and cities 14.3 percent.

The president of the Tennessee Municipal League (TML) for 1981-82, Mayor Randy Tyree of Knoxville (and an announced candidate for governor in 1982), has disclosed a TML plan to form a coalition with the Tennessee County Services Association and a dozen or so other organizations to work for a comprehensive reform of the state's tax system. This also is a revival of several previous undertakings; political realists probably would rate its chances of success to be rather low.

The troubles of the Blanton administration helped make an East Tennessean a Republican governor. Those troubles, involving a suspect pardoning policy, bid-rigging in highway contracts, and charges of extortion in the grant of liquor licenses, led to the conviction and sentencing of a number of administrators by federal courts, including Blanton himself (whose case is on appeal), a scandal of unusual proportions in Tennessee history. Two members of the legislature suffered penalties for violation of law, and one member of the legislative staff was suspended pending investigation of wrong-doing.

The battle between the judiciary and the legislature over the distribution of legislative seats continued off and on during the 1970s. The census of 1980 disclosed population shifts that necessitated a further reapportionment. The most spectacular change shown by the census was the growth around the fringes of the metropolitan areas. The reapportionment that followed the census did not arouse too much controversy, although the reapportionment of Congressional seats drew more comment. Tennessee shared modestly in the growth of the "Sun Belt," and the number of representatives to the lower national House increased by one. A new congressional district was created to the south, east, and northeast of Nashville. Most of the Tennessee congressional delegation continue to occupy safe seats.

Citations to Sectional Headings

CHAPTER I

Alexis De Tocqueville, *Democracy in America* (1835), ch. 4.
Harvey Walker, "Myths and Realities of the State Constitutional System," in W. Brooke Graves, ed., *Major Problems in State Constitutional Revision* (Chicago: Public Administration Service, 1960), 13.
Journal and Proceedings of the Limited Constitutional Convention (Nashville: State of Tennessee, 1953), 1162.
Albert L. Sturm, *Trends in State Constitution-Making, 1966–1972* (Lexington, Ky.: Council of State Governments, 1973), 92.

CHAPTER II

Ernst Freund, *Standards of American Legislation* (Chicago: Univ. of Chicago Press, 1917), 202.
John Stuart Mill, *On Liberty* (1859), ch. 1.
James Madison, *The Federalist* (1788), No. XLIV.
John Locke, *An Essay Concerning the True Original, Extent, and End of Civil Government* (Second Treatise) (1690), ch. 9.

CHAPTER III

Excerpts, U.S. Constitution.
Jasper Berry Shannon, *Toward A New Politics in the South*, 16.
Hugh A. Bone and Austin Ranney, *Politics and Voters* (New York: McGraw-Hill, 1963), 95.
U.S. v. *Classic*, 313 U.S. 299, 329.
Mill, *On Liberty*, ch. 1.

CHAPTER IV

Bone and Ranney, 95.

Lee S. Greene and Jack E. Holmes, "Tennessee" in Havard, ed., 165.
Ibid., 186
William Buchanan and Agnes Bird, *Money as a Campaign Resource,* 89.
Ibid., 90.
De Tocqueville, ch. 29.

CHAPTER V

Malcolm E. Jewell, "The Changing Face of State Legislatures" in Lee S.
    Greene, Malcolm E. Jewell, and Daniel R. Grant, *The States and the
    Metropolis* (University: Univ. of Alabama Press, 1968), 63.
Reynolds v. *Sims,* 377 U.S. 533, 565.
Poem from the *New York Times,* April 8, 1958, p. 28.

CHAPTER VI

Quinn v. *Hester,* 135 Tenn. 373, 380 (1916).
William J, Keefe, "The Function and Powers of the State Legislatures," in
    Alexander Heard, ed., *State Legislatures in American Politics* (Engle-
    wood Cliffs, N.J.: Prentice-Hall, 1966), 39.
John C. Wahlke, "Organization and Procedure," in Heard, ed., 132.
Alan Rosenthal, *Legislative Performance in the States: Explorations of
    Committee Behavior* (New York: Free Press, 1974), 82.
Ibid., 2.

CHAPTER VII

Headnote, *TCA,* 1, 566.
Keefe, 60.
Herbert Kaufman, *Policies and Politics in State and Local Government*
    (Englewood Cliffs, N.J.: Prentice-Hall, 1963), 40.
Leonard D. White, *The Federalists: A Study in Administrative History*
    (New York: Macmillan, 1948), 52.
Ibid., 114–15.
Shakespeare, *The Merchant of Venice.*
Wallace McClure, *State Constitution-Making,* 214.

CHAPTER IX

Aaron Wildavsky, "Political Implications of Budgetary Reform," *Public
    Administration Review* 21:4 (Autumn 1961), 184.
Mill, *Representative Government,* ch. 5.
President's Committee on Administrative Management, *Administrative
    Management in the Government of the United States* (Washington,
    Jan. 1937), 20.

Fred I. Greenstein, "The Changing Pattern of Urban Party Politics," in Lee S. Greene, ed., *City Bosses and Political Machines, Annals of the American Academy of Political and Social Science,* 353 (May 1964), 8.
President's Committee, *Administrative Management,* 20.

CHAPTER X

De Tocqueville, ch. 47.
Bank of Commerce and Trust Co. v. Senter, 149 Tenn. 569, 593 (1923).
Mill, *Representative Government,* ch. 14.
Ibid.

CHAPTER XI

Institute of Judicial Administration, *Preliminary Report on the Judicial System of Tennessee* (June 1971), 6.
Ibid., 7.
Ibid., 6.
Blackstone, *Commentaries.*
State v. *Grosvenor* 149 Tenn. 158, 167 (1923).
Institute of Judicial Administration, 16.
John Stuart Mill, *Utilitarianism* (1863), ch. 5.

CHAPTER XII

James Thurber, *Further Fables for Our Time* (New York: Simon & Schuster, 1956), 166 Copr. © 1956 James Thurber. Originally printed in *The New Yorker.*
Dick Netzer, *Economics and Urban Problems: Diagnoses and Prescriptions* (New York: Basic Books, 1970), 171.
Ibid., 174.
John Stuart Mill, *Principles of Political Economy: With Some of Their Applications to Social Philosophy* (1848), Book V, ch. 7.

CHAPTER XIII

City of Clinton v. *Cedar Rapids and Missouri River R.R. Co.,* 24 Iowa 455, 475 (1868).
Charles M. Kneier and Guy Fox, *Readings in Municipal Government and Administration* (New York: Rinehart, 1953), 271.
A.D. Lindsay, *The Essentials of Democracy* (London: Oxford Univ. Press, 1930), 72.
Advisory Commission on Intergovernmental Relations, *Urban America and the Federal System* (Washington: Government Printing Office, Oct. 1969), 31.

CHAPTER XIV

Charles R. Adrian, *State and Local Governments* (New York: McGraw-Hill, 1967), 157.

Richard S. Childs, *Civic Victories: The Story of an Unfinished Revolution* (New York: Harper, 1952), 11.

Elmer E. Cornwell, Jr., "Bosses, Machines, and Ethnic Groups," in Greene, ed., *City Bosses and Political Machines*, 33.

Greenstein, 7.

Joseph Sweat, "A Question of Fairness: Adequate Money to Meet Municipal Street Needs," *Tennessee Town and City* (Feb. 1974), 7.

CHAPTER XV

State of Maryland v. *Baltimore and Ohio R.R. Co.*, 3 Howard 534, 550 (1845).

Mill, *Representative Government*, ch. 15.

The Commission on Intergovernmental Relations: A Report to the President (June 1955), 53.

Advisory Commission on Intergovernmental Relations, *Urban America and the Federal System*, 29.

G. Theodore Mitau, *State and Local Government: Politics and Processes* (New York: Scribner's, 1966), 385.

CHAPTER XVI

Advisory Commission on Intergovernmental Relations, *Urban America and the Federal System*, 7, 8.

Charles R. Adrian, *State and Local Governments*, 3d ed. (New York: McGraw-Hill, 1972), 89.

Harvey C. Mansfield, "The States in the American System," in *The Forty-eight States: Their Tasks as Policy Makers and Administrators* (New York: American Assembly, 1955), 32.

The Commission on Intergovernmental Relations, 50.

Netzer, 179–80.

CHAPTER XVII

Havelock Ellis, *On Life and Sex* (New York: Doran, 1922), ch. 13.

CHAPTER XVIII

Health in Tennessee: A Statistical Overview (Nashville: Tennessee Dept. of Public Health, 1973), 1.

O. Henry, "The Discounter of Money," *Roads of Destiny*, (New York: Doubleday, 1925), I, 48.

CHAPTER XIX

Stanley J. Folmsbee, Robert E. Corlew, and Enoch L. Mitchell, *Tennessee, A Short History*, 268.
John A. Fairlie and Charles Maynard Kneier, *County Government and Administration* (New York: Century, 1930), 341.
TCA, 49–222.
State v. *Meador*, 153 Tenn. 634, 637 (1925).
Advisory Commission on Intergovernmental Relations, *Urban America and the Federal System*, 39.
Herman E. Spivey, "University Governance as a Function of University Mission," in *The Wisdom to Govern: Lectures in Honor of Lee S. Greene* (Knoxville: Univ. of Tennessee, 1974), 58.
Brown v. *Board of Education*, 347 U.S. 483, 493 (1954).

CHAPTER XX

Lord Byron, *Childe Harold's Pilgrimage*, Canto the Fourth (1818), CLXXVIII.
LeRoy P. Graf and Ralph W. Haskins, eds., *The Papers of Andrew Johnson* (Knoxville: Univ. of Tennessee Press, 1970), Vol. 2, p. 504.

CHAPTER XXI

Foster v. *Roberts*, 142 Tenn. 350, 355 (1919).
TCA, 48–116.
Henry D. Lloyd, *Wealth Against Commonwealth* (1849), ch. XXXV.
Fascination, Inc. v.*Hoover*, 39 Cal. 2d 260, 270 (1952).
Mill, *Principles of Political Economy*, Book V. ch. 11.
Kenneth P. Cantor, "Warning: The Automobile is Dangerous to Earth, Air, Fire, Water, Mind and Body," in Garrett DeBell, *The Environmental Handbook* (New York: Ballentine, 1970), 197.
Benjamin J. Taylor and Fred Witney, *Labor Relations Law* (Englewood Cliffs, N.J.: Prentice-Hall, 1971), 6.

CHAPTER XXII

Richard H. Slavin, quoted in *The Land Use Puzzle* (Lexington, Ky.: Council of State Governments, 1974), title page.
Robert Burns, *To a Mouse* (1785).

Selected Bibliography

The statutes of the State of Tennessee are contained in the printed volumes *Public Acts of Tennessee* and *Private Acts of Tennessee*. Some volumes in past years have included both types of statutes. These acts are arranged in chronological order by sessions of the General Assembly. The volumes also include resolutions and appropriation bills. Public acts are those of general application; the private acts relate to individual communities and, on rare occasions in the past, to individual persons. The statutes currently in force in the state are contained in the *Tennessee Code Annotated*. Periodic supplements are provided. The code, however, does not include the private acts, the resolutions, or the appropriation measures, and, since Tennessee still uses a great deal of private, or special, legislation, the code will not always provide a complete or accurate survey of local governmental powers and duties. Official copies of all acts are maintained by the secretary of state.

Journals of both houses are published; these journals indicate the bare bones of legislative activity, but they can be misleading, for certain types of action, such as motions to reconsider, appear to be more significant than they are. Furthermore, the votes recorded in the journals are not accurately taken and recorded on private or special acts.

Records of debates in the two houses are not published. Since 1955, the State Library and Archives have maintained audio-tapes of proceedings and debates in the Assembly. They can be heard in the state library at Nashville.

Records of committee hearings are not published and receive only summary attention in the public press. House and Senate rules are published, as are the reports of the Tennessee Legislative Council Committee.

The decisions of the Supreme Court of Tennessee have been fully reported in the *Tennessee Reports* (the official record) and in the *South-*

western Reporter (published by West Publishing Company in St. Paul and unofficial, but reliable). Some decisions of the appellate courts have been published in the Southwestern series and all have been officially published in the *Tennessee Appeals Reports* and similar series for the Court of Criminal Appeals. The official reports have all ceased with the 1971 reports, and in the future the reader will have to rely on the Southwestern series, long published not only in the series but in separate bindings under the title, *Tennessee Decisions;* from 1971 on, these reports will be certified as official. Trial court decisions are not published but may be examined in the offices of the clerks of those courts. Briefs and papers connected with trial court cases are on file in the clerks' offices.

The secretary of state is required by law to index and publish rules of the Tennessee departments.

Documents relating to local units of government are elusive. The charters of cities are found in the statute books, but the powers and responsibilities have been broadened by other pieces of legislation, both public and private. A program of codification of municipal ordinances has been under way for some years, under the aid and inspiration of the Municipal Technical Advisory Service at the University of Tennessee, and the charters and ordinances of the cities could be found in offices of recorders or clerks of cities. Occasionally charters and ordinances of the larger cities are collected and published, but no regularly observed publication program of this sort exists. The powers and duties of counties are to be found in the statutes, general and special.

Since its establishment in 1945, the Bureau of Public Administration of the University of Tennessee has paid particular attention to the publication of materials dealing with Tennessee state and local government. The Bureau has also attempted wherever possible to promote the publication of materials dealing with the Tennessee Valley Authority. In this way a considerable body of material has been made available on the structure and policy of Tennessee state and local agencies. Some attention has been given to the politics of Tennessee. Nevertheless, much remains to be done.

So far very little has been published on judicial politics in Tennessee. In recent years, some studies of legislative behavior have been undertaken. The subject of apportionment has been rather widely covered, and the effects of reapportionment are now receiving some attention. Party voting in the legislature has received some notice. The relationship of the governor to the legislature has received some attention, but as this relationship is now changing, added study is desirable. The attitudes and actions of the individual voter in Tennessee offer a field for further exploration. Forty years have passed since a general study of the Tennessee municipalities has been published; a new one is badly needed. County studies have been developed more recently. There is no general book describing the four large cities of Tennessee, although some good histories of single cities have been written.

Several important areas of policy in the State of Tennessee could well be made subjects of publications. The study of natural resource administration published in 1948 by the University of Tennessee Press is, of course, no longer valid; new environmental considerations invite further attention. Business regulation in Tennessee is wrapped in the deepest obscurity, as far as general public knowledge is concerned, and the same thing may be said of the state's role in many other fields such as agriculture and forestry.

The historical societies and the historians of Tennessee have been busy, and the short bibliography that follows gives some indication of the range and usefulness of that productivity. In particular, the University of Tennessee Press has been developing an increasing list of publications useful for the student of Tennessee history and government; a number of the studies of the Bureau of Public Administration have benefited from the aid of the Press.

The *Tennessee Blue Book* is a manual of Tennessee government that provides useful basic information. Unfortunately the printings are not large enough, and copies are often hard to secure.

Most, but not all principal agencies of the state publish periodic reports. For reasons that are by no means clear these reports do not come out promptly, and it is often difficult to secure copies. In some cases the reports have been as much as four years late. An interesting and useful magazine, *The Tennessee Conservationist,* is published by the Department of Conservation.

We are indebted to Dr. Sam B. Smith for permission to use entries from his *Tennessee History: A Bibliography* (Knoxville: University of Tennessee Press, 1974). We wish also to express our gratitude to Antionette Thompson and Joseph Stafford who have assisted in the preparation and the verification of this bibliography.

Abbreviations

(1) *APSR*   *American Political Science Review*
(2) *ETHSP*   *East Tennessee Historical Society Publications*
(3) *JOP*   *Journal of Politics*
(4) *JSH*   *Journal of Southern History*
(5) *MVHR*   *Mississippi Valley Historical Review*
(6) *THQ*   *Tennessee Historical Quarterly*
(7) *WTHSP*   *West Tennessee Historical Society Publications*

BOOKS AND MONOGRAPHS

Abbott, Lyndon E., and Lee S. Greene. *Municipal Government and Administration in Tennessee.* University of Tennessee *Record, Extension Series* 15:1. Knoxville, 1939.

Abernethy, Thomas P. *From Frontier to Plantation in Tennessee: A Study in Frontier Democracy.* Chapel Hill: Univ. of North Carolina Press, 1932; rpt. Univ. of Alabama Press, 1967.

Alexander, Truman Hudson. *Austin Peay, Governor of Tennessee.* Kingsport: Southern Publishers, 1929.

Anderson, Margaret. *The Children of the South.* New York: Farrar, 1966.

Ashcraft, Virginia. *Public Care: A History of Public Welfare Legislation in Tennessee.* University of Tennessee *Record* 50:8. Knoxville: Bureau of Public Administration, 1947.

Avery, Robert S. *Experiment in Management: Personnel Decentralization in the Tennessee Valley Authority.* Knoxville: Univ. of Tennessee Press, 1954.

Bain, Richard C. *Convention Decisions and Voting Records.* Washington: Brookings Institution, 1960.

Barteau, C.R. *A brief review: what has been done in Tennessee, the kind of government we are under, the kind of government our fathers gave us, Tennessee and the institution of African slavery-How shall she maintain it?* Hartsville, Tenn.: Plaindealer Book and Job Printing Office, 1861.

Bartley, Numan V. *The Rise of Massive Resistance: Race and Politics in the South during the 1950's.* Baton Rouge: Louisiana State Univ. Press, 1969.

Billington, Monroe Lee. *The Political South in the Twentieth Century.* New York: Scribner's, 1975.

Boyce, Everett Robert, ed. *The Unwanted Boy: The Autobiography of Governor Ben W. Hooper.* Knoxville: Univ. of Tennessee Press, 1963.

Brock, Robert M. *Knox County Government: A Citizen's Handbook.* Knoxville: Bureau of Public Administration, Univ. of Tennessee, for Knox County Library Board, 1959.

Brown, Louie A. *Measurements of Poverty in East Tennessee,* Institute of Regional Studies, East Tennessee State Univ., Monograph No. 1. Johnson City: The Institute, 1965.

Brown, Virginia Holmes. *The Development of Labor Legislation in Tennessee.* University of Tennessee *Record* 48:6. Knoxville: Bureau of Public Administration, 1945.

Buchanan, William, and Agnes Bird. *Money as a Campaign Resource: Tennessee Democratic Senatorial Primaries, 1948–1964.* Citizens' Research Foundation Study, No. 10. Princeton: The Foundation, n.d.

Butler, Hilton. *The Tennessean and His Government.* New York: Silver Burdett, 1941, 1946.

Caldwell, Joshua W. *Studies in the Constitutional History of Tennessee.* Cincinnati: Robert Clarke Co., 1895; 2d ed., 1907.

Capers, Gerald M., Jr. *The Biography of a River Town—Memphis: Its*

Heroic Age. Chapel Hill: Univ. of North Carolina Press, 1939; rpt. by author, 1966.

Clapp, Gordon R. *The TVA: An Approach to the Development of a Region.* Chicago: Univ. of Chicago Press, 1955; rpt. New York: Russell, 1971.

Clayton, W.W. *History of Davidson County, Tennessee.* Philadelphia: J.W. Lewis and Co., 1880; rpt. Nashville: Elder, 1971.

Cole, William E. *The Tennessee Citizen.* Oklahoma City: Harlow, 1958; 2d ed., 1964.

Combs, William H., and William E. Cole, *Tennessee: A Political Study.* Knoxville: Univ. of Tennessee Press, 1940.

Cortner, Richard C. *The Apportionment Cases.* Knoxville: Univ. of Tennessee Press, 1970.

Coulter, E. Merton. *The South during Reconstruction, 1865–1877.* Vol. 8 of *A History of the South.* Baton Rouge: Louisiana State Univ. Press, 1947.

———. *William G. Brownlow: Fighting Parson of the Southern Highlands.* Chapel Hill: Univ. of North Carolina Press, 1937; rpt. Knoxville: Univ. of Tennessee Press, 1971.

Dahir, James. *Region Building: Community Development Lessons from the Tennessee Valley.* New York: Harper, 1955.

David, Paul T., Malcolm Moos, and Ralph M. Goldman. *Presidential Nominating Politics in 1952.* 5 vols. Baltimore: Johns Hopkins Univ. Press, 1954. (Vol. 3—*The South*—contains a section on Tennessee.)

Davidson, Donald. *The Tennessee.* Vol. 1: *The Old River, Frontier to Secession.* New York: Rinehart, 1946; rpt. Knoxville: Univ. of Tennessee Press, 1980. Vol. II: *The New River, Civil War to TVA.* New York: Rinehart, 1948.

Droze, Wilmon Henry. *High Dams and Slack Water: TVA Rebuilds a River.* Baton Rouge: Louisiana State Univ. Press, 1965.

Duffus, R.L. *The Valley and Its People: A Portrait of TVA.* New York: Knopf, 1944.

Durisch, L.L., and H.L. Macon. *Upon Its Own Resources: Conservation and State Administration.* University: Univ. of Alabama Press, 1951.

Dykeman, Wilma. *The French Broad.* New York: Rinehart, 1955; rpt. Knoxville: Univ. of Tennessee Press, 1965.

Eighmy, John Lee. *Churches in Cultural Captivity: A History of the Social Attitudes of Southern Baptists.* Knoxville: Univ. of Tennessee Press, 1972.

Federal Writers' Project. *Tennessee: A Guide to the State.* American Guide Series. New York: Viking, 1939; rpt. Hastings House, 1949; rpt. Somerset, 1972.

Folmsbee, Stanley J., Robert E. Corlew, and Enoch L. Mitchell. *History of*

Tennessee, 2 vols. New York: Lewis Historical Publishing Co., 1960.

————. *Tennessee, A Short History.* Knoxville: Univ. of Tennessee Press, 1969.

Fontenay, Charles L. *Estes Kefauver: A Biography.* Knoxville: Univ. of Tennessee Press, 1980.

Foster, Austin P. *Counties of Tennessee.* Nashville: State of Tennessee, 1923.

Gaston, Paul Morton. *The New South Creed: A Study in Southern Myth-making.* New York: Knopf, 1970.

Ginger, Ray. *Six Days or Forever? Tennessee v. John Thomas Scopes.* Boston: Beacon, 1958; rpt. New York: Quadrangle, 1969.

Glass, James J. *Regional Planning and Politics: Development Districts in Tennessee.* Knoxville: Bureau of Public Administration, Univ. of Tennessee, 1973.

Goodman, William. *Inherited Domain: Political Parties in Tennessee.* Knoxville: Bureau of Public Administration, Univ. of Tennessee, 1954.

Gore, Albert. *The Eye of the Storm: A People's Politics for the Seventies.* New York: Herder and Herder, 1970.

————.*Let the Glory Out: My South and Its Politics.* New York: Viking, 1972.

Gorman, Joseph Bruce. *Kefauver: A Political Biography.* New York: Oxford Univ. Press, 1971.

Govan, G.E., and J.W. Livingood. *Chattanooga Country, 1540–1962, From Tomahawks to TVA.* Chapel Hill: Univ. of North Carolina Press, 1963.

Graf, LeRoy P., and Ralph W. Haskins, eds. *The Papers of Andrew Johnson.* Vol. I. 1822–1851; Vol. II, 1852–1857; Vol. III, 1858–1860; Vol. IV, 1860–1861; V, 1861–1862; (other volumes in preparation.) Knoxville: Univ. of Tennessee Press, 1967 (1); 1970 (II); 1972 (III); 1976 (IV); 1979 (V).

Graham, Gene S. *One Man, One Vote: Baker v. Carr and the American Levellers.* Boston: Little, 1972.

Graham, Hugh Davis. *Crisis in Print: Desegregation and the Press in Tennessee.* Nashville: Vanderbilt Univ. Press, 1967.

Grantham, Dewey W. *The Democratic South.* Athens: Univ. of Georgia Press, 1963.

Grebstein, Sheldon Norman, ed. *Monkey Trial: The State of Tennessee vs. John Thomas Scopes.* Boston: Houghton, 1960.

Greene, Lee Seifert. *Lead Me On: Frank Goad Clement and Tennessee Politics.* Knoxville: Univ. of Tennessee Press, 1982.

Greene, Lee Seifert, and George Steven Parthemos. ''Tennessee Valley

Authority," pp. 283–96, in *American Government: Policies and Functions*. New York: Scribner's, 1967.

Greene, Lee S., Virginia Holmes Brown, and Evan A. Iverson. *Rescued Earth: A Study of the Public Administration of Natural Resources in Tennessee*. Knoxville: Univ. of Tennessee Press, 1948.

Greene, Lee S., and Evan A. Iverson. "Tennessee," in Paul W. Wager, ed. *County Government across the Nation*. Chapel Hill: Univ. of North Carolina Press, 1950.

Greene, Lee Seifert, and Robert Sterling Avery. *Government in Tennessee*. Knoxville: Univ. of Tennessee Press, 1962; 2nd ed., 1966.

Greene, Lee Seifert, David H. Grubbs, and Victor C. Hobday. *Government in Tennessee*. Knoxville: Univ. of Tennessee Press, 1975.

Grubbs, Donald H. *Cry from the Cotton: The Southern Tenant Farmers' Union and the New Deal*. Chapel Hill: Univ. of North Carolina Press, 1971.

Guess, Eleanor Keeble. *The First Fifteen Years: A History of the Tennessee State Planning Commission*. University of Tennessee *Record, Extension Series* 25:5. Knoxville: Bureau of Public Administration, 1949.

Hamer, Philip M. ed. *Tennessee: A History, 1673–1932*, 4 vols. New York: American Historical Society, 1933.

Havard, William C., ed. *The Changing Politics of the South*. Baton Rouge: Louisiana State Univ. Press, 1972; section by Lee S. Greene and Jack E. Holmes, "Tennessee: A Politics of Peaceful Change," pp. 165–200.

Hawkins, Brett W. *Nashville Metro: The Politics of City-County Consolidation*. Nashville: Vanderbilt Univ. Press, 1966.

Heard, Alexander. *A Two-Party South?* Chapel Hill: Univ. of North Carolina Press, 1952.

Hobday, Victor C. *An Analysis of the 1953 Tennessee Home Rule Amendments*. Knoxville: Bureau of Public Administration, Univ. of Tennessee, 1956; 2d ed., 1976.

———.*Sparks at the Grassroots: Municipal Distribution of TVA Electricity in Tennessee*. Knoxville: Univ. of Tennessee Press, 1969.

Hodge, Clarence L. *The Tennessee Valley Authority: A National Experiment in Regionalism*. Washington: American Univ. Press, 1938; rpt. New York: Russell & Russell, 1968.

Holly, J. Fred, and Bevars D. Mabry. *Protective Labor Legislation and Its Administration in Tennessee*. Knoxville: Univ. of Tennessee Press, 1955.

Holmes, Jack E., Walter N. Lambert, and Nelson M. Robinson. *The Structure of County Government in Tennessee*. Knoxville: Bureau of Public Administration, Univ. of Tennessee, 1966.

Holt, Andrew D. *The Struggle for a State System of Public Schools in*

Tennessee, 1903–1936. New York: Teachers College, Columbia Univ., 1938.

Hopkins, Anne H. *Issues in the Tennessee Constitution.* League of Women Voters, m.p. 1976.

Hopkins, Anne, H., and William Lyons, *Tennessee Votes, 1799–1976.* Knoxville: Bureau of Public Administration, Univ. of Tennessee, 1978.

Howard, Edith Foster. *Riverfront: The Protection of Municipal Waterfronts in Tennessee.* University of Tennessee *Record, Extension Series* 25:1. Knoxville: Bureau of Public Administration, 1949.

Howard, George C., Jr., and Edith Foster Howard. *City-County Educational Relationships in Tennessee.* Knoxville: Bureau of Public Administration, Univ. of Tennessee, 1950.

Hubbard, Preston J. *Origins of the TVA: The Muscle Shoals Controversy, 1920–1932.* Nashville: Vanderbilt Univ. Press, 1961; rpt. New York: Norton, 1968.

Isaac, Paul E. *Prohibition and Politics: Turbulent Decades in Tennessee, 1885–1920.* Knoxville: Univ. of Tennessee Press, 1965.

Jewell, Malcolm E., and Lee S. Greene. *The Kentucky and Tennessee Legislatures.* Lexington: Dept. of Political Science, Univ. of Kentucky, 1967.

Johnson, Harry L., ed. *State and Local Tax Problems.* Knoxville: Univ. of Tennessee Press, 1970.

Johnson, Joseph E. *Assessment Administration in Knox County and Knoxville.* Knoxville: Bureau of Public Administration, Univ. of Tennessee, 1959.

———. *Current and Delinquent Tax Collection in Knox County, Tennessee.* Knoxville: Bureau of Public Administration, Univ. of Tennessee, 1960.

Johnson, Karen S., and Thayer Watkins. *Delineation of Development Districts in Non-Appalachian Tennessee.* Memphis: Bureau of Business and Economic Research, Memphis State Univ., 1969.

Johnson, Stanley P. *Tennessee Citizenship.* Richmond, Va.: Johnson Publishing Co., 1939.

———. *The Tennessee Handbook.* Knoxville: Univ. of Tennessee, 1938.

Johnson, Stanley P., and Julian Harriss. *The Tennessee Syllabus and Handbook.* Knoxville: Univ. of Tennessee, 1940.

Karns, Thomas Conner. *The Government of the People of the State of Tennessee.* Philadelphia: Eldredge and Brother, 1896.

Kelley, Harry F., Jr. *Dimensions of Voting in the Tennessee House of Representatives in 1967.* Knoxville: Bureau of Public Administration, Univ. of Tennessee, 1970.

Kelley, Harry F., Jr., and Charles E. Patterson, Jr. *The Tennessee*

Bureaucrat: A Survey of State Administrators. Knoxville: Bureau of Public Administration, Univ. of Tennessee, 1970.

Key, V.O., Jr. Southern Politics in State and Nation. New York: Knopf, 1949.

Killebrew, Joseph B., et al. Introduction to the Resources of Tennessee. Nashville: Tavel, Eastman and Howell, 1874.

Knox, John Ballenger. The People of Tennessee: A Study of Population Trends. Knoxville: Univ. of Tennessee Press, 1949.

Kull, D.C. Budget Administration in the Tennessee Valley Authority. University of Tennessee Record, Extension Series 24:3. Knoxville: Bureau of Business Research and Bureau of Public Administration, 1948.

Lacy, Eric R. Vanquished Volunteers: East Tennessee Sectionalism from Statehood to Secession. Johnson City: East Tennessee State Univ. Press. 1965.

Lambert, Walter N. Governments in Knox County. Knoxville: Bureau of Public Administration, Univ. of Tennessee, 1965.

Larsen, William F. New Homes for Old: Publicly Owned Housing in Tennessee. University of Tennessee Record, Extension Series 44:7. Knoxville: Bureau of Public Administration, 1948.

Lee, David D. Tennessee in Turmoil: Politics in the Volunteer State, 1920–1932. Memphis: Memphis State Univ. Press, 1979.

Lepawsky, Albert. State Planning and Economic Development in the South. Washington: National Planning Assoc., 1949.

Lilienthal, David E. TVA: Democracy on the March. New York: Harper, 1944; 20th anniversary edition, 1953.

———. The Journals of David E. Lilienthal. Vol. I: The TVA Years, 1939–1945. New York: Harper, 1964.

Long, Herman H., and Vivian W. Henderson. Negro Employment in Tennessee State Government: A Report from Nashville Community Conference on Employment Opportunity. Nashville: Tennessee Council on Human Relations, 1962.

Lyons, William, and Larry W. Thomas. Legislative Oversight: A Three State Study. Knoxville: Bureau of Public Administration, Univ. of Tenn., 1978.

Mauney, Connie Pat. Evolving Equality: The Courts and Desegregation in Tennessee. Knoxville: Bureau of Public Administration, Univ. of Tenn., n.d.

McBain, Howard Lee, and Seymour A. Mynders. How We Are Governed in Tennessee and the Nation. Knoxville: Southern School Supply, 1909.

McClure, Wallace. State Constitution-Making, with Especial Reference to Tennessee. Nashville: Marshall and Bruce, 1916.

Marshall, Jim B. *Fiscal Administration of County Roads: Three Tennessee Counties*. Knoxville: Bureau of Public Administration, Univ. of Tennessee, 1960.

Martin, Roscoe C., ed. *TVA: The First Twenty Years*. University and Knoxville: Univ. of Alabama Press and Univ. of Tennessee Press, 1956.

Miller, William D. *Mr. Crump of Memphis*. Baton Rouge: Louisana State Univ. Press, 1964.

Moore, John R., ed. *The Economic Impact of TVA*. Knoxville: Univ. of Tennessee Press, 1967.

Moore, John Trotwood, and Austin P. Foster. *Tennessee: The Volunteer State, 1769–1923*. 4 vols. Nashville: Clarke, 1923.

O'Rourke, Timothy G. *The Impact of Reapportionment*. New Brunswick, N.J.: Transaction Books, 1980.

Overman, Edward S. *Taxation of Public Utilities in Tennessee*. Knoxville: Univ. of Tennessee Press for Bureau of Public Administration and Bureau of Business and Economic Research, 1962.

Paullin, Charles O. *Atlas of the Historical Geography of the United States*. Washington and New York: Carnegie Institution of Washington and American Geographical Society of New York, 1932.

Peirce, Neil R. *The Border South States: People, Politics, and Power in the Five Border States*. New York: Norton, 1975.

Perry, Jennings. *Democracy Begins at Home: The Tennessee Fight on the Poll Tax*. New York: Lippincott, 1944.

Phelan, James. *History of Tennessee: The Making of a State*. Boston: Houghton, 1888.

Plaas, Hyrum, and Keith J. Ward. *Surveying Emergency Medical Services: A Handbook for Action*. Knoxville: Bureau of Public Administration, Univ. of Tennessee, 1968.

Plaas, Hyrum, and Charles A. Zuzak. *The Budgetary System in Tennessee*. Knoxville: Bureau of Public Administration, Univ. of Tennessee, 1969; 2d ed., 1977.

Pritchett, Charles Herman. *The Tennessee Valley Authority: A Study in Public Administration*. Chapel Hill: Univ. of North Carolina Press, 1943.

Ramsey, James G.M. *Annals of Tennessee to the End of the Eighteenth Century: Comprising Its Settlement, as The Watauga Association, from 1769 to 1777: A Part of North-Carolina; from 1777 to 1784; the State of Franklin, from 1784 to 1788; A Part of North-Carolina, from 1788 to 1790; the Territory of the U. States, South of the Ohio, from 1790 to 1796; the State of Tennessee, from 1796 to 1800*. Charleston, S.C.: Walker and James, 1853; rpt. Knoxville: East Tennessee Historical Society, 1972.

Roberts, Elliott. *One River—Seven States: TVA–State Relations in the Development of the Tennessee River.* Knoxville: Bureau of Public Administration, Univ. of Tennessee, 1955.

Robinson, Nelson M., and John R. Petty. *Public Utility Services in Tennessee: A Study for Subcommittee 1 of the Tennessee Legislative Council Committee.* Knoxville: Bureau of Public Administration, Univ. of Tennessee, 1966.

Sanford, Edward Terry. *The Constitutional Convention of Tennessee of 1796.* Nashville: Marshall and Bruce, 1896.

Satterfield, M.H. *Soil and Sky: The Development and Use of Tennessee Valley Resources.* Knoxville: Bureau of Public Administration, Univ. of Tennessee, 1950.

Schriver, William R., and Joseph D. Thoreson. *Major Sources of Social and Economic Data in Tennessee.* Knoxville: Occupational Research and Development Coordinating Unit, Univ. of Tennessee, 1968.

Scopes, John T., and James Presley. *Center of the Storm: Memoirs of John T. Scopes.* New York: Holt, 1967.

Scott, Mingo, Jr., *The Negro in Tennessee Politics and Governmental Affairs, 1865–1965: The Hundred Years Story.* Nashville: Rich Printing Co., 1965.

Selznick, Philip. *TVA and the Grass Roots: A Study in the Sociology of Formal Organization.* Berkeley: Univ. of California Press, 1949.

Shannon, Jasper Berry. *Toward a New Politics in the South.* Knoxville: Univ. of Tennessee Press, 1949.

Sheridan, Richard George. *Urban Justice: Municipal Courts in Tennessee.* Knoxville: Bureau of Public Administration, Univ. of Tennessee, 1964.

Siffin, Catherine Fox. *Shadow over the City: Special Legislation for Tennessee Municipalities.* University of Tennessee *Record, Extension Series* 27:3. Knoxville: Bureau of Public Administration, 1951.

Sims, Almon James. *A History of Extension Work in Tennessee: Twenty-Five Years of Service to Rural Life, 1914–1939.* Knoxville: Agricultural Extension Service, Univ. of Tennessee, 1939.

Sims, Carlton C. *County Government in Tennessee.* Ann Arbor: Edwards Bros., 1932.

Stewart, William H. *The Tennessee-Tombigbee Waterway: A Case Study in the Politics of Water Transportation.* University: Univ. of Alabama Press, 1971.

Tucker, David M. *Memphis Since Crump: Bossism, Blacks, and Civic Reformers, 1948–1968.* Knoxville: Univ. of Tenn. Press, 1980.

Welborn, David M., and Anthony E. Brown. *Regulatory Policy and Processes: The Public Service Commissions in Tennessee, Kentucky, and Georgia.* Knoxville: Bureau of Public Administration, Univ. of Tenn., 1980.

Wooster, Ralph A. *The People in Power: Courthouse and Statehouse in the Lower South, 1850–1860.* Knoxville: Univ. of Tennessee Press, 1969.
————. *Politicians, Planters, and Plain Folk: Courthouse and Statehouse in the Upper South, 1850–1860.* Knoxville: Univ. of Tennessee Press, 1975.
Zuzak, Charles A., Kenneth E. McNeil, and Frederic Bergerson. *Beyond the Ballot: Organized Citizen Participation in Metropolitan Nashville.* Nashville: Urban Observatory of Metropolitan Nashville—University Centers and Bureau of Public Administration, Univ. of Tennessee, 1971.

GOVERNMENT DOCUMENTS

Appalachian Regional Development Act of 1965: A Rationale and Model for Its Application in Tennessee. Nashville: Tennessee State Planning Office, 1965.
Report of the Commission on Community Services for Davidson County and the City of Nashville. *A Future for Nashville.* Nashville: The Commission, 1952.
Curran, Richard J., Jr. *State of Tennessee County Profile.* Nashville: State of Tennessee, 1969.
Freeman, Thomas H., IV. *An Economic History of Tennessee.* Nashville: Tennessee State Planning Office, 1965.
Hassler, Shirley. *Fifty Years of Tennessee Elections, 1916–1966.* Nashville: Office of the Secretary of State, State of Tennessee, 1968.
————. *Fifty Years of Tennessee Primary Elections, 1918–1968.* Nashville: Office of the Secretary of State, State of Tennessee, n.d.
Tennessee Statistical Abstract, 1971, 1974, 1977, 1980. Knoxville: Center for Business and Economic Research, Univ. of Tennessee, 1971.

ARTICLES

Abernethy, Thomas P. "The Origin of the Whig Party in Tennessee." MVHR 12 (March 1926), 504–22.
Alexander, Thomas B. "Whiggery and Reconstruction in Tennessee." JSH 16 (Aug. 1950), 291–305.
Anderson, George C. "The Constitutional Basis of Taxation in Tennessee." *Tennessee Law Review* 15 (1938), 280–87.
————. "Tennessee's Railroad and Public Utilities Commission." *Tennessee Law Review* 16 (1941), 974–78.
Avery, Robert S. "The TVA and Labor Relations: A Review." *JOP* 16 (Aug. 1954), 413–40.
Bailey, Kenneth K. "The Enactment of Tennessee's Anti-evolution Law." *JSH* 16 (1950), 472–90.

Barnhart, John D. "The Tennessee Constitution of 1796: A Product of the Old West." *JSH* 9 (Nov. 1943), 532–48.

Bejack, L.D. "The Chancery Court." *Tennessee Law Review* 20 (1948), 245–54.

Berenson, William M., Robert D. Bond, and J. Leiper Freeman. "The Wallace Vote and Political Change in Tennessee." *JOP* 33 (May 1971), 515–20.

Bergeron, Paul H. "Politics and Patronage in Tennessee during the Adams and Jackson Years." *Prologue* 2 (1970), 19–24.

Black, Roy W., Sr. "The Genesis of County Organization in the Western District of North Carolina and in the State of Tennessee." *WTHSP* 2 (1948), 95–118.

Boone, George S. "An Examination of the Tennessee Law of Administrative Procedure." *Vanderbilt Law Review* 1 (1947–48), 339–75.

Buck, A.E. "Administrative Reorganization in Tennessee." *National Municipal Review* 12 (Oct. 1923), 592–600.

Chandler, Walter. "The Judicial System of Tennessee: Its Beginning and Now." *Tennessee Law Review* 16 (1940), 519–28.

Clapp, Gordon R. "TVA: A Democratic Method for the Development of a Region's Resources." *Vanderbilt Law Review* 1 (1948), 183–93.

Cole, William E. "Impact of TVA upon the Southeast." *Social Forces* 28 (May 1950), 435–40.

Combs, William H. "An Unamended State Constitution: The Tennessee Constitution of 1870." *APSR* 32 (1938), 514–24.

Davidson, Donald. "Political Regionalism and Administrative Regionalism." *The Annals of the American Academy of Political and Social Science 207* (Jan. 1940), 138–43.

Denney, Raymond W. "The Tennessee Constitutional Convention." *Tennessee Law Review* 23 (1953), 15–23.

Dunn, Larry W. "Knoxville Negro Voting and the Roosevelt Revolution, 1928–1936." ETHSP 43 (1971), 71–93.

Edwards, Charles P. "Theoretical and Comparative Aspects of Reapportionment and Redistricting: With Reference to *Baker v. Carr.*" *Vanderbilt Law Review* 15 (1961–62), 1265–91.

Ewing, Cortz A.M. "Early Tennessee Impeachments." *THQ* 16 (1957), 291–334.

Felsenthal, Edward. "Kenneth Douglas McKellar: The Rich Uncle of the TVA." *WTHSP* 20 (1966), 108–22.

Fink, Miriam L. "Judicial Activities in Early East Tennessee." ETHSP 7 (1935), 38–49.

Folmsbee, Stanley J. "The Origin of the First 'Jim Crow' Law." *JSH* 15 (May 1949), 235–47.

Graham, Jeanne. "Kenneth McKellar's 1934 Campaign: Issues and Events." *WTHSP* 18 (1964), 107–29.

Grant, Daniel R. "Metropolitics and Professional Political Leadership: The Case of Nashville," *Annals* 353 (May 1964), 72–83.

———. "Metropolitan Problems and Local Government Structure: An Examination of Old and New Issues." *Vanderbilt Law Review* 22 (1968–69), 757–73.

Greene, Lee S. "Personnel Administration in the Tennessee Valley Authority." *JOP* 1 (May 1939), 171–94.

———. "The Southern State Judiciary." *JOP* 10 (Aug. 1948), 441–63.

Greene, Lee S., and Victor C. Hobday. "A Short Inquiry into Tennessee County Court Apportionment by the Federal Judiciary." *Tennessee Law Review* 37 (Spring 1970), 528–37.

Grubbs, David H. "Legal Aspects of City-County Consolidation in Tennessee." *Tennessee Law Review* 30 (1962–63), 499–516.

Hawkins, Brett W. "Public Opinion and Metropolitan Reorganization in Nashville." *JOP* 28 (May 1966), 408–18.

Holly, J. Fred. "The Co-operative Town Company of Tennesse: A Case Study of Planned Economic Development." ETHSP 36 (1964), 24–86.

Holt, Albert C. "The Economic and Social Beginnings of Tennessee." *Tennessee Historical Magazine* 7 (1921), 194–230, 252–313; 8 (1924), 24–86.

Howard, T.L. "The Justice of the Peace System in Tennessee." *Tennessee Law Review* 13 (Dec. 1934), 19–38.

———. "Tax Delinquency in Tennessee, Administrative Aspects." *Tennessee Law Review* 14 (June 1936), 219–31.

Isaac, Paul E. "The Problems of a Republican Governor in a Southern State: Ben Hooper of Tennessee, 1910–1914." *THQ* 27 (1968), 229–48.

Jones, Thomas B. "The Public Lands of Tennessee." *THQ* 27 (1968), 13–36.

Katzenbach, Nicholas de B. "Some Reflections on *Baker vs. Carr.*" *Vanderbilt Law Review* 15 (1961–62), 829–36.

Keebler, Robert S. "Our Justice of the Peace Courts: A Problem in Justice." *Tennessee Law Review* 9 (1930), 1–21.

Kitchens, Allen Hampton. "Political Upheaval in Tennessee: Boss Crump and the Senatorial Election of 1948." *WTHSP* 16 (1962), 104–26.

Lacy, Eric Russell. "Tennessee Teetotalism: Social Forces and the Politics of Progressivism." *THQ* 24 (Fall 1965), 219–40.

Lancaster, Robert. "What's Wrong with *Baker v. Carr?*" *Vanderbilt Law Review* 15 (1961–62), 1247–64.

Longley, Lawrence D. "The Effectiveness of Interest Groups in a State Legislature." *THQ* 26 (Fall 1967), 279–94.

McCarthy, Charles J. "Land Acquisition Policies and Proceedings in TVA—A Study of the Role of Land Acquisition in a Regional Agency." *Ohio State Law Journal* 10 (1949), 46–63.

McCarthy, James Remington. "The New Deal in Tennessee." *Sewanee Review* 42 (1934), 408–14.

McClure, Wallace. "Governmental Reorganization, A Constitutional Need in Tennessee." *Tennessee Historical Magazine* 2 (1916), 89–97.

McKinley, Charles. "The Valley Authority and Its Alternatives." *APSR* 44 (Sept. 1950), 607–31.

Majors, William R. "Gordon Browning and Tennessee Politics, 1949–1953." *THQ* 28 (1969), 166–81.

———. "The Political Scene in Twentieth-Century Tennessee: A Bibliography and Evaluation." *WTHSP* 24 (1970), 97–105.

Manning, John W. "County Consolidation in Tennessee." *APSR* 22 (1928), 733–35.

Miller, William D. "The Browning-Crump Battle: The Crump Side." *ETHSP* 37 (1965), 77–88.

Mooney, Chase C. "The Question of Slavery and the Free Negro in the Tennessee Constitutional Convention of 1834." *JSH* 12 (Nov. 1946), 487–509.

Overton, Elvin E. "The Judicial System in Tennessee and Potentialities for Reorganization." *Tennessee Law Review* 22 (1964–65), 501–72.

Parker, Eugene L., Jr. "Tax Problems Presented by the Tennessee Constitution." *Vanderbilt Law Review* 4 (1950–51), 116–44.

Parks, Norman L. "Tennessee Politics Since Kefauver and Reece: A 'Generalist' View." *JOP* 28 (Feb. 1966), 144–68.

Prewitt, Alan M. "The Judicial Structure in Tennessee." *Tennessee Law Review* 29 (1961–62), 1–18.

Price, David E., and Michael Lupfer. "Volunteers for Gore: The Impact of a Precinct-Level Canvass in Three Tennessee Cities." *JOP* 35 (May 1973), 410–38.

Pritchett, C. Herman. "The Development of the Tennessee Valley Authority Act." *Tennessee Law Review* 15 (1938), 128–41.

Ray, Joseph M. "The Influence of the Tennessee Valley Authority on Government in the South." *APSR* 43 (Oct. 1949), 922–32.

Rouse, Franklin O. "The Historical Background of Tennessee's Administrative Reorganization Act of 1923." *ETHSP* 8 (1936), 104–20.

Satterfield, M.H. "TVA-State-Local Relationships." *APSR* 40 (Oct. 1946), 935–49.

———. "Intergovernmental Cooperation in the Tennessee Valley." *JOP* 9 (Feb. 1947), 31–58.

Sims, Cecil. "The Limited Constitutional Convention in Tennessee." *Tennessee Law Review* 21 (1949), 1–8.

THESES AND DISSERTATIONS

Bailey, Kenneth K. "The Enactment of Tennessee's Anti-evolution Law." Master's thesis, Vanderbilt Univ., 1949.

Baker, Todd A. "The Office of Knox County Sheriff: An Administrative Study." Master's thesis, Univ. of Tennessee, 1959.

———. "The Politics of Innovation." Diss., Univ. of Tennessee, 1968.

Bennett, James D., II. "Struggle for Power: The Relationship between the Tennessee Valley Authority and the Private Power Industry, 1933–1939." Diss., Vanderbilt Univ., 1969.

Bentley, Hubert Blair. "Andrew Johnson, Governor of Tennessee, 1853–1857." Diss., Univ. of Tennessee, 1972.

Bergeron, Paul Herbert. "Political Struggles in Tennessee, 1839–1843." Master's thesis, Vanderbilt Univ., 1962.

Bird, Agnes Thornton. "Resources Used in Tennessee Senatorial Primary Campaigns, 1948–1964." Diss., Univ. of Tennessee, 1967.

Blackburn, Walter W. "Tennessee Urban and Regional Planners: A Survey and Analysis of Professional Practitioners." Master's thesis, Univ. of Tennessee, 1972.

Bolin, Imogene Wright. "Planning in Metropolitan Nashville and Davidson County, Tennessee, before and after Consolidation." Master's thesis, Univ. of Tennessee, 1968.

Boyd, Stephen D. "The Campaign Speaking of Frank Clement in the 1954 Democratic Primary: Field Study and Rhetorical Analysis." Diss., Univ. of Illinois, 1972.

Bradley, Leonard K. "Gubernatorial Transition in Tennessee: The 1970–71 Experience." Master's thesis, Univ. of Tennessee, 1973.

Brandon, Elvis Denby. "The Background and Operation of the Commission System in Memphis, Tennessee." Master's thesis, Duke Univ., 1952.

Bronaugh, Mae M. "The Crump-Browning Political Feud—1937–1938." Master's thesis, Memphis State Univ., 1959.

Brown, Philip G. "An Examination of Pressure Politics in Tennessee with Emphasis on the Activities of Six Interest Groups during the Eighty-fifth General Assembly." Master's thesis, Univ. of Tennessee, 1970.

Cameron, Addie Jane. "County Consolidation in Tennessee." Master's thesis, Univ. of Tennessee, 1940.

Cason, Palmer Preston. "History of Tennessee's Court System from Its Beginning to 1834." Master's thesis, George Peabody College, 1930.

Cheney, Frances N. "Historical and Bibliographical Study of the Administrative Departments of the State of Tennessee." Master's thesis, Columbia Univ., 1940.

Collins, George Douglas. "An Inventory of Some of the Governmental Agencies and Problems of Tennessee." Master's thesis, Univ. of Tennessee, 1932.

Coomer, James Chester. "The Growth and Development of the Republican Party in Tennessee: 1948–1966." Master's thesis, Georgia State College, 1968.

————"The Impact of Reapportionment on the Tennessee Legislative Process: An Analysis of the Tennessee General Assembly, 84th and 85th Sessions, Diss., Univ. of Tennessee, 1975.

Cushing, Arthur Leavitt. "A Comparative Analysis of the North Carolina and Tennessee Tax Support of Public Education." Master's thesis, Middle Tennessee State Univ., 1967.

Davis, Claude J. "Local Governmental Services and Industrial Development." Master's thesis, Univ. of Tennessee, 1951.

————. "Vocational Licensing in Tennessee." Diss., Univ. of Tennessee, 1957.

Diamond, Michael Jerome. "The Negro and Organized Labor as Voting Blocs in Tennessee, 1960–64." Master's thesis, Univ. of Tennessee, 1965.

Duggins, Edward Cameron. "The Background for Regulation of the Railroads in Tennessee." Master's thesis, Univ. of Tennessee, 1939.

Durbin, W.J. "Studies in the Financial History of Tennessee, 1860–1883." Master's thesis, Univ. of Tennessee, 1925.

England, Lurad R. "The Development of Public Vocational Education in Tennessee." Diss., George Peabody College, 1952.

Everett, Robert B. "The 1948 Senatorial Primary in Tennessee: A History and an Analysis." Master's thesis, Memphis State Univ., 1962.

Fox, Elbert Leonard. "A History of Populism in Tennessee." Master's thesis, George Peabody College, 1930.

Freeman, Thomas Harvey. "An Analysis of Planning Regions in Tennessee as Delineated by the Tennessee State Planning Commission—1963 and 1965." Master's thesis, Univ. of Tennessee, 1967.

Gardner, James B. "Political Leadership in a Period of Transition: Frank G. Clement, Albert Gore, Estes Kefauver, and Tennessee Politics, 1948–1956." Diss., Vanderbilt Univ., 1978.

Garrett, Gordon M. "The 1955 Tennessee Annexation Law and its Implementation in Sixteen Cities." Master's thesis, Univ. of Tennessee, 1960.

Garriott, William C., Jr. "The Effects of Environment on Public Planning: The Case of Appalachian Planning in Tennessee." Master's thesis, Vanderbilt Univ., 1969.

Griffith, Chester Clinton. "Constitutional and Legal Status of Compulsory Education in Tennessee." Master's thesis, George Peabody College, 1935.

Harrison, Joseph W. "The Bible, the Constitution and Public Education: A Case Study of Religious Instruction in the Public Schools of Knoxville and Knox County, Tennessee." Master's thesis, Univ. of Tennessee, 1961.

Harriss, Julian. "The First Twenty Years of Tennessee's Reorganized State Administration, 1923-1943." Master's thesis, Univ. of Tennessee, 1946.

Hawkins, Brett W. "Sources of Opposition and Support for Metropolitan Reorganization: The Nashville Experience." Diss., Vanderbilt Univ., 1964.

Hearn, Edell Midgett. "Public Educational Changes through Legislation in Tennessee 1953-1959." Diss., Univ. of Tennessee, 1959.

Hicks, John H. "Congressional Career of B. Carroll Reece, 1920-1948." Master's thesis, East Tennessee State Univ., 1968.

Higginbotham, Sanford W. "Frontier Democracy in the Early Constitutions of Tennessee and Kentucky, 1772-1799." Master's thesis, Louisiana State Univ., 1941.

Hill, Claude M., Jr. "The Administration of Educational Services of the State of Tennessee State Board of Education." Master's thesis, George Peabody College, 1954.

Hinton, Harold B. "County Government in Tennessee." Master's thesis, Vanderbilt Univ., 1920.

Hodges, James A. "The Tennessee Federation of Labor, 1919-1939." Master's thesis, Vanderbilt Univ., 1959.

Horton, Allison Norman. "Origin and Development of the State College Movement in Tennessee." Diss., George Peabody College, 1953.

Howard, T. Levron. "Federal Payments in Lieu of Taxation with Emphasis on the Program of the Tennessee Valley Authority." Diss., Univ. of Wisconsin, 1943.

Keen, Herbert F. "Certain Phases of Tennessee Legislation." Master's thesis, George Peabody College, 1926.

King, Roger Earl. "The Tennessee Legislative Council Committee: Reflection of Political Realities." Master's thesis, Middle Tennessee State Univ., 1968.

Klimasewski, Theodore J. "Political Party Regions in Tennessee: A Study in Electoral Geography." Diss., George Peabody College, 1970.

Lambert, Walter N. "The Effect of Federal Grants-in-Aid on Natural Resource Administration in Tennessee." Master's thesis, Univ. of Tennessee, 1967.

Layman, Edith Belle. "Tennessee's Action on the Proposed Amendments to the Constitution of the United States." Master's thesis, Univ. of Tennessee, 1934.

LeBlanc, Hugh L. "Personnel Administration in the State of Tennessee." Master's thesis, Univ. of Tennessee, 1950.

Lewis, Fred Alvin. "A Study of Retirement Plans for Employees of Tennessee Municipalities." Master's thesis, Univ. of Tennessee, 1948.

Locke, Jerry Ross. "The Politics of Legislative Reapportionment in Tennessee: 1962." Master's thesis, Univ. of Tennessee, 1963.

Longley, Lawrence Douglas. "Interest Group Effectiveness and Interaction in the Tennessee General Assembly." Master's thesis, Vanderbilt Univ., 1964.

Lord, Gerald D. "Federal Centralization versus Local Values: A Case Study of Federal-Local Relations in the Knoxville–Knox County Community Action Committee." Master's thesis, Univ. of Tennessee, 1969.

McArthur, Robert E. "The Impact of Metropolitan Government on the Rural-Urban Fringe: The Nashville–Davidson County Experience." Diss., Vanderbilt Univ., 1967.

McCorkle, Charles Howard. "Taxation in Tennessee." Master's thesis, Vanderbilt Univ., 1936.

McCoy, William J. "The Tennessee Political System: The Relationship of the Socioeconomic Environment to Political Processes and Policy Outputs." Diss., Univ. of Tennessee, 1970.

McKinney, Ellie Allene. "Personnel Administration in the State Government of Tennessee." Master's thesis, Univ. of Tennessee, 1945.

Macpherson, Joseph T., Jr. "Democratic Progressivism in Tennessee: The Administrations of Governor Austin Peay, 1923–1927." Diss., Vanderbilt Univ., 1969.

Majors, William R. "Gordon Browning and Tennessee Politics." Diss., Univ. of Georgia, 1967.

Matteson, R. P. "Private Legislation Affecting Local Governments in Tennessee." Master's thesis, Univ. of Tennessee, 1931.

Mikesell, Phillip Dean. "The Impact of Nashville's Metropolitan Consolidation on Administrative Departments: A Study of Change and Non-Change." Master's thesis, Vanderbilt Univ., 1968.

Minton, John D. "The New Deal in Tennessee, 1932–1938." Diss., Vanderbilt Univ., 1959.

Moore, Allen Harris. "Decision Making in Legislative Apportionment: The Tennessee Case, 1965." Master's thesis, Vanderbilt Univ., 1967.

Napier, William Jackson. "An Examination of the Responsibility of the State of Tennessee in Urban Development, with Emphasis on the Role, Actual and Theoretical, of the State Planning Office." Master's thesis, Univ. of Tennessee, 1967.

Neiswender, Roger D. "Planning, Programming, and Budgeting Systems Within the Tennessee County Government Structure: A Feasibility Study of Montgomery County, Tennessee." Master's thesis, Univ. of Tennessee, 1971.

Nichols, George Chester. "Tennessee, Tennesseans and Railroad Conventions, 1845–1852." Master's thesis, Univ. of Tennessee, 1963.

O'Donniley, Ronald Don. "A Case Study of Metropolitan Nashville and Davidson County, Tennessee's Application for a Model Cities Grant: The Decision-Making Process in Selecting a Model Cities Neighborhood." Master's thesis, Univ. of Tennessee, 1969.

Pere, Peter J. "Capital Budgeting: the Implications for Theory of the Tennessee Experience." Master's thesis, Univ. of Tennessee, 1965.

Petty, John Rife. "A Comparative Study of the Institutionalization of the Tennessee House of Representatives and the U.S. House of Representatives." Master's thesis, Univ. of Tennessee, 1971.

Pieper, Archibald Franklin. "Workmen's Compensation in Tennessee." Master's thesis, Univ. of Tennessee, 1954.

Priest, Marshall F., Jr. "Politics in Tennessee—the 1948 Democratic Gubernatorial Primary." Master's thesis, Memphis State Univ., 1963.

Quillen, Anna. "The Relationship of Municipal Electric Power Boards, the Tennessee Valley Authority, and Local Governments." Master's thesis, Univ. of Tennessee, 1948.

Richardson, Charles H. "A History of Municipal Government in Knoxville since 1911." Master's thesis, Univ. of Tennessee, 1945.

Rippa, Sol Alexander. "The Development of Constitutional Democracy in Tennessee, 1790–1835." Master's thesis, Vanderbilt Univ., 1950.

Robison, Robert M. "A History of Internal Improvement in Tennessee to 1840: A Study of Legislative Supervision." Master's thesis, George Peabody College, 1931.

Rouse, Franklin Owen. "The Reorganization of the Administrative Machinery of Tennessee." Master's thesis, Univ. of Tennessee, 1934.

Sheridan, Richard G. "Judicial Administration of Water Rights Law in Tennessee." Master's thesis, Univ. of Tennessee, 1963.

Smart, John C. "Budgetary Decision-Making in Knoxville and Knox County." Master's thesis, Univ. of Tennessee, 1967.

Stanbery, George W., II. "The Tennessee Constitutional Convention of 1870." Master's thesis, Univ. of Tennessee, 1940.

Stephenson, Claude B., Jr. "Intergovernmental Relationships in Soil and Forest Resources Administration in Tennessee." Master's thesis, Univ. of Tennessee, 1945.

Summerford, William A. "The Selection and Removal of Judges in Tennessee and Alternative Techniques." Master's thesis, Middle Tennessee State Univ., 1969.

Sweeten, Charles Hugh. "Tennessee Municipalities and TVA Power." Master's thesis, Univ. of Tennessee, 1966.

Watters, Charles William, "Judicial Selection in Tennessee and Missouri: A Comparative Analysis of the Quality and Performance of Judges." Master's thesis, Univ. of Tennessee, 1961.

Appendix: Constitution
of the State of Tennessee

(Reproduced from *Tennessee Constitutional Manual*, Department of State, October 1, 1978. In this version, sectional headings are often omitted.)

PREAMBLE
Four introductory clauses and the enacting clause are omitted here.

ARTICLE I.

DECLARATION OF RIGHTS.

SECTION 1. That all power is inherent in the people, and all free governments are founded on their authority, and instituted for their peace, safety, and happiness; for the advancement of those ends they have at all times, an unalienable and indefeasible right to alter, reform, or abolish the government in such manner as they may think proper.

SECTION 2. That government being instituted for the common benefit, the doctrine of non-resistance against arbitrary power and oppression is absurd, slavish, and destructive of the good and happiness of mankind.

SECTION 3. That all men have a natural and indefeasible right to worship Almighty God according to the dictates of their own conscience; that no man can of right be compelled to attend, erect, or support any place of worship, or to maintain any minister against his consent; that no human authority can, in any case whatever, control or interfere with the rights of conscience; and that no preference shall ever be given, by law, to any religious establishment or mode of worship.

SECTION 4. That no political or religious test, other than an oath to support the Constitution of the United States and of this State, shall ever be required as a qualification to any office or public trust under this state.

SECTION 5. That elections shall be free and equal, and the right of suffrage, as hereinafter declared, shall never be denied to any person entitled thereto, except upon a conviction by a jury of some infamous crime, previously ascertained and declared by law, and judgment thereon by court of competent jurisdiction.

SECTION 6. That the right of trial by jury shall remain inviolate, and no religious or political test shall ever be required as a qualification for jurors.

SECTION 7. That the people shall be secure in their persons, houses, papers and possessions, from unreasonable searches and seizures; and that general warrants, whereby an officer may be commanded to search suspected places, without evidence of the fact committed, or to seize any person or persons not named, whose offences are not particularly described and supported by evidence, are dangerous to liberty and ought not to be granted.

SECTION 8. That no man shall be taken or imprisoned, or disseized of his freehold, liberties or privileges, or outlawed, or exiled, or in any manner destroyed or deprived of his life, liberty or property, but by the judgment of his peers, or the law of the land.

SECTION 9. That in all criminal prosecutions, the accused hath the right to be heard by himself and his counsel; to demand the nature and cause of the accusation against him, and to have a copy thereof, to meet the witnesses face to face, to have compulsory process for obtaining witnesses in his favor, and in prosecutions by indictment or presentment, a speedy public trial, by an impartial jury of the County in which the crime shall have been committed, and shall not be compelled to give evidence against himself.

SECTION 10. That no person shall, for the same offence, be twice put in jeopardy of life or limb.

SECTION 11. That laws made for the punishment of acts committed previous to the existence of such laws, and by them only declared criminal, are contrary to the principles of a free Government; wherefore no *Ex post facto* law shall be made.

SECTION 12. That no conviction shall work corruption of blood or forfeiture of estate. The estate of such persons as shall destroy their own lives shall descend or vest as in case of natural death. If any person be killed by casualty, there shall be no forfeiture in consequence thereof.

SECTION 13. That no person arrested and confined in jail shall be treated with unnecessary rigor.

SECTION 14. That no person shall be put to answer any criminal charge but by presentment, indictment or impeachment.

SECTION 15. That all prisoners shall be bailable by sufficient sureties, unless for capital offences, when the proof is evident, or the presumption great. And the privilege of the writ of *Habeas Corpus* shall not be suspended, unless when in case of rebellion or invasion, the General Assembly shall declare the public safety requires it.

SECTION 16. That excessive bail shall not be required, nor excessive fines imposed, nor cruel and unusual punishments inflicted.

SECTION 17. That all courts shall be open; and every man, for an injury done him in his lands, goods, person or reputation, shall have remedy by due course of law, and right and justice administered without sale, denial, or delay. Suits may be brought against the State in such manner and in such courts as the Legislature may by law direct.

SECTION 18. The Legislature shall pass no law authorizing imprisonment for debt in civil cases.

SECTION 19. That the printing presses shall be free to every person to examine the proceedings of the Legislature; or of any branch or officer of the government, and no law shall ever be made to restrain the right thereof. The free communication of thoughts and opinions, is one of the invaluable rights of man and every citizen may freely speak, write, and print on any subject, being responsible for the abuse of that liberty. But in prosecutions for the publication of papers investigating the official conduct of officers, or men in public capacity, the truth thereof may be given in evidence; and in all indictments for libel, the jury shall have a right to determine the law and the facts, under the direction of the court, as in other criminal cases.

SECTION 20. That no retrospective law, or law impairing the obligations of contracts, shall be made.

SECTION 21. That no man's particular services shall be demanded, or property taken, or applied to public use, without the consent of his representatives, or without just compensation being made therefor.

SECTION 22. That perpetuities and monopolies are contrary to the genius of a free State, and shall not be allowed.

SECTION 23. That the citizens have a right, in a peaceable manner, to assemble together for their common good, to instruct their representatives, and to apply to those invested with the powers of government for redress of grievances, or other proper purposes, by address or remonstrance.

SECTION 24. That the sure and certain defense of a free people, is a well regulated militia; and, as standing armies in time of peace are dangerous to freedom, they ought to be avoided as far as the circumstances and safety of the community will admit; and that in all cases the military shall be kept in strict subordination to the civil authority.

SECTION 25. That no citizen of this State, except such as are employed in the army of the United States, or militia in actual service, shall be subjected to punishment under the martial or military law. That martial law, in the sense of the unrestricted power of military officers, or others, to dispose of the persons, liberties or property of the citizen, is inconsistent with the principles of free government, and is not confided to any department of the government of this State.

SECTION 26. That the citizens of this State have a right to keep and to bear arms for their common defense; but the Legislature shall have power, by law, to regulate the wearing of arms with a view to prevent crime.

SECTION 27. That no soldier shall, in time of peace, be quartered in any house without the consent of the owner; nor in time of war, but in a manner prescribed by law.

SECTION 28. That no citizen of this State shall be compelled to bear arms, provided he will pay an equivalent, to be ascertained by law.

SECTION 29. That an equal participation in the free navigation of the Mississippi, is one of the inherent rights of the citizens of this State; it cannot, therefore, be conceded to any prince, potentate, power, person or persons whatever.

SECTION 30. That no hereditary emoluments, privileges, or honors, shall ever be granted or conferred in this State.

SECTION 31, showing the boundaries of the state, is omitted here.

SECTION 32. That the erection of safe and comfortable prisons, the inspection of prisons, and the humane treatment of prisoners, shall be provided for.

SECTION 33. That slavery and involuntary servitude, except as a punishment for crime, whereof the party shall have been duly convicted, are forever prohibited in this State.

SECTION 34. The General Assembly shall make no law recognizing the right of property in man.

ARTICLE II.

DISTRIBUTION OF POWERS.

SECTION 1. The powers of the Government shall be divided into three distinct departments: the Legislative, Executive, and Judicial.

SECTION 2. No person or persons belonging to one of these departments shall exercise any of the powers properly belonging to either of the others, except in the cases herein directed or permitted.

LEGISLATIVE DEPARTMENT

SECTION 3. The Legislative authority of this State shall be vested in a General Assembly, which shall consist of a Senate and House of Representatives, both dependent on the people. Representatives shall hold office for two years and Senators for four years from the day of the general election, except that the Speaker of the Senate and the Speaker of the House of Representatives, each shall hold his office as Speaker for two years or until his successor is elected and qualified, provided however, that in the first general election after adoption of this amendment Senators elected in districts designated by even numbers shall be elected for four years and those elected in districts designated by odd numbers shall be elected for two years. In a county having more than one senatorial district, the districts shall be numbered consecutively.

SECTION 4. The apportionment of Senators and Representatives shall be substantially according to population. After each decennial census made by the Bureau of Census of the United States is available the General Assembly shall establish senatorial and representative districts. Nothing in this Section nor in this Article II shall deny to the General Assembly the right at any time to apportion one House of the General Assembly using geography, political subdivisions, substantially equal population and other criteria as factors; provided such apportionment when effective shall comply with the Constitution of the United States as then amended or authoritatively interpreted. If the Constitution of the United States shall require that Legislative apportionment not based entirely on population be approved by vote of the electorate, the General Assembly shall provide for such vote in the apportionment act.

SECTION 5. The number of Representatives shall be ninety-nine and shall be apportioned by the General Assembly among the several counties or districts as shall be provided by law. Counties having two or more Representatives shall be divided into separate districts. In a district composed of two or more counties, each county shall adjoin at least one other county of such district; and no county shall be divided in forming such a district.

SECTION 5a. Each district shall be represented by a qualified voter of that district.

SECTION 6. The number of Senators shall be apportioned by the General Assembly among the several counties or districts substantially according to population, and shall not exceed one-third the number of Representatives. Counties having two or more Senators shall be divided into separate districts. In a district composed of two or more counties, each county shall adjoin at least one other county of such district; and no county shall be divided in forming such a district.

SECTION 6a. Each district shall be represented by a qualified voter of that district.

SECTION 7. The first election for Senators and Representatives shall be held on the second Tuesday in November, one thousand eight hundred and seventy; and forever thereafter, elections for members of the General Assembly shall be held once in two years, on the first Tuesday after the first Monday in November. Said elections shall terminate the same day.

SECTION 8. Legislative Sessions—Governor's Inauguration—The General Assembly shall meet in organizational session on the second Tuesday in January next succeeding the election of the members of the House of Representatives, at which session, if in order, the Governor shall be inaugurated. The General Assembly shall remain in session for organizational purposes not longer than fifteen consecutive calendar days, during which session no legislation shall be passed on third and final consideration. Thereafter, the General Assembly shall meet on the first Tuesday next following the conclusion of the organizational session unless the General Assembly by joint resolution of both houses sets an earlier date.

The General Assembly may by joint resolution recess or adjourn until such time or times as it shall determine. It shall be convened at other times by the Governor as provided in Article III, Section 9, or by the presiding officers of both Houses at the written request of two-thirds of the members of each House.

SECTION 9. No person shall be a Representative unless he shall be a citizen of the United States, of the age of twenty-one years, and shall have been a citizen of this State for three years, and a resident in the county he represents one year, immediately preceding the election.

SECTION 10. No person shall be a Senator unless he shall be a citizen of the United States, of the age of thirty years, and shall have resided three years in this State, and one year in the county or district, immediately preceding the election. No Senator or Representative shall, during the time for which he was elected, be eligible to any office or place of trust, the appointment to which is vested in the Executive or the General Assembly, except to the office of trustee of a literary institution.

SECTION 11. The Senate and House of Representatives, when assembled, shall each choose a speaker and its other officers; be judges of the qualifications and election of its members, and sit upon its own adjournments from day to day. Not less than two-thirds of all the members to which each house shall be entitled shall constitute a quorum to do business; but a smaller number may adjourn from day to day, and may be authorized, by law, to compel the attendance of absent members.

SECTION 12. Each House may determine the rules of its proceedings, punish its members for disorderly behavior, and, with the concurrence of two-thirds, expel a member, but not a second time for the same offence; and shall have all other powers necessary for a branch of the Legislature of a free State.

SECTION 13. Senators and Representatives shall, in all cases, except treason, felony, or breach of the peace, be privileged from arrest during the session of the General Assembly, and in going to and returning from the same; and for any speech or debate in either House, they shall not be questioned in any other place.

SECTION 14. Each House may punish, by imprisonment, during its session, any person not a member, who shall be guilty of disrespect to the House, by any disorderly or any contemptuous behavior in its presence.

SECTION 15. Vacancies. When the seat of any member of either House becomes vacant, the vacancy shall be filled as follows:

(a) When twelve months or more remain prior to the next general election for legislators, a successor shall be elected by the qualified voters of the district represented, and such successor shall serve the remainder of the original term. The election shall be held within such time as provided by law. The legislative body of the replaced legislator's county of residence at the time of his or her election may elect an interim successor to serve until the election.

(b) When less than twelve months remain prior to the next general election for legislators, a successor shall be elected by the legislative body of the replaced legislator's county of residence at the time of his or her election. The term of any Senator so elected shall expire at the next general election for legislators, at which election a successor shall be elected.

(c) Only a qualified voter of the district represented shall be eligible to succeed to the vacant seat.

SECTION 16. Neither House shall, during its session, adjourn without the consent of the other for more than three days, nor to any other place than that in which the two Houses shall be sitting.

SECTION 17. Bills may originate in either House; but may be amended, altered or rejected by the other. No bill shall become a law which embraces more than one subject, that subject to be expressed in the title. All acts which repeal, revive or amend former laws, shall recite in their caption, or otherwise, the title or substance of the law repealed, revived or amended.

SECTION 18. A bill shall become law when it has been considered and passed on three different days in each House and on third and final consideration has received the assent of a majority of all the members to which each House is entitled under this Constitution, when the respective speakers have signed the bill with the date of such signing appearing in the Journal, and when the bill has been approved by the Governor or otherwise passed under the provisions of this Constitution.

SECTION 19. After a bill has been rejected, no bill containing the same substance shall be passed into a law during the same session.

SECTION 20. The style of the laws of this state shall be, "Be it enacted by the General Assembly of the State of Tennessee." No law of a general nature shall take effect until forty days after its passage unless the same or the caption thereof shall state that the public welfare requires that it should take effect sooner.

SECTION 21. Each House shall keep a journal of its proceedings, and publish it, except such parts as the welfare of the state may require to be kept secret; the ayes and noes shall be taken in each House upon the final passage of every bill of a general character, and bills making appropriations of public moneys; and the ayes and noes of the members on any question, shall, at the request of any five of them, be entered on the journal.

SECTION 22. The doors of each House and of committees of the whole shall be kept open, unless when the business shall be such as ought to be kept secret.

SECTION 23. Each member of the General Assembly shall receive an annual salary of $1,800.00 per year payable in equal monthly installments from the date of his election, and in addition, such other allowances for expenses in attending sessions or committee meetings as may be provided by law. The Senators, when sitting as a Court of Impeachment, shall receive the same allowances for expenses as have been provided by law for the members of the General Assembly. The compensation and expenses of the members of the General Assembly may from time to time be reduced or increased by laws enacted by the General Assembly; however, no increase or decrease in the amount thereof shall take effect until the next general election for Representatives to the General Assembly. Provided, further, that the first General Assembly meeting after adoption of this amendment shall be allowed to set its own expenses. However, no member shall be paid expenses, nor travel allowances for more than ninety Legislative days of a regular session, excluding the organizational session, nor for more than thirty Legislative days of any extraordinary session.

This amendment shall take effect immediately upon adoption so that any member of the General Assembly elected at a general election wherein this amendment is approved shall be entitled to the compensation set herein.

SECTION 24. Appropriation of public moneys. No public money shall be expended except pursuant to appropriations made by law. Expenditures for any fiscal year shall not exceed the state's revenues and reserves, including the proceeds of any debt obligation, for that year. No debt obligation, except as shall be repaid within the fiscal year of issuance, shall be authorized for the current operation of any state service or program, nor shall the proceeds of any debt obligation be expended for a purpose other than that for which it was authorized.

In no year shall the rate of growth of appropriations from state tax revenues exceed the estimated rate of growth of the state's economy as determined by law. No appropriation in excess of this limitation shall be made unless the General Assembly shall, by law containing no other subject matter, set forth the dollar amount and the rate by which the limit will be exceeded.

Any law requiring the expenditure of state funds shall be null and void unless, during the session in which the act receives final passage, an appropriation is made for the estimated first year's funding.

No law of general application shall impose increased expenditure requirements on cities or counties unless the General Assembly shall provide that the state share in the cost.

An accurate financial statement of the state's fiscal condition shall be published annually.

SECTION 25. No person who heretofore hath been, or may hereafter be, a collector or holder of Public Moneys, shall have a seat in either House of the General Assembly, or hold any other office under the State Government, until such person shall have accounted for, and paid into the Treasury, all sums for which he may be accountable or liable.

SECTION 26. No Judge of any Court of law or equity, Secretary of State, Attorney General, Register, Clerk of any court of Record, or person holding any office under the authority of the United States, shall have a seat in the General Assembly; nor shall any person in this State hold more than one lucrative office at the same time; provided, that no appointment in the Militia, or to the office of Justice of the Peace, shall be considered a lucrative office, or operative as a disqualification to a seat in either House of the General Assembly.

SECTION 27. Any member of either House of the General Assembly shall have liberty to dissent from and protest against, any act or resolve which he may think injurious to the Public or to any individual, and to have the reasons for his dissent entered on the journals.

SECTION 28. In accordance with the following provisions, all property real, personal or mixed shall be subject to taxation, but the Legislature may except such as may be held by the State, by Counties, Cities or Towns, and used exclusively for public or corporation purposes, and such as may be held and used for purposes purely religious, charitable, scientific, literary or educational, and shall except the direct product of the soil in the hands of the producer, and his immediate vendee, and the entire amount of money deposited in an individual's personal or family checking or savings accounts. For purposes of taxation, property shall be classified into three classes, to wit: Real Property, Tangible Personal Property and Intangible Personal Property.

Real Property shall be classified into four (4) subclassifications and assessed as follows:

(a) Public Utility Property, to be assessed at fifty-five (55%) per cent of its value;

(b) Industrial and Commercial Property, to be assessed at forty (40%) per cent of its value;

(c) Residential Property, to be assessed at twenty-five (25%) per cent of its value, provided that residential property containing two (2) or more rental units is hereby defined as industrial and commercial property; and

(d) Farm Property, to be assessed at twenty-five (25%) per cent of its value.

House trailers, mobile homes, and all other similar movable structures used for commercial, industrial, or residential purposes shall be assessed as Real Property as an improvement to the land where located.

The Legislature shall provide tax relief to elderly low-income taxpayers through payments by the State to reimburse all or part of the taxes paid by such persons on owner-occupied residential property, but such reimbursement shall not be an obligation imposed, directly or indirectly, upon Counties, Cities or Towns; provided, that such tax relief for the years 1973 through 1977 shall be not less than an amount equal to the State, County, and Municipal Taxes on Five Thousand ($5,000) Dollars worth of the full market value (or One Thousand Two Hundred Fifty ($1,250) Dollars of the assessed value) of property used for a residence by any taxpayer over sixty-five (65) years of age for a period of one (1) year prior to the date of assessment; provided further, that such relief shall not extend to persons having a total annual income from all sources in excess of Four Thousand Eight Hundred ($4,800) Dollars.

The Legislature may provide tax relief to home owners totally and permanently disabled, irrespective of age, as provided herein for the elderly.

Tangible Personal Property shall be classified into three (3) subclassifications and assessed as follows:

(a) Public Utility Property, to be assessed at fifty-five (55%) per cent of its value;

(b) Industrial and Commercial Property, to be assessed at thirty (30%) per cent of its value; and

(c) All other Tangible Personal Property, to be assessed at five (5%) per cent of its value; provided, however, that the Legislature shall exempt Seven Thousand Five Hundred ($7,500) Dollars worth of such Tangible Personal Property which shall cover personal household goods and furnishings, wearing apparel and other such tangible property in the hands of a taxpayer.

The Legislature shall have power to classify Intangible Personal Property into subclassifications and to establish a ratio of assessment to value in each class or subclass, and shall provide fair and equitable methods of apportionment of the value of same to this State for purposes of taxation. Banks, Insurance Companies, Loan and Investment Companies, Savings and Loan Associations, and all similar financial institutions, shall be assessed and taxed in such manner as the Legislature shall direct; provided that for the year 1973, or until such time as the Legislature may provide otherwise, the ratio of assessment to value of property presently taxed shall remain the same as provided by law for the year 1972; provided further that the taxes imposed upon such financial institutions, and paid by them, shall be in lieu of all taxes on the redeemable or cash value of all of their outstanding shares of capital stock, policies of insurance, customer savings and checking accounts, certificates of deposit, and certificates of investment, by whatever name called, including other intangible corporate property of such financial institutions.

The ratio of assessment to value of property in each class or subclass shall be equal and uniform throughout the State, the value and definition of property in each class or subclass to be ascertained in such manner as the Legislature shall direct. Each respective taxing authority shall apply the same tax rate to all property within its jurisdiction.

The Legislature shall have power to tax merchants, peddlers, and privileges, in such manner as they may from time to time direct, and the Legislature may levy a gross receipts tax on merchants and businesses in lieu of ad valorem taxes on the inventories of merchandise held by such merchants and businesses for sale or exchange. The portion of a Merchant's Capital used in the purchase of merchandise sold by him to non-residents and sent beyond the State, shall not be taxed at a rate higher than the ad valorem tax on property. The Legislature shall have power to levy a tax upon incomes derived from stocks and bonds that are not taxed ad valorem.

This amendment shall take effect on the first day of January, 1973.

SECTION 29. The General Assembly shall have power to authorize the several Counties and incorporated towns in this State, to impose taxes for County and Corporation purposes respectively, in such manner as shall be prescribed by law; and all property shall be taxed according to its value, upon the principles established in regard to state taxation. But the credit of no County, City or Town shall be given or loaned to or in aid of any person, company, association or corporation, except upon an election to be first held by the qualified voters of such county, city or town, and the assent of three-fourths of the votes cast at said election. Nor shall any county, city or town become a stockholder with others in any company, association or corporation except upon a like election, and the assent of a like majority. But the counties of Grainger, Hawkins, Hancock, Union. Campbell, Scott, Morgan, Grundy, Sumner, Smith, Fentress, Van Buren, and the new County herein authorized to be established out of fractions of Sumner, Macon and Smith Counties, White, Putnam, Overton, Jackson, Cumberland, Anderson, Henderson, Wayne, Cocke, Coffee, Macon, Marshall, and Roane shall be excepted out of the provisions of this section so far that the assent of a majority of the qualified voters of either of said counties voting on the question shall be sufficient when the credit of such county is given or loaned to any person, association or corporation; Provided, that the exception of the counties above named shall not be in force beyond the year one thousand eight hundred and eighty: and after that period they shall be subject to the three-fourths majority applicable to the other counties of the State.

SECTION 30. No article manufactured of the produce of this State, shall be taxed otherwise than to pay inspection fees.

SECTION 31. The credit of this State shall not be hereafter loaned or given to or in aid of any person, association, company, corporation or municipality: nor shall the State become the owner in whole or in part of any bank or a stockholder with others in any association, company, corporation or municipality.

SECTION 32. No Convention or General Assembly of this State shall act upon any amendment of the Constitution of the United States proposed by Congress to the several States; unless such Convention or General Assembly shall have been elected after such amendment is submitted.

SECTION 33. No bonds of the State shall be issued to any Rail Road Company which at the time of its application for the same shall be in default in paying the interest upon the State bonds previously loaned to it or that shall hereafter and before such application sell or absolutely dispose of any State bonds loaned to it for less than par.

ARTICLE III.

EXECUTIVE DEPARTMENT.

SECTION 1. The Supreme Executive power of this State shall be vested in a Governor.

SECTION 2. The Governor shall be chosen by the electors of the members of the General Assembly, at the time and places where they shall respectively vote for the members thereof. The returns of every election for Governor shall be sealed up, and transmitted to the seat of Government, by the returning officers, directed to the Speaker of the Senate, who shall open and publish them in the presence of a majority of the members of each House of the General Assembly. The person having the highest number of votes shall be Governor; but if two or more shall be equal and highest in votes, one of them shall be chosen Governor by joint vote of both Houses of the General Assembly. Contested elections for Governor shall be determined by both Houses of the General Assembly, in such manner as shall be prescribed by law.

SECTION 3. He shall be at least thirty years of age, shall be a citizen of the United States, and shall have been a citizen of this State seven years next before his election.

SECTION 4. Governor's term. The Governor shall be elected to hold office for four years and until a successor is elected and qualified. A person may be eligible to suceed in office for additional four-year terms, provided that no person presently serving or elected hereafter shall be eligible for election to more than two terms consecutively, including an election to a partial term.

One succeeding to the office vacated during the first eighteen calendar months of the term shall hold office until a successor is elected for the remainder of the term at the next election of members of the General Assembly and qualified pursuant to this Constitution. One succeeding to the office vacated after the first eighteen calendar months of the term shall continue to hold office for the remainder of the full term.

SECTION 5. He shall be commander-in-chief of the Army and Navy of this state, and of the militia, except when they shall be called into the service of the United States: But the militia shall not be called into service except in case of rebellion or invasion, and then only when the General Assembly shall declare, by law, that the public safety requires it.

SECTION 6. He shall have power to grant reprieves and pardons, after conviction, except in cases of impeachment.

SECTION 7. He shall, at stated times, receive a compensation for his services, which shall not be increased or diminished during the period for which he shall have been elected.

SECTION 8. He may require information in writing, from the officers in the executive department, upon any subject relating to the duties of their respective offices.

SECTION 9. He may, on extraordinary occasions, convene the General Assembly by proclamation, in which he shall state specifically the purposes for which they are to convene; but they shall enter on no legislative business except that for which they were specifically called together.

SECTION 10. He shall take care that the laws be faithfully executed.

SECTION 11. He shall, from time to time, give to the General Assembly information of the state of the government, and recommend for their consideration such measures as he shall judge expedient.

SECTION 12. In case of the removal of the Governor from office, or of his death, or resignation, the powers and duties of the office shall devolve on the Speaker of the Senate; and in case of the death, removal from office, or resignation of the Speaker of the Senate, the powers and duties of the office shall devolve on the Speaker of the House of Representatives.

SECTION 13. No member of Congress, or person holding any office under the United States, or this State, shall execute the office of Governor.

SECTION 14. When any officer, the right of whose appointment is by this Constitution vested in the General Assembly, shall, during the recess, die, or the office, by the expiration of the term, or by other means, become vacant, the Governor shall have the power to fill such vacancy by granting a temporary commission, which shall expire at the end of the next session of the Legislature.

SECTION 15. There shall be a seal of this State, which shall be kept by the Governor, and used by him officially, and shall be called the Great Seal of the State of Tennessee.

SECTION 16. All grants and commissions shall be in the name and by the authority of the State of Tennessee, be sealed with the State Seal, and signed by the Governor.

SECTION 17. A Secretary of State shall be appointed by joint vote of the General Assembly, and commissioned during the term of four years; he shall keep a fair register of all the official acts and proceedings of the Governor; and shall, when required lay the same, and all papers, minutes and vouchers relative thereto, before the General Assembly; and shall perform such other duties as shall be enjoined by law.

SECTION 18. Every Bill which may pass both Houses of the General Assembly shall, before it becomes a law, be presented to the Governor for his signature. If he approve, he shall sign it, and the same shall become a law; but if he refuse to sign it, he shall return it with his objections thereto, in writing, to the house in which it originated; and said House shall cause said objections to be entered at large upon its journal, and proceed to reconsider the Bill. If after such reconsideration, a majority of all the members elected to that House shall agree to pass the Bill, notwithstanding the objections of the Executive, it shall be sent, with said objections, to the other House, by which it shall be likewise reconsidered. If approved by a majority of the whole number elected to that House, it shall become a law. The votes of both Houses shall be determined by yeas and nays, and the names of all the members voting for or against the Bill shall be entered upon the journals of their respective Houses.

If the Governor shall fail to return any bill with his objections in writing within ten calendar days (Sundays excepted) after it shall have been presented to him, the same shall become a law without his signature. If the General Assembly by its adjournment prevents the return of any bill within said ten-day period, the bill shall become a law, unless disapproved by the Governor and filed by him with his objections in writing in the office of the Secretary of State within said ten-day period.

Every joint resolution or order (except on question of adjournment and proposals of specific amendments to the Constitution) shall likewise be presented to the Governor for his signature, and on being disapproved by him shall in like manner, be returned with his objections; and the same before it shall take effect shall be repassed by a majority of all the members elected to both houses in the manner and according to the rules prescribed in case of a bill.

The Governor may reduce or disapprove the sum of money appropriated by any one or more items or parts of items in any bill appropriating money, while approving other portions of the bill. The portions so approved shall become law, and the items or parts of items disapproved or reduced shall be void to the extent that they have been disapproved or reduced unless repassed as hereinafter provided. The Governor, within ten calendar days (Sundays excepted) after the bill shall have been presented to him, shall report the items or parts of items disapproved or reduced with his objections in writing to the House in which the bill originated, or if the General Assembly shall have adjourned, to the office of the Secretary of State. Any such items or parts of items so disapproved or reduced shall be restored to the bill in the original amount and become law if repassed by the General Assembly according to the rules and limitations prescribed for the passage of other bills over the executive veto.

ARTICLE IV.
ELECTIONS.

SECTION 1. Right to vote—Election precincts—Military duty. Every person, being eighteen years of age, being a citizen of the United States, being a resident of the State for a period of time as prescribed by the General Assembly, and being duly registered in the county of residence for a period of time prior to the day of any election as prescribed by the General Assembly, shall be entitled to vote in all federal, state, and local elections held in the county or district in which such person resides. All such requirements shall be equal and uniform across the state, and there shall be no other qualification attached to the right of suffrage.

The General Assembly shall have power to enact laws requiring voters to vote in the election precincts in which they may reside, and laws to secure the freedom of elections and the purity of the ballot box.

All male citizens of this State shall be subject to the performance of military duty, as may be prescribed by law.

Section 2. Laws may be passed excluding from the right of suffrage persons who may be convicted of infamous crimes.

Section 3. Electors shall, in all cases, except treason, felony, or breach of the peace, be privileged from arrest or summons, during their attendance at elections, and in going to and returning from them.

Section 4. In all elections to be made by the General Assembly, the members thereof shall vote *viva voce,* and their votes shall be entered on the journal. All other elections shall be by ballot.

ARTICLE V.

Impeachments.

Section 1. The House of Representatives shall have the sole power of impeachment.

Section 2. All impeachments shall be tried by the Senate. When sitting for that purpose the Senators shall be upon oath or affirmation, and the Chief Justice of the Supreme Court, or if he be on trial, the Senior Associate Judge, shall preside over them. No person shall be convicted without the concurrence of two-thirds of the Senators sworn to try the officer impeached.

Section 3. The House of Representatives shall elect from their own body three members, whose duty it shall be to prosecute impeachments. No impeachment shall be tried until the Legislature shall have adjourned *sine die,* when the Senate shall proceed to try such impeachment.

Section 4. The Governor, Judges of the Supreme Court, Judges of the Inferior Courts, Chancellors, Attorneys for the State, Treasurer, Comptroller, and Secretary of State, shall be liable to impeachment, whenever they may, in the opinion of the House of Representatives, commit any crime in their official capacity which may require disqualification; but judgment shall only extend to removal from office, and disqualification to fill any office thereafter. The party shall, nevertheless, be liable to indictment, trial, judgment and punishment according to law. The Legislature now has, and shall continue to have, power to relieve from the penalties imposed, any person disqualified from holding office by the judgment of a Court of Impeachment.

Section 5. Justices of the Peace, and other civil officers, not hereinbefore mentioned, for crimes or misdemeanors in office, shall be liable to indictment in such courts as the Legislature may direct; and upon conviction, shall be removed from office by said court, as if found guilty on impeachment; and shall be subject to such other punishment as may be prescribed by law.

ARTICLE VI.

Judicial Department.

Section 1. The judicial power of this State shall be vested in one Supreme Court and in such Circuit, Chancery and other inferior Courts as the Legislature shall from time to time, ordain and establish; in the Judges thereof, and in Justices of the Peace. The Legislature may also vest such jurisdiction in Corporation Courts as may be deemed necessary. Courts to be holden by Justices of the Peace may also be established.

Section 2. The Supreme Court shall consist of five Judges, of whom not more than two shall reside in any one of the grand divisions of the State. The Judges shall designate one of their own number who shall preside as Chief Justice. The concurrence of three of the Judges shall in every case be necessary to a decision. The jurisdiction of this Court shall be appellate only, under such restrictions and regulations as may from time to time be prescribed by law; but it may possess such other jurisdiction as is now conferred by law on the present Supreme Court. Said Court shall be held at Knoxville, Nashville and Jackson.

SECTION 3. The Judges of the Supreme Court shall be elected by the qualified voters of the State. The Legislature shall have power to prescribe such rules as may be necessary to carry out the provisions of section two of this article. Every Judge of the Supreme Court shall be thirty-five years of age, and shall before his election have been a resident of the State for five years. His term of service shall be eight years.

SECTION 4. The Judges of the Circuit and Chancery Courts, and of other inferior Courts, shall be elected by the qualified voters of the district or circuit to which they are to be assigned. Every Judge of such Courts shall be thirty years of age, and shall before his election, have been a resident of the State for five years, and of the circuit or district one year. His term of service shall be eight years.

SECTION 5. An Attorney General and Reporter for the State, shall be appointed by the Judges of the Supreme Court and shall hold his office for a term of eight years. An Attorney for the State for any circuit or district, for which a Judge having criminal jurisdiction shall be provided by law, shall be elected by the qualified voters of such circuit or district, and shall hold his office for a term of eight years, and shall have been a resident of the State five years, and of the circuit or district one year. In all cases where the Attorney for any district fails or refuses to attend and prosecute according to law, the Court shall have power to appoint an Attorney *pro tempore*.

SECTION 6. Judges and Attorneys for the State may be removed from office by a concurrent vote of both Houses of the General Assembly, each House voting separately; but two-thirds of the members to which each House may be entitled must concur in such vote. The vote shall be determined by ayes and noes, and the names of the members voting for or against the Judge or Attorney for the State together with the cause or causes of removal, shall be entered on the Journals of each House respectively. The Judge or Attorney for the State, against whom the Legislature may be about to proceed, shall receive notice thereof accompanied with a copy of the causes alleged for his removal, at least ten days before the day on which either House of the General Assembly shall act thereupon.

SECTION 7. The Judges of the Supreme or Inferior Courts, shall, at stated times, receive a compensation for their services, to be ascertained by law, which shall not be increased or diminished during the time for which they are elected. They shall not be allowed any fees or perquisites of office nor hold any office of trust or profit under this State or the United States.

SECTION 8. The jurisdiction of the Circuit, Chancery and other Inferior Courts, shall be as now established by law, until changed by the Legislature.

SECTION 9. The Judges shall not charge juries with respect to matters of fact, but may state the testimony and declare the law.

SECTION 10. Judges or Justices of the Inferior Courts of Law and Equity, shall have power in all civil cases, to issue writs of *certiorari* to remove any cause or the transcript of the record thereof, from any inferior jurisdiction, into such court of law, on sufficient cause, supported by oath or affirmation.

SECTION 11. No Judge of the Supreme or Inferior Courts shall preside on the trial of any cause in the event of which he may be interested, or where either of the parties shall be connected with him by affinity or consanguinity, within such degrees as may be prescribed by law, or in which he may have been of counsel, or in which he may have presided in any inferior Court, except by consent of all the parties. In case all or any of the Judges of the Supreme Court shall thus be disqualified from presiding on the trial of any cause or causes, the Court, or the Judges thereof, shall certify the same to the Governor of the State, and he shall forthwith specially commission the requisite number of men, of law knowledge, for the trial and determination thereof. The Legislature may by general laws make provision that special Judges may be appointed, to hold any Courts the Judge of which shall be unable or fail to attend or sit; or to hear any cause in which the Judge may be incompetent.

SECTION 12. All writs and other process shall run in the name of the State of Tennessee and bear test and be signed by the respective clerks. Indictments shall conclude, "against the peace and dignity of the State."

SECTION 13. Judges of the Supreme Court shall appoint their clerks who shall hold their offices for six years. Chancellors shall appoint their clerks and masters, who shall hold their offices for six years. Clerks of the Inferior Courts holden in the respective Counties or Districts, shall be elected by the qualified voters thereof for the term of four years. Any Clerk may be removed from office for malfeasance, incompetency or neglect of duty, in such manner as may be prescribed by law.

Section 14. No fine shall be laid on any citizen of this State that shall exceed fifty dollars, unless it shall be assessed by a jury of his peers, who shall assess the fine at the time they find the fact, if they think the fine should be more than fifty dollars.

ARTICLE VII.

State and County Officers.

Section 1. County government. The qualified voters of each county shall elect for terms of four years a legislative body, a county executive, a Sheriff, a Trustee, a Register, a County Clerk and an Assessor of Property. Their qualifications and duties shall be prescribed by the General Assembly. Any officer shall be removed for malfeasance or neglect of duty as prescribed by the General Assembly.

The legislative body shall be composed of representatives from districts in the county as drawn by the county legislative body pursuant to statutes enacted by the General Assembly. Districts shall be reapportioned at least every ten years based upon the most recent federal census. The legislative body shall not exceed twenty-five members, and no more than three representatives shall be elected from a district. Any county organized under the consolidated government provision of Article XI, Section 9, of this Constitution shall be exempt from having a county executive and a county legislative body as described in this paragraph.

The General Assembly may provide alternate forms of county government including the right to charter and the manner by which a referendum may be called. The new form of government shall replace the existing form if approved by a majority of the voters in the referendum.

No officeholder's current term shall be diminished by the ratification of this article.

Section 2. Vacancies. Vacancies in county offices shall be filled by the county legislative body, and any person so appointed shall serve until a successor is elected at the next election occurring after the vacancy and is qualified.

Section 3. There shall be a treasurer or Treasurers and a Comptroller of the Treasury appointed for the State, by the joint vote of both Houses of the General Assembly, who shall hold their offices for two years.

Section 4. The election of all officers, and the filling of all vacancies not otherwise directed or provided by this Constitution, shall be made in such manner as the Legislature shall direct.

Section 5. Elections for Judicial and other civil officers shall be held on the first Thursday in August, one thousand eight hundred and seventy, and forever thereafter on the first Thursday in August next preceding the expiration of their respective terms of service. The term of each officer so elected shall be computed from the first day of September next succeeding his election. The term of office of the Governor and other executive officers shall be computed from the fifteenth of January next after the election of the Governor. No appointment or election to fill a vacancy shall be made for a period extending beyond the unexpired term. Every officer shall hold his office until his successor is elected or appointed, and qualified. No special election shall be held to fill a vacancy in the office of Judge or District Attorney, but at the time herein fixed for the biennial election of civil officers; and such vacancy shall be filled at the next Biennial election recurring [sic] more than thirty days after the vacancy occurs.

ARTICLE VIII.

Militia.

Section 1. All militia officers shall be elected by persons subject to military duty, within the bounds of their several companies, battalions, regiments, brigades and divisions, under such rules and regulations as the Legislature may from time to time direct and establish.

Section 2. The Governor shall appoint the Adjutant-General and his other staff officers;

the Major-Generals, Brigadier-Generals, and commanding officers of regiments, shall respectively appoint their staff officers.

SECTION 3. The Legislature shall pass laws exempting citizens belonging to any sect or denomination of religion, the tenets of which are known to be opposed to the bearing of arms, from attending private and general musters.

ARTICLE IX.
DISQUALIFICATIONS.

SECTION 1. Whereas Ministers of the Gospel are by their profession, dedicated to God and the care of souls, and ought not to be diverted from the great duties of their functions; therefore, no Minister of the Gospel, or priest of any denomination whatever, shall be eligible to a seat in either House of the Legislature. *(Editor's note: This section was invalidated by the United States Supreme Court on April 19, 1978, in the case styled McDaniel v. Paty et al.).*

SECTION 2. No person who denies the being of God, or a future state of rewards and punishments, shall hold any office in the civil department of this State.

SECTION 3. Any person who shall, after the adoption of this Constitution, fight a duel, or knowingly be the bearer of a challenge to fight a duel, or send or accept a challenge for that purpose, or be an aider or abettor in fighting a duel, shall be deprived of the right to hold any office of honor or profit in this State, and shall be punished otherwise, in such manner as the Legislature may prescribe.

ARTICLE X.
OATHS, BRIBERY OF ELECTORS, NEW COUNTIES.

SECTION 1. Every person who shall be chosen or appointed to any office of trust or profit under this Constitution, or any law made in pursuance thereof, shall, before entering on the duties thereof, take an oath to support the Constitution of this State, and of the United States, and an oath of office.

SECTION 2. Each member of the Senate and House of Representatives, shall before they proceed to business take an oath or affirmation to support the Constitution of this State, and of the United States and also the following oath: I ——————— do solemnly swear (or affirm) that as a member of this General Assembly, I will, in all appointments, vote without favor, affection, partiality, or prejudice; and that I will not propose or assent to any bill, vote or resolution, which shall appear to me injurious to the people, or consent to any act or thing, whatever, that shall have a tendency to lessen or abridge their rights and privileges, as declared by the Constitution of this State.

SECTION 3. Any elector who shall receive any gift or reward for his vote, in meat, drink, money or otherwise, shall suffer such punishment as the laws shall direct. And any person who shall directly or indirectly give, promise or bestow any such reward to be elected, shall thereby be rendered incapable, for six years, to serve in the office for which he was elected, and be subject to such further punishment as the Legislature shall direct.

SECTION 4. New Counties may be established by the Legislature to consist of not less than two hundred and seventy-five square miles, and which shall contain a population of seven hundred qualified voters; no line of such County shall approach the Court House of any old County from which it may be taken nearer than eleven miles, nor shall such old County be reduced to less than five hundred square miles.

[*A portion of section 4, which deals with boundaries of certain specific counties, is omitted here.*]

SECTION 5. The citizens who may be included in any new County shall vote with the County or Counties from which they may have been stricken off, for members of Congress, for Governor and for members of the General Assembly until the next apportionment of members to the General Assembly after the establishment of such new County.

ARTICLE XI.
MISCELLANEOUS PROVISIONS.

SECTION 1. All laws and ordinances now in force and use in this state, not inconsistent with this Constitution, shall continue in force and use until they shall expire, be altered or repealed by the Legislature; but ordinances contained in any former Constitution or schedule thereto are hereby abrogated.

SECTION 2. Nothing contained in this Constitution shall impair the validity of any debts or contracts, or affect any rights of property or any suits, actions, rights of action or other proceedings in Courts of Justice.

SECTION 3. Any amendment or amendments to this Constitution may be proposed in the Senate or House of Representatives, and if the same shall be agreed to by a majority of all the members elected to each of the two houses, such proposed amendment or amendments shall be entered on their journals with the yeas and nays thereon, and referred to the General Assembly then next to be chosen; and shall be published six months previous to the time of making such choice; and if in the General Assembly then next chosen as aforesaid, such proposed amendment or amendments shall be agreed to by two-thirds of all the members elected to each house, then it shall be the duty of the General Assembly to submit such proposed amendment or amendments to the people at the next general election in which a Governor is to be chosen. And if the people shall approve and ratify such amendment or amendments by a majority of all the citizens of the State voting for Governor, voting in their favor, such amendment or amendments shall become a part of this Constitution. When any amendment or amendments to the Constitution shall be proposed in pursuance of the foregoing provisions the same shall at each of said sessions be read three times on three several days in each house.

The Legislature shall have the right by law to submit to the people, at any general election, the question of calling a convention to alter, reform, or abolish this Constitution, or to alter, reform or abolish any specified part or parts of it; and when, upon such submission, a majority of all the voters voting upon the proposal submitted shall approve the proposal to call a convention, the delegates to such convention shall be chosen at the next general election and the convention shall assemble for the consideration of such proposals as shall have received a favorable vote in said election, in such mode and manner as shall be prescribed. No change in, or amendment to, this Constitution proposed by such convention shall become effective, unless within the limitations of the call of the convention, and unless approved and ratified by a majority of the qualified voters voting separately on such change or amendment at an election to be held in such manner and on such date as may be fixed by the convention. No such convention shall be held oftener than once in six years.

SECTION 4. The Legislature shall have no power to grant divorces; but may authorize the Courts of Justice to grant them for such causes as may be specified by law; but such laws shall be general and uniform in their operation throughout the State.

SECTION 5. The Legislature shall have no power to authorize lotteries for any purpose, and shall pass laws to prohibit the sale of lottery tickets in this State.

SECTION 6. The Legislature shall have no power to change the names of persons, or to pass acts adopting or legitimatizing persons, but shall, by general laws, confer this power on the Courts.

SECTION 7. Interest. The General Assembly shall define and regulate interest, and set maximum effective rates thereof.

If no applicable statute is hereafter enacted, the effective rate of interest collected shall not exceed ten (10%) percent per annum.

All provisions of existing statutes regulating rates of interest and other charges on loans shall remain in full force and effect until July 1, 1980, unless earlier amended or repealed.

SECTION 8. The Legislature shall have no power to suspend any general law for the benefit of any particular individual, nor to pass any law for the benefit of individuals inconsistent with the general laws of the land; nor to pass any law granting to any individual or individuals, rights, privileges, immunities, or exemptions other than such as may be, by the same law extended to any member of the community, who may be able to bring himself within the provisions of such law. No corporation shall be created or its powers increased or diminished by special laws but the General Assembly shall provide by general laws for the organization of all corporations, hereafter created, which laws may, at any time, be altered or repealed, and no such alteration or repeal shall interfere with or divest rights which have become vested.

SECTION 9. The Legislature shall have the right to vest such powers in the Courts of Justice, with regard to private and local affairs, as may be expedient.

The General Assembly shall have no power to pass a special, local or private act having the effect of removing the incumbent from any municipal or county office or abridging the term or altering the salary prior to the end of the term for which such public officer was selected, and any act of the General Assembly private or local in form or effect applicable to a particular county or municipality either in its governmental or its proprietary capacity shall be void and of no effect unless the act by its terms either requires the approval of a two-thirds vote of the local legislative body of the municipality or county, or requires approval in an election by a majority of those voting in said election in the municipality or county affected.

Any municipality may by ordinance submit to its qualified voters in a general or special election the question: "Shall this municipality adopt home rule?"

In the event of an affirmative vote by a majority of the qualified voters voting thereon, and until the repeal thereof by the same procedure, such municipality shall be a home rule municipality, and the General Assembly shall act with respect to such home rule municipality only by laws which are general in terms and effect.

Any municipality after adopting home rule may continue to operate under its existing charter, or amend the same, or adopt and thereafter amend a new charter to provide for its governmental and proprietary powers, duties and functions, and for the form, structure, personnel and organization of its government, provided that no charter provision except with respect to compensation of municipal personnel shall be effective if inconsistent with any general act of the General Assembly and provided further that the power of taxation of such municipality shall not be enlarged or increased except by General act of the General Assembly. The General Assembly shall by general law provide the exclusive methods by which municipalities may be created, merged, consolidated and dissolved and by which municipal boundaries may be altered.

A charter or amendment may be proposed by ordinance of any home rule municipality, by a charter commission provided for by Act of the General Assembly and elected by the qualified voters of a home rule municipality voting thereon or, in the absence of such act of the General Assembly, by a charter commission of seven (7) members, chosen at large not more often than once in two (2) years, in a municipal election pursuant to petition for such election signed by qualified voters of a home rule municipality not less in number than ten (10%) per cent of those voting in the then most recent general municipal election.

It shall be the duty of the legislative body of such municipality to publish any proposal so made and to submit the same to its qualified voters at the first general state election which shall be held at least sixty (60) days after such publication and such proposal shall become effective sixty (60) days after approval by a majority of the qualified voters voting thereon.

The General Assembly shall not authorize any municipality to tax incomes, estates, or inheritances, or to impose any other tax not authorized by Sections 28 or 29 of Article II of this Constitution. Nothing herein shall be construed as invalidating the provisions of any municipal charter in existence at the time of the adoption of this amendment.

The General Assembly may provide for the consolidation of any or all of the governmental and corporate functions now or hereafter vested in municipal corporations with the governmental and corporate functions now or hereafter vested in the counties in which such municipal corporations are located; provided, such consolidations shall not become effective until submitted to the qualified voters residing within the municipal corporation and in the county outside thereof, and approved by a majority of those voting within the municipal corporation and by a majority of those voting in the county outside the municipal corporation.

SECTION 10. A well regulated system of internal improvement is calculated to develop, the resources of the State, and promote the happiness and prosperity of her citizens; therefore it ought to be encouraged by the General Assembly.

SECTION 11. Exemptions from execution. There shall be a homestead exemption from execution in an amount of five thousand dollars or such greater amount as the General Assembly may establish. The General Assembly shall also establish personal property exemptions. The definition and application of the homestead and personal property exemptions and the manner in which they may be waived shall be as prescribed by law.

SECTION 12. Inherent value of education—Public schools—Support of higher education. The State of Tennessee recognizes the inherent value of education and encourages its support. The General Assembly shall provide for the maintenance, support and eligibility standards of a system of free public schools. The General Assembly may establish and support such postsecondary educational institutions, including public institutions of higher learning, as it determines.

SECTION 13. The General Assembly shall have power to enact laws for the protection and preservation of Game and Fish, within the State, and such laws may be enacted for and applied and enforced in particular Counties or geographical districts, designated by the General Assembly.

SECTION 14. *(Editor's Note: This section was stricken by the referendum held March 7, 1978. However, in presenting the proposal to the voters, the Constitutional Convention of 1977 made no provision for renumbering the following sections.)*

SECTION 15. No person shall in time of peace be required to perform any service to the public on any day set apart by his religion as a day of rest.

SECTION 16. The declaration of rights hereto prefixed is declared to be a part of the Constitution of this State, and shall never be violated on any pretense whatever. And to guard against transgression of the high powers we have delegated, we declare that every thing in the bill of rights contained, is excepted out of the General powers of the government, and shall forever remain inviolate.

SECTION 17. No County office created by the Legislature shall be filled otherwise than by the people or the County Court.

SCHEDULE

The schedule of the constitution is omitted here.

Index

Government in Tennessee was originally designed in Linotype Times Roman by Hugh Bailey. The third edition was set in the Mergenthaler Variable Input Phototypesetter equivalent. The type face was chosen for its legibility and clean design—the same qualities that no doubt were sought when Times Roman was originated in 1932 by Stanley Morison, the noted typographer.

Serving as a design motif for the book is the state flag, which flies atop the capitol at Nashville (depicted on the title page). The flag displays three stars, representing the three Grand Divisions of the state, which are enclosed by a circle—a symbol of unity.

This volume was composed by Williams Company, Chattanooga, Tennessee; printed by Thomson-Shore, Inc., Dexter, Michigan; and bound by John H. Dekker and Sons, Inc., Grand Rapids, Michigan. The book is printed on paper which bears the watermark of the S. D. Warren Company and is designed for an effective life of at least three hundred years.

THE UNIVERSITY OF TENNESSEE PRESS : KNOXVILLE